The IBM PC
Its Applicat...

Laurence Press
Small Systems Group

Wiley IBM PC Series: Series Editor, Laurence Press, Ph.D.

A Wiley Press Book
JOHN WILEY & SONS, INC.
New York · Chichester · Brisbane · Toronto · Singapore

Publishers: Judy Wilson and Dianne Littwin
Series Editor: Laurence Press
Managing Editor: David Sobel
Composition & Make-Up: Editing, Design & Production, Inc.

Library of Congress Cataloging in Publication Data

Press, Laurence.
  The IBM PC and its applications.

  (Wiley IBM PC series)
  Includes index.
  1. IBM Personal Computer.   I. Title.   II. Series.
QA76.8.I2594P744   1984   001.64   83-25939
ISBN 0-471-88440-5

Printed in the United States of America

84, 85 10 9 8 7 6 5 4 3 2 1

To my wife, Marcela, who has shown me
so many ways to see the world.

MORE THAN TWO MILLION PEOPLE HAVE LEARNED TO PROGRAM, USE, AND ENJOY MICROCOMPUTERS WITH WILEY PRESS GUIDES.

The Wiley IBM PC Series
Laurence Press, Series Editor

*APL for the IBM PC, Rose
*BASIC Keywords for the IBM PC, Adamis
*Business BASIC for the IBM PC, Adamis
 CP/M for the IBM: Using CP/M-86, Fernandez & Ashley
*dBase II for the IBM PC, Greenberg & Greenberg
*Decision Making: A Management Science Guide for the IBM PC, Hesse
 Digital Communications Programming on the IBM PC, Schwaderer
*The Electronic Link: Using the IBM PC to Communicate, Magid & Boeschen
*File and Database Management Programs, Hecht
*What If. . . ? A User's Guide to Spreadsheets on the IBM PC, Williams
*The IBM PC in the Corporation, Walden
 IBM PC: Data File Programming, Brown & Finkel
*IBM PC Pascal, Conlan
 PC DOS: Using the IBM PC Operating System, Ashley & Fernandez
 PC Graphics: Charts, Graphs, Games and Art on the IBM PC, Conklin
*Word Processing with the IBM PC, Hewes & Grout

*Forthcoming

iv

Acknowledgments

Writing the acknowledgments and the dedication is easily the most pleasant step in writing a book. It feels good to have a chance to say "thanks" to those who helped the most.

Myron Hecht, my colleague on a related project, will certainly recognize some of the ideas in this book. So will Ken Young, a constant source of enthusiastically delivered information. The reviewers, Hal Jennings and Steve Walton, gave me encouragement and suggested many valuable changes after reading the first draft. The same goes for Andrew Williams and Dave Schwaderer.

The staff at John Wiley and Sons have also lent their support. Judy Wilson and Dianne Littwin went along with the idea of a series on the IBM PC, and Dianne has overseen this book as both editor and publisher. Doreen Jasquith has guided it quickly and smoothly through the 1001 steps that a manuscript goes through.

Portia Isaacson, at Future Computing, was midwife to the IBM PC Series. Every book in the series owes a debt of gratitude to Jeannette Maher, at IBM, but I suspect that she has helped me more than any of the others.

Credit for moral support goes to the same people as always. My wife, Marcela, the kids, and my parents head the list. When I would begin to burn out, Nate Horowitz could usually get me to sit in a cafe for a while, Lew Whitaker supplied laughs and diskettes, Aki Runchal kibbitzed and lent a printer, and Jorge Parachoques did his bit to keep me smiling during the summer.

Trademarks

The following titles are trademarked or copyrighted by these companies:

Apple, Apple II/II + /IIe by Apple Computer, Inc. ■ *Ascom* by Dynamic Microprocessor Associates ■ *Citation* by Eagle Enterprises ■ *Condor* by Condor Computer Corporation ■ *Copy II PC* by Central Computer Software ■ *CorrectStar, WordStar* by MicroPro International Corporation ■ *CP/M, CP/M-86* by Digital Research Corporation ■ *dBase II* by Ashton-Tate, Inc. ■ *Desq* by Quarterdeck Software ■ *Fancy Font* by SoftCraft ■ *Final Word* by Mark of the Unicorn ■ *Grammatik* by Aspen Software ■ *IBM, IBM PC* by International Business Machines, Inc. ■ *Intelliterm* by Microcorp ■ *Jetdrive, Jspool* by Tall Tree Systems ■ *Keyswrapper, Xeno-Copy* by Vertex Systems ■ *Knowledgeman* by Micro Data Base Systems ■ *MBA* by Context Management Systems ■ *Memory/Shift* by North American Business Systems ■ *MultiLink* by Software Link, Inc. ■ *MultiPlan, Windows, Word, MSDOS* by Microsoft Corporation ■ *1-2-3* by Lotus Development Corporation ■ *PAC-MAN* by Bally Midway Manufacturing Company ■ *Palantir* by Designer Software ■ *PC-Talk* by The Headlands Press, Inc. ■ *PC-Write* by Quicksoft ■ *Peachtext* by Peachtree Software, Inc. ■ *pfs* by Software Publishing Corporation ■ *Plan-80* by Executive Software, Inc. ■ *Prokey* by RoseSoft ■ *Superwriter, SuperCalc* by Sorcim Company ■ *System Backup* by Norell Data Systems ■ *Terminal Emulation Package* by Persoft, Inc. ■ *T.I.M.* by Innovative Software, Inc. ■ *UCSDp* by Softech Microsystems ■ *UNIX* by Bell Laboratories ■ *VisiCalc, VisiOn* by VisiCorp ■ *Think Tank* by Living Video Text ■ *Volkswriter* by Lifetree Software, Inc. ■ *Writer's Pack* by Digital Marketing

A complete list of company names and addresses appears in Appendix F.

Contents

Preface

Since World War II, computers have moved from the lab, to behind corporate glass walls, to some people's desks. Many feel that they will soon be on every desk. After all, when telephones first came into offices, they stood on pedestals in the center of the room so they could be shared.

This book was written primarily for people who still do not have computers on their desks—managers, administrators, and professionals. Most of these "knowledge workers" have no computer experience, but they may suspect that a personal computer could enhance their productivity. The book should also be of use to those with some experience with personal computers, perhaps in just one or two applications or with a first generation machine, who are interested in upgrading to an IBM PC or a PC-compatible computer. A third group of readers are those who work with large computers and are now seeking to understand personal computers in order to integrate them into their organizations and data processing departments.

The book was written for the "intelligent layman." The only prerequisite is curiosity, but that is not to say that the subject is trivial or that you can plan on learning it all with a quick skimming of this or any other book.

Beware of books written by people who "had never even seen a computer until just a year ago." True, they may be sensitive to your questions and uncertainties, but they may also be confused and therefore confusing. There are technical terms and concepts involved, and I don't gloss over them, burying them in glib similes. Doing so would leave you vulnerable to sales snow jobs and confuse you in the long run, convincing you that the subject is beyond your comprehension. It is not. Instead, technical terms are explained in context (they are set in italics), and as you will see, they are not difficult to understand.

WHAT IS COVERED?

The book is organized into three parts:

1. Introduction: An overview of personal computing, the IBM PC, and its applications

2. Application Basics: An introduction to word processing, spreadsheet processing, data management, and remote and local communication
3. Software and Hardware Selection: This section covers the same applications as Part 2, but with the emphasis on evaluating software and determining hardware requirements.

After reading the first part, either you can read the second and third parts in order, or if one application is critical, you can skip ahead. For instance, if you are most interested in spreadsheet processing and want to get started right away, read Chapters 6, 10, and 12 after finishing Part 1.

The book concentrates on the IBM PC and its applications but keeps them in the context of the history of personal computing and likely future trends and developments. That is necessary, because in computing and electronics today, there is almost no such thing as the present, only the past, the passing, and the future. A framework is presented for evaluating software and hardware that has not yet been developed.

The book is about the things you can do with a PC without being a programmer. However, even with packaged software, there may be circumstances in which technical help, generally light programming, is necessary to set up or slightly extend a program, and those are pointed out.

HANDS-ON EXPERIENCE

Driving a car is not difficult, is it? But it would be difficult to understand a book on what a car is and how to drive one without ever having seen a car. The same goes for personal computers. If you are a beginner, the more hands-on experience you can get as you read this book, the better.

That experience should begin as soon as possible, but you should definitely get some practice before starting Part 2. At the very least, visit a computer store for a demonstration. Make an appointment, so you won't be rushed, and be sure that the demonstration centers around your application. Better yet, spend more leisurely time trying a friend's PC or one at work or perhaps at a community college. Best of all, get your own PC right now, and use it as you read.* Regardless of when you get a PC, plan on rereading the appropriate chapters a month or so after you have been using it for real applications.

Have you already been using a personal computer for some applications? If so, Part 1 and the chapters in Part 2 that cover those applications may be reviews, but I would still recommend reading them over quickly. That will make sure we are using terms consistently, and there will doubtless be a few mini-epiphanies where something is presented in a slightly different way than you have seen it before. However, people with prior experience

---

*If you want to make some quick hardware decisions, read Chapters 1 and 2, and the hardware sections of Chapters 11–14. For the sorts of applications we are concerned with, a 256K memory, and two double-sided disk drives would be a reasonable configuration.

will probably find Part 3 most valuable, since it points out factors to consider and questions to ask in selecting software and configuring a PC.

Readers with experience on large computers but not personal computers should also read quickly through Part 1, but they too will get the most from the application oriented chapters. Because of their background, they will not need as much hands-on experience to supplement their reading. Having driven a truck or bus teaches you a lot about driving a car.

THE REST OF THE SERIES

For in-depth coverage of a particular application and detailed comparisons of particular programs, see the companion volumes in this series:
Word Processing with the IBM PC, by Hewes & Grout
What if . . . ? A User's Guide to Spreadsheets on the IBM PC, by Williams
File and Database Management Programs, by Hecht
The Electronic Link: Using the IBM PC to Communicate, by Magid and Boeschen
Digital Communications Programming on the IBM PC, by Schwaderer
Other books in the series will be useful to a variety of readers, ranging from beginners interested in operating system training or introductory programming through advanced users looking for more technical depth.

PART ONE
Personal Computing and the IBM PC

This part concentrates on the PC itself, rather than its applications. The first chapter sets the stage, introducing personal computing in general as well as the IBM PC. The standard hardware components of a PC, the keyboard, display, memory, disk, printer, and central processing unit (CPU) are covered in depth in Chapter 2. Chapter 3 covers other hardware options and fills you in on how the various system components interface and how to buy your PC. Part I concludes with a chapter on system software, stressing operating systems.

Part I was written assuming that you have no experience with computers, large or small. Even if you have worked with mainframe or other personal computers in the past, I would recommend at least a quick reading of this part. We will establish some common terms, and no matter what your background, there will be spots at which something is seen from a slightly different perspective than yours.

CHAPTER ONE
What Is a Personal Computer?

Figure 1-1 is a photo of the IBM Personal Computer or PC for short. It is small enough to sit on or next to your desk and is fairly nice looking (and not bad as a status symbol). When switched on, a PC is relatively quiet and doesn't get noticeably warm or consume much electricity. There should be a year or so between service calls, and it is cheap enough that you or your company can probably justify putting one on your desk. A personal computer, like a "personal telephone," is small, cheap, unobtrusive, reliable, and designed to be used by one person at a time.

The IBM PC is the star of this book, and we will have a lot to say about it, but our major emphasis will be on what you can do with a PC, things like writing, communicating with other computers, storing and retrieving information, and spreadsheet modeling. If the PC is the star of the book, the plot centers on its uses or *applications,* as a computer person would say.

Who would use a PC for writing, communicating, storing files, or creating spreadsheets? Mention personal computers to most people, and they either imagine a child shooting down arcade game rocketships or a technical wizard working in a research lab. But this book is neither for children nor technicians. The applications covered are of most interest to what Peter Drucker called "knowledge workers," professionals, managers, and administrators. If you do that sort of work, whether on your own or in a large organization, a personal computer can be a useful tool.

What about prerequisites? Did you get a C— in high school algebra even though you had all the formulas written in tiny print on the palm of your hand? Don't you have to be good at math or know a lot about computers and programming to use a PC? No. The applications we are concerned with have nothing to do with math (beyond arithmetic), and IBM and others have already written the programs you will be using. All that is required is curiosity and a perceived need. There is no doubt in my mind that you can learn to use a PC, as long as you see it as a needed or useful tool.

Figure 1-1. The IBM PC is the star of this book. In this photo, you see the main components of a typical PC. The disk drives, memory, and CPU are in the box under the video display. Disks are inserted through the horizontal slots in the front. The keyboard is attached by a coiled cable so you can find a comfortable typing position, and the printer is on the left. (Courtesy of IBM Corporation)

That is not to say that the subject is trivial; there is a lot to be learned. You don't have to learn it all at once to get started; after a few hours you can be doing useful work with a PC. But don't jump in without preparation. Although this book is written for beginners, it won't patronize you by glossing over important concepts, even if they are a little technical. To do so would leave you at the mercy of salespeople, and even more important, would undermine your confidence. For instance, it might be possible to cover the applications in this book without explaining the ASCII code, but it isn't difficult to understand and if you don't learn what "ASCII" means, you will be intimidated every time you hear or read the term.

INTERACTING WITH A PC

Have you ever tried an arcade game like Pacman? If not, do so next time you see one. You will learn something, because an arcade game is a computer that has been programmed to play a game. It is programmed to display objects on the screen, move them about according to certain rules, detect collisions between them, note when you press a button or move one of the controls, and so forth.

Even though this book is not about games, playing one will give you a feel for the sorts of things a computer can do. In fact, if you have never used a computer before, make your first program a game. Don't get an arcade game; get a word-oriented game, perhaps an adventure, board game, or simulation. (Some starting games are suggested in Appendix A.) Playing the game will give you the feel of the keyboard, and you will begin to get a feel for the kinds of things personal computers do and how they are operated. As you will see, they are programmed to be used conversationally or *interactively*. There is a dialogue between you and the PC.

Let's see what one of those person-computer dialogues is like. When you take a PC out of its shipping box and set it up, you have a collection of components like those in Figure 1-1. The electronic boxes sitting on your desk are the computer *hardware*. Figure 1-2 shows a diagram of the PC hardware components, and each is explained in this chapter.

But if you are going to play a game, you will also need *software*, a program for playing the game. There are hundreds of PC game programs on the market, so you have a wide choice, but let's assume that you will buy a TIC-TAC-TOE program, since it is simple and familiar. A *program* is just a list of instructions for the computer to follow. By following the instructions

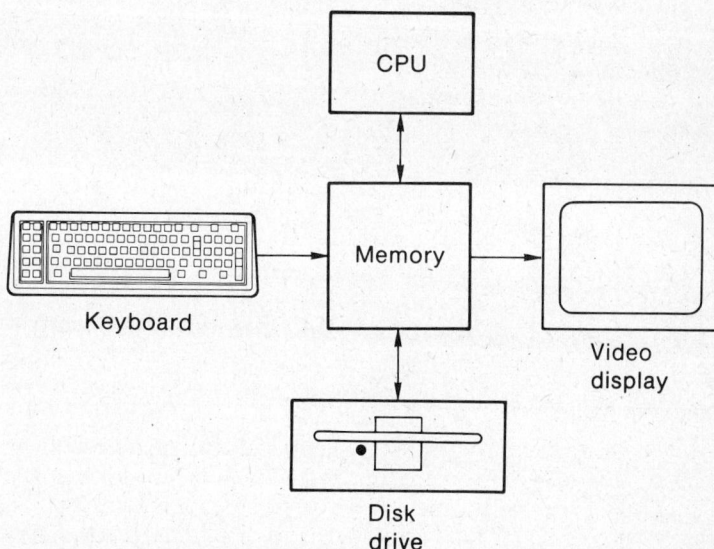

Figure 1-2. This diagram shows how the PC components connect. The memory is center stage. Whatever you type on the keyboard, print, or display goes through the memory. Information coming from or going to the disk drives is also channeled through the memory.

in the TIC-TAC-TOE program, the computer will be able to play the game with you.

You can think of examples of "programs" in other contexts: a recipe is a list of instructions for a cook to follow, a do-it-yourself kit might come with a list of assembly instructions, or when you invite someone for a visit, you might give him or her a list of instructions for getting to your house (see Figure 1-3). In all of these examples, if someone mechanically follows or executes the instructions, the desired result is achieved. The same is true of your PC. In mechanically executing the TIC-TAC-TOE program, it plays the game.

Okay, a recipe is a list of instructions for a cook and a program is a list of instructions for a computer; but recipes are printed in cookbooks, where are programs? Your TIC-TAC-TOE program would be recorded on a magnetic

1. Preheat oven to 350 degrees
2. Sift 1 3/4 cups of flour.
3. Resift the flour with 1 cup of sugar.
4. Add 1/2 cup of soft butter.
5. Add 2 eggs.
6. Add 1/2 cup of milk.
7. Add 1/2 teaspoon of salt.
8. Add 1 3/4 teaspoons of baking powder.
9. Add 1 teaspoon of vanilla.
10. Beat vigorously for 2 to 3 minutes.
11. Grease a 9- by 13-inch pan.
12. Bake for 30 minutes in the greased pan.

Figure 1-3. If a cook follows these instructions faithfully, the result is a cake. A recipe for making a cake is like a computer program. It is a list of instructions for a cook to follow, and a program is a list of instructions for a computer to follow. Like an unquestioning cook, the PC also executes its instructions, doing whatever it has been programmed to do.

Give a cook a different recipe and you get a different dish. Similarly, you can use your PC for different things by loading different programs into its memory. A word processing program turns your PC into a machine to help you write, whereas a TIC-TAC-TOE program turns it into a game player.

Figure 1-4. Programs and data are stored on magnetic disks. They work like audio cassettes, but store computer data, not sounds. Information is recorded on the surface of the disk, which rotates inside a protective cover. To change programs on your PC, you would insert a disk into a drive and the new program would be copied from the disk into the memory. It would replace the old program in memory, just as recording a new song on a tape erases any song that was recorded earlier. (Courtesy of Panasonic)

disk like the one shown in Figure 1-4. To use it, you would put the disk in the slot in the front of one of the *disk drives*, in the unit beneath the display in Figure 1-1. The program would then be *loaded* or read from the disk into the memory of the PC and executed.

But wait, we're getting a little ahead of ourselves—what is a disk and disk drive? Disks are like the cassettes used in tape recorders and hi-fi sets. Just as your voice or music can be recorded on magnetic tape, computer data and instructions can be recorded on a magnetic disk. The surface of a disk is made of material similar to that on the surface of recording tape, but it is round like a phonograph record, not long and thin like a tape. When the computer reads or writes the disk, a motor spins it like a phonograph record on a turntable (but at 360 RPM). If you glance back at Figure 1-4, you see that the disk actually rotates inside a protective cover, and information is read and written through the oblong opening.

The TIC-TAC-TOE program would be read from the disk into the memory of the PC. Check the directions of the arrows in Figure 1-2 and you will find that the memory is in the center of the computer. Whatever is typed on the keyboard goes into the memory, information is transferred both ways between the memory and disk, and information to be printed or displayed is sent from the memory to the printer or video screen. Most important, the program that the PC is executing must be in its memory (see Figure 1-5).

Once the TIC-TAC-TOE program was loaded from the disk to the memory, it could be executed. The first step in the program, and therefore the first thing the PC would do, would be to explain the rules of the game to the user (you) by writing out a display screen like the one in Figure 1-6. As you see, the program has displayed the board and is asking for your choice of symbols, X or O. When you typed your selection on the keyboard, it would ask whether you wanted to go first or second. If you said "first," the program would ask for your move. Then it would show you its move on the screen, and ask for your next move, and so on (see Figure 1-7). The dialogue between you and the PC would continue until the game was over. You can see why we used the terms "interactive" or "conversational" in describing personal computers.

In summary, the TIC-TAC-TOE program would be loaded into memory from a disk. Once in memory, it would be executed, and then you and the PC would have a "conversation" in which the game was played. The keyboard and video display would be used during the conversation; you would enter your moves through the keyboard and the PC would "speak" to you using its display. After you were finished playing, you could load another program (it would replace the TIC-TAC-TOE program) and use your PC for something else.

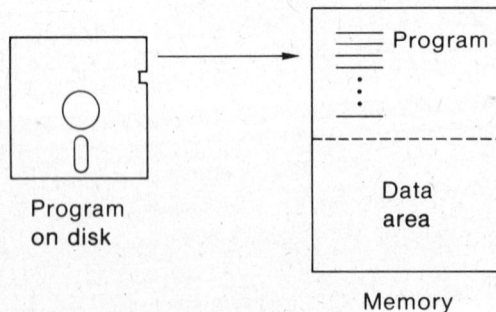

Program on disk

Program

Data area

Memory

Figure 1-5. Like some people, a computer cannot do anything without a program. Before a program can be executed, it must be loaded from its disk into the memory of the PC. Only part of the memory is used to hold the program; the rest is available for the data you will be working on.

```
Let's play TIC-TAC-TOE. When
it is your turn to move, just      |   |
move the cursor to the square   ---+---+---
you want to play in and hit        |   |
the ENTER key.                  ---+---+---
                                   |   |

Do you want X or 0?
```

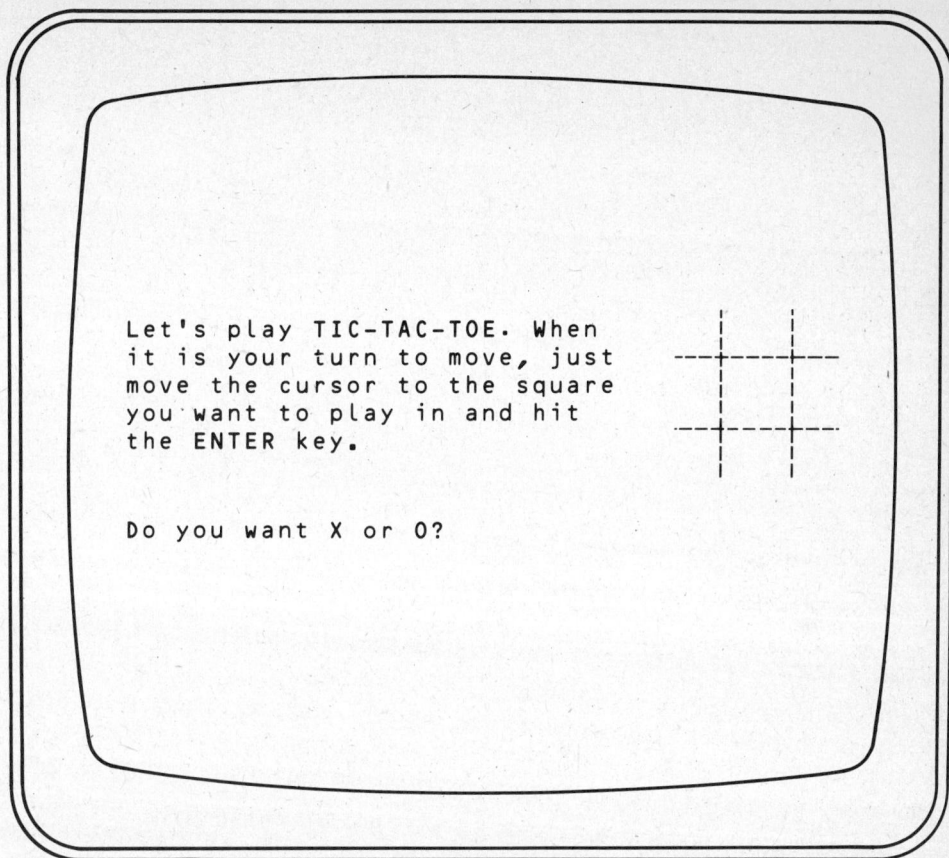

Figure 1-6. If you have never used a computer before, a game playing program is a good way to begin. It will get you used to the keyboard and give you a feel for the sorts of things computers do.

There is a conversation between a PC and its user. In this example, the computer has just displayed an explanation of the game, and asked the user to choose a symbol. The user would reply by typing either X or O, and then the PC would ask who should go first. The user would answer and the game would begin. The dialogue would continue until the game was over.

We still have not mentioned the other two components in Figure 1-2, the central processing unit or CPU and the printer. The *CPU* actually carries out the instructions in memory. One by one, the instructions are transferred from the memory to the CPU and executed. When it finishes one instruction, it goes on to the next, and so on. Choosing the next move in a TIC-TAC-TOE game might require the execution of several hundred instructions in this rather tedious, plodding manner, but since the instructions are fetched from memory and executed in millionths of seconds, the PC appears to decide its next move immediately.

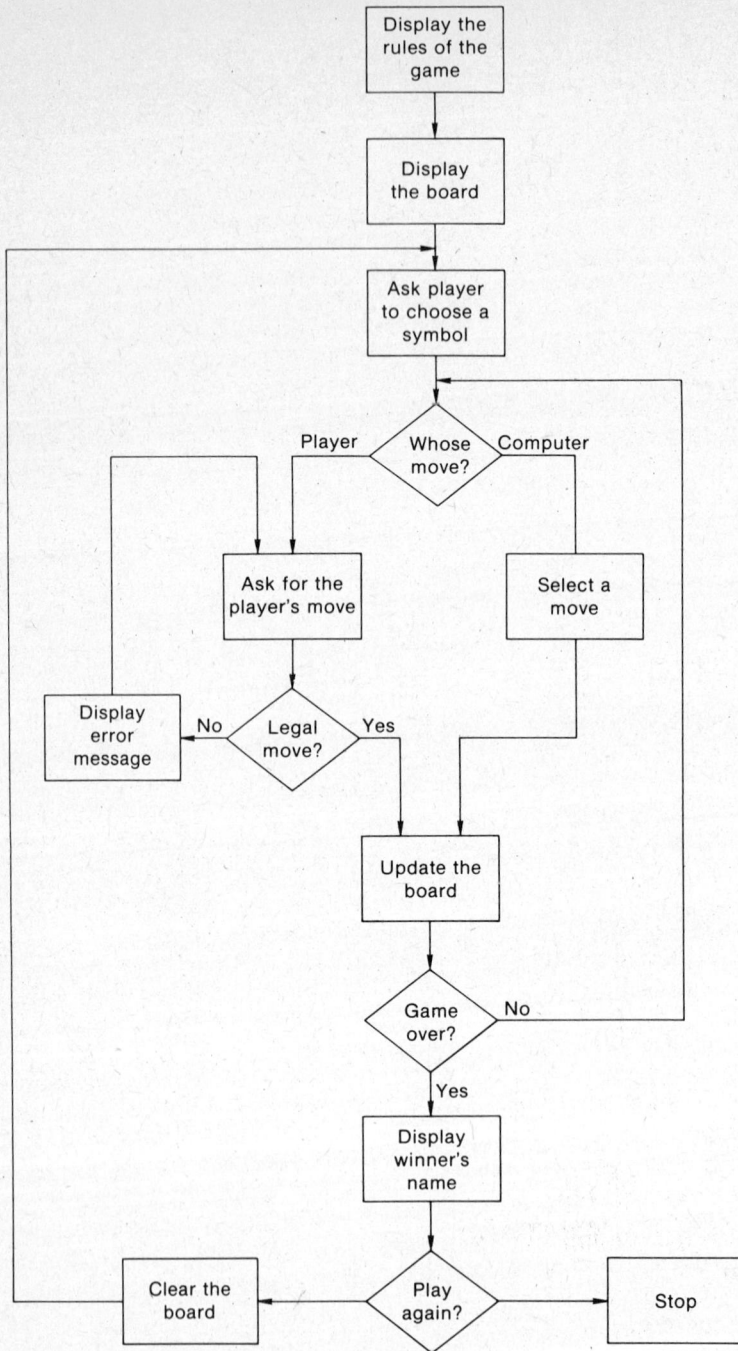

Figure 1-7. This diagram spells out the logic of a TIC-TAC-TOE program; it tells exactly what the PC should do in order to play the game. Spend some time tracing through this flow chart, and imagine what would be showing on the PC display at each step in the game.

The *printer* does just that, it prints information from the memory of the computer. For instance, a TIC-TAC-TOE program could be set up to record a transcript of the game on the printer. More practical applications, like printing letters, financial plans, or electronic mail messages from other computers, are more likely.

HISTORY OF PERSONAL COMPUTING*

The Idea of Personal Computing

A picture of a personal computer is beginning to emerge. The hardware is packaged in a few relatively small boxes designed to sit on or next to your desk. The same hardware may be used for many different applications if you have the appropriate software. To use your PC for writing, you would need a word processing program, to communicate with another computer, a communications program, and so on. The PC is designed to be used interactively or conversationally by one person at a time, and, more important, that person is a manager or professional, not a computer technician. It is a tool.

Do you suppose that the IBM PC was the first personal computer along these lines? Probably not. It turns out that today's personal computers have evolved out of years of speculation, research, and development regarding the idea of personal computing, its orientation toward nontechnical people, and the technology underlying it.

It is hard to say where an idea begins, but for me the father of personal computing was Vannevar Bush (see Figure 1-8). Bush was a professor at the Massachusetts Institute of Technology (MIT) and directed the Office of Scientific Research and Development during World War II. In July 1945, he published an article in the *Atlantic Monthly* speculating on a machine to help scientists cope with the proliferation of scientific documents. Bush's research had been with mechanical computers for solving engineering problems, but the hypothetical machine he described in that article was not for engineering; it was for organizing documents and writing. His hypothetical machine, dubbed Memex, contained a library of scientific notes and documents. Documents could be written, displayed, annotated, and associated with other documents. The user moved from one document to the next by manipulating the controls of the Memex console.

Science fiction? Bush's speculation on the technology that might be used to implement a Memex machine was not accurate, but his conception of an electronic assistant for knowledge workers was. By the late 1950s, it had become clear to a few people that the digital computer could be used in the way Bush had suggested. One of these was Douglas Englebart at the Stanford Research Institute (SRI) in Palo Alto, California. In 1962, he

*If you are really impatient to get on with it, you can skip this section on history, but it really won't take very long to read, and it is nice to give credit to the innovators.

Figure 1-8. Vannevar Bush was known for his research on servomechanisms and for the design of several "differential analyzers," mechanical computers for engineering problems. The differential analyzer shown here was hardly a personal computer, but Bush was the first to speculate on what one might do. In 1945, feeling the need for some help in keeping up with his scientific reading and writing, he wrote an article entitled "As We May Think," speculating on a machine to assist with writing, annotating, and filing documents. His vision inspired some of the early developments that led to the PC. (Courtesy of the National Museum of American History, The Smithsonian Institution)

published a report on how the computer could be used to "augment human intellect." In that report, he paid his respects to Bush, by reprinting much of the *Atlantic Monthly* article and discussing it at length. During the 1960s, Englebart and his colleagues built a prototype personal computer. They developed hardware and software for writing, filing material, and communicating with colleagues. Many of today's state of the art ideas were operating in Englebart's laboratory by 1965.

The other hotbed of early work on the idea of personal computing was MIT, where Bush himself was still involved. One of the leaders at MIT was Joseph Licklider, who envisioned a "man-machine symbiosis". In an influential paper published in 1960, he reasoned that, since people and computers have different characteristics, different fortes, they should be able to complement each other in interactive problem solving. Licklider was active in directing research at MIT and in obtaining funding for the development of interactive computing tools from the Advanced Research Projects Agency (ARPA) of the U.S. Department of Defense.

In order to appreciate the work of people such as Bush, Englebart, and Licklider, we must bear in mind that very few people were using computers interactively before the late 1960s. Computers were kept behind glass walls. Programmers and data entry workers used keypunch machines to create decks of punched cards that were submitted in batches for processing. (Thus the term *batch processing* as opposed to interactive computing.) Hours or even days would pass before a job got on the computer, was run, and the results came back.

Computers for the People

The interactive computer systems developed at MIT and SRI were intended for knowledge workers, not computer professionals. Others carried this orientation even further, to the man (or child) on the street.

In the early 1960s, Bob Albrecht, then at Control Data Corporation, began teaching children programming. By the end of the decade, he had formed the first walk-in computer center, used primarily by children, and was publishing a bimonthly newspaper called *People's Computer Company (PCC)*. PCC combined the counterculture values of the time with an enthusiasm for humanistically applied technology. It was computing's contribution to the appropriate technology movement. In fact, PCC was part of the Portola Institute, which included the *Whole Earth Catalog* among its projects.

Of course, Albrecht was not the only one interested in computing for nontechnicians. In 1963, John Kemeny and Thomas Kurtz persuaded Dartmouth College to make an introductory computing course mandatory for all liberal arts students. Part of their faith in the feasibility of doing so grew out of the success of an experiment in which they found that it was easy to teach programming concepts using the Dartmouth Oversimplified Programming Experiment (DOPE), which was extended to form the BASIC programming language. By the early 1970s, Alan Kay and his colleagues at the Xerox corporation had constructed a prototype "Dynabook," a very powerful personal computer designed to be programmed and used by children. Around the same time, Seymour Papert and his colleagues at MIT were developing LOGO, another powerful system for children.

The conception of interactive computers as easy-to-use tools grew out of this era. With their roots in the 1960s, early personal computer developers valued decentralization and cooperation. Computers should not be controlled by a technical elite and kept in corporate centers, they should be on everyone's desk. Early personal computerists were somewhat anarchistic—they enjoyed owning their own tools—but cooperation was also valued. The early papers of Licklider and others working on interactive computing make constant reference to computers as facilitating collaboration and "communities of users."

The Technology

Researchers at MIT were interested in interactive systems almost from the beginning of electronic computers. The Whirlwind computer, built to monitor radar data in 1950, seems to have been the first machine to use a video display for interaction with the operator. Three generations of experimental computer followed the Whirlwind at MIT: the TX-0, the TX-2, and the LINC (don't ask me what happened to the TX-1). These machines were used by students and faculty at MIT to develop the first software for interactive applications. Pioneering interactive programs were written for engineering analysis, the solution of mathematical problems, communication with remote computers, computer-aided design and graphics, and sophisticated games.

The LINC (Laboratory Instrument Computer) was the last of these experimental machines, and it could be argued that it was the first personal computer. Whereas the Whirlwind and TX (transistorized, experimental) machines were formidable room-fillers, the LINC was relatively small (see Figure 1-9). It was designed to be used by one person at a time, and had a keyboard for input and a video display for output. Most important, there was a small cartridge tape drive, used for saving programs and data in the same manner as we use the disk drive on the PC.

The LINC was first demonstrated in 1962 and redesigned for production in 1963. MIT produced 29 LINCs, and the Digital Equipment Corporation made 21 more. A minimal system sold for $43,600. Whether or not you consider the LINC the "first" personal computer depends upon your criteria. It was designed for interactive use and had a keyboard, display, and file system. On the other hand, it wasn't nearly as reliable, comfortable to be around, affordable, or powerful as an IBM PC.

Time-Sharing

A few researchers at MIT or SRI could afford relatively large, expensive computers as prototype personal computers; however, most could not. The computers of the 1950s and 1960s were too large and too expensive to give one to everyone who wanted to develop systems for interactive problem solving. This difficulty led to the invention of *time-sharing*, sharing one computer among many simultaneous users.

The idea was simple. Connect many teletypewriters (keyboard/printer combinations) to a single, large computer. The computer would be programmed to divide its time between the users, working for a fraction of a second on one person's job then switching to the next in round robin fashion. If there was nothing to do for a particular user when his or her time slot came up, the computer would skip that person and go on to the next one (see Figure 1-10).

If 20 users were connected to the computer, they would each get about one twentieth of its time. Even in those days, computers were pretty fast, and since the people at the teletypewriters could be counted on to spend

Figure 1-9. The Laboratory Instrument Computer (LINC) was arguably the first personal computer. The LINC was used interactively by one person at a time, and could also be connected to laboratory instruments. It was small by the standards of the day, had a keyboard and video display, and used tape cartridges for storing programs and data. Fifty LINCs were built at MIT and the Digital Equipment Corporation. The first was demonstrated at MIT in 1962, and the production model, shown here, became available in 1963. (Courtesy of Digital Equipment Corporation)

some time typing or thinking about what to do next, it seemed that one twentieth of the time of a large computer would be plenty for each user. The idea sounded reasonable in 1960, and indeed it was. Interactive computing really began to take off when time-sharing systems became available. Much of the software we use on our PCs was conceived and developed on time-sharing systems.

Again, it is impossible to credit a single person as the inventor of time-sharing. Christopher Strachey published an influential paper on time-sharing in 1959. Joseph Licklider, John McCarthy, and others at MIT were early advocates, and encouraged ARPA to fund experiments in time-sharing. Depending upon who you ask, the first time-sharing system was either at MIT, at the System Development Corporation in Santa Monica, California, or at Bolt, Beranek and Newman, a Boston R & D company

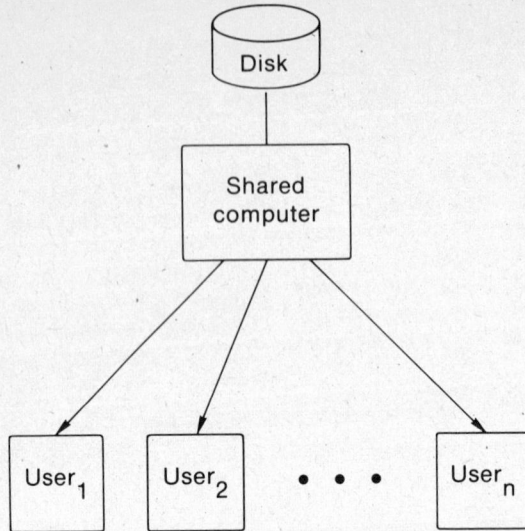

Figure 1-10. Interactive computing came into its own with the invention of time-sharing. Several users were connected to a single large computer and disk. The first time-sharing work stations were usually keyboards with printers, teletypewriters borrowed from the field of telegraphy. They were followed by the familiar computer terminal, which combines a keyboard with a video display.

In time-sharing, the computer divides its time between the users, spending a fraction of each second executing each of their programs. If the system is well designed and not overloaded, each user has the illusion of being the only one using the computer. Time-sharing brought the cost of interactive computing down to the point where many people could use the systems and develop new applications.

closely affiliated with MIT. Regardless, by 1964 these and important university systems at Berkeley and Dartmouth were operating.

Electronics

Of course, all of this has taken place in the midst of nearly magical progress in electronics. The transistor effect was first demonstrated by William Shockley, John Bardeen, and Walter Brattain at Bell Laboratories in 1947. By the early 1950s people were thinking of fabricating several transistors, along with the connections between them, in a single unit. By 1959 Texas Instruments, under the direction of Jack Killy, had done so and was marketing the first integrated circuits, called *ICs* or *chips*. The progress in electronics hasn't abated, and it won't for some time to come. The electronic components inside the 69-inch-high LINC cabinet would fit on a single circuit board in your PC. That electronic magic, in conjunction with the ideas and techniques we have been discussing, gives us today's PC.

You may come across such terms as large scale integration (*LSI*), or very large scale integration (*VLSI*) used to describe chips. These terms are used loosely as a measure of the number of components on a chip and the degree of complexity of the organization of the components. The large chips in a PC, for instance the CPU, fall in the VLSI category, and the newer memory chips are somewhere on the borderline. Some of the supporting chips would be classified as medium or even small scale integration. The most exotic chip is the optional math coprocessor (see Figure 1-11), which compresses 65,000 electronic devices onto a ⅓ inch square. The chip itself is buried inside the plastic or ceramic case that connects it to the outside world and dissipates heat.

Chip densities continue to increase at a spectacular rate, and we will have million-transistor chips in the 1990s. The nonmechanical parts of a computer as powerful as a PC will be pocket sized at that time.

As we continue with the story of the IBM PC and its applications, we will return from time to time to historical developments. Doing so will help us keep things in perspective, and we can pay our respects to the folks who made all this fun possible. You can also refer to Appendix B for a quick overview of your PC's "family tree."

Figure 1-11. The Intel 8087 math coprocessor chip, which is optional on the PC, contains 65,000 devices on a ⅓ inch square. The active element in the center is welded to contacts that are used to connect it to the outside world. The chip is encased in plastic or ceramic material, which protects it and dissipates heat. (Reprinted by permission of Intel Corporation, Copyright 1984)

THE FUTURE

Table 1-1 summarizes what has happened since personal computers became commercial products. They have already gone through three generations, and with all the progress in electronics and the attention personal computers are getting these days, you can expect many more changes. New IBM PC models have already been introduced since the first one in 1981, and there will be others.

Short term projections are easy to make in the computer field because there is a lead time between the introduction of new components and their incorporation into products that you and I can purchase. For example, the IBM PC has an optional hard disk with a capacity of 10 million characters, but the suppliers of small disk drives are already offering 50 million character units. It is only a matter of time until these higher capacity drives are available for the PC. Greater speed and capacity and falling costs are on the horizon for all PC components.

I would also expect to see your personal computer and telephone get closer together. As mentioned above, data communication is a primary PC application. With electronic progress being what it is, your PC will soon be

Table 1-1. Generations of Business/Professional Personal Computers

	Generation		
	I (1975)	II (1978)	III (1981)
Early computer manufacturers	MITs, IMSAI, Polymorphic	Apple, Radio Shack, Digital Microsystems	IBM, Victor, Wicat
CPU	8080	8085, 6502, Z-80	8086/8, 68000
Typical RAM memory	16K	64K	256K
Number of transistors in a typical system	50,000	300,000	3,000,000
Major operating systems	None	CP/M, TRS-DOS, Apple DOS	MS-DOS, CP/M-86, UNIX family
New application software	None	Word processing Spreadsheets Data management Communication	Local communication
New system software	Microsoft BASIC interpreter	Many language processors and floppy disk OS	Screen-oriented, Multitaskins OS

Personal computers emerged as commercial products in 1975, with the introduction of the Altair computer from MITS. The CPU and other chips that will be used in the next generation are already in production or advanced stages of design, so crystal ball gazing is fairly easy.

powerful enough to begin taking over some voice communication work as well. It won't be too long until personal computers can double as telephones, sophisticated answering machines, and automatic dialers at a reasonable cost. Merging the personal computer, telephone, and answering machine will not only give more function, it will also clear off desk space.

My desk was a small, simple thing in 1975, with just a phone, in basket, Rolodex file, and radio (see Figure 1-12). Today it is huge. A PC sits on a large, L-shaped extension, and the phone has been joined by an answering machine. With a little luck, the future will bring me a smaller, simpler desk.

Not only will the phone and answering machine disappear into the computer, the components will get smaller. For instance, the current PC disk drives are about 3½ inches high and 5½ inches wide, but smaller units are already available from the drive manufacturers. As chip densities rise, the electronic components all shrink, and the TV-like PC display unit will someday give way to a flatter display that may even be hung on the wall. All of this will reduce the desk space taken up by a personal computer, its *footprint*.

Software progress will also help to clear the cluttered desktops. As software becomes more sophisticated, it will be convenient to use the PC for more functions, and switching from one task to another will be easier. When that happens, the Rolodex files, in basket shelves, and manila folders will begin disappearing from desk tops.

The problems of putting very powerful personal computers on every desk are not technological. Prototypes of such machines exist today. When businesses first acquired telephones, they often put them on pedestals in the middle of the office, but by the 1950s, they had proliferated and moved to everyone's desk. Today we take personal telephones for granted, but it remains to be seen whether we will all have personal computers and clean desks in, say, 1990 or 2000. Problems of standardization and mundane business matters concerned with support, production, and logistics will have to be solved if we are to put computers on every desk; the technical part is relatively easy.

If the future sounds so rosy that you are thinking of putting this book aside and waiting five years for the "ultimate" personal computer, don't. Imperfect as it is by tomorrow's standards the IBM PC is simply amazing by yesterday's standards. It can serve as a useful tool today, and your experience with it will help you to understand your requirements when the time comes to replace it.

BACK TO THE PRESENT

This chapter has answered the question asked in the title. We have seen what a personal computer is, how it may be used, and where it came from. If you haven't already done so, you should get some hands-on experience before reading on. If you already have a PC, you can begin with a game playing program. If you are still in the shopping stage, visit a store and try a

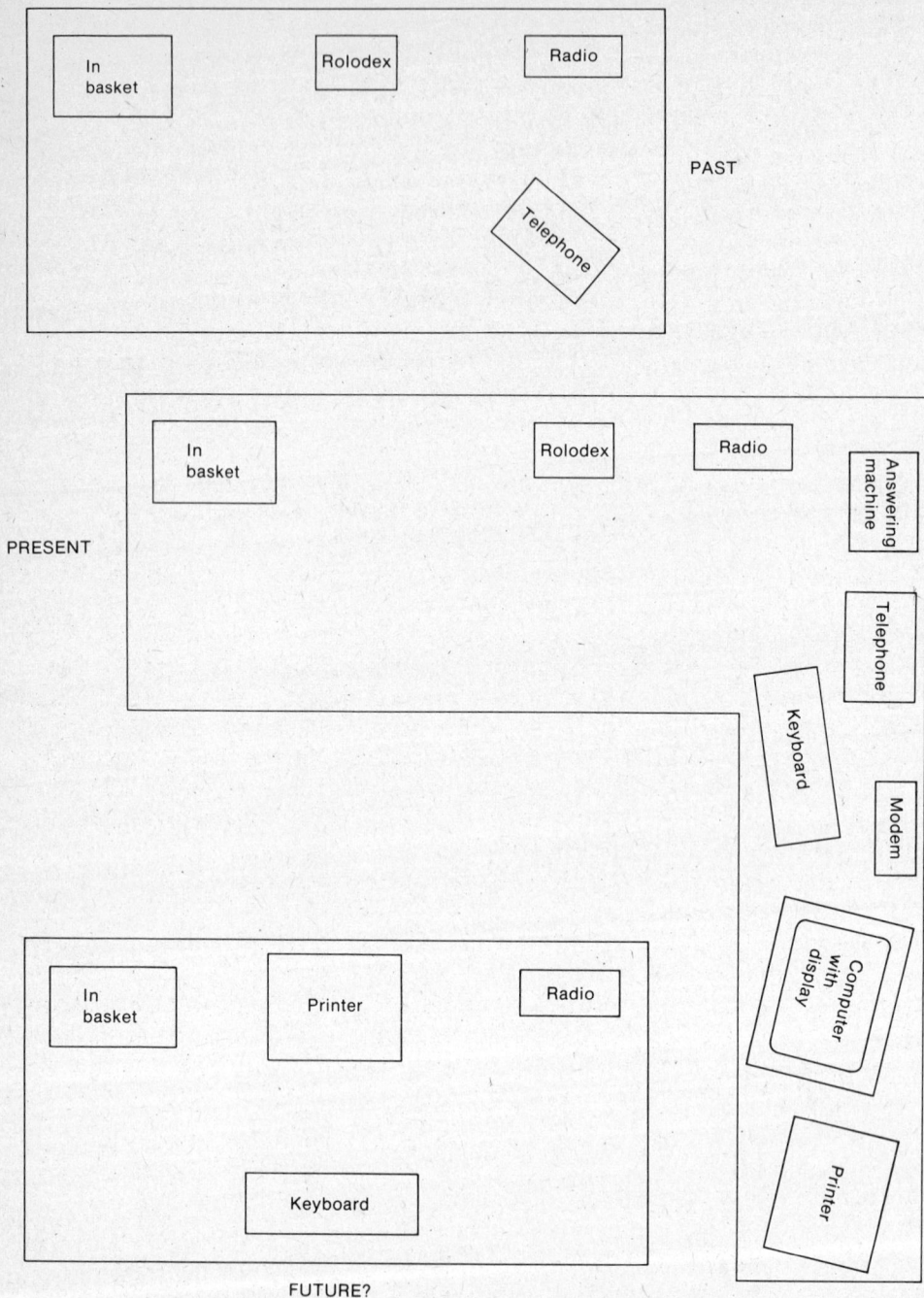

Figure 1-12. Is this progress? In 1975, my desk was small and simple, today it is twice as large and has less free space. With a little luck, personal computer technology will have it looking simple again by 1990 or 2000.

PC out. Play some games, and ask for a "serious" demonstration. Don't worry about seeing it all on the first visit, there will be others.

The remainder of Part I takes a closer look at the PC and its components. By the end of Part I, you should know how the components work and what your choices are, and have a fairly good idea of what you will be getting, where to get it, and what questions to ask. Part II moves on to the important application areas mentioned above: word processing, file management, local communication, remote communication, and spreadsheet modeling. There is a chapter devoted to each application, covering what it is and how it can be used. In Part III, the emphasis switches from "what is an application?" to "what should I buy?" There is a general chapter on software evaluation, followed by separate chapters on software evaluation and the hardware implications of each of our applications.

By the time you reach the end of the book, you will have a good overview of the IBM PC and its applications. You will know what you need and where to look for it. For an in-depth follow-up on one of the applications, you can refer to other books in the PC Series covering word processing, file management, communication, and spreadsheet modeling.

CHAPTER TWO
The Standard Components

The first chapter presented a quick overview of the PC and its components; this one looks more closely. We will examine the keyboard, display, memory, disk, printer, and CPU, seeing how each works and pointing out the choices you have to make in configuring a PC. If you keep your applications in mind as you read this chapter, you should pretty well know what you need by the end. To keep things in perspective, we will also speculate on the evolution of each of the components over the next few years. The next chapter talks about a few other components you might be interested in and gets down to the details of shopping for a PC.

THE KEYBOARD

The primary PC *input device* is the keyboard. Although there are rudimentary devices for drawing on or speaking into a PC, most of what you enter will be typed on a keyboard. The keyboard is an important part of any personal computer, and you can rest assured that the PC keyboard is a good one. It is sturdy, feels as good as the door on a Rolls Royce, is comfortable to type on, and is functionally complete. Figure 2-1 shows a diagram of the PC keyboard. At first glance it is similar to a typewriter, but a closer look reveals significant differences.

Function Keys

For a start, there are ten *function keys* on the left side of the keyboard. They are labeled F1 to F10, because they do not have predetermined functions; the way they are used is determined by the program. For instance, in a word processing application, F1 might be used for the command to delete a word from a document, whereas in a file management application, it might be used to sort a data file. Since the meanings of these function keys are assigned by the software and they are free to change, they are often called *soft function keys*.

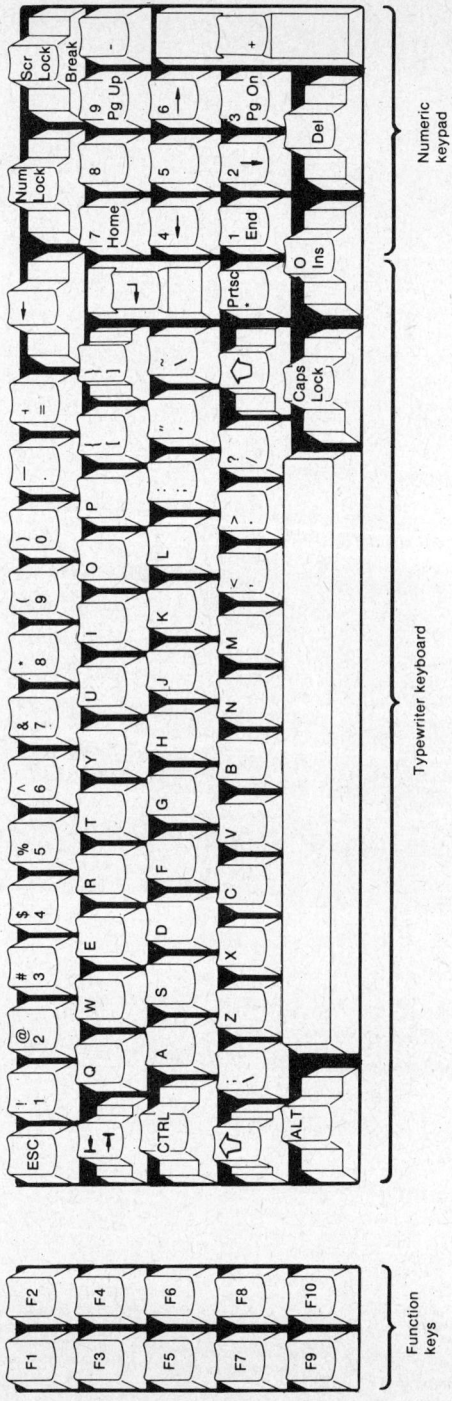

Figure 2-1. This keyboard has a number of keys not found on a typewriter. For instance, there are ten function keys (F1–F10) on the left and special cursor control keys and extra number keys on the right.

The right hand side of the keyboard also has keys that are not found on a standard typewriter. There is a rectangular group of keys laid out like the numeric keypad on an adding machine. These can be used instead of the number keys along the top row to speed numeric data entry, but each has a second meaning when not shifted. The "2," "4," "6," and "8" keys have arrows on them, pointing down, left, up, and right. They are used for moving the cursor around the display screen. But what is the cursor?

Cursor Control Keys

The *cursor* is a special symbol on the display screen that is used to keep track of where you are. In word processing, for example, it shows where the next character you type will go, or in a spreadsheet program, the cursor shows which spreadsheet cell you are working on at the present time. In order to distinguish it from the regular characters on the display screen, the cursor symbol has a unique shape and often blinks on and off. The shape and blinking can be changed by the program, but it is usually a blinking underline character or rectangle. So the cursor is just a pointer on the screen; now let's get back to the keyboard.

The "1" and "7" on the numeric keypad also double as cursor control keys when they are not shifted. As you see, they say "Home" and "End" and are usually used to move the cursor to the top and bottom of the screen, respectively. I say they are *usually* used for cursor control, because in reality, a program can use them for any function. However, not using a key to do what its name implies would be confusing, and not many programmers would do that.

Other Special Keys

There are other special keys, for instance "Ins," "Del," "PgUp," and "PgDn," which are used to insert and delete characters or move the display up or down. The exact way they work depends upon the program, but it will be clear in all cases. The "PrtSc" key causes the contents of the screen to be printed. It usually works as advertised, but it may not in some circumstances, depending upon your printer, display, and software. The "PrtSc" key sounds handy at first, but you will seldom use it, since the application programs for communication, word processing, and so forth all have more flexible printing commands.

The "Ctrl" (*control*) and "Alt" (*alternate*) keys will be used in many programs, so they are important. They work like the "shift" key on a typewriter. If you are using a typewriter and you hit the "shift" key, what happens? Nothing. By itself, the "shift" key doesn't cause anything to be typed; it changes the meanings of the other keys from lower case to upper case. The control and alternate keys are also used to change the meanings of the other keys. For instance, I am using a word processing program as I write this. If I hit the "T" key, the letter T appears as the next character on the line, but if I hold down the control key with my little finger and then hit "T," the program interprets it as a delete word command, and deletes the word the cursor is pointing to. That may sound confusing at first, but have faith—you will adjust quickly.

There are a few other keys that you won't find on a typewriter keyboard, and their meanings will be made clear in the context of the programs you use. But what about the regular typewriter keys, the ones in the middle of the keyboard?

The Middle of the Keyboard

The best known typewriter keyboard layout is the one used on the IBM Selectric typewriter, so you would expect that IBM would have copied it exactly for the PC. For the most part they did copy both the high quality of the typewriter keyboard and its layout, but there are some differences. The most noticeable, and widely criticized, distinction is that the shape and position of the "tab," "shift," and "return" keys are different. If you are a touch typist who is used to the Selectric keyboard, you may find yourself making a few typos when you move to the PC.

Depending upon the arrangement and size of your desk, you may also find that the keyboard cord, which unfortunately attaches to the back of the PC, is too short. This can be a particular problem if you prefer sitting with the keyboard on your lap, as I frequently do.

Most people have little trouble with the nonstandard keys and the cord length, but if you do, you have a couple of alternatives. Several companies manufacture oversize keycaps, which you can put on the "shift," "tab," and "return" keys. If you are a touch typist, they may have some effect, though they don't seem to change anything for my quasi-touch typing. There are also extra-length cables on the market for those whose desk and comfort dictate their use. If you really insist on Selectric compatibility, there are even companies that sell replacement keyboards, but be sure to try the feel before buying one.

Past and Present

The keyboard on your PC evolved from the typewriter, first patented in 1868 by Christopher Sholes, Carlos Glidden, and Samuel Soule. Several of the keys and functions can also be traced to teletypewriters, notably the Teletype which dates back to 1924, and dedicated word processors, dating back to 1964.

Like all of the other peripheral components of a personal computer, keyboards will become "smarter" in the future. You may have heard people speak of *intelligent* or *dumb* peripherals, and while those terms are not rigorously defined, an intelligent device is one that has considerable autonomous capability; it can do relatively complex things on its own without using the rest of the PC.

The PC keyboard is fairly intelligent. It is controlled by its own internal microcomputer, buried under the keys. The internal microcomputer is programmed to let the PC know whenever a key is pressed or released, to diagnose the keyboard for malfunction (when the system is first turned on), to check for stuck keys, to make sure there is only one signal sent when a key is pressed, and to generate repeat signals at a regular rate when one is held down continuously. The small microcomputer inside the keyboard is similar in structure to the one in the PC, but it has a smaller memory and is slower. The only conceptual difference is that its program is never changed; it always runs a keyboard control program. Like the microcomputer in a video game, household appliance, or auto ignition system, it is dedicated to a single job.

It turns out that all of the PC peripherals, the printer, disks, and display, are fairly intelligent. Their controllers are either designed around special purpose LSI chips or microcomputers of their own. In the future, we will see very intelligent peripherals (*VIPs*), with internal microcomputers as powerful as the CPU used in the PC. Unless I miss my guess, it will also be possible to change the programs running in those peripheral control computers, thereby redefining their characteristics.

A more intelligent keyboard would be reconfigurable. It would be possible to redefine keyboard meanings to suit the job at hand (even the legends on the keycaps would be changeable), but those changes are fairly minimal. Since it is largely mechanical and constrained by the size of the human hand, adding intelligence will not have as signficant an effect on future keyboards as it will on other components. Most work will go into increased comfort and appearance, and one day soon the PC may have a cableless keyboard (like its little brother, the PC Jr), which could cut cost and increase comfort. Reduced cost of the electronic components, increased manufacturing volumes, and international competition will also help lower prices.

THE DISPLAY*

The display is the primary *output device* on your PC; you will use it and the keyboard for most of your interaction. Whereas IBM offers only one keyboard with the PC, there are two display options, the *Monochrome* Display and the *Color/Graphics* Display. You will have to select one or the other (very few will get both), so we will describe each. Let's begin with the Monochrome Display.

Monochrome and Color/Graphics Options

The Monochrome Display is divided into 25 lines of 80 characters each. It is a *green-phosphor* display, which means that the characters usually appear

---

*The display is made of two components, the screen you look at and an electronic adapter inside the PC. For now, we will consider them as a single unit, but in Chapter 3, we will have to look a little closer.

light green against a dark green background. If you look closely at the characters, you will see that they are made up of tiny dots, like the images on a television screen. With the Monochrome Display, each character is made up of a *matrix* of up to 7 by 9 dots inside a 9 by 14 dot rectangle (see Figure 2-2).

Since you spend a lot of time looking at your PC display screen, you want it to be easy on your eyes; and the Monochrome Display is. The 9 by 14 dot matrix results in very readable, well defined characters. The green phosphor display is easier to look at than the white-on-black displays that you commonly see, though there is tentative evidence that amber displays (when the room light is low) and those showing dark characters on a light background are even better. The Monochrome Display is flicker-free and is covered with an antiglare coating. A first class job.

The second choice is the Color/Graphics Display. As you can guess from the name, there are two differences: it can display 16 different colors and it can display graphics as well as characters. The part about color is self-explanatory, but what do we mean by *graphics*?

With a graphics display, the computer can be programmed to turn each individual display dot on or off. Instead of having 25 lines of 80 *characters* you have 200 lines of 320 *dots*. Since each dot can be turned on or off, it is possible to draw pictures and graphs on the screen; hence the name "graphics." Of course, the more dots you can put on the screen the smoother the drawing looks, and the display can be programmed to double the *resolution* on the screen to 200 lines of 640 dots, if you need the extra detail. Of course, there is no such thing as a free lunch, so something must be given up to use the high-resolution mode. Can you guess what it is? Color. If a PC is programmed to show high resolution graphics, you are back to a black-and-white display.

Before going on, I want to give you one more term, so you will understand it when you see it in ads or someone uses it. Do you suppose that computer scientists really use a simple word like "dots" to describe the points on the

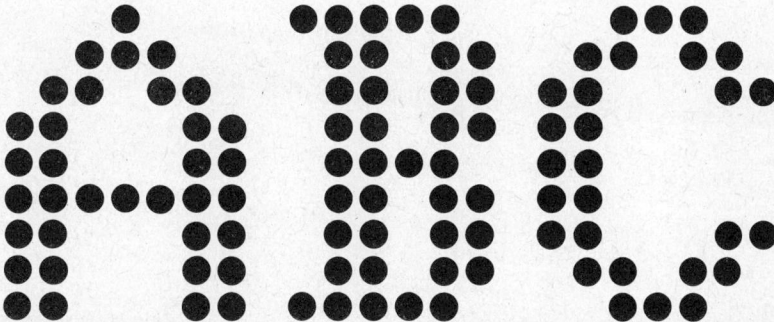

Figure 2-2. The 9 by 14 dot-matrix used in the IBM Monochrome Display gives clear, well separated characters. It is easy on the eyes. Character quality with the lower resolution Color/Graphics Display is not as good, since characters are formed on an 8 by 8 matrix.

screen? No. They call them *pixels*, which is short for "picture elements," but it means "dots."

Which One Is For You?

At this point you might be wondering why anyone would want a Monochrome Display when they could have a Color/Graphics Display. Part of the answer is in the quality of characters. The Monochrome Display constructs characters using a 9 by 14 matrix whereas the Color/Graphics Display uses an 8 by 8 matrix. That means the character quality and separation are noticeably better with the Monochrome Display. Not only that, but, with many programs, the Monochrome Display changes faster than the Color/Graphics Display, which cuts down on flicker. These factors, coupled with the pleasant green phosphor, means that the Monochrome Display is easiest on your eyes and is probably the one you want if you will be using your PC several hours a day, say, for word processing. Moreover, it will save you money.

Of course, graphics programs won't work with the Monochrome Display, so you would not be able to play many of the arcade style games on the market or use *business-graphics programs* that draw pie charts, bar graphs, and so forth on the screen (see Appendix A for more on business graphics). Choosing displays is not easy; be sure to spend some time looking at both before making the decision.

If your application dictates the Color/Graphics Display, but you have a significant amount of character-oriented work, like spreadsheets or word processing, lean toward software that allows you to select the colors in which characters will be displayed. That will give you the opportunity to place black characters on a white background, which, as I pointed out above, is easier on your eyes. The ability to vary the brightness of the display in order to match the ambient light will also help with eyestrain if you are using a color monitor.

It's a Memory-Mapped Display

Let's see how the display works in conjunction with the memory. As we saw in Figure 1-2, information going to the display comes from the memory. Figure 2-3 is a closer look at how the display is actually implemented on the PC. A portion of the memory is set aside as a *display buffer*, and whatever characters are in the buffer area are simultaneously displayed on the screen. If the screen has room for 2,000 characters (25 lines of 80 characters), there are 2,000 corresponding locations in the memory buffer. The location and exact size of the buffer depends upon whether you have the Monochrome or Color/Graphics Display installed. Since you may come across the term, you should know that a display that works like this, in which the contents of a portion of memory are continuously displayed on the video screen, is called a *memory-mapped* display.

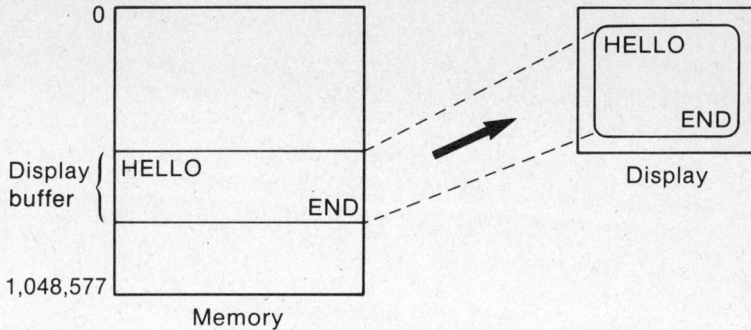

Figure 2-3. With a memory mapped display such as the one on the PC, a portion of the memory is set aside for the screen image. Whatever information the program places in that area will be seen on the screen. With the Color/Graphics Display, more memory must be set aside in order to specify the color of each display dot.

Past and Future

As we saw in Chapter 1, the first computers to use video displays for interactive applications were developed at MIT in the 1950s. Both the devices and approaches to using them were influenced by those pioneering projects. Games also come to mind when thinking back on early displays. Sophisticated space war games were developed on the TX-0 at MIT in the early 1960s, but William Higinbotham, a physicist at the Brookhaven National Laboratories, had already constructed a video game that simulated a tennis match in 1958. Nolan Bushnell's Pong, which started Atari, really got the commercial ball rolling in 1973.

In the past, memory has been a major cost component with graphic displays, in which individual dots can be turned on and off. Since graphic displays are more flexible than character-oriented displays, and memory prices are falling rapidly, we can expect a trend toward graphic displays. Furthermore, resolutions will increase as the cost of memory and control electronics drops.*

There is also a lot of electronic circuitry in a video display, so look for both significant cost savings and increased intelligence. Where a dumb display might be given a command to display a character or dot in a certain position, an intelligent display could handle commands like "display a red square," "rotate the square," "enlarge it," "move it to the left," or "place it in a window in the top half of the screen and clip off its corners if they don't fit." As you can imagine, an intelligent display would take some load off the rest of the PC. The difficulties in building intelligent displays are associated not

*According to Richard Canning, a well-known data processing expert, a minimum resolution in the neighborhood of 200,000 dots is desirable for business graphics. My subjective experience would confirm this estimate.

only with our ability to fabricate them economically, but also with defining and adopting appropriate control-language standards.

Not only will future displays be cheaper and smarter, they will be smaller and will use less power. Various (monochromatic) flat screen technologies are making inroads into the territory occupied by the TV-like cathode ray tube (*CRT*) on your PC. Flat screens will make for relatively portable computers, since they are smaller, lighter and more rugged, and use less power. They will also help with the desk clutter caused by the PC in your office.

THE MEMORY

If the IBM PC is the star of this book, the memory is the star of the PC. As we saw in Chapter 1, everything coming in or going out of a computer passes through its memory. Not only that, but the program being executed must be in the memory. Memory is important today, and memory requirements will

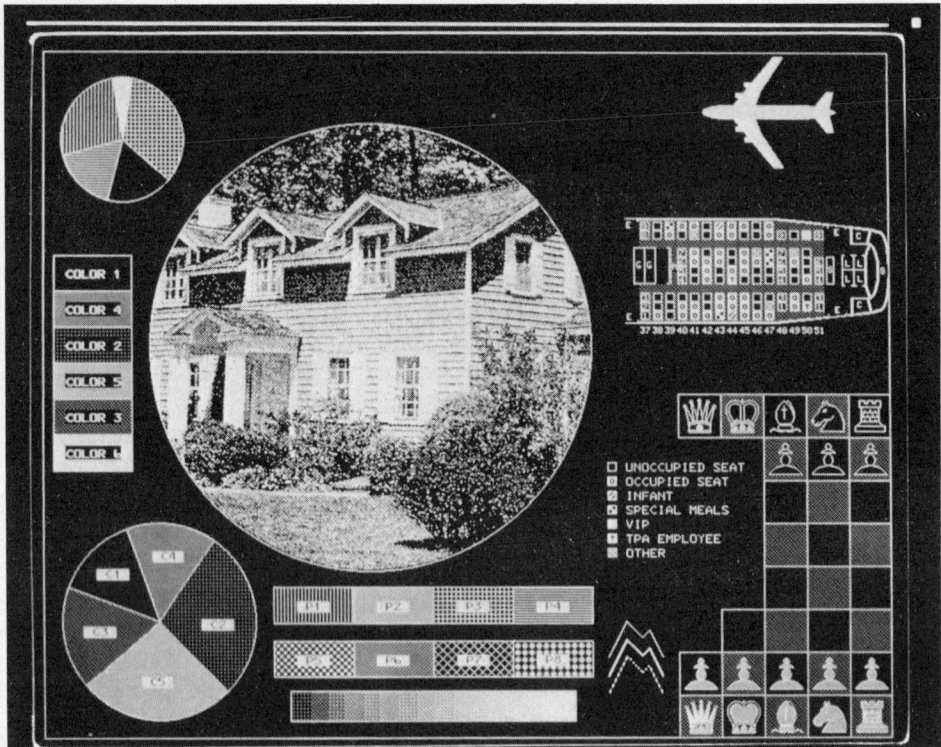

Figure 2-3.5. In not too many years, personal computers will have high resolution, graphic displays such as this one from a large IBM computer. As you see, drawings, pictures, and text with varying fonts can be combined in one image. The software to exploit this sort of display will be a major undertaking. (Courtesy of IBM Corporation)

grow in the future as software complexity increases. But we're getting ahead of ourselves a little.

You know what it means to have a lot of money or a lot of shoes, but what does it mean to have a lot of memory in your computer?

The basic unit of computer memory is the *byte*. Generally speaking, one byte can hold a single character. So if my name (Larry Press) were stored in the memory of a PC, how many bytes would it require? Eleven (don't forget to count the space).

The PC I am using to write this book has a memory capacity of 589,824 bytes. Since the numbers get kind of high, computer people generally speak of *kilobytes* or simply *KB* in describing memories. One kilobyte is 1,024 bytes. A little arithmetic (589,824 divided by 1,024) shows that my PC has a 576KB memory. To put that in some perspective, a double-spaced typed page has about 2,000 characters on it, depending on margins, and the chapters in this book average around 45,000 characters. That means a double-spaced page takes about 2KB of memory and a chapter about 44KB.

How Much Is Enough?

You might wonder why I have such a large memory if a complete book chapter takes only 44KB. Recall that the program you are using must also be in memory. As you see in Figure 2-4, the word processing program I am using ties up another 40KB, and the operating system (the system-control program, which will be discussed in Chapter 4) uses 24KB more. That still leaves quite a bit of space, but what if I wanted to work on several chapters at once, or on two documents, perhaps an outline with notes along with the chapter? Or if I were running a spreadsheet program, having a large memory would enable me to create large spreadsheets.

Still, for doing just one thing, 576KB is probably more than enough. But it

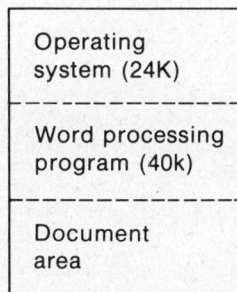

```
┌─────────────────────┐
│ Operating           │
│ system (24K)        │
│ - - - - - - - - - - │
│ Word processing     │
│ program (40k)       │
│ - - - - - - - - - - │
│ Document            │
│ area                │
└─────────────────────┘
```

Figure 2-4. This figure shows how memory is used while a program, the word processor being used to write this book in this example, is running. The operating system takes 24KB, the word processing program 40KB, and the remainder of the memory is available for data, in this case, Chapter 2 of the book you are reading. Even if a program can work in a limited memory, it may be slowed down by frequent transfers of program segments and text to and from the disk.

is possible to use your PC to do more than one thing at a time, and in that case, 576KB begins to disappear rather quickly. We will return to the topic of running several programs simultaneously in Chapter 4.

There is a second reason for wanting a large memory. In many cases, programs run faster in large memories than small. Can you see why? What happens if my word processing program runs out of memory? With some programs that would be the end of the line, but with most programs a portion of the document would automatically be written out to the disk to make room for new material, and writing information on a disk is time consuming (by computer standards). Similarly, if a program is complex, but you don't have much memory, it must be broken into sections, which are brought in from the disk only when needed. Again, bringing in a program section takes time, slowing the PC down.

Okay, memory is good and, since software products are becoming more complex, you will want still more in the future, but how much should you get? I would say you will want at least 256KB for the sort of applications we are concerned with in this book. You should have a reason for getting less. Looking to the future, that recommendation will probably rise to at least 512KB, but if you don't need it already, you might hold off since memory prices are constantly falling, and as we will see, you can add memory later.

Representing Data

Let's see how characters are actually represented in memory. Recall that each character is stored in a byte. Each byte may be broken down into eight *bits* (short for *binary digits*) each of which can be set to either a zero or a one. In Figure 2-5, all of the bits in the first byte are set to zero, the second byte has them all set to one, and in the third byte they are mixed. In order to represent characters, we merely need to make up a code of ones and zeros. Figure 2-6 shows part of the code that is used in the PC. As you see, each letter of the alphabet has its own unique combination of ones and zeros, just

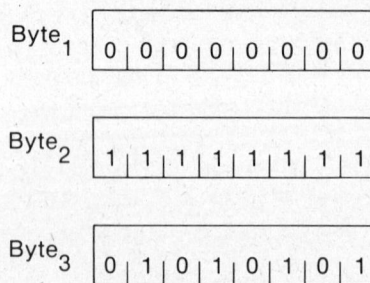

Byte$_1$: 0 0 0 0 0 0 0 0

Byte$_2$: 1 1 1 1 1 1 1 1

Byte$_3$: 0 1 0 1 0 1 0 1

Figure 2-5. Each byte of memory can be subdivided into eight bits. A bit, or binary digit, is set to either one or zero. In the first byte, each bit is set to zero, in the second they are all ones, and they are mixed up in the third. Characters are stored using codes made of ones and zeros.

A:	0	1	0	0	0	0	0	1		N:	0	1	0	0	1	1	1	0
B:	0	1	0	0	0	0	1	0		O:	0	1	0	0	1	1	1	1
C:	0	1	0	0	0	0	1	1		P:	0	1	0	1	0	0	0	0
D:	0	1	0	0	0	1	0	0		Q:	0	1	0	1	0	0	0	1
E:	0	1	0	0	0	1	0	1		R:	0	1	0	1	0	0	1	0
F:	0	1	0	0	0	1	1	0		S:	0	1	0	1	0	0	1	1
G:	0	1	0	0	0	1	1	1		T:	0	1	0	1	0	1	0	0
H:	0	1	0	0	1	0	0	0		U:	0	1	0	1	0	1	0	1
I:	0	1	0	0	1	0	0	1		V:	0	1	0	1	0	1	1	0
J:	0	1	0	0	1	0	1	0		W:	0	1	0	1	0	1	1	1
K:	0	1	0	0	1	0	1	1		X:	0	1	0	1	1	0	0	0
L:	0	1	0	0	1	1	0	0		Y:	0	1	0	1	1	0	0	1
M:	0	1	0	0	1	1	0	1		Z:	0	1	0	1	1	0	1	0

Figure 2-6. This table shows a portion of the ASCII coding scheme for representing characters in a computer. These are the codes for the capital letters only, and similar codes have been assigned other characters. The 96 printable characters also include lowercase letters, numerals, and punctuation marks. In addition to the printing characters, there are codes for various controls like carriage return and line feed.

like Morse code uses dots and dashes. Can you figure out how your initials would be represented in memory? My initials, LP, would be:

```
0 1 0 0 1 1 0 0
0 1 0 1 0 0 0 0
```

Where do you suppose this code came from—was it invented by IBM for the PC? No. It is part of a standard code, called the *ASCII code*, which is used by nearly all computer manufacturers (ASCII stands for the American Standard Code for Information Interchange). It is interesting to note that the PC is the first IBM computer to use the ASCII code exclusively; until now, IBM computers have used their own coding scheme.

Figure 2-6 shows only part of the ASCII code, the uppercase letters. In addition, there are lowercase letters, numbers, and punctuation. Altogether, there are 96 printing characters (including "space"). In addition to the printing characters, the PC uses 12 of the ASCII control codes, like "carriage return," "line feed," and "ring the bell." Those 12, plus the 96 printing characters, take care of 108 codes, but it turns out that with an eight-bit byte there are 256 possible codes, so 148 remain. IBM has decided to use those codes for all sorts of special characters. A few examples are shown in Figure 2-7, but remember that they are not standard; they are specific to the PC.

We should note that the ASCII code is not the only way to represent data stored in your PC's memory. It is used to represent characters that will be printed, compared, and manipulated in various ways, but it is not used to store numbers that will be used for computation. If a number is to be used

☺	:	0	0	0	0	0	0	0	1
♡	:	0	0	0	0	0	0	1	1
ü	:	1	0	0	0	0	0	0	1
é	:	1	0	0	0	0	0	1	0
£	:	1	0	0	1	1	1	0	0
α	:	1	1	1	0	0	0	0	0
β	:	1	1	1	0	0	0	0	1
⌐	:	1	1	0	1	1	0	0	1
Γ	:	1	1	0	1	1	0	1	0

Figure 2-7. IBM uses 108 of the standard ASCII codes in the PC, but since there are 256 unique permutations of zeros and ones in a byte, 148 codes remain. These examples illustrate a few of the 148 special display symbols that IBM chose for the PC. The first two could be used in a game program, the next three would be handy in Europe, and the Greek alphabet is included for mathematicians. The last two symbols would be used in making simple drawings (they would be used as the corners of a rectangle).

for arithmetic, rather than just to be printed or compared, it would be stored in memory in a different way, often as a binary number.

For instance, a telephone number or social security number would be stored as regular ASCII codes, since a program would not be doing arithmetic on them. (It doesn't make a lot of sense to multiply phone numbers!) However, if a payroll program used a person's hourly wage and the number of hours they worked, these items would be stored as binary numbers so they could be multiplied to give the gross pay. An understanding of binary numbers is not needed for this book, but if you are curious about how they work, you can get the idea in Appendix C.

Read Only Memory

You will doubtless come across the term *ROM*, which stands for read only memory. ROM is different than the memory we have been discussing, because it is permanently recorded at the factory and cannot be changed. Other than that, it behaves like the usual *read/write memory*. Do you have any home video games? The program cartridges used in those games are just ROM chips with game playing programs stored in them. To change programs on your PC, you load a new program into memory from a disk, but to change programs on a video game, you change the memory itself along with its permanent program. When the CPU is executing instructions, it doesn't "care" whether they are stored in ROM or read/write memory.

Why would anyone want to use ROM when it seems less flexible than read/write memory? Because it does not erase when you turn off the power, ROM is handy for programs that you use almost all the time. They never have to be loaded into memory; they are just there as soon as you turn on the power. On the PC, portions of the operating system are always needed, so IBM has stored them in ROM. Also, because many people program in the BASIC language, a portion of the Basic programming system is also in ROM. A program to check for hardware malfunction automatically whenever the PC is turned on is also stored in ROM.

Why do you suppose the video game companies use ROM? For a start, if you can change programs by changing memory, you don't need a disk drive on the system, which lowers the initial cost of the game machine. Just as important is the problem of program piracy. Anyone with a PC can make a copy of most programs. Even those that are "copy protected" are not that hard for a technician to copy. But copying a program from one ROM cartridge to another requires equipment and skill that most people do not have.

There are two other terms you may encounter: *EPROM* and *RAM*. EPROM is erasable ROM. It can be erased and rewritten, but doing so requires special equipment, so it does not figure into your use of the PC. RAM, which stands for random access memory, is just another term that is used for the usual read/write memory we have been speaking of all along. Since RAM is a somewhat misleading term, we will stick with "read/write," but you should know what it means if someone tells you they have "64KB of RAM."

Past and Future

Early computers used all sorts of things for memory, even mechanical components. George Stibitz built a computer out of electrical relays (switches that could be opened or closed electrically) at Bell Laboratories in 1939. Each really was one bit of memory (open and closed represented 1 and 0), and Stibitz' computer had a 32 byte memory. Various electronic techniques were developed, but none were truly successful until the magnetic core, devised in 1949 by Jay Forrester for use on the Whirlwind Computer at MIT. Magnetic core memories used tiny donut shaped iron circles to represent zeros and ones. If it was magnetized in a clockwise direction it was a one, otherwise a zero. These were finally superseded by memory chips, such as those used in the PC.

The memory chips used in the Altair, the first personal computer aimed at the general public (1975), had a capacity of 1K bits or 128 bytes each. The memory chips in the first IBM PCs held 16K bits, today's PC uses 64K bit chips, and both American and Japanese companies are already manufacturing 256K bit memory chips. You can draw the graph for yourself. The prices fall in half and the capacities double every two to three years. By the early 1990s we can look forward to 4-million-bit chips costing well under $100.00. That is good news. It means that the memory needed for increasingly complex software will be available, and desktop computers with several million bytes of memory will be common in the near future.

DISK DRIVES

The IBM PC uses magnetic disks for auxiliary storage. When you purchase a new program, it will come on a disk. If you create a data file, whether it is a memo to your boss, a company payroll file, a financial plan, or whatever, it will be saved on disk. Data and programs are written from memory to disk or read from disk into the memory. In either case, the transfer erases whatever was there before, just as recording a new song on a cassette tape erases the one that had been on that part of the tape. If you save a file on disk, an old file of the same name is lost, and if you load a program from disk, the program that had been in memory is erased.

Floppy Disks

Chapter 1 introduced disks like the one in Figure 1-4. They are like small phonograph records that can be used for playing or recording. Information is recorded in concentric circles or *tracks* on the disk surface, using a *read/write head* similar to the one used in a tape recorder. Figure 2-8 shows how the access mechanism inside the drive steps the read/write head from track to track. Some drives record on only one side of the disk (the bottom) and others record on both sides. Two sided drives have twice the capacity, and IBM charges more for them. A disk written on a single sided drive can be read on a double sided system, but obviously it doesn't work the other way around. By the way, you don't have to worry about which disk track something is on, since, as we will see, the operating system is responsible for that.

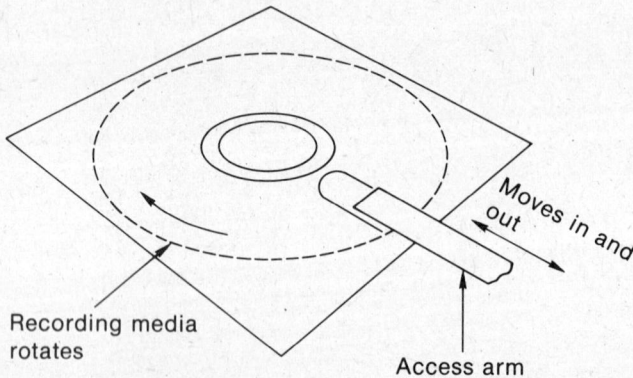

Figure 2-8. A disk drive is similar in concept to a record player. The recording medium rotates inside a protective jacket (see Figure 1-4), and information is read and written through a small magnetic head attached to an access arm. The information is recorded in concentric tracks on the disk, so the access arm must be able to move in toward the center and out toward the edge. All of this is taken care of automatically, in a fraction of a second. If your drive is single sided, the information is recorded on the "bottom" of the disk, the side away from the label.

The disks we have seen so far are made of flexible material, so they are called *floppy* or *flexible disks*. If some disks are flexible, you are probably thinking that others must be inflexible, and you are correct. You can get both *floppy* and *hard disk* drives for your PC (hard disks like those used in the PC are often called *fixed* or *Winchester disks*). There are a number of differences between hard disks and floppy disks; let's go over them.

Hard Disks

The biggest difference between the standard PC and the model XT is that the latter includes a hard disk. The first difference between floppy and hard disks is their capacity. Have you been wondering how much information will fit on a disk? Will it hold ten book chapters, 1,000 customer records, or what? Like memory, disk capacity is measured in bytes or kilobytes. A floppy disk for your PC holds about 160K or 320K bytes, depending upon whether it is single or double sided and on the operating systems you are using. But IBM's hard disk has a 10 million byte (ten *megabyte* or *MB* for short) capacity, equivalent to about 30 double sided floppy disks. A hard disk drive is also faster, since more information is stored on each track (less access arm movement), the access arm moves faster, and information is read and written at a higher rate of speed because the disk rotates ten times faster.

If a hard disk is both faster and capable of holding more, there must be a catch. For a start, hard disk drives are more expensive than floppy drives. They are also noisier, heavier, and more delicate. The heads or disk may be damaged if they are jostled about. Finally, a floppy disk is removable, whereas the medium in a conventional hard disk drive is fixed in place. That means that if your hard disk is filled up, you must erase something in order to add a new file or program. With a floppy system, you just use a new disk.

It will also be necessary to make *backup* copies of files on a hard disk. With the PC-XT, you must use floppy disks for backup, but those wishing to copy very large files might find that too slow and cumbersome. (You would not want to copy 30 disks every day.) A number of vendors offer alternative media for backup, for example, high speed tape cartridges or in one case even video tape. There are also removable hard disks on the market, but IBM does not offer one at this time. There were some questions about the reliability of the earliest removable hard disks, and the cost of the media is much higher than for a floppy disk, but these disks are useful both for file backup and for on-line use.

Your Choice

Which should you get? For a start, do you need the capacity of a hard disk? You can make a rough estimate of your needs with a little arithmetic. We already gave estimates for the storage requirements of written text; how about another example? What if you stock 1,000 items in your business; how much disk would it take to store your entire inventory file? Start by estimating the number of characters for each inventory record, for example:

Stock number	10 characters
Item name	25 characters
Quantity on hand	5 characters
Quantity on order	5 characters
Date of last order	6 characters
Reorder quantity	5 characters
Total	51 characters

A first approximation would be the number of records (1,000) times the number of characters in a record, or 51,000 bytes. Now, there will be overhead, and you need to anticipate growth, but it is not likely that you would go to a hard disk just to accommodate this file.

But capacity is not the only thing to consider in evaluating hard disks. As already mentioned, they are faster than floppy disks. Furthermore, they are more convenient; let's see why. You will be using your PC for a number of things. For instance, you may use it to write reports, a book, or correspondence, for remote communications, or for business forecasting. With a floppy disk system, you would amass up quite a library of disks:

A word-processing program disk
Disks for each book chapter or report
A disk for correspondence
A communication program disk
A communication file disk
A spreadsheet program disk
Disks with spreadsheet forecasting models

As you see, it can mount up. As I look around my office, there are about 200 disks. A hard disk can help organize things, save the time to locate and swap disks, and save operating errors by simplifying procedures. As time goes on and software becomes more complex, hard disks (like large memories) will become even more worthwhile. Finally, floppy disks are vulnerable to coffee spills, being dropped and stepped on, being left in the sun to warp, and so forth.

If you decide that the cost of a hard disk is justified, you will need at least one floppy disk drive to go with it. The floppy will be used for making backup copies of important programs and data files, and since software is sold on floppy disk, you need at least one floppy drive for reading new programs when they arrive, even if you transfer them straight to a hard disk. Ironically, one of the biggest problems you may encounter with a hard disk has to do not with the disk itself, but with software distribution. Many companies use techniques to render their software uncopyable, in order to stop unauthorized copying. Unfortunately, these *copy protection* techniques can keep a legitimate user from being able to copy the program to a hard disk.

What happens if you add up your estimated disk requirements and find you need more than the 10MB of the PC-XT? Sticking with IBM products, you can add a second 10MB hard disk, and other vendors offer hard disk options for the PC with capacities ranging as high as 1 billion bytes. Of course, a disk drive that size will not fit in the PC cabinet.

If you decide on a floppy disk system, you should get two double sided drives. The second drive not only doubles your storage capacity, it also saves a lot of time. You will save time swapping disks in and out of a single drive, be able to organize your disk library more conveniently, and need far fewer disks. The extra cost of double sided drives is also offset by increased convenience and capacity.

A slight variation for you to consider is the *slimline drive*. This kind is functionally equivalent to standard floppy disk drives but only half as tall. That means you can fit two drives into one of the openings in the front of the PC, enabling you to have either four floppy drives in the cabinet or two floppy drives and a hard disk. This is a nice way to save space and cut down on clutter. As of this writing, IBM does not offer slimline drives for the PC, but several other vendors do.

Past and Future

Disk technology owes much to the work of Alan Shugart. He worked on IBM's first commercial disk, which was used in their model 305 RAMAC (random access computer). Built in the 1950s, the RAMAC disk was bigger than a refrigerator and used a stack of 24 inch platters to store less information than fits on the five inch hard disk in a PC-XT. While at IBM, Shugart also invented the floppy disk, which was first used as a console device for loading diagnostic programs and basic control codes into large IBM computers. The floppy disk seemed like such a good idea that he left IBM to manufacture them in 1973, and as such he was also responsible for their early commercial development.

As with memory, the capacity of both floppy and hard disks is steadily increasing, while cost and size decrease. The IBM PC uses industry-standard 5¼ inch disks, but many companies are manufacturing disks ranging from 2½ to 4 inches (both hard and floppy). Unfortunately, no standard size and format has been adopted yet for these smaller drives. Owing to improvements in recording techniques, reduced costs of electronics, and increased production volumes, we can look forward to 100-megabyte hard disks in desktop PCs.

The capacity of floppy disks is also rising rapidly. Yesterday's eight inch disk held 256K bytes, today's three inch disk holds a million, and 10MB drives are coming. Still, many predict the demise of the floppy. Removable hard disks are available, offering considerably more capacity. If they prove reliable and the cost of media comes down much further, they might begin cutting into the floppy's territory.

Bubble memories also compete with the floppy disk. They are fully electronic devices with capacities in the floppy disk ballpark. Since they are not mechanical, and therefore not subject to damage when banged around a bit, bubble memories are often used in portable computers. They remain more costly than floppies of similar capacity and are not usually removable, but they are subject to the same sort of progress as other electronic devices.

Audio and video disk technologies hold the promise of ultra-high capacities for computer storage. At present, they are read-only or write-once devices, but that will not always be the case. However, the power requirements of these laser based devices are such that they will probably not be part of a personal computer for many years, if ever. For the next few years, our PCs will doubtless stick with magnetic recording.

As with the other components, you can also expect to see more intelligence in your disk drives. They will be able to read disks written on other manufacturers' systems and execute complex basic commands like "sort the payroll file into alphabetical order and signal the CPU when you are finished."

THE PRINTER

There are many factors to consider in selecting a printer: speed, character quality, control and flexibility, form handling, size, noise, reliability, and interfacing. As with the other components, your applications, the ways in which you plan to use your PC, will determine which printer you need. To get started, let's see how printers work.

Printer Types and Character Quality

There are two basic types of printer, *dot-matrix* and *formed-character*. Dot-matrix printers are similar to video displays in that they create characters by either printing or not printing dots in a rectangular grid. Figure 2-9 shows how a dot-matrix printer works. As the print head moves across the page, dots are either printed or not, forming the characters. As with displays, character quality is better with some dot-matrix printers than others. Figure 2-10 compares the character quality of the IBM Matrix Printer with a 5 by 9 matrix to that of a printer with a 4 by 6 matrix.

In general, a printer that uses a large number of dots in the matrix, say 9 by 18, will produce better looking characters than one that uses a smaller matrix. Newer printers also stagger the dots slightly and use more and smaller dots, so quality is improving. Not only do many small dots make for clear characters, but the printer manufacturer has more flexibility in designing the *font* or typestyle used for each character. Notice, for example,

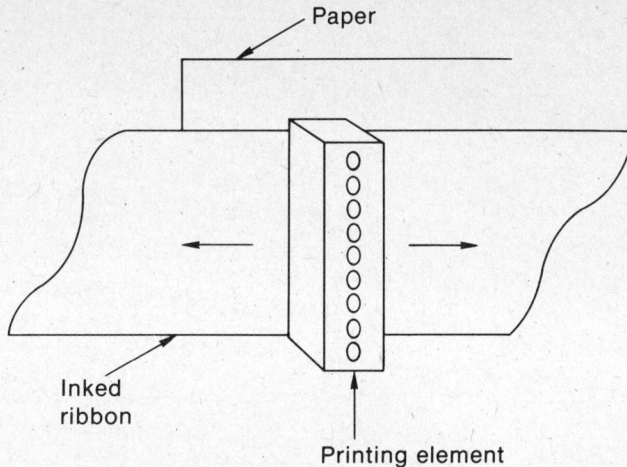

Figure 2-9. With a dot-matrix printer, small pins are struck against an inked ribbon in order to form the characters. The printing element moves after each column of dots is printed. Even a slow printer requires hundreds of print/no-print decisions per second, and therefore printers have internal microcomputers programmed to control the printing process.

how cramped the characters from the 4 by 6 matrix in Figure 2-10 are. There are no *descenders*, dots below the print line, on characters like "g."

Another technique for improving dot-matrix print quality is to make multiple passes of the print head, shifting the dots slightly each time to fill in the spaces (see Figure 2-11). If the printer makes just one pass over the material, it will be relatively fast, but the quality will suffer. If it makes two, speed will be cut, but appearance will be better. Dot-matrix printers often offer two or more *print quality modes*, for instance a high speed *draft mode* or a high quality (but slow) *correspondence mode*.

IBM currently offers four dot-matrix printers for the PC (see Table 2-1 on page 44). The top-of-the-line Color Printer offers three different modes, whereas the Compact Printer only offers one. Of course, there are many other vendors of dot-matrix printers for your PC. If you decide to look at other printers, compare character quality using identical paper and ribbons. Look carefully at difficult characters like X, a, f, g, j, k, p, q, r, w, y, 4, 5, *, @, $, and &. They are likely to be extra light or to have cramped fonts.

To this point, we have been speaking of printing characters, but, like displays, most dot-matrix printers have an *all-points-addressable (APA) graphics mode* as well. In APA graphics mode, they can be programmed to print or not print individual dots, thereby drawing pictures and graphs or producing characters with custom designed character fonts (see Figure 2-12 on page 45). If you decide on a dot-matrix printer and the APA graphics mode is optional, you should probably get it.

When looking at APA graphic printers, keep software compatibility in mind. In character mode, all printers accept standard ASCII codes and print

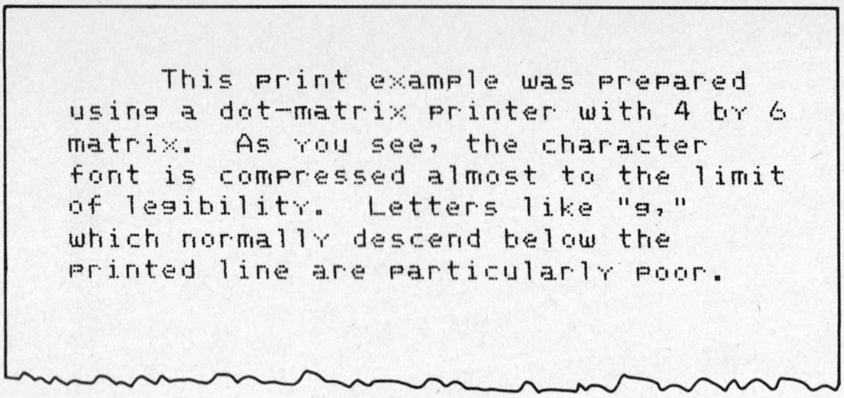

```
         This print example was prepared
   using a dot-matrix printer with 4 by 6
   matrix.  As you see, the character
   font is compressed almost to the limit
   of legibility.  Letters like "g,"
   which normally descend below the
   printed line are particularly poor.
```

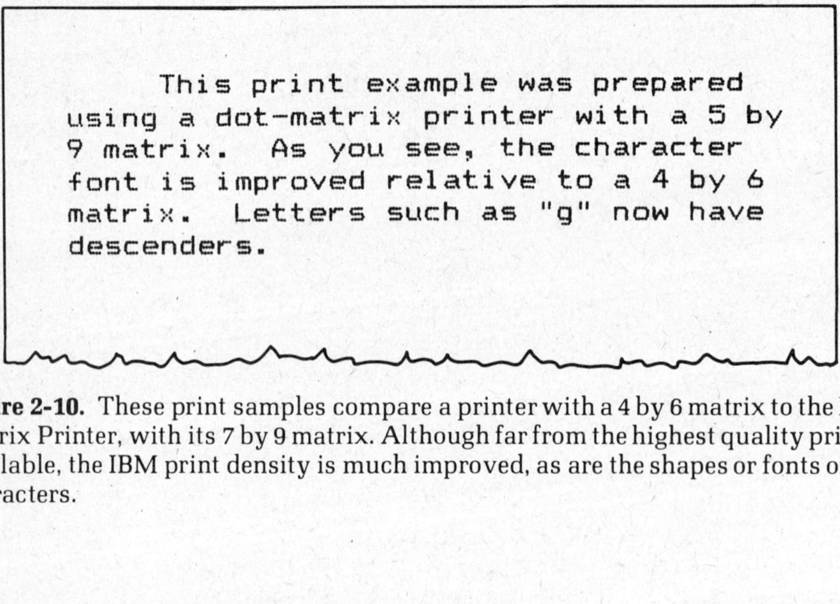

```
         This print example was prepared
   using a dot-matrix printer with a 5 by
   9 matrix.  As you see, the character
   font is improved relative to a 4 by 6
   matrix.  Letters such as "g" now have
   descenders.
```

Figure 2-10. These print samples compare a printer with a 4 by 6 matrix to the IBM Matrix Printer, with its 7 by 9 matrix. Although far from the highest quality printer available, the IBM print density is much improved, as are the shapes or fonts of the characters.

the corresponding characters; however, there are no standards for graphics mode. Therefore, be sure the printer you get is compatible with whatever graphic software you plan to use. A good question to ask in this regard is whether or not the printer is 100% compatible with the IBM Graphics and Color Printers while in graphics mode.

Software compatibility problems can also crop up in character mode if you go beyond the ASCII printing characters. In Figure 2-7 we saw that the PC is capable of displaying many nonstandard special characters, but many printers will be unable to do so. The original IBM Matrix Printer was not able to display those characters, and few printers from other manufacturers are able to either. Of course, many people get along without IBM's special characters.

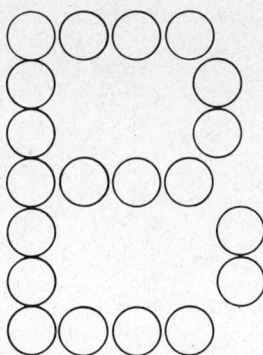

THIS PRINT SAMPLE IS 1 PASS,
12 CPI AT 550 CPS

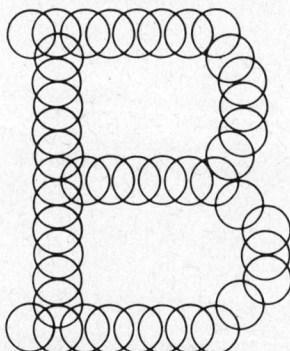

THIS PRINT SAMPLE IS 2 PASS,
12 CPI AT 150 CPS

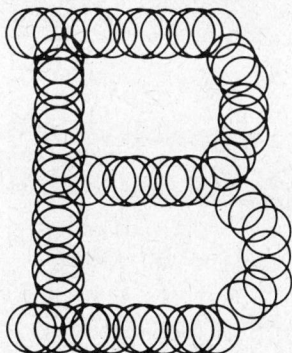

THIS PRINT SAMPLE IS 3 PASS,
12 CPI AT 100 CPS

Figure 2-11. Character appearance may be improved by making multiple passes over the line to fill in the spaces between the dots. Of course, the print speed is cut for each additional pass. Printers that use many small diameter pins also produce better looking results. (Courtesy of Jim Adkisson and Florida Data Corporation)

Table 2-1. Selected characteristics of IBM printers. This table shows selected characteristics of the printers IBM offers for the PC at the present time. The Color Printer is the top of the line in speed, flexibility, and character quality and the Compact Printer is most economical. Of course, many other companies manufacture printers for the PC, so your choice is much wider. In evaluating other printers, be careful to assess software compatibility, particularly in APA graphics mode or when printing characters outside of the standard ASCII set. A given program may not work with a printer, or it may work but produce graphs that are out of proportion.

	Compact	Matrix	Graphic	Color
IBM Model number	5181, model 1	5152, model 1 (no longer available)	5152, model 2	5182, model 1
Type	Thermal dot-matrix	Impact dot-matrix	Impact dot-matrix	Impact dot-matrix
Interface	Serial	Parallel	Parallel	Parallel
Paper	Thermal	Plain	Plain	Plain
Print quality modes	1	4	4	6*
Speed (characters per second)	50	80	80	200 (draft mode) 110 (text mode) 35 (near letter quality mode)
Color	No	No	No	Yes
All-points-addressable graphics	Yes	No	Yes	Yes
Proportional spacing	No	No	No	Yes
Subscripts and superscripts	No	No	No	Yes
Automatic justification	No	No	No	Yes
Number of printable characters	191	157	197	253
Feed	Friction	Pin	Pin	Pin or friction
Maximum paper width (inches)	8.5	9.5	9.5	14.875

*Although there are arguably 12 printing modes on the Color Printer, your nearsighted author cannot see a noticeable quality difference.

A formed-character printer is more like a standard typewriter. Each letter of the alphabet is embossed on the printing element, and to print a character, the element rotates until the character is in front of the ribbon, where it is struck by a small hammer. In some printers, the printing element

THE FREE PRESS

THE NEWSLETTER OF THE PRESS AND PLOTKA FAMILIES

ISSUE 2   JUNE, 1984

Figure 2-12. In all-points-addressable (APA) graphics mode, a dot-matrix printer can print or not print each individual dot. That means you can print drawings, graphs, or special symbols. Here we see a graphic printer used to print characters with user designed type fonts. Of course, the printer runs relatively slowly in APA graphics mode.

is shaped liked a "golfball" in a Selectric typewriter, in some it is flattened out to resemble a flower (these elements are called *daisy wheels*), and in others it is thimble shaped. The shape of the printing element will not be important to you. On the other hand, if you get a formed-character printer, make sure that there is a ready supply of printing elements available and that you like the font choices.

Which is best for you? Dot-matrix printers are faster, more reliable, smaller, and cheaper than formed-character printers. But there is no doubt that what they print came from a computer, not a typewriter. People turn to formed-character printers when they need high quality output, such as that illustrated in Figure 2-13. In fact, you often hear formed-character printers referred to as *letter quality*.

Both formed-character and dot-matrix printers have some capability for special type effects (see Figure 2-14). In general, a formed-character printer achieves these effects through precision placement of the print element and the dot-matrix printer through alternative font definitions. The formed characters look better and can be placed anywhere on the page, whereas the

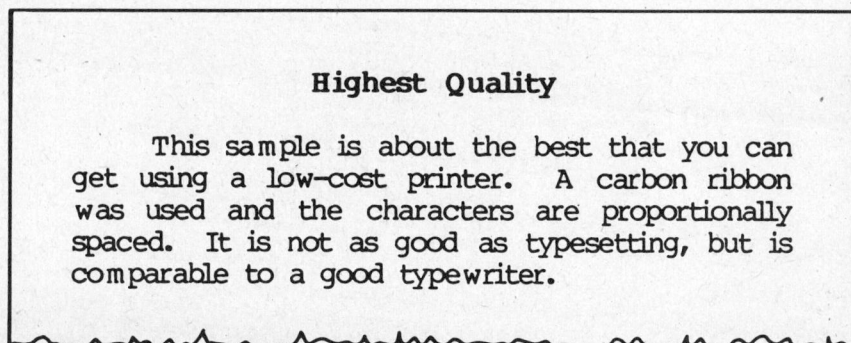

Highest Quality

This sample is about the best that you can get using a low-cost printer. A carbon ribbon was used and the characters are proportionally spaced. It is not as good as typesetting, but is comparable to a good typewriter.

Figure 2-13. This is an example of high quality, formed-character printing. It is shown actual size, but if the output were reduced by a commercial printer, the appearance would be closer to that of set type.

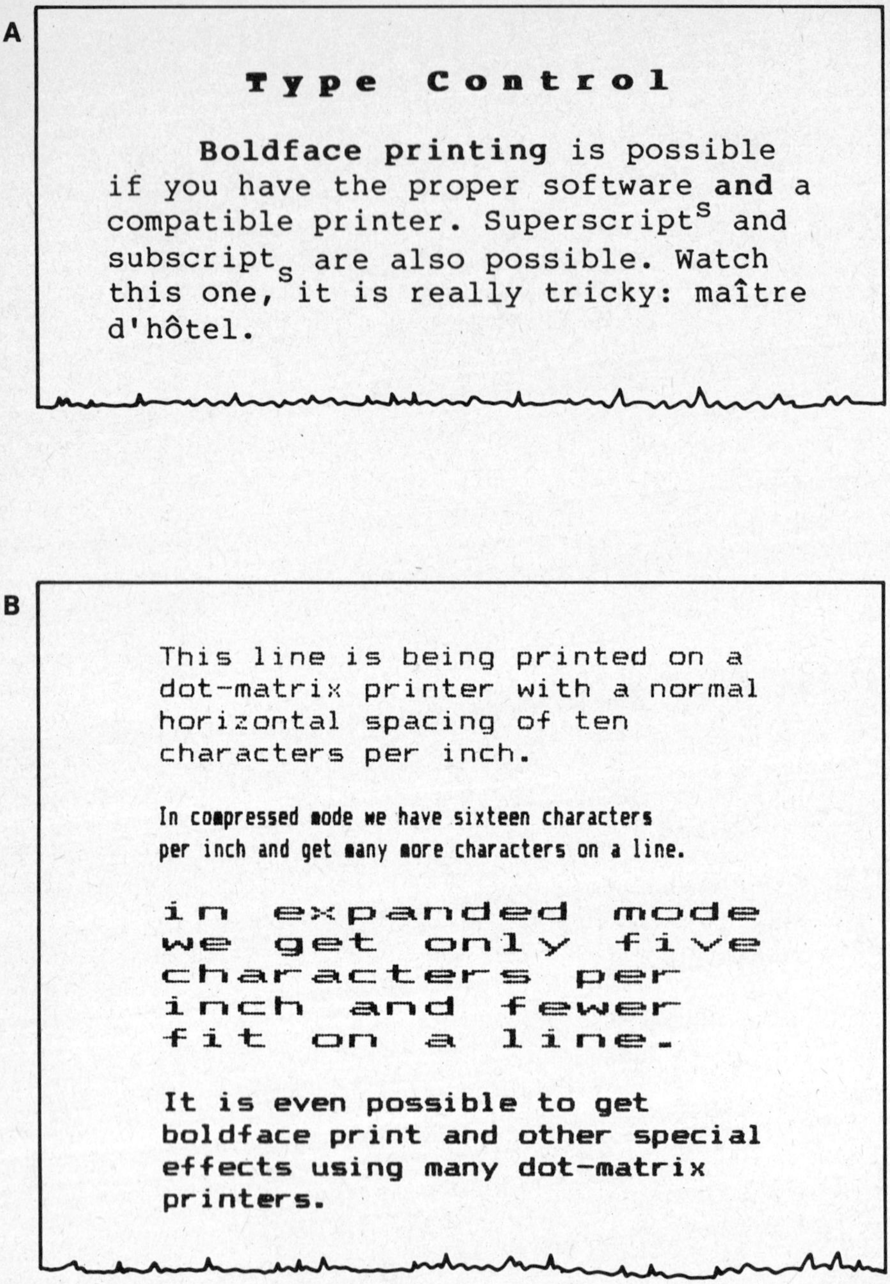

A

Type Control

Boldface printing is possible if you have the proper software **and** a compatible printer. Superscript^S and subscript$_S$ are also possible. Watch this one, it is really tricky: maître d'hôtel.

B

This line is being printed on a dot-matrix printer with a normal horizontal spacing of ten characters per inch.

In compressed mode we have sixteen characters per inch and get many more characters on a line.

in expanded mode we get only five characters per inch and fewer fit on a line.

It is even possible to get boldface print and other special effects using many dot-matrix printers.

Figure 2-14. These examples illustrate the special type effects that are available with a formed-character printer (a) and the IBM Matrix Printer (b). The formed character printer achieves effects by precision placement of characters on the page. For instance, the boldface is achieved by printing a character, shifting the print element 1/120 of an inch, and reprinting it. The different fonts are built into the IBM printer; the program can switch it from one mode to another.

dot-matrix printer is able to vary character size and style. Don't forget that it takes software as well as the appropriate printer to achieve these effects. Special type effects are a likely place for printer/software incompatibility to turn up.

Only you know whether you need the appearance of formed-characters, but remember that people's expectations change. A publisher or customer who might have been turned off by a computer written manuscript or letter in the past might see it as a status symbol today.

To this point, we have spoken only of *impact* printers, which strike an inked ribbon against the paper. There are many nonimpact printing techniques as well. Some of these, for instance ink-jet or laser printing, are still expensive by PC standards, but the print quality is excellent and prices are dropping. They have resolutions of hundreds of dots per inch, and produce very sharp characters and graphics. At the other end of the spectrum are nonimpact printers, such as the IBM Compact Printer, that use special thermal or electrosensitive paper. They are cheap, quiet, and reliable, but the paper is often ugly. However, rapid strides are being made in plain paper thermal printers, ink-jet, and other technologies. High resolution nonimpact printers seem to be the wave of the future.

Speed and Amenities

Printer speeds are usually advertised in characters per second (CPS). Dot-matrix printers typically range from 80 to 500 CPS, whereas formed-character speeds are 10 to 80 CPS. No doubt about which are faster.

Although manufacturers advertise speeds in CPS, that can be misleading. In printing a page, only part of the time is spent actually printing the characters. A good deal of time is spent spacing between lines and pages, so the *slew* rate, the rate at which paper moves through the printer, is important as well as CPS. Bidirectional printing also saves time, as does a *logic seeking* print head, which can move straight to the next character position, even as the paper is moving. In case you think this is mere quibbling, look at Table 2-2. As you see, CPS can be quite misleading as a measure of actual speed or *throughput*.

Does speed matter to you? That depends upon how much you have to print, and on whether or not you have to be there waiting while the printer does its work. If you print many short documents and have to feed the paper by hand, you will waste a lot of time waiting for a slow printer. A long manuscript will take a lot of time with a slow printer, even if it can run unattended. Make an estimate of your printing load. For instance, if you will be sending mass mailings of 100 letters a day, time an actual letter and multiply by 100.

Speed is also affected by printer *buffering*. Since characters are transferred from the PC to the printer faster than they can actually be printed, all printers have internal memory buffers for holding characters waiting to be printed. These buffers are usually very small, holding perhaps

Table 2-2. Effective versus rated speeds of selected printers. These are the results of an experiment run by Tim Barry of *Infoworld Magazine*. He found that the actual time to print a 3,466 character document was not directly related to character printing rates because some printers move the paper and position the printing element much faster than others. The print speeds are shown in characters per second.

Printer	Rated Speed	Time to Print	Effective Speed
TI 820	150	38	91
Centronics 704	180	44	79
LA-36 Decwriter	60	68	51
IDS-440	198	70	50
IDS-460	150	74	47
Anadex DP 8000	112	89	39
Centronics 700	60	112	31
Okidata micro 80	80	137	25

256 bytes. However, several companies sell auxiliary printer buffers with considerably more capacity (see Figure 2-15). Let's say you have a 10,000 character letter to print and a 16K byte printer buffer installed on your PC. The letter would be transferred to the printer buffer at electronic speeds, and while it was printing, the PC would be free to do something else.

Pay attention to amenities as well. At 80 CPS, a formed-character printer is noisy and vibrates quite a bit. It would require a sturdy table. Regardless of what sort of printer you have, if noise is a serious problem, you can put it in a sound deadening enclosure like the one shown in Figure 2-16. An 80 CPS formed-character printer would also be fairly large, not the sort of

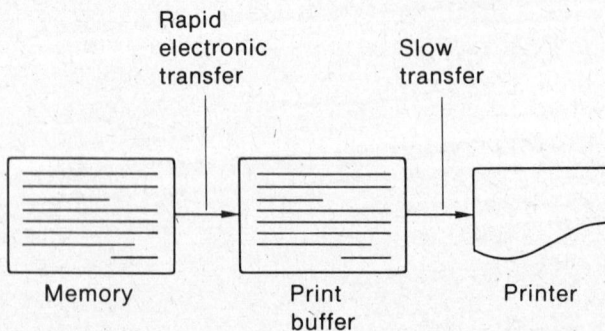

Rapid electronic transfer

Slow transfer

Memory   Print buffer   Printer

Figure 2-15. Information to be printed can be transferred at electronic speeds to a buffered printer. It is held in the buffer memory while being printed, and the PC is freed up to do something else. Some printers come with integral buffers, but they are usually quite small. If you do a lot of printing, look at stand-alone buffers that can be installed between the PC and its printer.

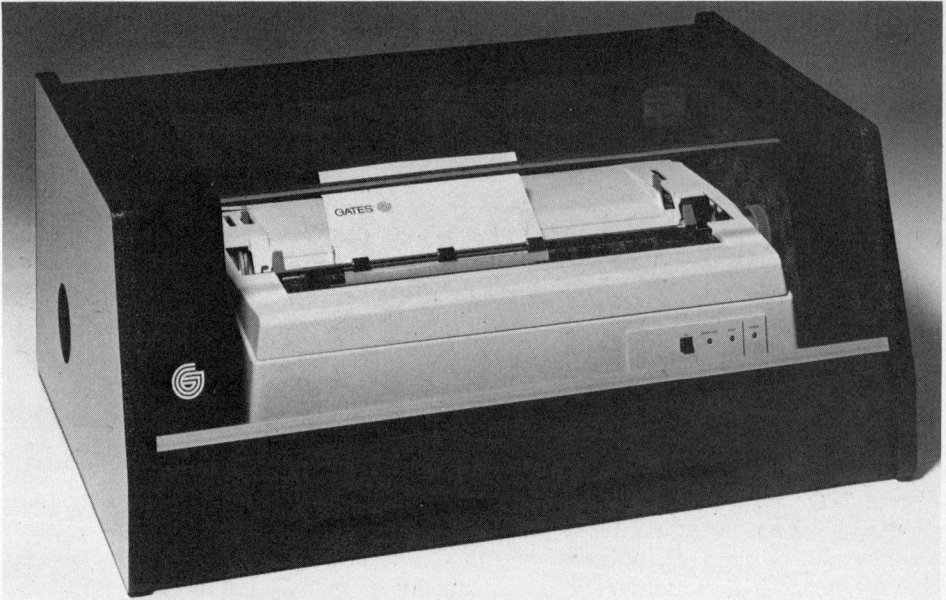

Figure 2-16. If noise is a problem in your environment, an enclosure such as the one around this printer will help. (Courtesy of Gates Acoustinet, Inc.)

thing you would want on an executive desk. Check the footprint size of a printer, don't forget to look at the printer stand if there is one, and anticipate where the paper will sit.

Paper Handling

With a typewriter, you insert single sheets of paper one at a time, and when one is finished, you take it out and insert a second. With a computer printer, you can choose between single sheets and *continuous forms*, in which the sheets are joined together at a perforated edge (see Figure 2-17). Continuous forms are nice if you are printing out something long like a draft manuscript, a spreadsheet, or a long list of salespeople and their year-to-date production. Even if your printer is slow, you can start a job and go for a cup of coffee or a run around the block. The PC would be programmed to skip across the edges of the pages, and when you got back the job would be finished.

On the other hand, printing single letters on your company letterhead would be more convenient if you had a printer that used single, unattached sheets. Which will you use most, single sheets or continuous forms?

For feeding single sheets, you want a printer that works like a typewriter, in which the paper is held against the platen and pulled through by friction. A *friction feed* printer works fine for single sheets, but for continuous forms, you might like a more positive feeding mechanism. With a *pin feed*,

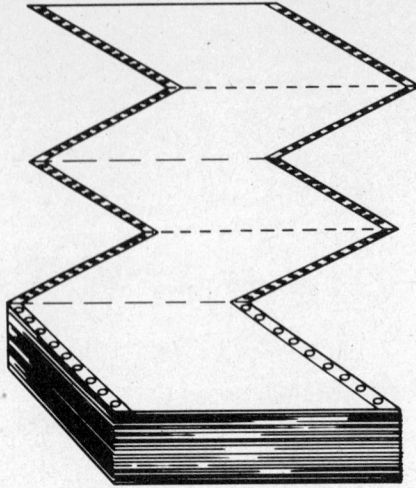

Figure 2-17. With continuous forms, the pages are joined at serrated edges and pinfeed holes are punched into strips along the sides. These strips are also serrated so they can be torn off. Standard sheet widths range from 8½ to 15 inches, but special forms such as gummed labels or continuous index cards might be narrower. If you will be using odd-sized forms, be sure your printer can accommodate them.

the paper is pulled through the printer by pins that fit into holes along the sides of the paper. With a good friction feed mechanism, you can get away with continuous forms in some situations, but if you anticipate using thick forms or gummed labels, or if you will need perfect registration, look for a pin feed printer.

The IBM Matrix Printer comes standard with pin feed, but you can add friction feed as an option. Even if you seldom use it, it is handy to have when you do need it. By the way, you may hear the term *forms tractor*. A forms tractor is a detachable pin feed mechanism that adjusts to handle paper of different widths. A forms tractor is useful when you must use extra wide or extra small paper and when you have thick forms or gummed labels that cannot be wrapped around a platen. Before you get a printer, decide your minimum and maximum paper widths. If you plan to print everything from four inch gummed labels to 15 inch computer paper for wide reports, pay particular attention to the mechanical paper handling of the printer.

If you will be doing a lot of printing on single sheets, for instance mailings on letterhead stationery, there are two other options to consider. One is a *sheet and envelope feeder* that automatically inserts cut paper into the printer (see Figure 2-18). This is not cheap but will save time. Your second option is to have special forms made up, in which your letterhead is attached to continuous paper with a light adhesive. You print it using a standard tractor feed, then remove the sheets from the backing.

Figure 2-18. This printer has a sheet feeder attached to it. It automatically feeds cut sheets such as your letterhead stationery. (Courtesy of Okidata Corporation)

Reliability

Reliability is an important factor, since the mechanical components of your PC, the printer and disk drives, will cause more trouble than the electronic parts like the memory and CPU. But it is difficult to judge reliability. Can you imagine walking into a dealership and being told that a printer is unreliable? Some manufacturers publish data on mean time between failures (*MTBF*), but many don't. Besides, are these figures truly comparable? You will have to rely on your judgment. Pay attention to the quality of construction of the case and the mechanical components. You can tell a well made mechanism from a cheap one. Try to estimate the mechanical complexity. A simple printer with few moving parts will be easier to work on and will break less often. If it is a dot-matrix printer, ask what is involved in replacing the print head when it wears out. Can you do it yourself, and how much will the replacement cost? Touch the print head after it has been running for a while; it should not be too hot. Be sure to find out who will repair the printer. When you have narrowed the choice down, call a repair shop and ask the technician about the reliability and ease of working on the printers you are considering.

Past and Future

Like the keyboard, your PC printer traces its roots back to the days of telegraphy and the early typewriters. Royal E. House patented the first printing telegraph, which used an inked ribbon and printed on a strip of paper, in 1846. Basic design improvements were made by Emile Baudot in the 1860s. This telegraphic equipment evolved into the stock ticker (remember ticker tape parades?) in 1867 and the ubiquitous Teletype in 1924. If you ever get a chance to look at the complex electro-mechanical mechanism of a Teletype, you will appreciate the evolution of impact printers up to the present day. The printer on my first personal computer was a ten CPS Teletype, which broke almost daily. By replacing mechanical devices with electronics and improving designs, engineers have given us fast, reliable, low cost printers.

Looking to the future, we see printers with increased intelligence and memory responding to basic commands from the CPU like "print this report using 12 point roman type, and interrupt me when you are finished."

I would also expect to see graphic dot-matrix printers replacing formed-character printers as technology and people's attitudes about what is acceptable appearance change. Dot-matrix printers are more flexible, being able, for instance, to alter fonts or draw graphs. If people can see that sort of flexibility on their video displays, they will want it on printed copy as well. The same motivation will ensure that color printers are more common in the future than today. It would also seem that nonimpact printers will eventually replace impact printers, since they should be more reliable, make less noise, and offer higher resolutions.

CPU

The central processing unit (CPU) controls all of the components we have been discussing; it executes the program. If an instruction in a program says:

```
PRINT "LARRY"
```

it is the CPU that is responsible for moving the ASCII codes for the characters in my name to the display buffer so that they will appear on the display screen. Of course, in using your PC, you are totally unaware of these microscopic activities. Just as you can drive without understanding how the car works or recognize a Van Gogh painting without understanding your perceptual system, you can use a PC without understanding how the CPU works. However, a little basic literacy will make you comfortable with the terms you encounter.

The CPU in your PC is a single LSI chip made by Intel Corporation, not IBM. (Since 1982, however, IBM has been a major stockholder in Intel.) Of course, IBM is not Intel's only customer; the same model 8088 CPU chip is used in other personal computers. As we shall see in the next chapter, many of them are somewhat compatible with the PC.

Word Length

You may have heard the PC referred to as a "16 bit" computer. That is to say that the *word length* of the CPU is 16 bits. Do you remember the term bit? We saw it earlier when discussing the representation of data in memory; a bit was one of the zero/one positions used in the code for a character. To say that the 8088 is a 16 bit CPU is to say that its basic, machine level instructions operate on 16 bits (two bytes) at a time. Generally speaking, that means it gets more work done with each instruction than an eight bit CPU and less than a 32 bit CPU.

But word length has a second component, the amount of information that moves between the memory and CPU at one time. As the CPU executes a program, the instructions are brought one at a time from the memory and executed. When it finishes one, it fetches the next one from memory and continues. The results of an instruction go the other way. If the CPU adds two numbers together, the sum must be transferred back into the memory. As you can guess, a lot of information moves through the "pipe" between the CPU and memory (see Figure 2-19). With the 8088, only eight bits (one byte) move between memory and the CPU at a time; it is therefore an 8/16 bit

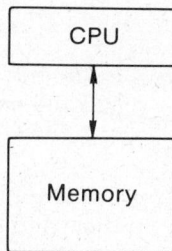

Figure 2-19. Instructions and data move back and forth between the memory and CPU at electronic speeds. In the PC, the path between the CPU and memory is eight bits wide, and one byte is transferred at a time. However, once something is in the CPU, perhaps the number to be added, it is able to work on 16 bits at a time. Since it has an eight bit data path, and performs 16 bit operations, the Intel 8088 CPU used in the PC is said be an 8/16 bit CPU.

CPU. Internally, it works with 16 bit information, but it transfers it in and out in eight bit chunks.

The 8088 used in the PC is the least powerful of a compatible family of CPUs made by Intel. The next one up, the 8086, is identical to the 8088, except that it is a true 16 bit CPU, transferring 16 bits to and from the memory. It is a good bet that future IBM PCs will remain compatible with the original, by using more powerful CPU chips in the Intel family.

Address Space, Coprocessors, Memory Management, and Protection

The word length is the most talked about characteristic of a CPU, but the *address space* is even more important. The address space is the maximum amount of memory the CPU was designed to work with. In the case of the 8088, that is 1,048,576 bytes, or one megabyte (1,024 × 1,024 bytes). See Figure 2-20.

The PC also has an optional *math coprocessor*, an extra chip that speeds up arithmetic and other mathematical operations by adding 68 mathematical instructions to the 8088's repertoire. If your program makes use of it, the coprocessor can make dramatic improvements in the speed of computation. We have run tests of a variety of programs and found that

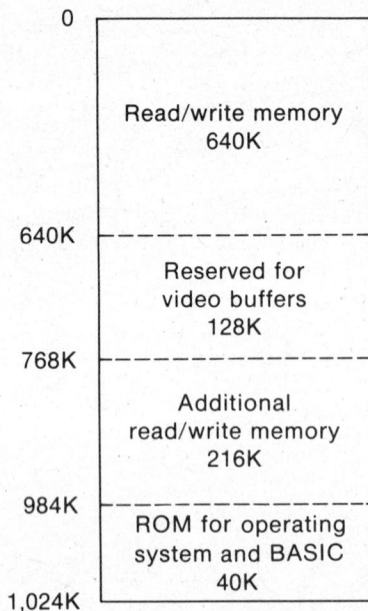

```
0  ┌─────────────────────┐
   │                     │
   │  Read/write memory  │
   │        640K         │
   │                     │
640K ├ ─ ─ ─ ─ ─ ─ ─ ─ ─ ─┤
   │    Reserved for     │
   │    video buffers    │
   │        128K         │
768K ├ ─ ─ ─ ─ ─ ─ ─ ─ ─ ─┤
   │     Additional      │
   │  read/write memory  │
   │        216K         │
984K ├ ─ ─ ─ ─ ─ ─ ─ ─ ─ ─┤
   │  ROM for operating  │
   │  system and BASIC   │
   │        40K          │
1,024K └─────────────────────┘
```

Figure 2-20. This map of memory shows how IBM has decided to use the megabyte address space of the Intel 8088 CPU. Parts of the operating system and the BASIC language processor (we'll say more about these in Chapter 4) are stored in ROM, at the high end of memory. Although IBM has reserved the 216KB above the video buffers for future ROM, some people use that area for read/write memory.

computation speed improves by a factor of four to 20 times with the 8087 installed. Of course, nothing will change if the program doesn't use the 8087 or if the display, printer, or disk is the factor that limits computation speed. So don't elect the 8087 option unless the software you plan to run uses it and execution speed is limited by the CPU rather than by one of the other components. Finally, if you decide not to get an 8087 at first, there is no problem adding one later on, and the price will probably be lower.

You may also hear of *memory management* and *protection* chips. These are not available for the 8088, but are for the more powerful members of the Intel CPU family. They will become increasingly important as software becomes more complex. If two programs are running at the same time, but one has an error in it, these chips can keep the bad program from inadvertently modifying the other one. They can also be used to pull a portion of a program into memory from the disk automatically when it is needed.

A Mainframe CPU?

The term *mainframe* is often used to describe very large computers that are used for processing large batches of transactions such as monthly payroll or inventory reports or for time-sharing by many users. The IBM 370 is one of IBM's mainframes, and it turns out that IBM offers the option of augmenting the standard Intel 8088 CPU on the PC with a 370-compatible CPU.

The 370 CPU option, called the XT/370, enables you to run much of the software written for the IBM 370. The XT/370 option roughly doubles the cost of a basic PC, so you might be wondering who would want it. Large organizations that already had IBM 370 mainframe computers installed might be able to use software they had been developing over the years. Programmers in these organizations who were writing mainframe software might find it more convenient to do so on an XT/370, then transfer the programs to the mainframe when they were finished. The XT/370 also facilitates the sort of communication between personal computers and mainframes that we will discuss in Chapter 9. Or, you just may need to run some software on your PC that requires more memory than the Intel 8088 can address, and the XT/370 has an address space of 4MB.

But wait. Can you really plus 4MB of memory into an IBM PC? Not really. In fact, with the XT/370 option in a PC you have only 512KB of memory, and for technical reasons only 480KB of that is available. Let's say you have a program written for a 370 mainframe computer that uses two MB of memory. How can you run it on an XT/370 with only 480KB?

The answer is provided by what is called *virtual memory*. As you see in Figure 2-21, the *real memory* in the system is only 480KB, but up to 4MB of hard disk space may be set aside as virtual memory. The virtual memory is divided into small segments called *pages*, which can be transferred automatically between the real memory and the virtual memory on the

XT/370 CPU

Real memory
(480 KB)

Virtual memory
(4 MB)

Hard disk
(10 MB)

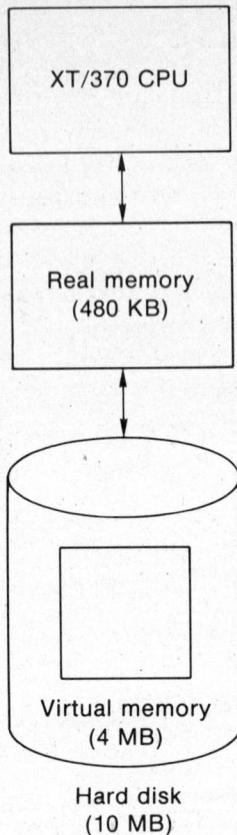

Figure 2-21. With the XT/370 CPU option, a PC can execute programs written for the IBM System 370 computer, which can address much more than 480KB of real memory. In order to use programs larger than 480KB, a segment of up to 4MB is set aside on the hard disk. That segment is used as virtual memory. When the CPU refers to a location that is not in real memory, the page (portion of the virtual memory) containing that location is automatically read in from the disk (see Figure 2-22).

disk. This is illustrated in Figure 2-22. When the CPU attempts to read something from location "X," the hardware checks to see whether the page containing that address is in real memory at the time or is stored in virtual memory on the disk. If it is in real memory, the information is immediately transferred to the CPU. If not, the missing page is automatically read into real memory, and the information then transferred to the CPU.

In either case, the CPU gets the proper information, and the decision whether or not to read a page from the disk is made automatically by the XT/370 hardware. As far as the CPU is concerned, it cannot tell whether the information came immediately from real memory or it was first read in from virtual memory. It is as if the computer *virtually* has 4MB of memory,

```
                    ┌──────────────────────────┐
                    │                          │
                    │      XT/370 CPU          │
                    │                          │
                    └──────────────────────────┘
                      │                    ▲
   Request for information    Requested information
      at address X
                      │                    │
                      ▼
                    ◇ Is address ◇  Yes
                    ◇ X in real  ◇ ────────►
                    ◇ memory     ◇
                    ◇    ?       ◇
                      │ No
                      ▼
            ┌──────────────────────┐
            │  Automatically read  │
            │  the page containing │
            │  address X from      │
            │  disk to real memory │
            └──────────────────────┘
```

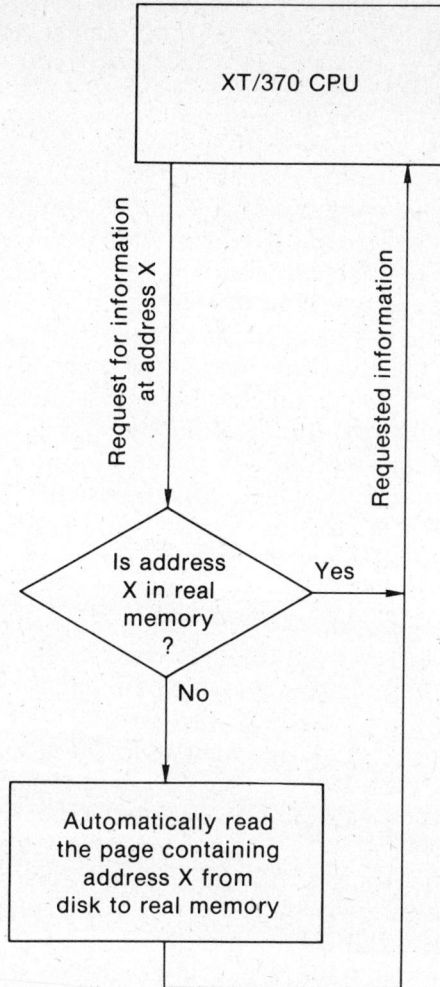

Figure 2-22. This diagram shows how the virtual memory illustrated in Figure 2-21 is managed. The CPU requests information from location X without regard to where it is actually stored. If the page containing location X is in real memory, the information is passed immediately back to the CPU; otherwise, the page is read from the virtual memory area on the disk into memory, and then the requested information sent to the CPU. All of this is hidden from the CPU; it is handled automatically by the memory management hardware. As far as the CPU is concerned, the computer has over 4MB of memory.

Note that the same decision making process would occur if information were being sent from the CPU to the memory. It would still be necessary to have the correct page in memory so that it could be updated.

when in fact the real memory is only 480KB. This is the memory management function referred to in the previous section.

Past and Future

The basic organization, or *architecture,* of the CPU used in the PC, or, for that matter, any other commercially available computer, was worked out during the 1940s by the people who developed the very first electronic computer, the ENIAC, at the University of Pennsylvania. J. Presper Eckert and John W. Mauchley headed that project, which included people like the eminent mathematician John von Neumann among its participants. In 1946 von Neumann, along with Arthur Burks and Herman Goldstine, wrote a report for the U.S. Army entitled "Preliminary Discussion for the Logical Design of an Electronic Computer." Reading that report leaves no doubt that von Neumann would have been able to pick up an 8088 manual and be writing machine language programs in half an hour. Basic CPU organization has not changed since that time; in fact, researchers speculating on new ideas for CPU architecture still refer to the status quo as *von Neumann machines.*

While he would be familiar with the architecture of the CPU in your PC, von Neumann would have been flabbergasted by the actual construction. Your IBM PC is a much more powerful computer than the 30 ton ENIAC was.

The basic ideas have stayed the same, but the technology has evolved beyond imagination, and it is continuing to evolve rapidly. As personal computer CPUs have increased in power, chip manufacturers have implemented the basic architecture of larger computers in one or a few chips. That trend will doubtless continue. Your PC uses a 16 bit CPU today, which resembles the minicomputers of the early 1970s. It won't be long until personal computer CPUs are like the 32 bit CPUs on today's larger minicomputers. They will have large address spaces, being able to address millions of bytes of memory, and will have the sort of memory management and protection capabilities discussed above. That translates into extremely powerful computers.

In the long run, we will doubtless see non-von Neumann CPUs, but that will not be before the next generation of personal computer has come on the scene. The next generation will have conventional CPUs and look a lot like larger computers do today.

CONCLUSION

We have taken a look at the standard components of a personal computer, the keyboard, display, memory, disk, printer, and CPU. In configuring your PC, you have to choose between the Monochrome and Color/Graphics

Displays, decide how much memory to buy, choose between floppy and hard disk drives, and pick out a printer.

If you will be spending long hours with your PC and working character data, the Monochrome Display is probably best. However, if you need graphics or color, you will have to get the Color/Graphics Display from IBM or else turn to another vendor. As far as memory goes, you will probably want at least 256KB. Even if the software you plan to use can get by with less memory, it may run faster with more and you will doubtless get more software later. On the other hand, adding memory is very simple, and you can always do so later.

If you spend a few hours thinking through your applications, you should also be able to decide whether the increased speed and capacity of a hard disk are justified. If you decide to stick with floppy disks, you will almost assuredly want two double sided drives. If the character quality is acceptable, you should probably get a dot-matrix printer. It will be relatively small, flexible, inexpensive, and fast. Regardless of the type of printer you select, don't forget to look at things like speed, convenience, form handling, and maintainability.

By now you should have a fairly good idea of what sort of configuration is best for you and your applications. Still, there are other devices you might want to get and many options to consider in shopping for your PC and putting it together. Chapter 3 covers these topics.

CHAPTER THREE
The Rest of the System

Chapter 2 covered the basic hardware components, those that are included in every PC. But there are other options for you to consider, and those that would be of most interest to a professional or managerial user will be covered in this chapter. In configuring a PC not only do you have to decide what components to buy, but you also have to know how they interconnect, how they plug together, so we will review expansion options and the standard interfaces between the PC and its peripherals. With all that under your belt, you still have to decide where to get your PC, so we will also look at your shopping options. Finally, there are a lot of people other than IBM trying to sell you PC components and even complete, PC compatible and portable computers, so we will say a few words about them.

OTHER DEVICES

Every PC will have the standard input/output devices described in Chapter 2, but there are others that may be of interest to a professional or managerial user, either now or in the immediate future.

Voice Input/Output

In science fiction movies computers often converse with people in natural language, but your PC is far from fluent in English (or Japanese). There are two basic approaches to getting your PC to speak. One is *speech encoding*, in which it is used like a digital tape recorder. Sound patterns are recorded in memory and "played back" through a speaker. These may be words that are prerecorded by the manufacturer or spoken in through a microphone.

You have probably heard examples of prerecorded speech. It is used in many electronic toys and games. There are "talking" cars and elevators, computers give verbal stock quotes ("the-price-of-I-B-M-is—1-2-3") and tell you when a telephone number has been changed ("the-new-number-is—4-7-5—4-3-2-1"). These systems seem to be speaking in sentences, but they are just stringing together prerecorded words.

You have more flexibility if you can record your own speech through a microphone or telephone. In that case, the encoded speech goes into memory, where it can be saved on disk and played back later. Depending upon the quality of the recording hardware and software, it takes from 1,000 to 4,000 bytes of memory to record one second of speech with reasonable fidelity, so a sentence in a reading instruction program for children might easily require about 5K and a phone message 100K.

The alternative to speech encoding, *speech synthesis*, uses much less memory. The basic idea here is that the computer outputs phoneme codes to a synthesizer, which then "pronounces" the sounds through an amplifier and speaker. Since there are only a few phonemes in each word, the storage requirements are negligible. Furthermore, it is theoretically possible to have the computer "say" anything you feel like programming it to say.

Figure 3-1 shows how a speech synthesizer operates. It contains both a phoneme-driven synthesizer and a microcomputer. The computer in the synthesizer accepts standard ASCII characters from the PC and is programmed to "sound the words out" by analyzing them and coming up with the appropriate phoneme codes (its program is permanently stored in its own ROM). Those codes are then fed to the synthesis chip, which pronounces them through a speaker. It is very simple to program the PC in this case; it is just as though it were printing or displaying the words on a screen. The problem is that the quality of such systems may not be the highest. We have run tests with one synthesizer and found that people can recognize only about 50% of the words it "says." On the other hand, the performance of systems that have more extensive programs for sounding words out and are programmed to look up difficult words in a phonetic dictionary stored in ROM is better. Since these systems are all electronic, with no mechanical parts, we can expect to see their prices fall rapidly.

There are many potential applications of both speech encoding and speech synthesis, helping handicapped people, for example, or teaching

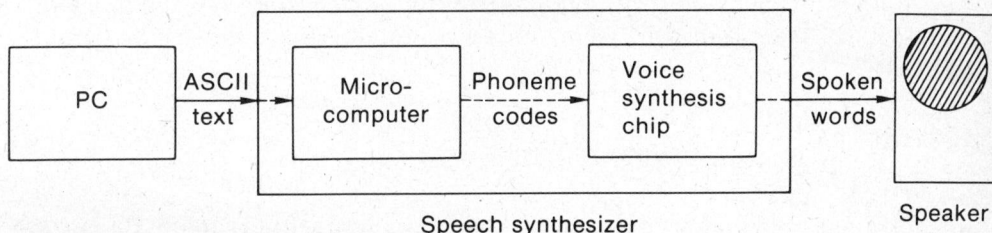

Speech synthesizer   Speaker

Figure 3-1. Programming a PC to "talk" using a speech synthesizer is as simple as programming it to print words on paper, since the words are sent as plain ASCII text. The speech synthesizer contains its own microcomputer, which has been programmed to convert the words coming in to the appropriate phoneme codes, which in turn are passed on to the synthesis chip for output to the speaker.

small children, but the one you are likely to find on your desk is telephone management. It is not difficult to imagine using a PC as an "intelligent answering machine" that can record spoken messages for playback to you, forwarding to another phone, or permanent storage on disk. This will become practical when disk and memory capacities grow and recording techniques improve, and both are happening now. Getting the phone into your computer is an important step toward the simplified desk of Figure 1-11.

Voice Recognition

While good progress is being made toward the goal of using a computer as a digital tape recorder and voice synthesizer, the problem of recognizing what someone says is much more difficult. There are systems for your PC today that are capable of very simple voice recognition tasks. For example, you could control cursor movement by recording patterns for the words "up," "down," "right," and "left," and then pronouncing them into a microphone to move the cursor.

Note some of the limitations in that example. First of all, the systems within the PC price range have to be "trained" to your voice, because your "up" sounds different than mine. In this example, we have limited the vocabulary to four words. Increasing the number of candidate words concomitantly increases the chance of erroneous recognition or of "not sure what you said, please repeat" messages. Furthermore, the words must be said one at a time, not run together in a naturally spoken sentence, and there had better not be any background noise, for that would cause problems.

With time, these limitations will begin to lift. There are already systems available (though not for a PC) that can discriminate among several hundred words with fair accuracy, as long as they are spoken separately. However, even if a recognition system correctly identified every word, it would in no sense be "understanding" what was said. These days a lot is being heard in both the United States and Japan about "artificial intelligence," but people have been trying to build machines that understood the meaning of (typed) natural language input since the earliest days of computing. To me that goal seems far away, but there are those who would disagree.

Alternative Ways to Point

The purpose of the cursor control keys is to point at a place on the screen. If you want to delete a character while using your word processor, you point to it with the cursor, then give a command to delete it. If you want to change a cell in a spreadsheet, you point to it by moving the cursor, then type in the new values or formulas. In selecting command alternatives from a menu, you often point to your choice by moving the cursor, then hit the ENTER key to make the selection. But the cursor control keys are just one means of pointing; there are others.

Have you gotten a chance to try a video game yet? Video games usually use a joystick for moving objects around on the screen, and joysticks are available for the PC, but their precision is limited relative to other pointing devices, such as the *mouse* (see Figure 3-2). The mouse was developed as a pointing device in the early 1960s, and many manufacturers are now offering mice that are compatible with the PC. You move the mouse over the tabletop (some work optically, requiring a special pad on the surface) and the cursor follows your hand movements. A mouse will have from one to three buttons on the top for signaling to the PC when it is pointing at the spot you want. You can move the cursor quickly with a mouse, and with a little practice you will be able to control it easily. However, using a mouse means taking your hand off the keyboard, and of course the PC must be programmed to use the mouse.

A mouse can also be used for freehand drawing, in doing design work, and in preparing figures for reports. A *digitizing tablet* is an alternative to the mouse for such applications. It is similar in that a pen or a device that looks like a mouse is moved over a special grid on the user's desk to control the cursor. The difference is that with a digitizing tablet the computer knows exactly where the pen is on the grid, whereas with a mouse it only senses relative motion, the direction in which the mouse moves. If you plan to be drawing figures, try both out to see which you can control more easily.

Figure 3-2. A mouse may be used instead of the cursor control keys for pointing at spots on the screen. As the hand size device is moved around on the tabletop, the cursor moves on the screen. When you get it where you want it, perhaps pointing at an appropriate menu choice, you hit one of the buttons on the top. (Courtesy of Microsoft)

Why All the Fuss?

Both the mouse (today) and voice recognition (in the future) are being touted as very important devices for the business and professional PC user. Why? Because it is felt that most managers and professionals will not use a keyboard, since they consider it low status clerical work and are unwilling to spend the time learning to type.

However, although typing on a typewriter might have low status implications, PCs are becoming status symbols. I know of one executive who has his hidden in a $10,000 cabinet that automatically opens and places the keyboard in front of him when he presses a button. The attitudes and skills of people coming out of school today are certainly different than in the past. Furthermore, a mouse is just a pointing device. It can be used to designate something on the screen that you want to change or move and to select a command, but it cannot be used to enter information once you have the right place. You could not type a letter using just a mouse.

To use a mouse or other pointing device requires both extra hardware and special software. In the short run at least, your software choice with a mouse-oriented system will be limited (unless you will be doing a lot of freehand drawing). Only time will tell whether mice are a necessity or a fad, but even if you are attracted to them now, look before you leap.

Plotters

Plotters are not the people in the other department who are trying to step on your fingers on the way up the corporate ladder; they are computer output devices used to draw pictures and graphs. The basic idea is simple, as you see in Figure 3-3. The plotter has a pen that can be raised off the paper,

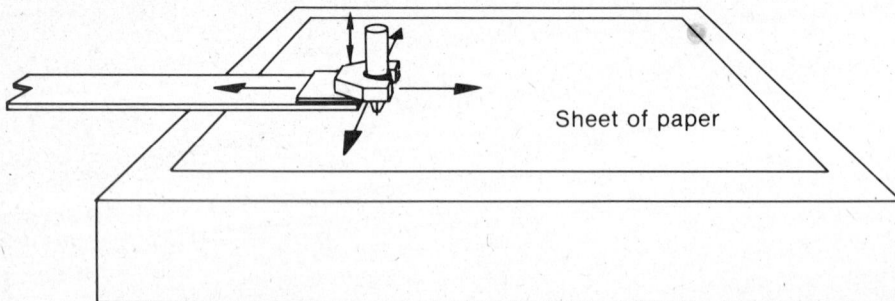

Sheet of paper

Figure 3-3. This diagram shows how a plotter works. A mechanism can raise or lower the pen and move it to any coordinate point on the page. If the pen is down when moved, it draws a line, so every drawing is made of line segments (a circle would be drawn as a many faceted polygon). Programming at the level of pen movement would be very tedious, so software packages are available that work at a much higher level, allowing you to produce, say, a bar chart with just a few commands and specifications.

lowered, and moved to any point on the page. Pictures drawn in this manner are really composed of many straight lines, and as you can imagine it is a rather tedious process. However, as a user you don't get involved with the low level drawing commands. You construct a figure on the screen, perhaps a pie chart, bar graph, or freehand drawing, save it on the disk, and then give the command to print it. The graphic software takes care of it from that point on; it deals with the hundreds of small pen movements.

There are other kinds of plotters besides the one diagrammed in Figure 3-3. Some have several pens, so that they can make color drawings (see Figure 3-4), and with others the paper moves under the pen(s). Regardless of the design, low cost plotters have one thing in common, they take quite a while to draw something. A chart or diagram may take several minutes to complete.

Graphic dot-matrix printers (those that can print individual dots) can also be programmed to make drawings and graphs. In that case, the picture

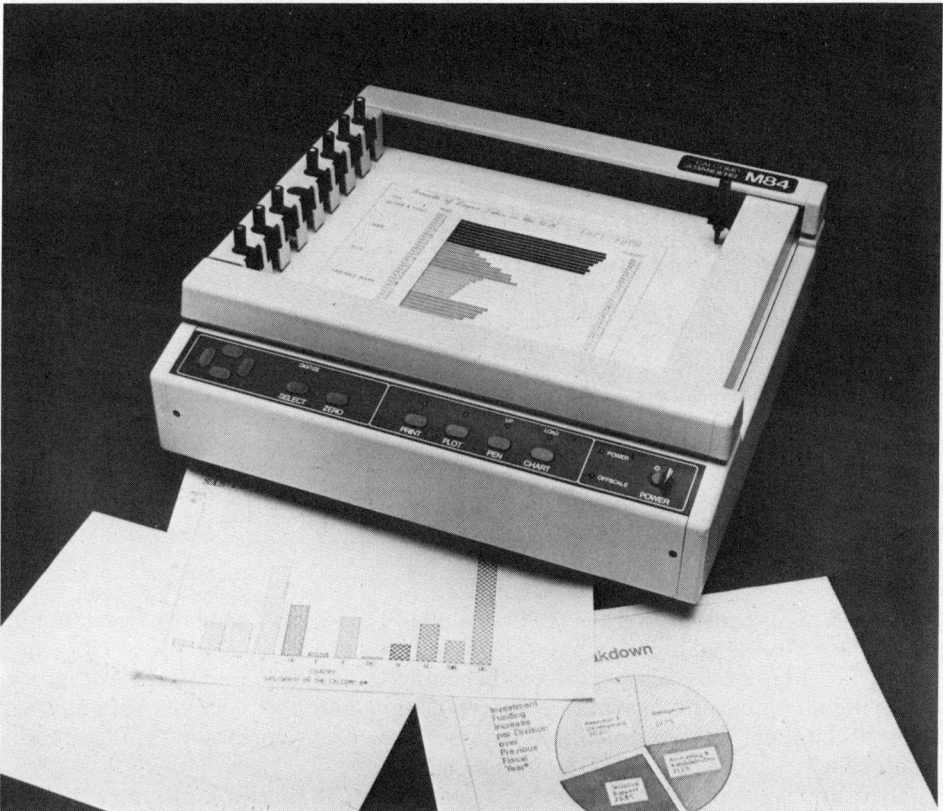

Figure 3-4. This plotter has 8 pens, each with a different color of ink. When it receives a "change color" command, it replaces the current pen in the rack on the left and picks up a new one. (Courtesy of Calcomp)

is made up of lots of dots, not straight lines, but the effect is similar. Plotting with a low cost dot-matrix printer is also fairly slow. Since the resolution and cost of dot-matrix printers are both improving rapidly, and everyone needs a printer anyway, I would expect a trend toward the replacement of plotters with printers as time passes.

PLUGGING IT ALL TOGETHER

We have spoken of the PC as a collection of components that work together, but how do they actually plug together, how are they packaged? Let's take a look inside the PC. If you already have one, just remove the screws in the back and slide the outer cover off. Don't be afraid, it's all very simple, no different from looking around under the hood of a car.

With the cover off, you see something like Figure 3-5 (a model XT would also have a hard disk and three additional expansion slots). On the bottom of the PC there is a green plastic *printed circuit board*, covered with chips plugged into sockets. That large board, called the *system board* or *mother*

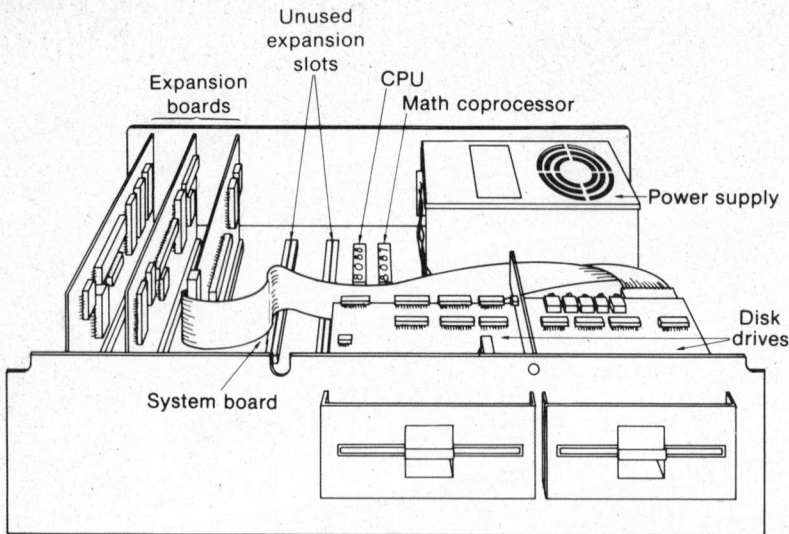

Figure 3-5. This drawing shows the inside of a PC. It looks mysterious at first, but it isn't. Don't be afraid to remove the cover and look around inside your PC; it's not nearly as complex as what you see beneath the hood of your car. Adding or removing an expansion board, or even replacing a bad disk drive, is very simple. Even if you don't do it yourself, you can see how easy working on a PC is for a technician.

There are five expansion slots on the system board. In this illustration, only three are being used. At least two slots, one for the disk control board and a second for a display controller, are used in every PC. Extra memory or other add-ons would go in the remaining slots. If this were a model XT, one of the disks would be a hard disk, and instead of five expansion slots, there would be eight.

board, contains many of the basic electronic components. For instance, the CPU is the large chip located to the left of the power supply. Look at it closely, and you will see that the model number, 8088, is printed on the top. Next to it, you find another of the large, 40 pin sockets. That is for the 8087 math coprocessor, and if you didn't order one as an option, the socket will be empty.

Can you find the disk drives? They are easy to spot in the front of the case. Notice that each is held in by just two screws and is attached by a plug and a flat, multiwire ribbon cable, so removing a drive takes only a minute or two. That sort of easy modularity makes servicing the PC simple. Look inside an electric typewriter and ask yourself which would be easier to maintain.

Behind the disk drives is the *power supply*. Its function is to convert the AC current coming from your wall plug into DC current at the voltage levels your PC needs. The power supply is designed to protect your PC. If the voltages are not right, it refuses to start the computer. The only thing you need to be aware of is its capacity. If you have a PC-XT, you have a heavy duty power supply, designed to power the hard disk. If you bought a PC without a hard disk and are planning to add one later, be sure that either the disk has its own power supply or your PC power supply has sufficient capacity. Make that your dealer's responsibility.

Room for Expansion

To the left of the power supply, you see several printed circuit boards that are plugged into the system board (see Figure 3-6). One of these *expansion boards* (or *expansion "cards"*) contains the electronics that controls your disk drives. Can you tell which one it is? Right. It's the one that's connected to the disk drive by a ribbon cable. How about the other boards?

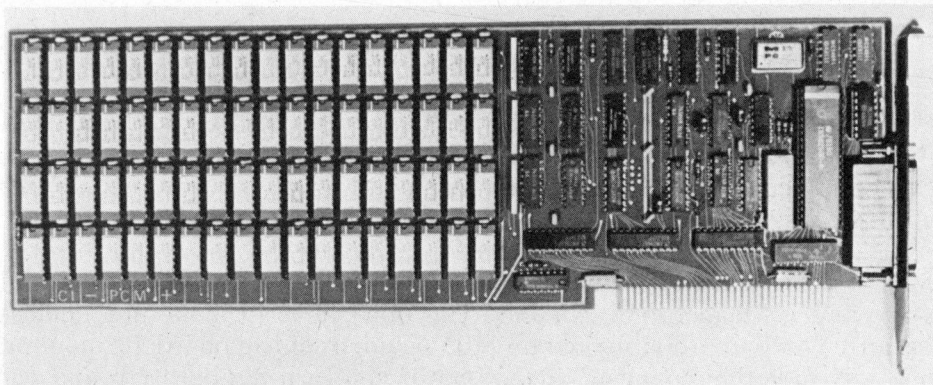

Figure 3-6. This is a typical PC expansion board. The plug on the lower right of the board fits into a slot on the PC system board. With a memory board such as this, you can add 512KB to your PC in a few minutes. (Courtesy of Chrislin Industries, Inc.)

Every PC is also equipped with a board that controls its video display. You can tell which it is by looking for the cable that plugs into the end of the board through the opening in the back of the cabinet. The cable runs from the video control board to the display monitor. Recall that IBM offers two display options, Monochrome and Color/Graphics. Each of these has its own board as well as its own monitor. If you get a Monochrome Board, you will need a monochrome monitor, and if you get the Color/Graphics Board you will need a color monitor to go with it. More on monitors below.

Is there room for extra expansion boards in your PC? On the PC-XT, the system board has connectors or *slots* for eight expansion boards, whereas the standard PC has just five. As we will see, there are many manufacturers who would like to fill these empty slots with their own expansion boards.

Where is the memory? Some memory chips are plugged into sockets on the system board, but you may have still more, depending upon the memory size of your system. The original PC system board was designed to use 16K bit memory chips, so only 64K bytes of memory would fit on it. If you wanted more, you had to add an extra memory board in an expansion slot. The newer system board uses 64K bit memory chips, so it is able to accommodate 256K bytes without going to an extra memory board, saving money and expansion slot space.

What if you decide to purchase the XT/370 option, installing the IBM System 370-compatible CPU? That would require not one, but three additional boards, plugged into expansion slots of a PC-XT. One of the three contains the 370 CPU and the memory management circuitry necessary to transfer virtual memory pages in and out of real memory, the second contains the real memory for the XT/370, and the third enables the PC to emulate certain models of IBM mainframe terminal.

Note that many expansion boards have more than one function. For example, do you have a Monochrome Display? If so, the board that controls the display also has the control circuitry for a printer.

The Outside World

I have been describing the interconnections within the PC, but how about the external devices? Figure 3-7 is a diagram of the back of a PC, where everything connects. You can use it as a point of reference in reading this section.

Let's start with the display. The PC in Figure 3-7 is set up for both Monochrome and Color/Graphics Displays, for the sake of illustration. If you want a Monochrome Display, you don't have to make any choices because you will probably just buy IBM's video control board, its monitor, and the cable that connects them. Even if you turn to another brand, the components should be fully IBM compatible.

With the Color/Graphics Display, there are three connection options. The first is to connect the PC to the antenna of a standard color TV set, using an *RF modulator*, which is just a device that tricks the TV into thinking your

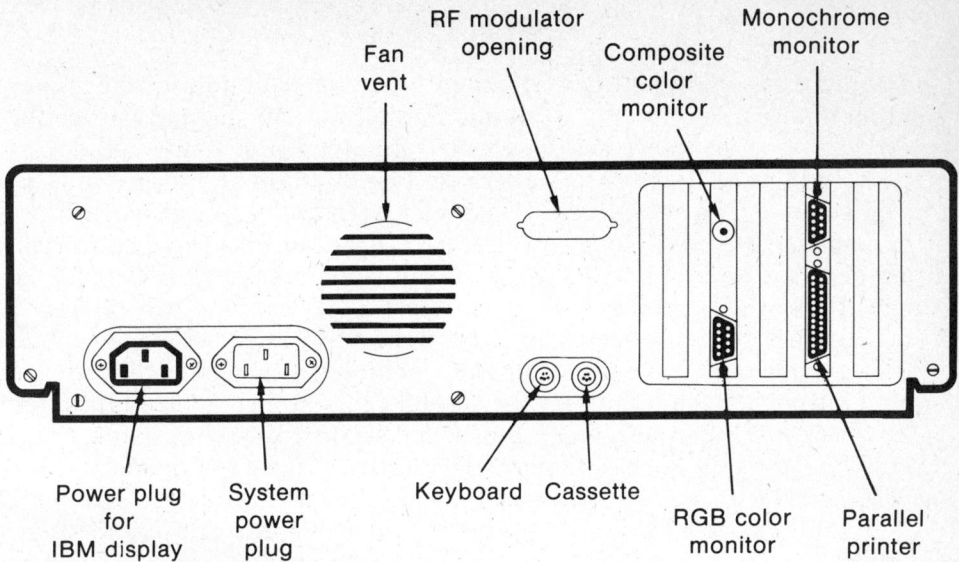

Figure 3-7. External devices plug into the PC from the back. For purposes of illustration, this system has both Monochrome and Color/Graphic Display Boards installed. The Color/Graphics board may be plugged into a composite monitor, an RGB monitor, or a standard TV set (using an RF modulator). Since an RGB monitor produces a sharper image, that is probably the one you would choose.

The Monochrome Display is controlled by a multifunction board. In addition to the display plug, it has a port for a printer. In the case of the Monochrome Display, you will probably get the board, cable, and monitor from IBM.

If you had other expansion boards that interfaced to the outside world, for instance a modem board or a serial input/output board, they would be in the adjacent unused slots.

computer is a TV program being broadcast on an unused channel. An RF modulator is electrically inefficient, limiting you to 40 character lines, so you should forget that alternative for serious use.

The other choices involve using video monitors. A monitor is like a high quality TV set without the circuitry for antenna input and channel selection. Instead of connecting to an antenna, the signal goes straight into the display. There are two types of color monitor, those that accept a *composite video* signal and those that need separate signals for the primary colors (red, green, and blue), RGB monitors.

RGB monitors generally produce the best images, since unscrambling a composite signal is not necessary (IBM's color monitor is an RGB). You will have to pay more for an RGB than for a composite video monitor, but my guess is that you will feel the extra cost is justified when you see the results. If you already have a TV set with an auxiliary input for a composite video signal, perhaps for a videotape recorder, try it out, using a word-processing or graphics program, but be critical in evaluating the quality of the image.

The Printer

The interfaces among hi-fi components are well standardized; every manufacturer's turntable plugs into any amplifier using a standard cable. Unfortunately, the interfaces between computer components are not as smooth. In the world of printers, there are two different standards: the *RS-232* or *serial* interface and the *Centronics* or *parallel* interface. Printers often come standard with one and offer the other as an option. The electrical differences are not important to you, but of course your PC must be compatible with its printer.

The IBM dot-matrix printer comes with the Centronics parallel interface, which, as you may have guessed, was established by Centronics, Inc., a prominent printer manufacturer. Since eight bits are transferred from the PC to the printer at a time ("in parallel"), and several control signals are also needed, the cable is fairly complex. If you buy a non-IBM printer with a parallel interface, you may still get the cable from IBM, but be sure your dealer guarantees compatibility of the PC, the cable, the printer, and your software.

Now, the cable plugs into the printer at one end, but how about the other end? If you have a Monochrome Display Board installed in your PC, you are ready to go, since it is a *multifunction board*, with a connector (or *port*) for a parallel printer as well as the IBM Monochrome Monitor. Look back at the fourth slot from the left in Figure 3-7, and you can see the two sockets.

If you have a Color/Graphics Display Board (the second slot from the left in Figure 3-7), you will need another board with a printer port. IBM will sell you a board with a single, parallel port on it, but that is not a very good deal, because, in addition to the cost of the board, it ties up one of the expansion slots while providing only one function. Many companies manufacture multifunction boards that include one or two parallel ports.

If your printer has a serial interface, things are a little more complicated, but not seriously so. The RS-232 serial interface was specified by a professional standards society, but unlike a standard for, say, screw threads, which is unambiguous, the RS-232 standard has been interpreted in slightly different ways by each manufacturer. This doesn't cause any major problems, just irritating hassles.

Figure 3-8 illustrates the problem. Everyone adheres to the standard to the extent of making compatible plugs and sockets. There is also universal agreement on the meanings of most of the critical pins in the plug: pins 1 and 7 are always used for electrical and signal-level ground, pin 2 for data transmit, and pin 3 for data receive. But two minor problems can occur. The first is the sexes of the connectors. A cable can be wired correctly but be female when it should be male or vice versa. The second problem has to do with *handshaking*, signaling when a device is busy. If you are printing something and the printer runs out of paper, it needs a way to signal to the PC to quit sending characters temporarily. It may even have to pause while it does a carriage return or feeds paper from one page to the next. The problem is that all printers don't use the same mechanism to signal that

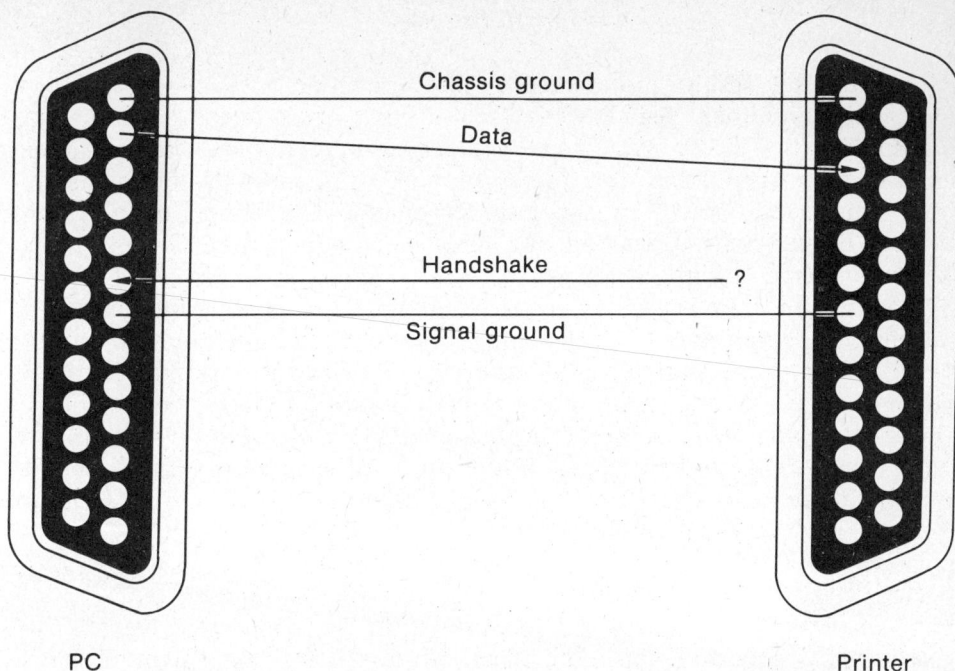

Figure 3-8. The cable connecting a device like a printer to a PC through a serial port usually has four wires in it. Two are used for electrical grounding, one for the signal ground, and the other, like the third connector in a wall plug, for power ground. The power ground is often left out, but that is a little risky. The data going to the printer travels through a third wire.

The pin assignments for those three wires are standardized, but unfortunately different printer manufacturers use different pins for the fourth wire, the one that signals when the printer is busy. A technician will have to make up a custom cable in most cases, and, if the printer manual is confusing (or not available), some trial and error may be necessary in order to get the printer-busy (handshaking) connection correct.

they are busy, so a cable that works with one printer will often not work with another.

The solution to either of these problems is simple: make a new cable. It will always be possible to get an RS-232 printer to work, but it may take some experimenting with cable configurations. Make that your dealer's responsibility.

The PC shown in Figure 3-7 does not have a serial port. The XT model comes with a standard serial port, but the PC doesn't. If you have a PC or need more than one serial port on an XT, you can buy an IBM serial interface board or, more likely, get a multifunction board with as many serial ports as you need. But why would you need more than one serial port? Because they are used for other input/output devices, not just printers.

Other Devices

Most other devices, for instance mice, plotters, modems for communication over telephone lines (see Chapter 8), and voice input/output systems, are available with RS-232 interfaces. In such cases, you may run into the same sorts of minor problems as with printers. I should also mention in passing that you need to set a few software parameters in the operating system when using devices connected to a serial port; again, that will be simple. Your dealer can handle it for you.

In some cases, external devices will interface through a *game port*. IBM planned the game port for video game joysticks, but some manufacturers have used it for mice and other devices. Again, IBM sells a game board, but game ports are available on many multifunction boards.

Finally, some devices, for example non-IBM disk or display controllers, have their own control boards that plug directly into one of the PC expansion slots.

SHOPPING

Shopping for a PC and shopping for a Chevrolet are similar in many ways. After doing some reading and talking to friends, you visit a dealer, get some literature, and discuss the models, options, and accessories that are available. You go for a test drive, return home to think it over, ask more questions, do some more reading, and visit another dealer or two.

Since you are reading this book, you must at least be at the stage of having decided on IBM. By this point you should have a good idea which model you need, the hard disk XT or the floppy disk PC, what type of printer you need, and, roughly, what your memory requirements are.* But whose components should you buy?

IBM Versus Brand X

When you buy a Chevrolet, you can get the radio from the dealer or from an independent shop. Pick up any computer magazine and you see ads from hundreds of companies that make IBM PC accessories. If you want to, you can get a stripped down PC and add memory, input/output ports, disks (hard or floppy), printers, video displays, and so forth from alternative vendors.

Is that a good idea? To some extent it probably is. There are two basic reasons for going outside of IBM: to get additional capability or to save money. As we have seen, there are a number of boards on the market that combine the functions of several IBM boards in one package. For instance,

---

*Each chapter in Part III has a section on hardware requirements that will help you refine your configuration.

let's say you have decided you need a game port, two serial ports (one for a printer and one for a modem), and 512KB memory. At the time of this writing, that would require four separate expansion boards from IBM, but many manufacturers combine all four in one board, at a considerable savings. Note that I said "at the time of this writing." Prices change, and new products are announced by IBM and others almost daily. Although specific offerings change, the basic idea will not, so consider alternatives to IBM components.

But does it make you nervous to buy "off brand" parts? Are you uneasy about buying Michelin tires or a Sears battery for your Chevrolet? In buying components from alternative suppliers, you have to worry about maintenance and compatibility. Computers are very reliable, but they do break sometimes. Before you buy anything, make sure you understand who could fix it for you and what they charge.

Compatibility is also a possible problem. Hardware compatibility is fairly easy to achieve. IBM has had a policy of encouraging companies to manufacture add-on components for the PC, and they have published detailed specifications for the hardware designer. You can be almost certain of hardware compatibility. Software may be more of a problem. Let's say you purchase a certain word processing program. Now, unless the software company has made a huge mistake, the program will work well with an IBM printer, but what if you buy someone else's printer? Or, perhaps you have decided you need both graphic capability and the high resolution characters of the IBM Monochrome Display. In that case, you would be interested in one of the alternative display boards on the market, but again, is it compatible with all of the software you will be using? Does it emulate the IBM displays properly?

Many of the components in a PC are purchased by IBM from other companies. For instance, the dot-matrix printer is made by Epson, and they have a model that is very close to the IBM printer. Surprisingly enough, the disk drives are also standard subassemblies and are safely purchased from second sources. There are also many color monitors (not display boards) that, if they can display the full 16 colors, can be considered without further compatibility worries. You can even purchase memory chips without being concerned about compatibility. Ask your dealer to check out these options as a way of saving money, but pay attention to the warranty periods of the substitute components as compared to IBM's.

The most likely places for compatibility problems are with non-IBM display boards, disk controllers, and printers. Run some tests with the software you plan to be using, and remember that a simple test may not show up problems. For instance, a printer might work well until you get it back to your office and try to print italics. If you will be doing any graphic printing, be sure your software works with your printer. Obviously, manufacturers do their best to be fully compatible, so you don't have to be too worried, but keep your eyes open. If you deviate from IBM, have your dealer guarantee the compatibility of the components and software you buy.

Your Dealer

Have you noticed how many times in the last few pages I have suggested that your dealer assume some responsibility? Selecting a dealer may be the most important step in the shopping process. What would you look for in a car dealer? You should want among other things a good price (but perhaps not rock bottom), reasonable financing if needed, a good parts and service department, knowledgeable and friendly salespeople you felt you could communicate with, a sense of honesty. Look for the same kinds of things in a computer dealer.

IBM has a chain of retail stores (called "Product Centers"). There are also independent dealers and non-IBM chains. For large purchases, you can deal directly with IBM. The fact that a dealer is part of a large chain doesn't guarantee that they have a lot of resources or skills. The individual dealerships are often independently owned; some may be excellent and others poor, although IBM is making a strong effort to train and qualify authorized dealers. There is even variation among the IBM Product Centers. Consider the individual dealer, not the reputation of a chain.

The fewer resources—friends, consultants, colleagues at work, club members and so forth—you have available, the more important your dealer will be. Be particularly cautious about guarantees of the compatibility of everything you purchase (hardware and software), and consider maintenance before committing yourself.

Maintenance

Maintenance is particularly important, not because your PC will break often (in roughly five machine years of operation, I have not had any problems with either of my PCs), but because when it does you will need it back in a hurry if you are using it in your business or professional work.

There are many options available. The IBM Customer Service Division offers maintenance contracts that fully cover the PC for a monthly fee. Like health insurance, it is expensive but relatively safe. A fixed fee maintenance contract also facilitates planning, since you know exactly what it will cost each month. IBM offers several options, including maintenance at your site and walk-in service centers. Their offerings and the way in which a given problem would be handled will vary from city to city, so ask detailed questions like where are parts stocked, what is the maximum turnaround time for any repair, where will the repair actually be done, and are loaner machines and components available while you are waiting for your PC to be returned.

IBM may very well not be the best bet for maintenance. Just as there are independent auto-service shops, there are independent computer-repair companies. There are national repair chains as well as local people. In many cases your dealer will have a well staffed and stocked service department. Check all of these alternatives out, and be sure to cover all the questions mentioned above in your maintenance agreement.

If you are part of a large organization planning to purchase many PCs, you can deal directly with IBM. IBM will offer you a quantity discount, although a dealer may well beat it. Many large companies still buy PCs from non-IBM stores. As a large organization, you should also expect discounts on software. If you will be purchasing, say, 100 copies of a certain word processing program, you certainly should not pay full price. Work your way up the distribution chain. Ask your local dealer for a discount, look into becoming a "dealer" yourself, go to the wholesale level or to the software publisher.

A large organization can also expect better terms on a maintenance contract, and you should consider the alternative of setting up your own in-house maintenance staff. The PC is highly modular and therefore easy to troubleshoot. A technician can swap a disk drive, printer, memory board, or other component in just a few minutes. With a small stock of spare parts and systems, it should be possible to maintain a large fleet of PCs, and IBM offers classes to train your service staff.

COMPATIBLE COMPUTERS

When the PC was introduced in 1981, IBM offered around half a dozen software packages to go with it; today there are thousands. There are twenty-plus companies advertising "PC compatible" computers, hoping to exploit this software base. This section will guide you if you are thinking of getting one of those machines.

But why would someone be tempted to buy a compatible computer rather than the PC itself? Certainly the PC can run all that software as well as its imitators. One reason might be value; the compatible machine could be cheaper, have more capacity, or both. A second reason, in the case of several of the compatible machines, is portability; they are designed to move around. This section looks at the question of compatibility, the next at portability.

Ergonomics and Quality

You may be surprised to find ergonomics included as a compatibility issue, but in order to be comparable to a well designed machine like the PC, a competitor must offer the same level of quality, design, and operator comfort.The styling, feel, and comfort of the keyboard, display size and clarity, viewing angle and glare resistance, quality of materials and construction, noise level, desk footprint, layout on the user's desk, and documentation standards must all be in the IBM ballpark.

Note that this can even mean copying IBM's mistakes. For instance, several compatible machines duplicate the layout of the IBM keyboard, even though most people seem to agree that the shift keys are awkwardly placed. However, if the manual that comes with a program written for the

PC is to be 100% applicable to the compatible machine, it must have the IBM keyboard, shift keys and all.

On the other hand, some ergonomic improvement is possible without sacrificing compatibility. For example, the keyboard cord can be longer or attach at the front of the machine instead of the back.

Component Capability and Capacity

In evaluating a PC compatible machine, look at each of the system components, comparing its capability with the PC. Most compatibles use the same CPU as IBM, the Intel 8088. Some use upward compatible members of the Intel CPU family, which will be fine unless you have a time sensitive program in which software executing too rapidly causes a problem. For those who need the extra speed, check to see if the 8087 math coprocessor is available.

The compatible machine should be able to accommodate as much memory as the PC on its system board. Of course, adding memory in expansion slots should also be possible.

For the keyboard, compatibility is largely a comfort and quality issue, as mentioned above. If there are keyboard layout differences, make sure all of the functions are at least duplicated. You will need the function keys, "Ctrl," "Alt," "Num Lock," "Shift Lock," and the other special keys.

Display compatibility involves both viewing comfort and clarity, and functional capability. Remember that the PC has both Monochrome and Color/Graphic Displays. A "compatible" machine without color or without graphics may not be suitable for your applications. Remember also that the PC can display many special symbols (Figure 2-7), and these must be duplicated by a compatible display. As with the keyboard, improving on the PC display may result in incompatibility. For instance, if the display offers higher resolution graphics or more colors than the PC, it would seem to be better. But if you get home and find that programs written for the standard PC graphics board won't work or that shapes or colors are different, you might not be so happy. If you will be using a composite video monitor, be sure it is supported as well.

To be compatible, a computer must be able to read and write IBM format disks. There are "compatible" computers on the market that don't even use standard 5¼ inch disk drives. Of course, drive capacity must also be greater than or equal to IBM's in order to qualify as compatible.

In most cases, the printer will be purchased separately from the computer, so all you need to worry about is the availability of the necessary serial or parallel port. In machines that include built-in printers, you can run into problems if the character set and graphics modes are not exactly like those of IBM's printer. As with any other printer, check it with the software you will be using.

Expansion Boards

To be IBM compatible, a computer must be able to use boards designed to plug into the IBM system board. Will you be using a modem board, an RS-232 board, or a memory expansion board? If so, test them, or get a compatibility guarantee from your dealer.

Having single boards work properly isn't the whole story when dealing with compatibility. Heat, power, and the number and size of the expansion slots may also cause problems. The computer must have enough expansion slots and a large enough power supply to handle the boards you plan to add. Be careful of the spacing of the slots on the system board; it may not be possible to fit a large board in. Cooling can also be a problem when you add a lot of boards, so see if the machine seems hot after running for a while, perhaps on a poorly ventilated shelf.

Software Compatibility

Software is the most complex dimension of compatibility. Perfect compatibility would be illegal, since IBM has copyrighted parts of the operating system and BASIC interpreter that are in the ROM of the PC. Not only that, but there are a few errors in the IBM ROM, and it would be silly to duplicate them faithfully. Finally, IBM offers new versions of its system from time to time, so compatibility is a moving target.

Forgetting about perfect compatibility (you will have to get a PC for that), what are the alternatives? Ideally, all programs written for the IBM PC would work perfectly just as they come from the package, but that won't always happen. Let's consider some places where software compatibility problems might occur.

Most obviously, a compatible computer must use 5¼ inch disk drives and the same recording format as the PC. If a system has, say, 3¼ inch drives, a program written for the PC would have to be transferred to the smaller format. This is usually done by means of the serial input/output (I/O) ports on the computers, either over telephone lines or with the two machines connected directly, and it requires the help of a technician.

Even if a program comes on a 5¼ inch disk, it may not work. It must be written for the proper operating system. Recall from Chapter 1 that the operating system is a central program that controls the interfaces between the application program, the user, and the PC hardware. We will discuss operating systems in detail in Chapter 4, but for the time being it is enough to know that IBM offers four choices: DOS, CP/M-86, PC/IX, and the UCSD p-System. Nearly all compatibles offer DOS, but perhaps not the others. If you contemplate using one of them, be cautious.

One of the most important functions of the operating system is handling input and output for application programs. An application program that issues requests to the operating system when it needs to read or write information, instead of issuing commands directly to the input and output devices, is fairly easy to transfer from one computer that uses that operating system to another. The operating system provides a well defined interface between the program and the computer hardware.

Therefore, a compatible machine should emulate all of the operating system I/O facilities in order to work with software that uses them. But what if an application program doesn't use the operating system for all of its input and output? In the interest of speed, some programs address the devices directly rather than passing their requests through the operating system. This is particularly true of word processors, spreadsheet programs, and graphics packages, which make heavy use of the display. In that case, the PC compatible computers must emulate IBM's display, so that programs that update it directly work as advertised. Always test a compatible machine using display intensive programs like word processors and games.

Finally, don't forget that problems can come up even when you try to use a program on a standard PC. For example, a certain word processing program may not work properly with a certain printer. These problems will still be there with a PC compatible computer.

PORTABILITY

There are two types of portable computer. The first are full function computers, which are descended from the Osborne computer introduced in 1981.* Several of these sewing-machine-sized portables are PC compatible (see Figure 3-9).

Although they are called "portables" a better term might be "*transportables*." Don't expect to throw one of these machines into a backpack and take off for the hills, but you can plan to bring it home over the weekend.

Bringing a PC or XT home from the office is a hassle because it is heavy, awkward to carry, and delicate. A portable should have a sturdy, padded handle and carrying case to make it easy to carry from your office to the trunk of your car and back. The read-write heads on the disk drives should be held in place mechanically when power is off, and shock absorbing mountings should be used for the drives. Chips may be soldered in place rather than plugged into sockets. That would make them better able to stand the potholes you drive your car over, but will cause slight problems with replacement. The boards must be held firmly in place by retainers. The cases and frames need to be strong and scuff resistant. In short, a transportable computer must be designed to take bumps.

Pay attention to the size and weight also. If it is too large, you will have trouble traveling on a plane. You may have to argue to convince an airline

---

*Unfortunately, Osborne had trouble coming up with other products and was subsequently forced to declare Chapter 11.

Figure 3-9. This PC compatible computer is transportable; it would be easy to put it in the trunk of your car and bring it home for the weekend. The single package contains all of the standard components but the printer, and there are ports on the side for connecting a printer if you bring one along. (Courtesy of COMPAQ Computer Corporation)

ticket agent to let you carry it on board. Once on board, it may not fit under the seat, and if it does, it will be where you want to put your feet. Carrying it from an airport parking lot to the ticket counter and then to a flight gate may stretch your arm. Test it by carrying it 100 yards or so or up a flight of stairs.

The second type of portable is designed to fit in a briefcase and is usually used in conjunction with a full function computer that is back in the office (see Figure 3-10). The first briefcase size portable was the Sony Typecorder, designed for note taking and text editing in the field. When you got back to the office, you transferred your Typecorder data to a desk top computer or word processor.

The Typecorder was nearly impossible to use because the display was very small (forty characters) and the text editing software primitive. However, that is all changing. Flat displays are much larger, cheaper, and power efficient today than in 1981, when the Typecorder was introduced. Furthermore, progress in CPUs and memories allows much more powerful software to be included with these briefcase computers. Finally, small disk

Figure 3-10. This computer is not PC compatible, but it is portable. You could put it in a briefcase or backpack as well as a car trunk. It is not designed to stand on its own, but would be used in conjunction with a PC back at the office. Information recorded while you were out would usually be transferred to your desktop PC through a serial input/output port. That could either be done over the telephone or, once you were back at the office, through a cable (like the one in Figure 3-8) connecting the serial ports on the two machines directly. (Courtesy of Sony Corporation of America)

drives have made briefcase size computers with auxiliary storage possible (the Typecorder had only a microcassette recorder).

These developments have brought the cost down and the power up to the point where you can work efficiently in the field, perhaps writing a memo or developing a spreadsheet, then come back to the office and transfer your work to a PC. Alternatively, it may be transferred to the PC over phone lines while you are still away. In evaluating one of these portables, pay close attention to the display quality, keyboard feel, and software power (some software will probably be included in read-only memory), as well as the amount of time it can run without charging the battery, how long it takes to charge it, and, if relevant, whether it has a built-in modem and software for communication. You can expect a lot from portable computers in the near future. Intel and others have low power versions of the 8088 CPU used in the PC, 256K memory chips are in production, and single chip modems are now available for connecting to telephone lines. The lap size IBM PC is almost upon us.

CHAPTER FOUR
System Software

Programs are generally divided into two classes: *systems software* and *applications software*. The majority of this book is concerned with applications programs, programs for doing work on a particular application, like word processing or spreadsheet modeling, but this chapter covers systems programs. The distinction is not razor sharp, but systems programs are tools that make the computer easier to use, regardless of the application. They are closer to being a part of the computer itself; they determine its personality. In fact, parts of the operating system on the PC are permanently stored in read only memory. We will look at two types of systems software, operating systems and programming language processors.

OPERATING SYSTEMS

The operating system is the only "component" of your PC that is not shown in Figure 1-2, because it is a program. But it is not just any program, it is the program that controls every aspect of the operation of the PC. The operating system provides two interfaces, one between the user and the PC and a second between the application program being used and the hardware. This section goes over the functions of an operating system and reviews some of the operating system options for the PC.

The User Interface

As mentioned above, portions of the operating system are stored permanently in ROM, so as soon as you switch your PC on, it is in control. The first thing the operating system is programmed to do is test portions of the PC hardware to see if it is functioning okay (hence the delay after you switch it on and nothing seems to be happening). If it is, the remaining

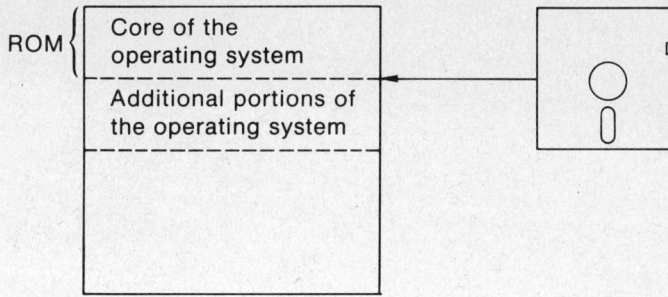

Figure 4-1. When you first turn power on, the portion of the operating system that is in ROM is in control of the PC. It is programmed to check the memory for malfunctions, and if everything is okay, to load in the remainder of the basic operating system. Still other parts may be loaded in only when the commands calling for them are given.

portion of the operating system is loaded in from disk (see Figure 4-1). Then it asks you the date and time and what you would like to do next.

In responding, you can choose among several commands like those listed in Figure 4-2 (the options vary somewhat, depending upon which operating system you are using).* You might start off by seeing how much space is left on one of your disks, then erasing an unneeded file, then loading and executing a word processing program in order to write a letter.

When you gave the command to run the word processing program, the operating system would look up its exact address in the directory on the disk, load the word processor into memory, and turn over control to it. From that point on, you would interact with the word processing program instead of the operating system. However, when you finished your word processing task, control would be returned to the operating system, which would wait for your next command. Once again, your choices would be those shown in Figure 4-2.

It turns out that there are ways of hiding this selection process in order to simplify system operation. For instance, you can set the operating system up so that as soon as it has finished checking for hardware malfunction it loads and executes a specified program. Game playing programs are often set up this way. You just put the game program disk in a drive and switch power on. After a pause for checking the hardware, the game is automatically loaded and executed. The operating system has been hidden for the sake of simplicity, as if a shell had been placed around it.

Computer designers spend a lot of time looking for ways to simplify the command selection process, and systems presenting a variety of *command interfaces* or *shells* have been designed. Instead of typing in the name of a command, for instance "erase" followed by the name of the file to be erased,

*For a complete explanation of the operating system commands for DOS or CP/M-86, see *CP/M for the IBM: Using CP/M-86* or *PCDOS: Using the IBM PC Operating System,* two of the books in the Wiley series on the IBM PC.

PCDOS Command	Function
PROGRAM NAME	Load the program into memory and execute it
FORMAT	Prepare a brand new disk for use
ERASE	Erase a file from a disk
COPY	Copy a file from one disk to another
DISKCOPY	Copy an entire disk
DIR	Examine the directory to see what files are on the disk
TIME	Change time
DATE	Change date
COMP	Compare two files to see if they are identical
DISKCOMP	Compare two disks to see if they are identical
SYS	Make a new copy of the operating system on another disk
CHKDSK	Check to see how much free space remains on a disk
TYPE	Display the contents of a file on the screen or print it
RENAME	Change the name of one of the files on a disk

Figure 4-2. These are typical operating system commands. The table shows the DOS command names. Commands for the same functions are provided in other operating systems although their names and details concerning their usage vary.

you might just point to a menu with "erase" as one choice. Or you might point to an *icon* that represents the erase command, perhaps a small picture of a trash can on the screen. Menu oriented command interfaces, in which you point to your choice, are well suited to systems equipped with mice or other pointing devices.

Using the picture of a trash can to represent the erase command is an attempt to simplify system operation by letting people refer to everyday reference points in controlling their PCs. The desktop is another commonly used metaphor that presents a familiar point of reference. In the 1960s researchers began designing operating systems in which the display screen simulated the top of a desk. Since there are a lot of things piled on top of most desks, the screen was divided into *windows,* separate areas used for different jobs and files (see Figure 4-3). Since a display screen is pretty small and a desk can get pretty cluttered, the windows must be able to overlap each other. In this case, commands can be given implicitly by moving the cursor to a given window or making a menu selection.

There is a great deal of interest in metaphors like the desktop and other PC control styles, but the simple command choice illustrated in Figure 4-2 is

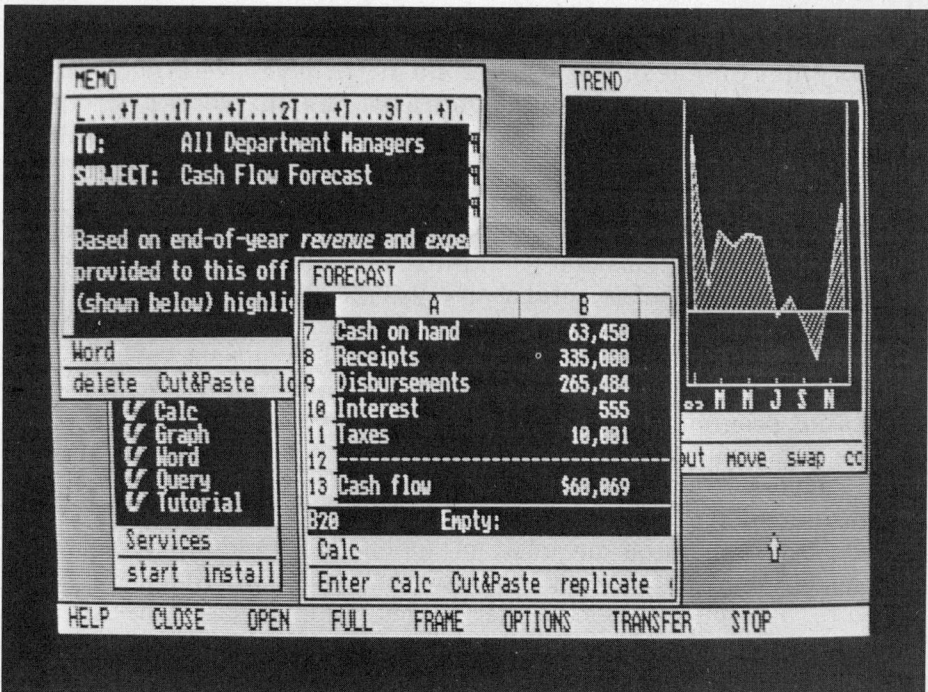

Figure 4-3. Window oriented interfaces are provided by several PC operating systems and operating system extensions. Each application is displayed in its own window, and windows can be resized or repositioned. Developers of window interfaces contend that they are simple to learn because of the similarity between the display and a desk with many folders on it. (Courtesy of VisiCorp)

still most common because that is the arrangement with which the PC started. Time will tell what sort of user interface style finally replaces it.

Interfacing with the Computer

We have been speaking of the operating system's role in interfacing between the user and the PC, but as you see in Figure 4-4 it also interfaces with the hardware. Most important, it takes care of the disk. (In fact, the acronym DOS stands for disk operating system.) The most critical task on the PC side is keeping track of the physical location of each file on a disk. It is your responsibility to remember which disk a particular file or program is on, but you don't have to know which tracks it uses within that disk. The operating system takes care of that by automatically updating a *directory* of the files on a disk whenever one is added, erased, or changed. If you forget what files you have put on a disk or can't remember the exact name you gave one, you can command the operating system to display the contents of the directory. Figure 4-5 shows the sort of information that is kept in the directory. Different operating systems may keep track of different file *attributes*, but the idea would be the same.

If you have a hard disk, or store many files on each floppy disk, you will want an operating system that can keep track of files in a *hierarchical directory*, like the one shown in Figure 4-6. If you have several hundred files on a disk, it will not be very helpful to see a listing of the names of all of them roll by on the screen when you ask to see the directory. Instead, you would like to work with a relevant subgroup, perhaps letters, business letters, or invoices.

The operating system also helps the programmer by providing for commonly used functions that would otherwise have to be part of nearly all application programs. For instance, every application program, be it a word processor, spreadsheet program, communication package, or data manager, reads and writes information to and from the disk, reads the keyboard, and writes to the display screen and printer. It would be wasteful if every application programmer had to write subprograms for input and output, so the operating system provides those subprograms. As operating systems become more powerful, more and more common input/output functions are being included in them, for instance, the ability to handle graphic displays is just beginning to be moved from application programs to operating systems. That affects the user in two ways. It saves programmer time and therefore cost, and it makes the interface between the PC and the user more uniform, since all programs, regardless of the application, read the keyboard and write to the display in a common manner.

Multitasking and Multiuser Operating Systems

In Chapter 1 we spoke of time-sharing systems, in which several people used a computer simultaneously. There are operating systems available for

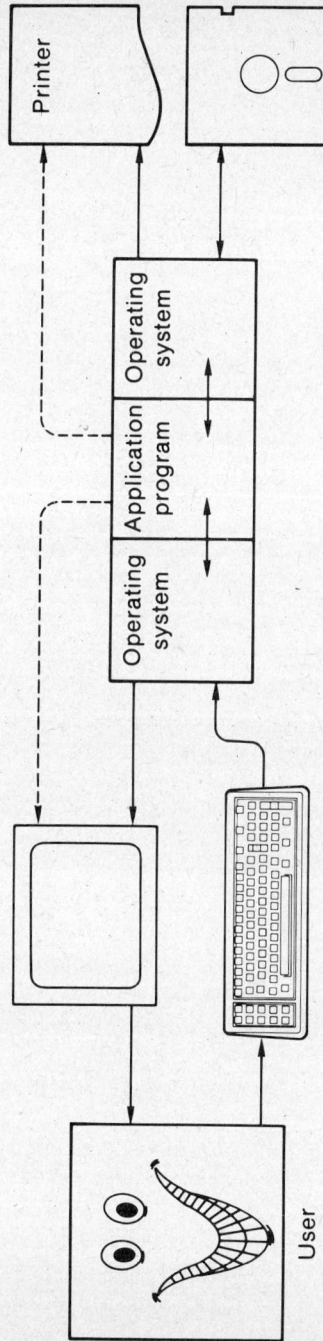

Figure 4-4. The operating system interfaces between the PC and the user and the PC and the hardware. For example, when you type something on the keyboard, it is read by the operating system then passed over to the application program. The most important hardware control functions of the operating system is reading and writing the disk and keeping track of what is on it and where everything is stored.

If, for the sake of increased speed, an application program bypasses the operating system to do its own input and output (dotted lines), it may be incompatible with future versions of the operating system or with "PC compatible" computers.

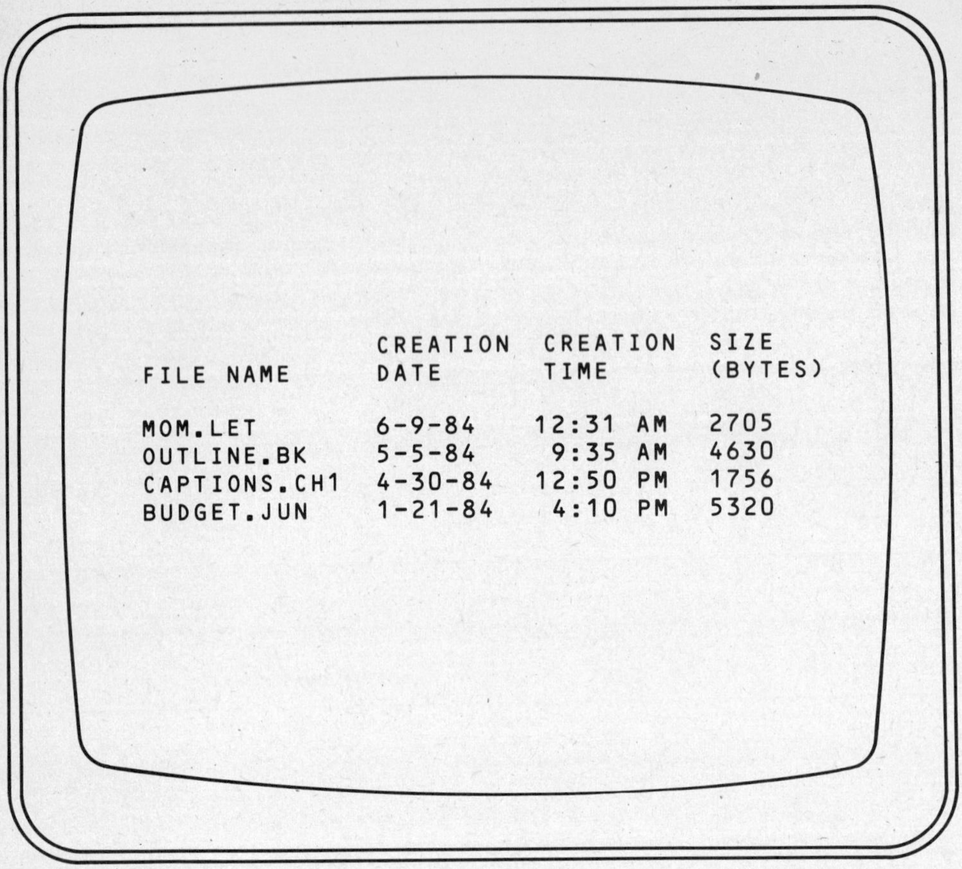

```
                   CREATION   CREATION   SIZE
    FILE NAME      DATE       TIME       (BYTES)

    MOM.LET        6-9-84     12:31 AM   2705
    OUTLINE.BK     5-5-84      9:35 AM   4630
    CAPTIONS.CH1   4-30-84    12:50 PM   1756
    BUDGET.JUN     1-21-84     4:10 PM   5320
```

Figure 4-5. This is the sort of information kept in the directory that the operating system maintains on each disk. The directory, like the operating system itself, is written on disk tracks set aside for the purpose. DOS keeps track of the name of the file, its creation date, creation time, and size. Other operating systems may keep track of fewer or more file attributes, but the basic idea will be the same. Note that the file names have been chosen to remind you of what the file contains, but restrictions on the length of the names are a little limiting.

the PC that turn it into a small time-sharing system. You would configure it with a hard disk, add a *terminal* (an integrated keyboard/display unit) for each user, and get a *multiuser* operating system. Since the focus of this book is personal computers as tools for individuals and multiuser systems are most commonly used in data processing applications, I will not say more about them.

Single-user *multitasking* operating systems are a different story. They are designed to be used by one person, who may be doing several things at one time. Multitasking operating systems began making the transition from larger computers to personal computers as soon as 16 and 32 bit CPUs became available. They didn't turn up sooner because they require a lot of

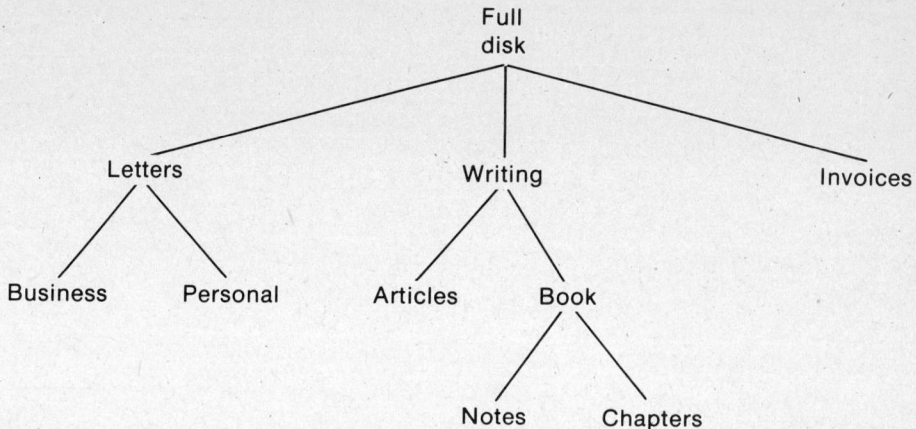

Figure 4-6. If you have a lot of files on a disk, which is particularly likely if it is a hard disk, you will want an operating system with hierarchical directories. DOS versions 2.0 and greater have this capability.

memory and are facilitated by the memory management and protection features that were not available on the earlier 8 bit models.

Can you foresee wanting to use your PC for several things simultaneously? At times, you will literally want to do two things at once. For instance, you might print a long report while creating a spreadsheet model, or you might be transmitting a large file to a remote computer at the same time as you are writing a report with your word processing program. That kind of thing will come up, but the most common reason for wanting a multitasking system is to make the transitions between tasks go faster.

Imagine that you are working on a proposal using your word processing program, and the boss calls on the phone and asks you how your department costs are running this month compared to your budget. If the budget was in a spreadsheet file and you do not have a multitasking system, you would have to go through the following steps:

Save the proposal on disk, and remove it from its drive
Remove the word processing disk from its drive
Find the disk with the spreadsheet program disk and insert it in its drive
Find the disk with the budget file and insert it in its drive
Execute the spreadsheet program and look at the budget

When the boss hung up, you would have to go through similar steps to restart the word processing job. In the meantime, the disks would probably have been left lying on your desk, and you probably would have spilled coffee on them.

If the spreadsheet and word processing programs had both been active under a multitasking operating system, you could have switched immediately from one to the other by moving the cursor or hitting a function key, depending upon the operating system. Ideally, when your PC was switched on in the morning, all the tasks you might work on during the day would be started up, though you would use only one, or perhaps two, simultaneously. It is clear that this sort of operation requires a hard disk, lots of memory to hold all of the active programs and files, and a sophisticated operating system. It may be beyond the capacity of your first PC, but not of your second.

IBM's Operating Systems

As of this writing, IBM offers five operating systems with the PC: DOS, CP/M-86, UCSD p-System, PC/IX, and, for those with the XT/370 CPU, VM/PC. What do you think the most important factor is in choosing among them? Is it technical, like speed or memory requirements? Is it the simplicity of the user interface? No, it is application software availability.

A given application program must be written to *run under* (be compatible with) an operating system. That means that once an operating system is decided on, only compatible application software may be used. For that reason, the most important characteristic of an operating system is how well it has caught on, how many application programs have been written for it. At this time, DOS is the clear leader on that score.

That is not to say that the others are totally out of the picture. The original version of CP/M was available on literally hundreds of brands of eight bit computers, so many application programs were developed to run under it. Although many of them were converted to run on the PC, the 16 bit version of CP/M (CP/M-86) has not done as well as its predecessor. Still, it is a significant factor and was the first of these operating systems to be offered in a multitasking version (called "Concurrent CP/M" by Digital Research, Inc., which developed it). If you will be using Concurrent CP/M, or any multitasking system, you should plan on a 512KB memory and a hard disk.

The p-System was developed at the University of California at San Diego, and has been made available on a wide variety of personal computers. In fact, the ease with which it and its applications can be transferred to a new computer is one of its main selling points. To a lesser extent than CP/M, the p-System was also available on eight bit computers. Be aware of efficiency in looking at the p-System. The generality that makes it easy to transfer from one computer to another takes its toll in terms of execution speed. That may not be noticeable in your case, but keep it in mind.

PC/IX, the latest PC operating system from IBM, is derived from UNIX, an operating system developed at Bell Laboratories in the early 1970s and widely used in universities. UNIX has many features that are handy for programmers, and they have been incorporated into PC/IX. It also comes with a powerful text editing program, developed by the company that adapted UNIX to the PC for IBM. Although UNIX was designed for multiple users, PC/IX is a single-user, multitasking operating system.

PC/IX is intended primarily for programmers, and if you or someone in your organization plans to use it, get a 512KB memory and a hard disk.

The VM/PC operating system is quite sophisticated but would be of interest only to those with the XT/370. If you have an XT/370, you need VM/PC for System 370 programs. Since the XT/370 is capable of operating in "standard" PC mode as well, and the VM/PC operating system is compatible with DOS, you would want to use it (as opposed to CP/M-86, PC/IX, or the p-System) when not in 370 mode.

Usually, you will select your application software first and use whichever operating system it is available for. In rare cases, this will force you to use two different operating systems, but you should do so only reluctantly. The necessity of dealing with two different user interfaces would cause training and skill retention problems. Furthermore, the data files created under one operating system could not be read by the other. It would be as if your PC had a split personality and was not even compatible with itself. If you do have to end up supporting more than one operating system, be sure to get a utility program that copies files from one disk format to the other.

Other Choices

The choice is further muddied by the fact that several independent companies offer operating systems for the PC. If you are interested in advanced capabilities like multitasking, multiple users, and window oriented user interfaces, you should look at the non-IBM alternatives. Pay particular attention to those claiming to be compatible with UNIX. Since it has been around for a long time, there are quite a few application packages available under it.

Finally, some companies offer user interface packages that are used in conjunction with the standard IBM operating systems (usually DOS). They are loaded in along with the operating system. You interact with the interface package, and it in turn deals with the operating system. Some of these are very sophisticated, offering multiple windows, to keep several jobs ready to go simultaneously, pass data from one job to another, and so forth. They may simplify your perception of the system, but they are essentially different operating systems, so be sure you are pleased with the choice of application programs that run under them.

Do you need one of these more sophisticated operating systems? Features like multitasking and a window oriented user interface are appealing. They can make PC operation easier to learn, speed up transitions between jobs, facilitate data sharing, and so forth, but you pay a price. They all require a lot of memory, and may require a mouse instead of the standard cursor control keys for pointing at the screen. Your choice of application software may be severely limited relative to the standard IBM operating systems. There may also be some loss of efficiency since overhead is incurred in these operating systems; computer horsepower is required to keep track of which task is running, where its program is in memory, how the windows are laid out on the screen, and other factors. Remember that the CPU used in the PC is at the low end of Intel's 16 bit line. It is being pushed pretty hard by these systems, especially if the 8087 math coprocessor is not used. Don't feel as though you have been left behind if you decide to stick with a simple operating system on your first PC.

Augmenting a Simple Operating System

If you decide to stick with DOS or another standard operating system, there are a number of utility programs available that augment them. In the future we can expect to see these capabilities made a part of standard operating systems, but for now they must be added on. Before describing these operating system extensions, a disclaimer is needed. Since they often work by actually changing a portion of the operating system, by *patching* it, they may run into the same sorts of incompatibilities as are found when moving from one operating system version to another. Patching an operating system may make it incompatible with some of your application software, and two different patches may not even be compatible. With that warning in mind, let's look at three operating system extensions, beginning with one that allows you to reassign and extend key meanings.

Reassigning Key Meanings

Since the interpretation of a key is determined by software, not by the keyboard hardware, it is possible to change the meaning of any key arbitrarily. But why would you want to do that? Let's consider an example or two.

I have a particularly tough time finding the "backspace" key on the standard keyboard unless I look for it. Look at the keyboard and you will see that it is on the top row of keys, far from the normal typing position. To make backspacing more convenient, I have switched the meanings of the "backspace" and "backward slash" keys. The new "backspace" is just below my left hand, where it is easily found.

It is also possible to generate more than one character when a key is hit. For instance, when typing letters, you might want to associate your name and the date with single keys (for instance "alt-n" for your name and "alt-d" for the date). Whenever you hit "alt-n," your name would be typed and "alt-d" would do the same for the date. Similarly, if you were using a word processing program to write a novel, you could assign the protagonist's name to a single key, rather than typing it every time it occurred. A single keystroke could also generate a system command, for example loading and executing a commonly used program.

Redefining your keyboard may seem like a fairly radical switch, but computers are very flexible machines. Some people go as far as to customize the entire keyboard. Historically, the typewriter keyboard was laid out to slow typists down, since key jams were a problem if you typed too fast. There have always been advocates of other, more efficient layouts, such as that proposed by August Dvorack in 1932. If you prefer, there is nothing to keep you from switching to a Dvorack key layout, or any other.

Programs for redefining the keyboard actually alter the portion of the operating system that interprets the codes transmitted from the keyboard to the PC. Since it takes only a second to read in a disk file that contains a new keyboard definition, you have the flexibility of defining different layouts for different tasks. For example, you may want to use one keyboard for word processing and a slightly different one for file management.

Electronic Disks

Which is faster, reading a file from a disk to memory or moving the same information around within the memory? That is like comparing Lois Lane to Superman. Disks are slow (by computer standards) with access times measured in hundredths of seconds, whereas memory operates at electronic speeds. Electronic disk emulators use a portion of memory as if it were a disk drive, simulating a disk functionally, but at higher speed. This not only improves the execution speed of the program you are running, it also cuts the time needed to make the transition from one task, such as editing a document, to another, like running a spelling checker or creating a spreadsheet. Electronic disks provide a means by which an application program that was not written to take advantage of the large memory possible in a PC can be sped up.

An electronic disk emulator divides the PC's memory into two regions, one that holds the operating system and whatever application program you are using at the time and a second that is used to emulate a disk drive (see Figure 4-7). When a program needs to read or write a disk file, the disk emulator performs a little sleight of hand. The instructions to read or write the disk are intercepted, and the data transfer takes place between the two sections of memory, rather than between the actual disk drive and the memory. This memory-to-memory movement is much faster, because no mechanical motion is involved, as it is with a disk.

To get a feel for the time a disk emulator might save, I ran a test comparing the time it took to proofread a 3,000 word article using a spelling checker program with an electronic disk and the time it took without one. With the conventional disk setup, it took 154 seconds, and with an electronic disk 67. In another test, copying a large file took only 1 second, compared to 14 seconds with conventional disks.* Note that these tests were run using floppy disks, and the differences would have been smaller with a hard disk.

These savings sound small, but they add up. For instance, if the program you are using for word processing is fairly large and complex, its author may have broken it up into several parts, which are temporarily read into memory from the disk when they are needed. An electronic disk essentially

*Table 13-6 shows further comparisons, made with file management software.

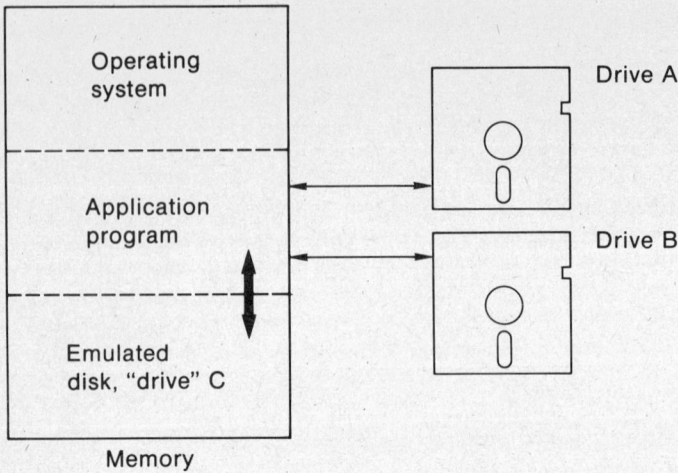

Figure 4-7. Modifying your operating system with a disk emulator will speed things up considerably, since records are transferred within memory at electronic speeds. When the application program requests that information be read from or written to drive C, the operating system merely moves it from one region of memory to the other. Depending upon the emulation package, it may be possible to have more than one electronic disk (drive D, etc.) active, and an electronic disk may have even greater capacity than a floppy disk.

eliminates the few-second delays when program segments are read. Similarly, when you move from one job to the next, say, from writing a document to checking its spelling, then back to a word processor for the next one, the delays for reading and writing programs and document files are nearly eliminated. Furthermore, the capacity of an emulated disk may be larger than that of a floppy disk (if you have sufficient memory).

Of course, a disk emulator requires additional memory. For example, a word processing program, spelling checker, and its dictionary can easily require between 200KB and 300KB. Add to that the space for the document you are working on, a backup copy, and the temporary space needed by the programs, and it is easy to come up with a 500KB electronic disk requirement. (If you do, be careful, because some electronic disk programs are limited to as little as 320KB).

Power fluctuation is another potential problem if you are using a disk emulator. If a storm or brownout causes the computer to lose power, the contents of memory, including everything in the emulated disk area, will be lost. In a conventional system, files that have been saved on disk will still be there after a power failure. If power is unreliable in your part of the country, you will have to make precautionary backup copies of your emulated disk files at frequent intervals. Another source of protection against power failures is a battery backup power supply for the PC.

But if the cost of the additional memory and power loss worries do not dissuade you, an electronic disk emulator will speed your PC up, even if you are using a simple operating system and application software that was designed with small memories in mind.

Print Spoolers

Spool stands for simultaneous peripheral operation on line. The term is borrowed from large computer operations in which there may be only one system printer and many users or jobs. In these cases, the printer may be tied up on someone else's job when you are ready to use it, so the material to be printed is diverted into a buffer area (on disk or in memory). When the printer finishes one job, the operating system starts it working on the next one waiting in the buffer.

You may not think there is much need for spooling with a PC, since there is only one user, but the same approach can let you print one job while working on the next. Imagine that you have just finished writing a long report using your word processor. If you have a slow printer, your PC could be tied up for quite a while while the report is printing. However, if you have a spooling utility program or your operating system already provides for that function, you can go on to your next task while the report prints.

Does that sound familiar? We saw that a printer equipped with a sufficiently large memory buffer would enable you to do the same thing; this is a way to do it without buying the extra hardware. But why would anyone ever buy a printer buffer in that case? There are three reasons: some of the CPU's time would be taken by a spooling utility, slowing the PC down during the overlapping job; the spooling utility would be more cumbersome to operate; and it may cause problems with the format of the printed material.

Before closing the book on these options for augmenting the operating system, I should note that they are all short term solutions. Functions such as reassigning key meanings, electronic disk emulation, and print spooling will all be provided by the operating system in the future. You should be aware of these options today, but with your next personal computer they will be standard equipment. Furthermore, since we see operating system vendors working on user interface facilities like window and menu oriented shells and standardized support for graphic input/ output devices, we can expect to see them used in the application programs of the future. It is possible to get ideas about future application software by looking at current system software developments, in the same way that today's new chips help us predict the hardware configuration of tomorrow's PCs.

LANGUAGE PROCESSORS

Can you name a few programming languages? BASIC, Pascal, PL/I, FORTRAN, COBOL, C, LOGO, and LISP are some of the languages available for the IBM PC. Many of the application programs you can get for your PC have been written in one of these languages. That sounds simple, but there is one problem: the IBM PC can't understand any of them. The PC can only execute programs written in the *machine language* of its CPU, the Intel 8088. BASIC, Pascal, and the others are *high level* languages, which are convenient for programmers, but unfortunately too complicated for your PC.

What do people do when something is written in a natural language such as English, but the reader speaks only French? Someone translates from English to French. The same thing happens with computer programs. The program would first be written in a high level language like Pascal, and then translated into machine language (see Figure 4-8). In computer jargon this translation process is referred to as *compilation*; the original version of the program is called the *source* program and the translated version is called the *object* program. To restate the process in these terms, the source program, written in a high level language such as Pascal, is compiled into its machine language equivalent, the object program.

Translation between natural languages like English and French is very difficult; it can be done only by highly trained people. Luckily, translating a program from a high level computer language to machine language is much simpler. It is so simple that we are able to program computers to do it for us. A few paragraphs back, there was a list of languages that are "available" for the PC. To be more precise, there are translating programs, or *compilers*, available for these languages. That means that if a programmer writes a program in one of them, the computer will take care of the translation into machine language.

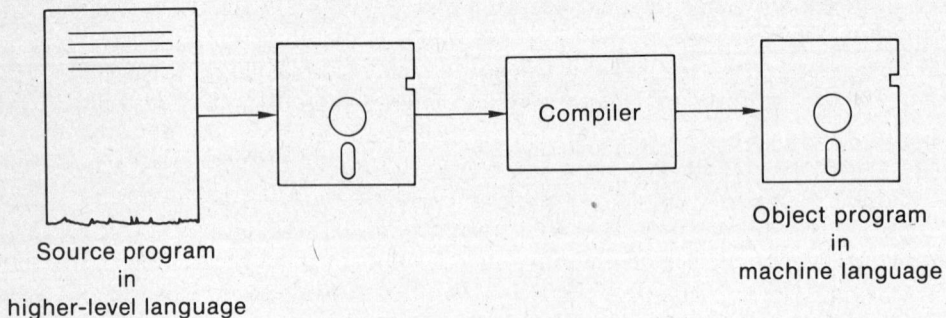

Source program
in
higher-level language

Compiler

Object program
in
machine language

Figure 4-8. Programs written in higher level languages must be translated into machine language before they can be executed. One approach is to translate the entire program before executing it, using a program called a compiler. The steps are illustrated in this figure. The program to be translated, the source program, is first keyed onto a disk (probably with a word processing program). The compiler then reads it from the disk and writes out the machine language translation, the object program.

When you purchase the program from a software company, they usually just give you the machine language version. That means it is ready to use without further processing, but you would not be able to make modifications to it without the source version. In the unusual event that you find you want a programmer to modify a program, be sure the source version is for sale at a reasonable price.

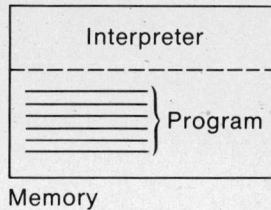

Memory

Figure 4-9. A second approach to getting from a higher level language to machine language is to interpret the program. The source program is loaded into the memory of the PC along with the interpreter. The interpreter is a program that translates one source instruction at a time and executes it before going on to the next. Interpreted programs execute much slower than compiled programs, but that doesn't matter if you are doing something that doesn't tax the computational power of the PC.

If you buy a program that is to be interpreted, you will get the source version, but will need the interpreter program to execute it. Even though you have the source program, the software vendor may protect it (legally and technically) to keep you from making modifications.

Bear with me for one important variation on this theme. You may have heard of *interpreters*, as opposed to compilers (see Figure 4-9). In fact, an interpreter for a simple version of BASIC is included in the ROM of your PC. An interpreter is akin to a compiler, but instead of translating the entire program into machine language before it can be executed, it translates one instruction at a time, as the program is being executed. As soon as an instruction is translated, it is executed, then the next one is translated and executed, and so forth. There are pros and cons to both compilers and interpreters (interpreters are easier to use, for example, but the programs run much slower), but for this discussion, one thing is clear: the interpreter must be in memory at the time you are using the program.

If you buy a program, say a communication package, that has been compiled into machine language, you will be able to load the program into your PC and run it. However, if the program is designed to be interpreted, the software vendor will send you the source program and in order to use it you will have to supply the interpreter. Since IBM includes a BASIC interpreter with every copy of DOS, many people sell programs written in BASIC, assuming the user will already have the interpreter.

There are further variations on the interpreter/compiler theme. For technical reasons, some compilers translate source programs into an *intermediate language* and interpret that version. Do you recall that one of the IBM operating systems was called the p-System? The p stands for "pseudo," since programs written for that operating system are all translated into an intermediate form, a language for hypothetical (pseudo) computer. Again, to use programs that were written in this manner, you would need an interpreter. Bear these differences in mind, so you won't get caught buying a program only to find you can't use it by itself. Find out whether any of the software you are thinking of buying requires an interpreter or other auxiliary *run time* program.

That's all we'll have to say about programming languages and language processors, because this book is about what you can do with a PC without programming. If you are curious to see a bit more, Appendix D presents a few programming concepts and examples. Be careful, though—some people get hooked on programming (others find it dull).

If you do get curious, and want to go further, you might take a class at a junior college or computer store. With relatively little study, you should be able to learn to use the BASIC interpreter that comes with the PC. For self-study, consider getting a book and one of the low cost language processors suggested in Appendix D. They will not make you an expert programmer, capable of writing your own word processor or operating system, but they will get you started.

PART TWO
Application Basics

Part II is organized around four important applications for knowledge workers: word processing, spreadsheet processing, data management, and communication. Each chapter begins with a brief history of the application and goes on to introduce the basic terms and concepts involved and shows what the application software does and how you might use it.

This part was written assuming that you have no prior computer experience, but before reading the chapter on a particular application, you should have had a hands-on demonstration in a computer store at the very least. Make sure the program is demonstrated using one of your applications, and if at all possible, spend some leisurely time at a computer club, with the people in your organization's data processing department, or at your own PC.

The chapters are independent of each other so that you can read straight through Part II, or if one application is of primary importance, you can skip straight to the appropriate product evaluation chapter in Part III. Regardless of the order you decide on, as you cover the various applications (in this book and in actual practice), your understanding will deepen because of the functional overlap between them. For example, the idea of editing is much the same, regardless of whether you are editing a document with a word processor, an electronic memo with a communication program, or a text field with a data management program. As you will see, many functions, like searching for character patterns, searching for records, sorting, formatting reports or macro commands, and importing and exporting data files, are relevant to several or all applications.

CHAPTER FIVE
Word Processing Basics

Word processing is simply using your PC as a writing tool, as a dynamic medium. My first experience with word processing was as an undergraduate in 1959. I enrolled in a programming class, and was shown how to use a keypunch, a machine that is something like a typewriter but is used for making punched cards. We were shown the keypunch so we could punch FORTRAN programs into cards that the computer could read, but it was obviously handy for writing more than just programs. You punched whatever you wanted to write into a deck of cards, one line of text per card, and then ran them through a punched card accounting machine, which listed them on its printer (see Figure 5-1). If you discovered a mistake, say a misspelling, only the card with the bad word had to be repunched. In no time, I was using this system for letters home and notes to girls.

Now, this writing system had some drawbacks. There were only uppercase letters, changing a single character on a card meant typing the whole card over, and sometimes corrections left you with very short lines. However, compared to typing, revision was easy, so programmers often prepared drafts of manuals and other technical documentation using punched cards. Whenever a line changed, that card was pulled out of the deck and the corrected one inserted in its place.

The problem of revisions leaving short lines was solved by using a computer instead of an accounting machine to print the text. The computer could be programmed to ignore the positions of the words on the cards; it just read them in and printed full lines. If one card didn't fill a line, the first words from the next one would. The cards were thought of as containing a long list of words that had no relationship to the format of the final printed page.

In order to control the format of the printed report, it was necessary to intersperse commands such as "start a new page here," "end of paragraph," or "set the left margin at ten character spaces." The commands might have been a little confusing, but since the only people using them were programmers, who were used to such things, they were easily learned.

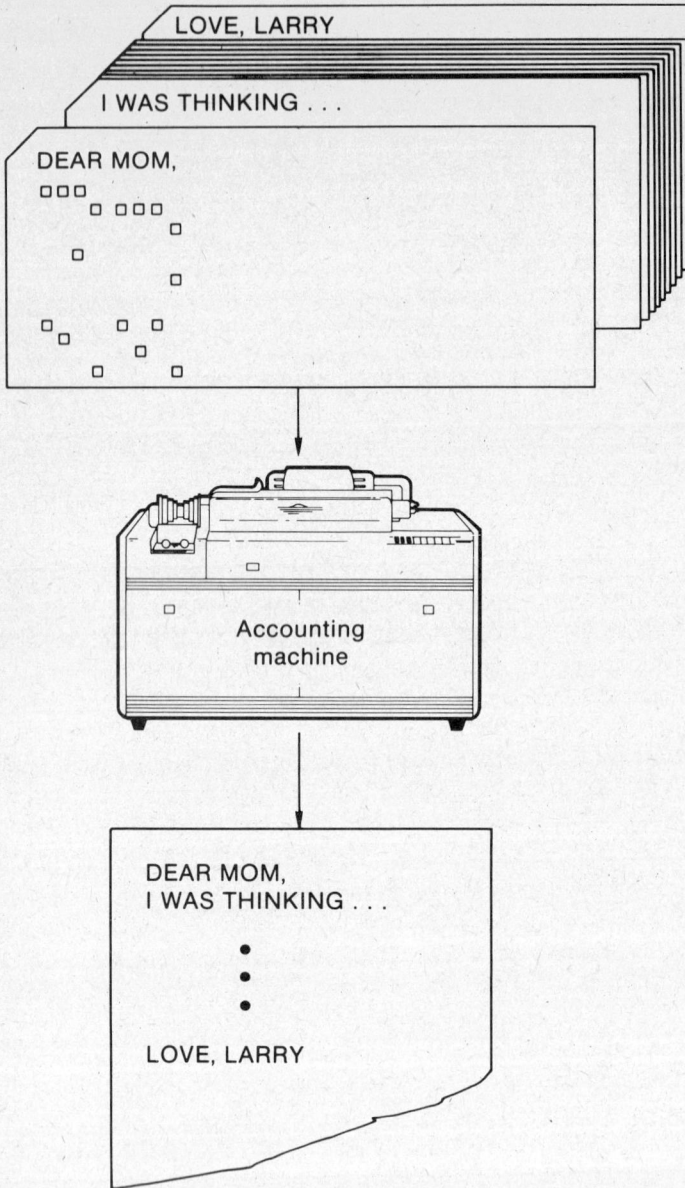

Figure 5-1. The roots of word processing go back to the days in which punched card accounting machines were used to print card decks with text punched in them. A document would be punched one line per card and run through the machine, which was set up to print whatever it found in the card. These machines were programmed using plugboards that looked something like an old-fashioned switchboard.

APPLICATIONS

1. You may use a word processing program for business and personal correspondence. A good typist can transcribe short letters faster with a typewriter than with a word processor, but if you are composing letters, or if they need revision, a word processor will save time and improve the quality of your correspondence.

2. A word processor will be a bigger help if you write relatively long documents, such as term papers, business plans, research reports, books about computers, magazine articles, screenplays, or family histories. Many writers have turned in their pencils and yellow pads for word processors because they find their writing goes faster and is freer.

3. A word processor can be used for assembling documents by pulling in pre-written "boilerplate" paragraphs. For instance, politicians might produce replies to constituents' mail using different paragraphs for supporters, critics, or people interested in various issues; a salesperson could insert standard material in "custom" proposals; or an attorney could include standard paragraphs in legal documents.

4. Another mass mailing application is sending nearly identical letters to many people by automatically filling in the blanks in a template letter. Systems such as this are often used for junk mail and bad news, like sending "personalized" collection letters to people whose accounts are past due, but they also may be used in a positive manner, for instance in following up on marketing leads.

5. Word processors can be handy in any situation in which you have forms to fill in. They are often used by lawyers to create wills or deeds that follow a fairly standard format. Repetitive forms such as invoices are also easy to prepare using word processors if you don't send out enough each month to justify setting up an automated billing system.

6. If you prepare documents for printing or formal presentation, a word processor can be a big help. For instance, a newsletter editor could compose and revise copy, and then print the final copy for pasteup. It is doubly handy because the format of the printout can be revised as easily as the contents of the articles. If a column comes out a half inch too long to fit on a page, you can shrink it by printing it out with each line a fraction of an inch closer together or with an extra character on each line. Special effects such as boldface printing, proportional spacing, or justification of columns would also be useful for a newsletter editor.

These programs were the ancestors of the print formatting portion of today's word processors.

A few years after I began writing letters on a keypunch, the card decks that programmers always carried around began to disappear. Instead, they began keeping their programs on magnetic tape or disk. Once a document was on disk or tape, the revision process had to be changed. One no longer simply re-punched a card, inserted it in the deck, and threw the old one away. Programs were developed for maintaining text and program files.

You punched cards describing your revisions and the tape or disk was altered accordingly. It was possible to change a single word or character within a line without retyping the entire line or to search through an entire file, substituting one word or symbol for another. These programs were the ancestors of the text editing portions of today's word processors.

As time-sharing systems became widespread during the 1960s, text editing programs were adapted for interactive operation, and they have evolved into line editors such as the EDLIN program that is part of DOS or ED, the CP/M-86 line editor. Revisions were made by typing the same sorts of commands on a terminal, and the document on the disk was updated. Line editors were frequently used for software documentation, and occasionally books were prepared using them.

These systems were used by programmers, but not by anyone else. In 1964, IBM changed all of that with the introduction of the Magnetic Tape Selectric Typewriter (see Figure 5-2). The MTST looked like a typewriter,

Figure 5-2. This photo shows IBM's Magnetic Tape Selectric Typewriter. When the MTST was introduced in 1964, IBM coined the term word processing. This model was used to compose material for printing. (Courtesy of IBM Corporation)

but documents could be stored on magnetic tape as well as printed. The machine was designed for nonprogrammers, and IBM coined the phrase "word processing" to describe what it did.

The MTST and its competitors evolved as designers and users worked with them, but the most important change was the addition of a video display for viewing text without having to print it on paper. Researchers at the Massachusetts Institute of Technology and the Stanford Research Institute had developed display oriented writing systems (on what were then large, expensive computers) as early as 1962, but it was not until the mid-1970s that they found their way into the commercial word processing marketplace.

Display oriented word processors laid the groundwork for personal computer word processing software. In 1976, a film-maker named Michael Shrayer got the idea of programming his personal computer to emulate a commercial word processor and began marketing a program called Electric Pencil. Many software companies have followed Shrayer's lead, and today's IBM PC with a good word processing program is scarcely distinguishable from a dedicated word processor.

With this history behind us, let's take a closer look at word processing on the PC. Anyone who has used a typewriter has a good point of reference for understanding word processing. When you hit a key on a typewriter, the corresponding letter is printed. If your PC is running a word processing program and you type a letter, it is entered into memory and immediately displayed on the video screen (see Figure 5-3).

Now let's say you wanted to write something, perhaps a letter to your mom. When you first loaded and executed your word processing program, you would be given a choice of commands similar to those in Figure 5-4. Since you were just starting the letter, you would choose the "create" option, and the screen would change to something like Figure 5-5, resembling a blank sheet of paper. You would begin typing your mom's

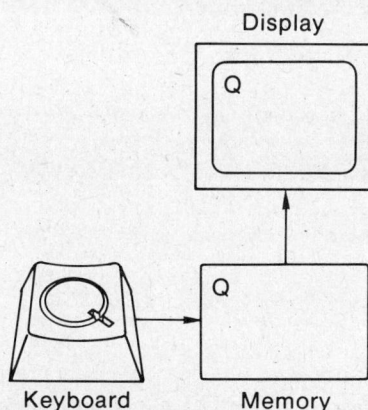

Figure 5-3. When running a word processing program, typed characters go into memory. The program continuously displays whatever is in memory, so that you can keep track of what you are writing.

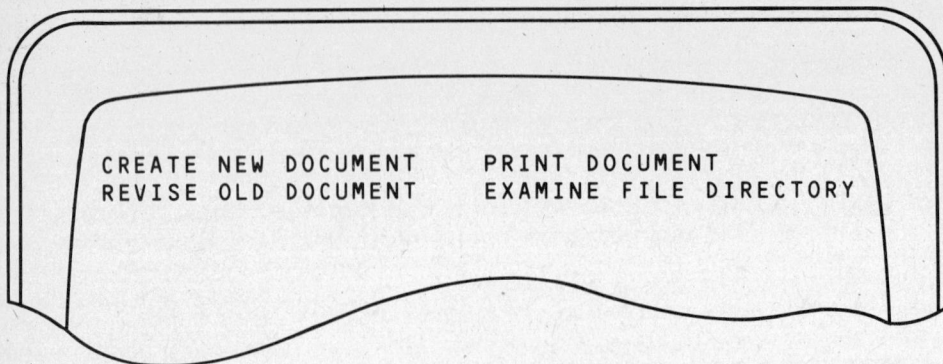

```
CREATE NEW DOCUMENT      PRINT DOCUMENT
REVISE OLD DOCUMENT      EXAMINE FILE DIRECTORY
```

Figure 5-4. When you first load and execute a word processing program you get a menu something like this one. You have the option of starting a new document or continuing to work on (revising) a partially completed document that has been saved. You can print a document that has been completed and saved on disk or examine the directory to see which files are on the disk if you have forgotten their names.

letter as if you were using a typewriter. As you typed, each character would go into memory and would be displayed.

As soon as you made your first mistake and saw how easy it was to fix, you would begin to like word processing. If you accidentally typed "Dear Mop" instead of "Dear Mom," you would fix it by simply hitting the "backspace" key and typing an "m." The "p" would be changed to an "m" in memory, and hence on the display. Since errors are so easily fixed, you could relax as you went on with the letter.

As you continued typing, and your letter began to fill the screen (see Figure 5-6), you would notice some curious things. First, when you got to the end of a line, it would not be necessary to hit the "enter" key (which corresponds to the "carriage return" on a typewriter). The program would automatically recognize that a line was full, and put the next word at the start of the following line. This is called *word wrapping*, and all word processing programs for your PC will do it for you. It might seem strange for a few minutes; you might find yourself typing unneeded carriage returns, but you would quickly find that letting the PC worry about margins speeds up your typing.

CURSOR MOVEMENT AND SCROLLING

You would also notice that there was a funny symbol on the screen, perhaps a blinking underline or rectangle, that moved as you typed. This very important character is the cursor, which we discussed in Chapter 2. In word processing, the cursor shows you where the next character you type will go. What would happen if you discovered you had made a spelling error several

```
PAGE 1 LINE 1                    EDITING LETTER.MOM

L                                          R
├─┼─┼─┼─┼─┼─┼─┼─┼─┼─┼─┼─┼─┼─┼─┼─┼─┼─┼─┤
```

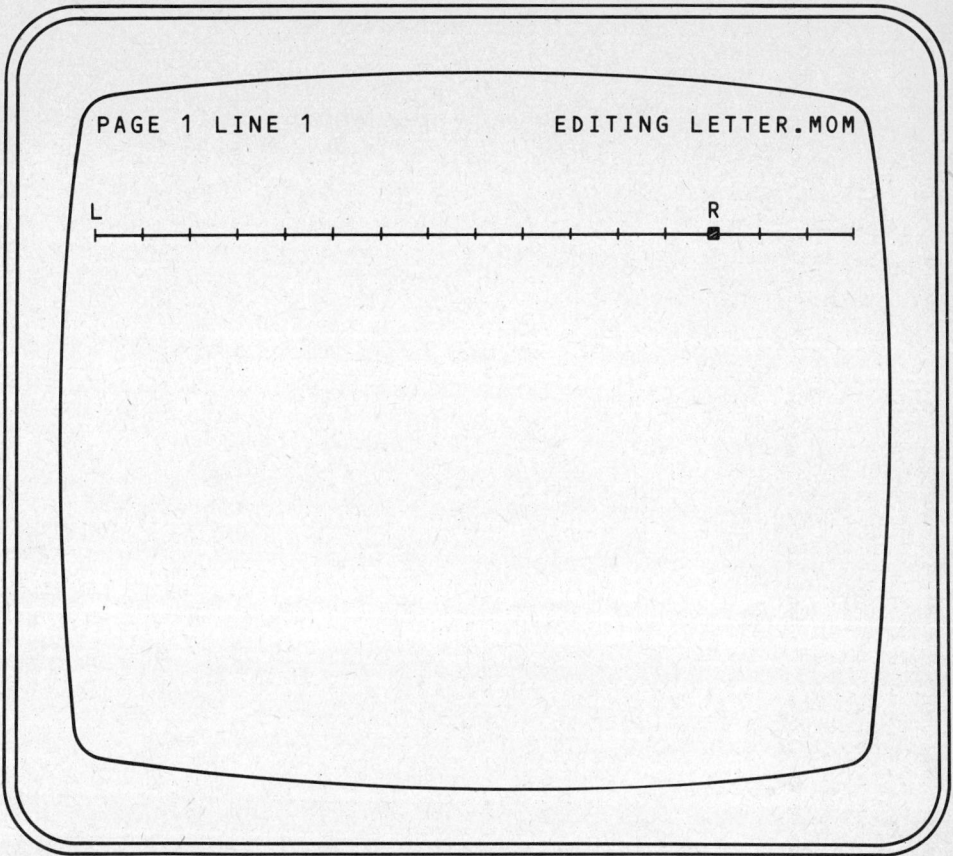

Figure 5-5. If you start a new document, you will get a screen something like this one. The top portion of the screen is an interaction area where the program displays status information like the name of the file you are editing and the current page, line, and character position of the cursor. The status area would also be used for other interaction with the operator, for instance to spell out menu options or to prompt you for input when necessary.

Just below the interaction area is a "ruler" that shows the current tab stops and margin settings. Below that is the screen area used as a window onto your document. Whatever you type goes into memory and is displayed in that window. Some programs may give you a larger text window by not having an interaction area, or by letting you eliminate it once you are proficient in the operation of the program.

sentences back? To fix the mistake, you would move the cursor to the bad word, correct the misspelling, return the cursor to the end of the letter, and continue typing. If the corrected word were longer or shorter, the text would be moved to make space for it.

How would you move the cursor to the place where the error occurred? There are three possibilities. With most word processing programs for the

```
PAGE 1 LINE 8                    EDITING LETTER.MOM
L                                                   R
┝──┼──┼──┼──┼──┼──┼──┼──┼──╱

Dear Mom,

    I was thinking the other day about
how you always said that I had learned
to read and write by the time I was
nine months old. Mom, I know you have a
great memory and are really objective,
but do you really think that ...
```

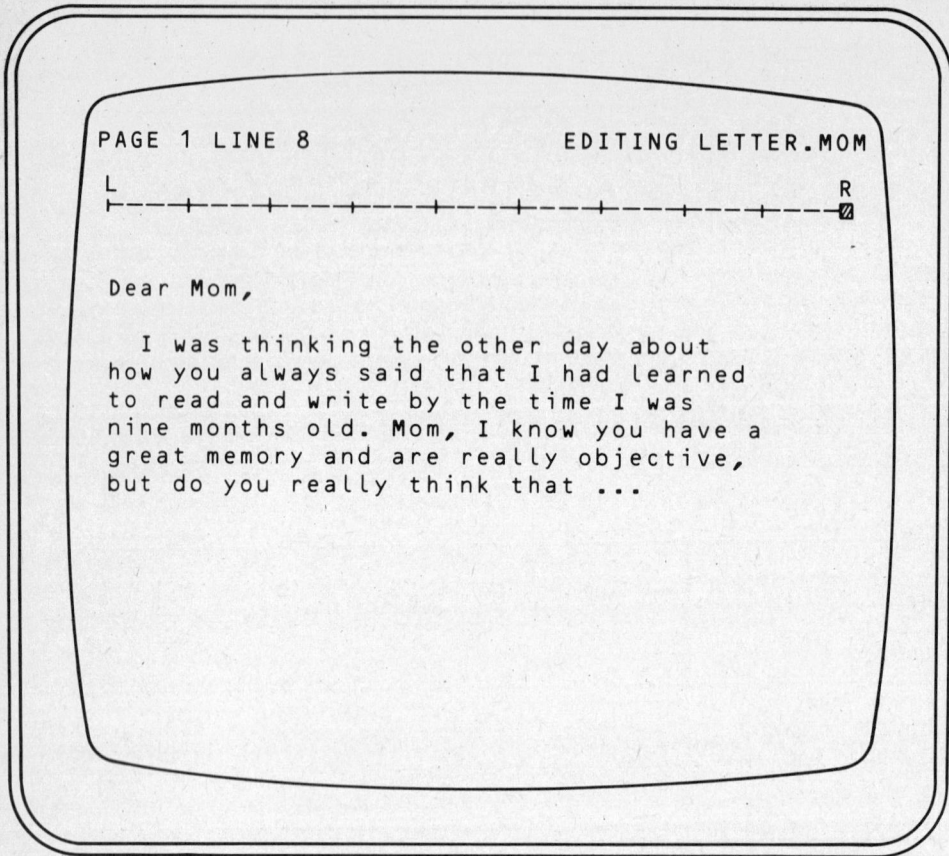

Figure 5-6. This is what you would see in the text window after you had typed in the first few lines of your letter. The words would have been automatically adjusted to the margins, and the cursor would be pointing to the next available character position. Any status information in the interaction area, for instance the cursor position or the percentage of memory remaining, would also have been updated.

PC, you would use the light colored cursor control keys on the right hand side of the keyboard, which were described in Chapter 2. Some programs let you use either the cursor control keys or control characters (the "control" key plus a character) for moving the cursor (see Figure 5-7). Though you might find it awkward at first, using the control key can be faster than cursor control keys, since your hands remain in the normal typing position. The third cursor movement option is a mouse or other direct pointing device, and some programs are set up to use a mouse, though most are not at this time.

   Having fixed the mistake, you would continue keying in your mom's letter. Since mothers like long letters from their children, it wouldn't be long before the screen filled up. When that happens, the text on the screen moves

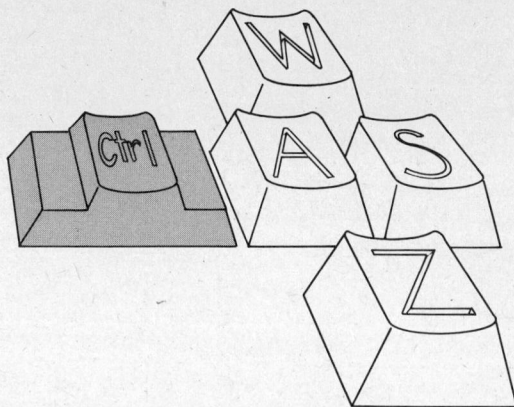

Figure 5-7. Many word processing programs let you move the cursor with control characters as well as the cursor control keys. By holding down the CONTROL key as you type, you change the meanings of the other keys. The arrangement shown here is common. The "W," "S," "Z," and "A" keys move the cursor up, right, down, and left, respectively, if the CONTROL key is held down while they are hit. This seems awkward at first, but since it doesn't take your hands away from the normal typing position, it can be faster than using the cursor control keys once you get used to it.

up one line to make room at the bottom for the next line. This is called *scrolling* because it resembles the movement of a continuous document as if it were "behind" the display screen (see Figure 5-8).

Remember that as you typed the letter to your mother, the characters were entered into the PC's memory. If you think of the display as being a window, through which a portion of the document in memory is visible, then scrolling is just moving the "window." What would happen if you remembered that something had been left out, and you wanted to return to the first part of the letter to add it? Most PC word processing programs let you scroll up or down a screenful at a time using the "page up" and "page down" keys. Most also enable you to scroll immediately to the beginning or end of the document, perhaps using one of the grey function keys on the left hand side of the keyboard.

SAVING YOUR WORK

Okay, back to your mother's letter. What would happen if something came up—something *very* important—and you couldn't finish the letter? You would save the half finished letter on a disk, perhaps by hitting a certain function key, and specifying a file name, like LETTER.MOM, when prompted by the program. The next day, when you were ready to finish the letter, you would execute the word processing program, and begin by

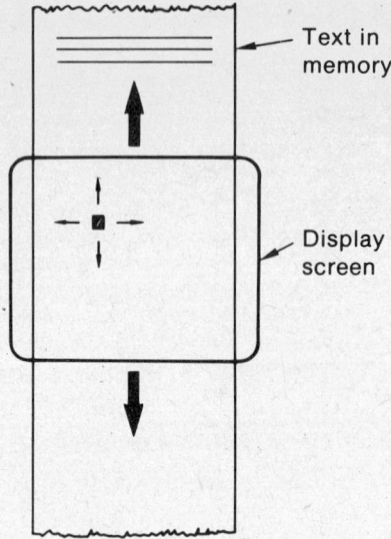

Figure 5-8. Think of the video display screen as a window through which a portion of the text in memory is visible. Moving the window to see a different part of the document is called scrolling. After you type for a while, the document in memory becomes too large to fit in the text window and the system automatically scrolls in order to make room for new text.

To read or change a part of the document that is not currently on the screen, you would move the window using scrolling commands such as PAGE UP, PAGE DOWN, START OF DOCUMENT, or END OF DOCUMENT. Once the proper text is in the window, you can move the cursor to point to any word or character. Depending upon your system, you either move the cursor with the cursor control keys, control codes, or a pointing device such as a mouse.

giving a command to REVISE the file LETTER.MOM. It would take a second to transfer the file from the disk to memory (you would see the little red light on the disk drive come on while it was being read), and you would be right back where you had left off the day before, ready to finish the letter.

If it has been a really long time since you wrote your mom, and you are feeling really guilty, the letter might finally fill your PC's memory. What happens then? Figure 5-9 maps the use of memory while you are running a word processing program. One portion is used by the operating system, the word processing program takes up another portion, and what remains is available as a *buffer* area for your document. With some programs, the size of the buffer area is fixed regardless of the amount of memory installed in your PC, resulting in some unusable space.

With most programs, when your letter got so long that the buffer became full, an early portion of it would automatically be transferred from memory to a temporary file on the disk in order to make room. That sounds simple, but what happens if you decide to return to the early part of the letter to

```
┌─────────────────────────┐
│                         │
│    Operating system     │
│                         │
├─────────────────────────┤
│                         │
│    Word processing      │
│       program           │
│                         │
├─────────────────────────┤
│                         │
│    Document             │
│      area               │
│                         │
├─────────────────────────┤
│                         │
│    Unused memory        │
│                         │
└─────────────────────────┘
```

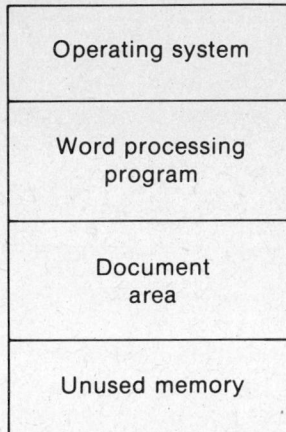

Figure 5-9. This is a map of memory use during word processing. A portion of the memory is devoted to the operating system and its reserved areas, and the rest is available for the word processing program and the buffer area for your document. Note that with many (but not all) programs, a portion of the memory will go unused, regardless of how much is installed in the PC. Limited memory can force the system designer to leave capabilities out of the word processing program or can slow operation by requiring frequent transfers of program or document segments between memory and the disk.

However, don't forget that even if your word processing program is unable to use the available memory fully, you can use that space for an electronic disk emulator, print spooler, or other operating system enhancement (see Chapter 4).

make another change? The word processing program must realize that the part you want to change is now on the disk and read it back into memory, perhaps saving another portion of the letter on disk temporarily.

Automatically transferring needed information back and forth between the disk and memory is called *paging* in computerese, and it takes a fairly clever program to do it. In large computers, paging is handled automatically by the hardware and operating system, but in today's PC the word processing program would have to keep track of which parts of the letter were in memory and which were on disk. That will change in future PC generations; the hardware and operating system will take care of paging, relieving applications programs such as word processors of the responsibility.

GETTING IT ON PAPER

Okay, you finally finish the letter. You probably don't want to invite your mother over to your place to read it on the display screen; you want to print it, to get a *hard copy*. With most word processing programs, you must save a document on the disk before it can be printed, so you would give a SAVE command, writing the letter on the disk, followed by a PRINT command. Usually a separate program is loaded in to do the printing when you give the PRINT command (see Figure 5-10).

The two programs that your word processing software are comprised of are referred to as the *editor* and the *formatter* or *print formatter*. The editor is used for creating and revising documents and the formatter for printing them out. In some word processing systems, the two functions are combined into one larger program, but in most they are separate, and the speed and ease of making transitions from editing to print formatting and back will be an important consideration in choosing a word processing program.

Before continuing, let's take a closer look at the printed version of your mother's letter. Designers of word processing software often say one of their goals is that what you see on the screen is what you will get on the printer. When a document is printed, it should come out exactly as it appeared on the screen during editing, with page numbering and titles, top, bottom, and side margins, page breaks, and so forth all printed as they were displayed. The advantage of having an exact preview of the final printout while you are editing a document is that it simplifies your conception of the system. There are no surprises when it is printed (like a letter ending with nothing but "Sincerely Yours" on the last page), since there seems to be only one version of the letter, whether it is printed or displayed on the screen.

But, as with many design principles, some compromises with this goal are necessary and desirable. Problems begin to come up when you look at

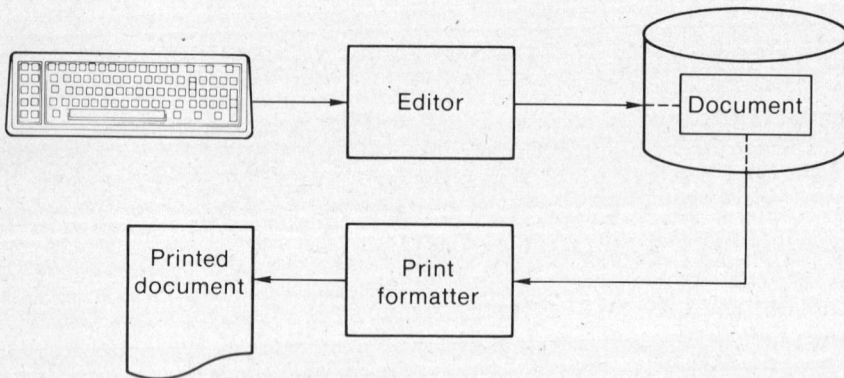

Figure 5-10. Word processing is a two stage operation, and a word processing package has two major subcomponents: an editor and a print formatter. First, the document is created and revised using the editing portion of the program. It is saved on disk and then printed using the formatting program.

In most systems, the editor and formatter are essentially separate programs that are loaded into memory from the disk when needed, but in some they are both kept in memory at all times. The latter scheme makes for quick operation since you can make the transition from editing to printing without delay; however, since both programs are in memory, there is less space for the document buffer.

the characteristics of the PC display and printer. For instance, the IBM dot-matrix printer is capable of printing italic characters, but the Monochrome Display cannot show this effect. A word processing program that dogmatically stuck to the principle of exact correspondence between the displayed and printed versions would not be able to print italics or underline words. Other printers sport features like *proportional spacing* of characters (more space for wide characters like M than for narrow characters like l), precise control over the spacing between lines, and subscripts and superscripts, which cannot be displayed on your PC.

Some effects might be possible to duplicate but still awkward. For instance, the IBM dot-matrix printer can print compressed characters. At 16.5 characters per inch, that is 132 characters on an eight inch line, but the display is only 80 characters wide. With horizontal scrolling, it is possible to compose extra wide documents, but editing them is clumsy.

Other problems with displaying exactly what will be printed are inherent in word processing tasks, because you may not know when you are editing a document exactly what will be printed. If you are planning to use your word processor for mass mailing or other kinds of standard documents, you won't know what words will be in the final printed versions of your document at the time it is created. You will use the editor only to create a template, which will be filled in later as the documents are printed.

As display and printer technology evolve, a closer match between displayed documents and drawings and printed ones will be possible, but for now PC owners must expect some compromises. With today's hardware, strict adherence to formatting everything on the screen would mean that instead of "what you see is what you get," it would be "what you see is all you *can* get."

If complete *on-screen* formatting, in which you always see what you will get, is not possible, what is the alternative? To some extent, all PC word processing programs rely on *print formatting commands* that are inserted in the text of the document (see Figure 5-11). These commands are like those used in the old days to control programs that printed documents from decks of punched cards; they control such things as margin sizes, line spacing, and justification. With most word processing programs, formatting commands are on separate lines in the text and set off some special punctuation (a "." in the example). These command lines would not be printed out; they would be interpreted in order to control the formatting program.

Embedded commands are also used to control printing. In Figure 5-11, we see a special character ("^B") before and after the word "new," which causes it to be printed in boldface type. Embedded commands are usually used for changes in type *attributes* or appearance, like underlining, subscripts and superscripts, compressed and expanded print, or italics.

To the extent that a word processing program relies on formatting commands to control the appearance of printed output, it will be necessary to imagine exactly what a document will look like when it is printed. The version you see on the screen, with formatting commands inserted, will not

```
.LM10
.RM45
.SP2
.JUST
.CTR
Lincoln's Address at Gettysburg
.LEFT
     Fourscore and seven years ago our
fathers brought forth on this
continent a^Bnew^B nation, conceived
in liberty, and dedicated to the
proposition that all men are created
equal.

     Now we are engaged in a great
civil war, testing whether that nation,
or any nation so conceived and so
dedicated, can long endure . . .
```

```
            Lincoln's Address at Gettysburg

        Fourscore and seven years ago our fathers

    brought forth on this continent a new nation,

    conceived in liberty, and dedicated to the

    proposition that all men are created equal.

            Now we are engaged in a great civil war,

    testing whether that nation, or any nation so

    conceived and so dedicated, can long endure....
```

Figure 5-11(a). In this display, we see the use of formatting commands to control the printing of a document. The first four lines set the left and right margins and cause the printout to be double spaced and the right margin to be justified. The CTR command causes the text that follows to be centered, and the LEFT command stops the centering. The ^ B, which is inserted before and after the word "new," starts and then stops boldface printing. At first, the formatting commands interspersed in your text may be confusing, but you soon get used to them and learn how they work. (b) Here we see the printed page corresponding to the display shown in a. Note that the title is centered, the lines are double spaced and justified, and the word "new" is indeed printed with boldface characters. A system that leaned toward on-screen formatting would try to have the video display appear as much like the printout as possible.

be exactly what you get on the printer. The closer your system comes to formatting documents on the screen exactly as they will be printed, the easier it will be to anticipate what the printed version will look like while you are editing it.

On the other hand, once you become familiar with the formatting commands for a particular program, it is easy to predict what a document will look like. Furthermore, on-screen formatting may slow you down while you are editing documents, because new editing commands must be learned and used. For instance, changing a paragraph from single to double spacing or rearranging it when margins change or a phrase is erased, leaving a short line, requires that it be redisplayed on the screen. With some word processing programs, you would have to give a command to *reformat* a paragraph after changing it. Even if reformatting were handled automatically, it would cause a slight delay. More important, the portion of the program that does the reformatting ties up some memory space. Whether the conceptual clarity of on-screen formatting is worth some loss of efficiency will depend upon how you plan to use your word processor. We will return to this tradeoff in Chapter 11, but for now let's get back to that letter for mom.

FURTHER REVISION, SEARCHING, AND BLOCK OPERATIONS

Before sending the letter off to your mother, you should read it over for mistakes. What if you find some spelling errors or just decide that, on second thought, you would like to change the letter? To revise the letter, you just reload the editor and make the changes. There are even some commands that make it easy to do.

Transposition of letters is a common error, for instance typing "teh" instead of "the." With a single SEARCH/REPLACE command, you could substitute "the" for "teh" throughout your letter. If you spotted other misspellings in the letter, you would use a simple SEARCH command to scroll quickly to the bad words, then retype them. Figure 5-12 illustrates the SEARCH/REPLACE command.

You may decide you want to change the emphasis in the letter by rearranging it—a little electronic cut and paste. If there was a paragraph in your letter asking your mom for a loan, you could use a BLOCK-MOVE command to move the paragraph from the end of the letter to the beginning. First, you would designate the text to be moved by moving the cursor to the beginning and the end of the block and marking them with a command. Most programs would change the color or intensity level of the marked block so you could visually verify that it was indeed the text you wanted to move. As soon as you saw that the block was correctly specified, you would move the cursor to the destination point and give a BLOCK-MOVE command. A second later, the marked paragraph would be moved from its original location near the end of the letter to the new spot near the beginning.

```
        L***ncoln's Address at Gettysburg

    Fourscore and seven years ago our
fathers brought forth on th***s
cont***nent a new nat***on,
conce***ved ***n l***berty, and
ded***cated to the propos***t***on
that all men are created equal.

    Now we are engaged ***n a great
c***v***l war, test***ng whether that
nat***on, or any nat***on so
conce***ved and so ded***cated, can
long endure. We are met on a great
battlef***eld of that war. We have
come to ded***cate a port***on of that
f***eld as a f***nal rest***ng place
for those who here gave the***r
```

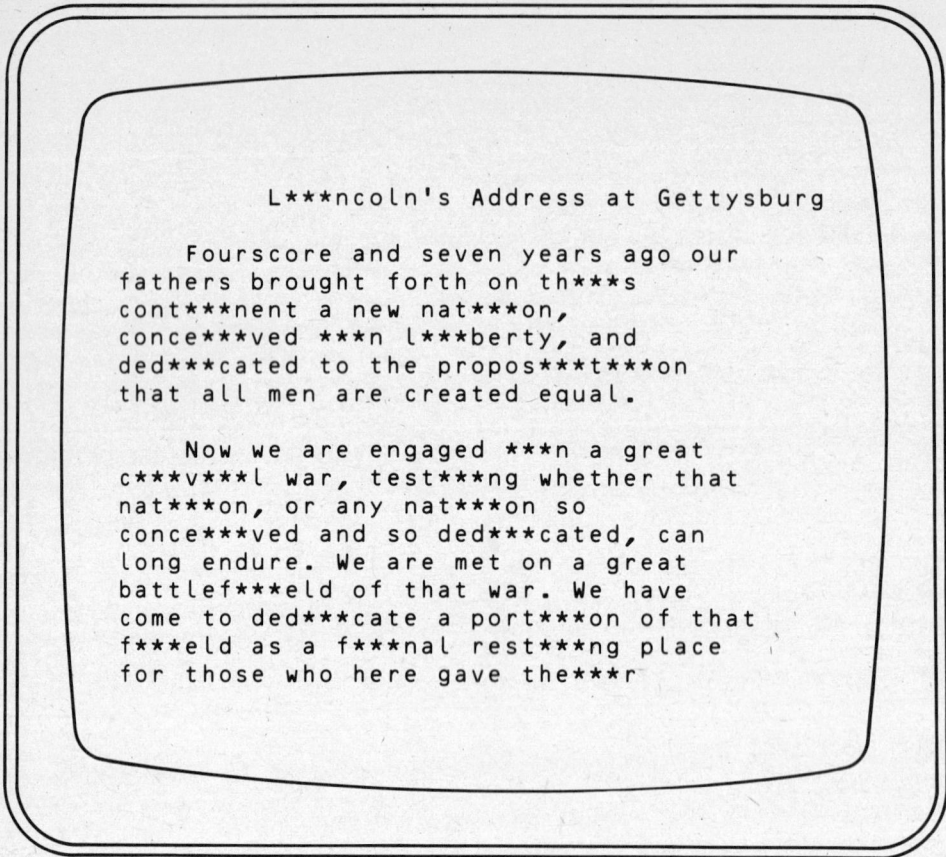

Figure 5-12. In this example, the search and replace function has been used to replace all occurrences of a specified search pattern, and the letter "i" with the character string "***." As you see, a string command completely transforms the text. This also shows why it is useful for your system to allow you to preview replacements before they are made; it is possible to inadvertently create nonsense at a rapid rate using a search and replace command.

Of course, you could change your mind about the money and use a BLOCK-DELETE command to get rid of that paragraph altogether. Or, if you are really desperate, you could use a BLOCK-COPY command to put the money paragraph at several different places in the letter.

When you were finished revising the letter, you would save the final version on disk and print out a fresh copy for your mom. But you might want to do more than send your mother letters with a word processor. Let's consider some other applications.

TEMPLATES FOR REPETITIVE DOCUMENTS

If you have a word processing program with the proper formatting capability, your PC can be used for repetitive documents. I'll bet the phrase "junk mail" comes to mind when you think of repetitive documents, but there are more dignified applications as well. You might use your word processor to generate personalized cover letters when you send out press releases on new products or brochures in response to inquiries. An author might send personalized inquiry letters to a list of publishers before writing a story, or a college might use a word processor to correspond with applicants or donors.

In order to use your PC in this manner, you would first use the editor to create a *template* document such as the one shown in Figure 5-13. The template is a general version of the letter to be sent, and each term beginning with the "@" character represents a reserved space that will be filled in to make a specific instance of the letter.

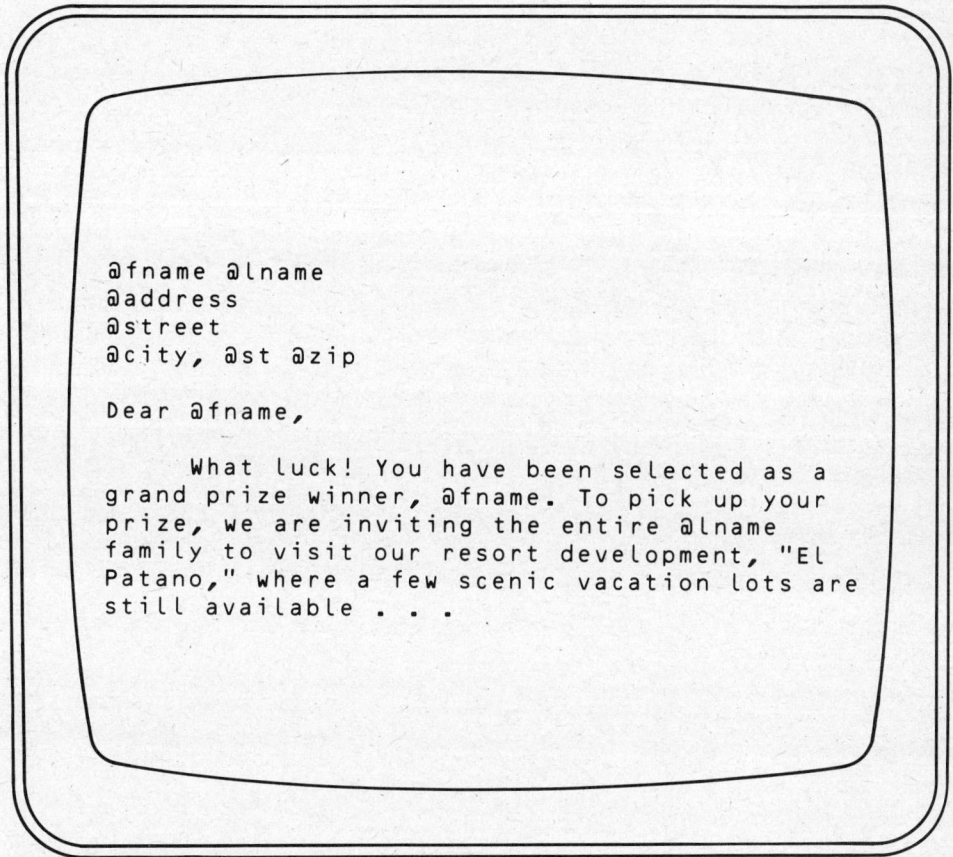

```
@fname @lname
@address
@street
@city, @st @zip

Dear @fname,

     What luck! You have been selected as a
grand prize winner, @fname. To pick up your
prize, we are inviting the entire @lname
family to visit our resort development, "El
Patano," where a few scenic vacation lots are
still available . . .
```

Figure 5-13. A template letter such as this would be used for repetitive letters. Each of the terms beginning with a "@" is a placeholder, to be filled in with data from a file on the disk. The data file would contain the first name, last name, street, city, state, and zip codes of everyone on the mailing list. The data from these records would be plugged into the blank spots in the template to produce personalized letters. Note that the first and last name values are used at different points in the letter.

The blanks will be filled in with data from a disk file at the time the letter is printed (see Figure 5-14). Are you wondering where the data file comes from in Figure 5-14? You might create it using the word processing editor or, depending on its size and structure, a separate file management program might be used (see Chapter 7).

In addition to just filling in blank spaces in the template, the input data might be used to control the content of the letter. For example, if you were using your PC to send out collection letters, the value for the "due date" space could determine which of several paragraphs were used to end the letter. Accounts with a fairly recent due date would get a gentle reminder and those that were long overdue would get something a little nastier.

ASSEMBLING DOCUMENTS

Assembled documents are a variation on the repetitive document theme. Prewritten "boilerplate" material may be stored on disk for incorporation into letters and other sorts of documents. Figure 5-15 shows how a politician might use boilerplate material in replying to mail and telegrams. The bottom half of the screen shows a template letter, such as we discussed above. In this example, the character "@" is used to mark places where blanks must be filled in, but, unlike the previous example, they would be filled in by an operator at the time the letter was being prepared, not with data from a disk file.

A special character is used to mark the spaces so that a SEARCH command may be used to move quickly from one blank space to the next (SEARCH for "@"). The operator would key in the person's name and the campaign issue for each letter as it was being composed.

In addition to this variable information, a prewritten closing paragraph could be read in from disk. In this example, there are five different closing

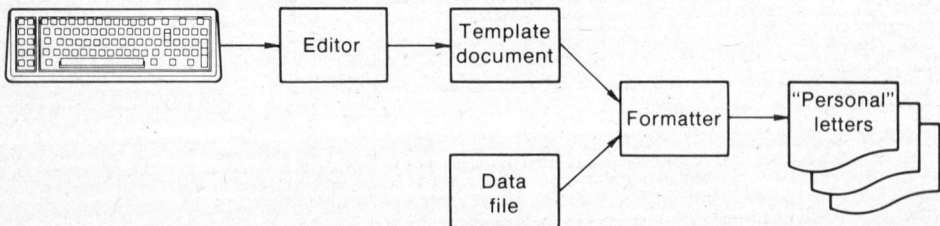

Figure 5-14. The word processing editor would be used to create the template, and the formatter would print the repetitive letters. If the data file were fairly small, you might create and maintain it using the word processing editor, treating it as if it were just a structured document. However, if the data file contained more than, say, 100 records, it might pay off to use a separate mailing list or file management program. If you do that, make sure it is compatible with your word processing program.

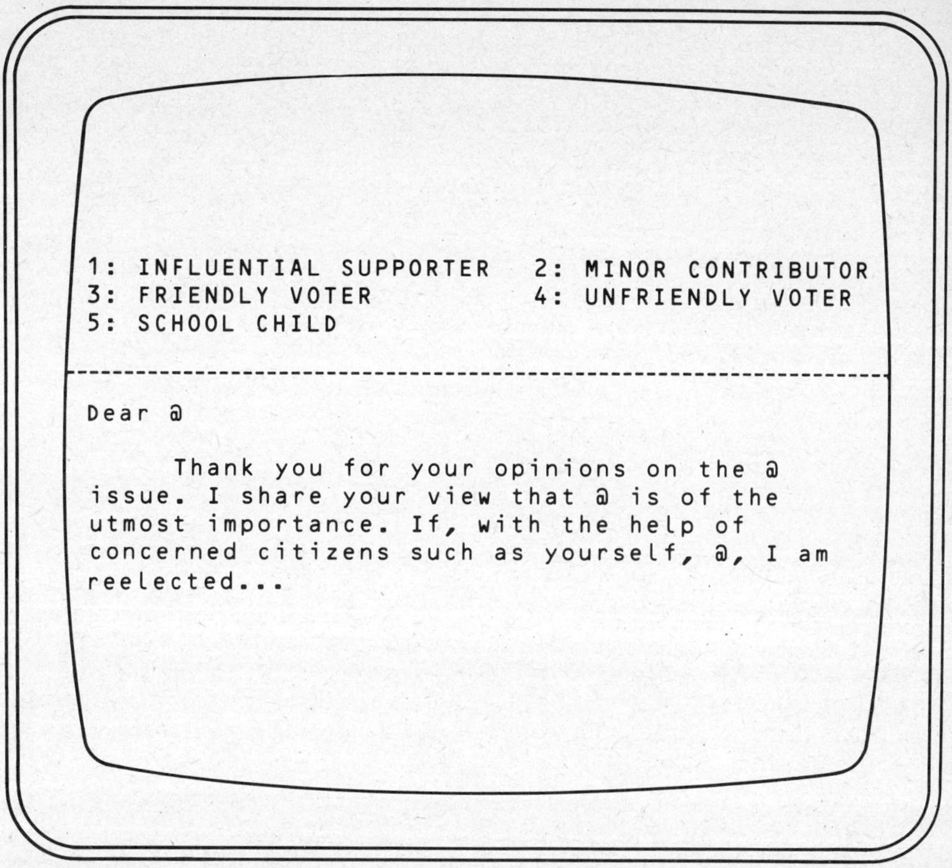

```
1: INFLUENTIAL SUPPORTER   2: MINOR CONTRIBUTOR
3: FRIENDLY VOTER          4: UNFRIENDLY VOTER
5: SCHOOL CHILD
------------------------------------------------------------

Dear @

     Thank you for your opinions on the @
issue. I share your view that @ is of the
utmost importance. If, with the help of
concerned citizens such as yourself, @, I am
reelected...
```

Figure 5-15. In this example, a template is being filled in manually while you use the editor. You would use the SEARCH command to move quickly from one instance of the "@" character to the next, and type in the name of the voter and the issue he or she was interested in.

In addition to filling in the template, one of five prewritten closing paragraphs could be included at the end of the letter. The menu, shown in the interaction area at the top of the screen, would be used in selecting the paragraph to be read in from disk.

paragraphs, and the operator would select the appropriate one using the menu shown in the upper half of the screen. The same sort of approach could be used in many applications; for instance, an attorney might fill in standard forms or incorporate standard paragraphs of legal jargon into wills or other documents.

This sort of operation is not as fully automatic as the mass mail application discussed above. Figure 5-16 illustrates the mechanics of filling in a template document and including prewritten material. A legal secretary might use a word processor to prepare deeds in this manner, and, although it would be faster than typing them, there would be a number of

Disk files

Template deed

Memory

Prewritten paragraphs

A
B
C
D

1

3

4

Printer

2

Keyboard

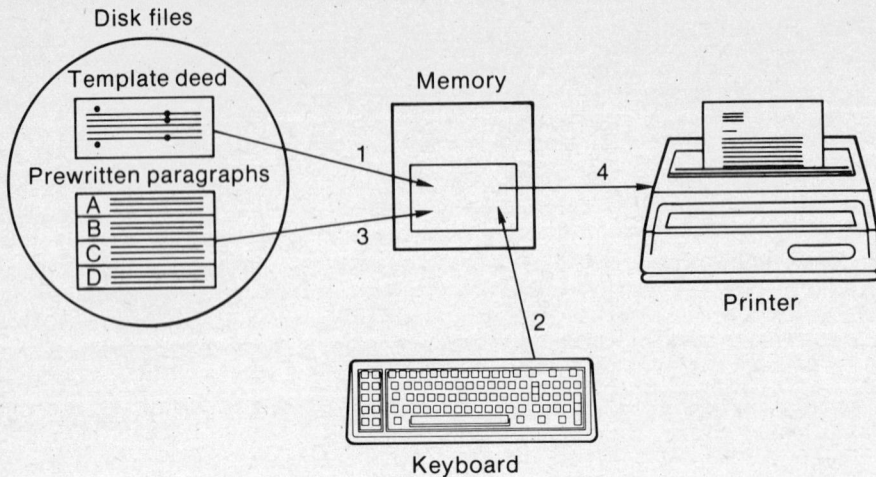

Figure 5-16. This figure shows the steps in preparing a document using prewritten paragraphs and a template. First, the template document is read into memory from the disk. Then the search command is used to find the "blank" places where the operator must enter information for this particular document. At some places, entire prewritten paragraphs or sections are read in from the disk. Finally, the finished document is printed out (in many systems, it must also be written onto the disk before printing). Even though this is faster than typing, a good deal of operator time is required.

manual steps. The template would have to be loaded, the blanks in the deed would be filled in, and the standard paragraphs inserted. Once the deed was finished, it would be saved on the disk and then printed.

WRITING AIDS

You may also be interested in programs to help with your writing. The most common are spelling checkers. You wouldn't want your mom to know you can't spell, would you? Spelling checkers are really dictionary look-up programs. There are many variations on the theme, but most operate in two phases (see Figure 5-17). In the first phase, the program makes a list of all the words in the document and checks each against a dictionary. If a word is found in the dictionary, it is assumed to be spelled correctly, otherwise it is added to a list of suspect words.

The first phase proceeds automatically, but during the second phase, the missed words are shown to you one at a time. You have three basic choices with each word (see Figure 5-18). If it is misspelled, you either correct it or mark it for later correction, depending upon the program. If it is spelled correctly, either you tell the program to add it to the dictionary or, if it were an uncommon word, you might give the command to ignore it.

Analysis phase:

```
┌──────────────┐
│ Your         │
│ document     │                    ┌──────────────┐              ┌──────────────┐
└──────────────┘ ╲                  │ Searching    │              │ List of      │
                   ╲──────────────▶ │ program      │ ───────────▶ │ misspelled   │
┌──────────────┐ ╱                  └──────────────┘              │ words        │
│              │ ╱                                                 └──────────────┘
│ Dictionary   │
└──────────────┘
```

Action phase:

```
┌──────────────┐
│ Your         │
│ document     │ ╲
└──────────────┘   ╲
                     ╲              ┌──────────────┐              ┌──────────────┐
┌──────────────┐ ◀───│              │ Action       │              │ Corrected    │
│ Dictionary   │      │             │ program      │ ───────────▶ │ document     │
└──────────────┘      │             └──────────────┘              └──────────────┘
                     ╱
┌──────────────┐   ╱
│ List of      │ ╱
│ misspelled   │
│ words        │
└──────────────┘
```

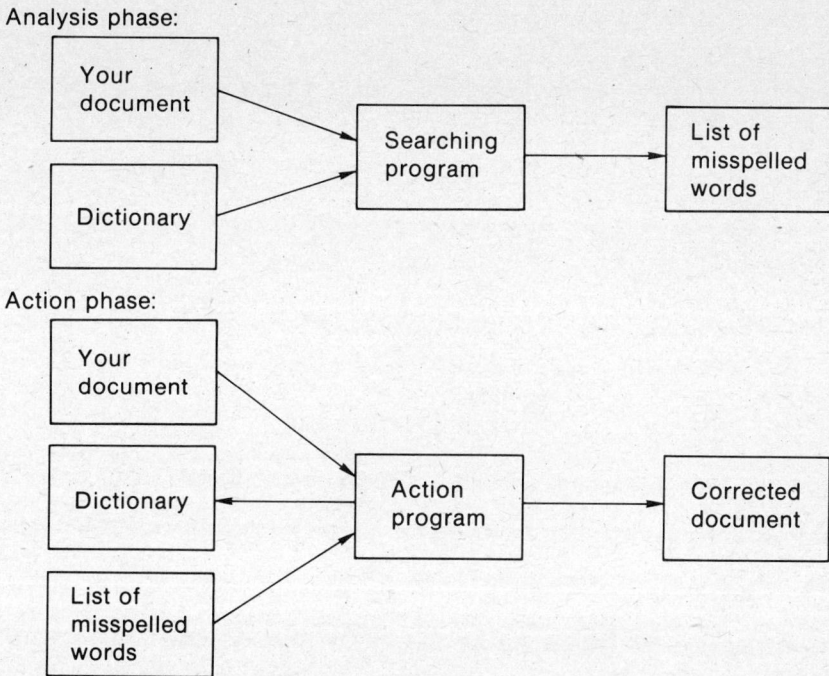

Figure 5-17. Spelling correction is a two step process. During the first phase, the text is searched for words that are not found in the spelling corrector's dictionary. The intermediate file of misspelled words becomes input for the second phase, in which you decide what action should be taken for each of the missed words.

Don't expect too much from a spelling checker. It will sea nothing wrong with this sentence because the word "sea" is in the dictionary. Some spelling checkers are thrown by hyphenated words or contractions; they would add the word "don" to the missed word list when proofreading the first sentence in this paragraph. When you first start using a spelling checker, you will be amazed at how many correct words show up on the missed words list because they were not in the dictionary that was distributed with the program; however, as you use the program and add words to the dictionary, that will become less of a problem. The rub is that, unless you are a very confident speller, you will want to look up each word before adding it to the program dictionary, and that is time consuming (I have added about 500 words to my spelling checker dictionary). The opposite problem occurs when the program dictionary comes with mis-spelled words in it or you inadvertently add one.

Spelling checkers are usually used after the fact to proofread a document, but some can be used to check the spelling of a word while you are writing. If a word you are questioning is not found in the dictionary, others with close spelling are suggested. Being able to check spelling while writing, without leaving your editing program, is handy. There are thesaurus

```
MISSPELLED WORD: compuuter

ACTION MENU
  A:  ADD TO DICTIONARY
  I:  IGNORE
  C:  CORRECT IN DOCUMENT


YOUR CHOICE  ▪
```

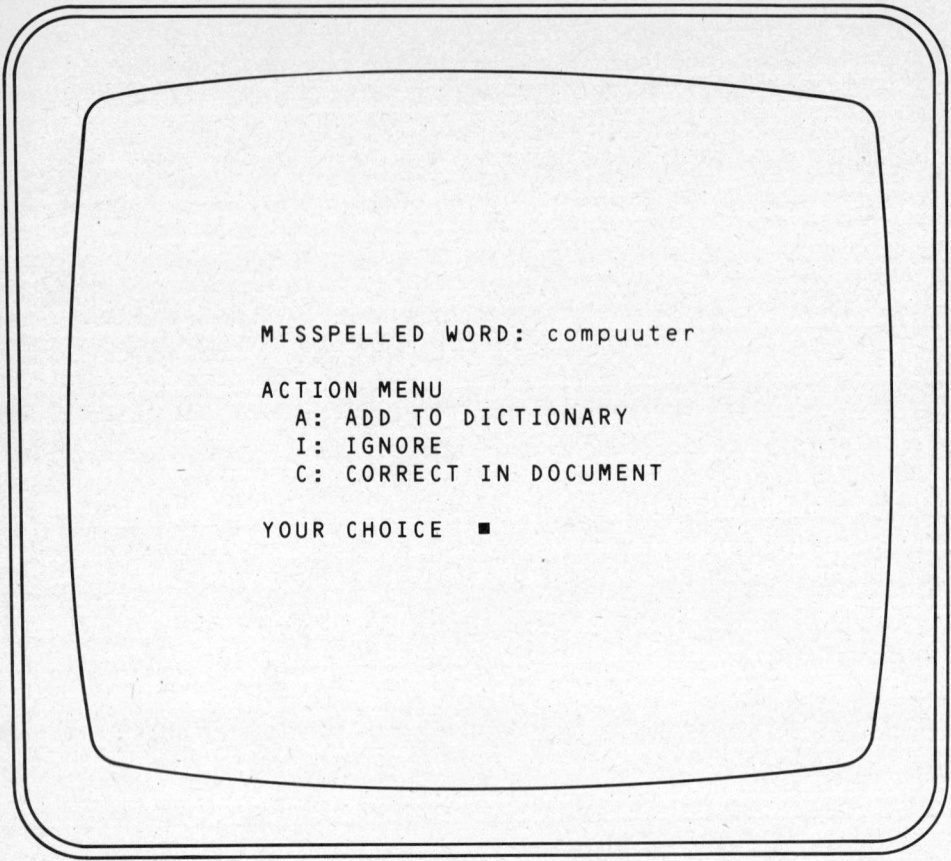

Figure 5-18. During the second phase of spelling correction, you must decide how each of the missed words should be handled. In the case illustrated, the word is really misspelled, so the operator would select choice C. This would cause the system to mark the word "computer" for correction (in some systems, you would correct it immediately). If the missed word had been correct and was one that is commonly used, perhaps "IBM" if you write about computers often, you would add it to the dictionary by selecting choice A. An uncommon, but correct, word, perhaps "Gettysburg," would be ignored.

programs that work in a similar manner. If you are stuck for a synonym of a word, you enter it and the program searches its thesaurus for suggestions. Again, to be truly helpful, a thesaurus program must be usable while you are editing a document.

Spelling checkers have been available for many years on time sharing systems and have migrated onto personal computers. One of the first spelling checkers came out of the Writer's Workbench project at Bell Laboratories; however, that project has gone beyond spelling checkers. Bell has also developed programs for finding punctuation errors, wordy diction, passive constructions, sexist phrases, split infinitives, incorrect use of

```
Passives

     This text contains a much higher percentage of
passive verbs (44%) than is common in good documents
of this type (22%). A sentence is in the passive
voice when its grammatical subject is the receiver
of the action.

 PASSIVE: The ball was hit by the boy.

When the doer of the action in a sentence is the
subject, the sentence is in the active voice.

 ACTIVE: The boy hit the ball.

The passive voice is sometimes needed

 1.  to emphasize the object of the sentence,

 2.  to vary the rhythm of the text, or

 3.  to avoid naming an unimportant actor.

 EXAMPLE: The appropriations were approved.

     Although passive sentences are sometimes needed,
psychological research has shown that they are harder
to comprehend than active sentences. Because of this,
you should transform as many of your passives to
actives as possible. You can use the style program to
find all your sentences with passive verbs in them, by
typing the following command when this program is
finished.
```

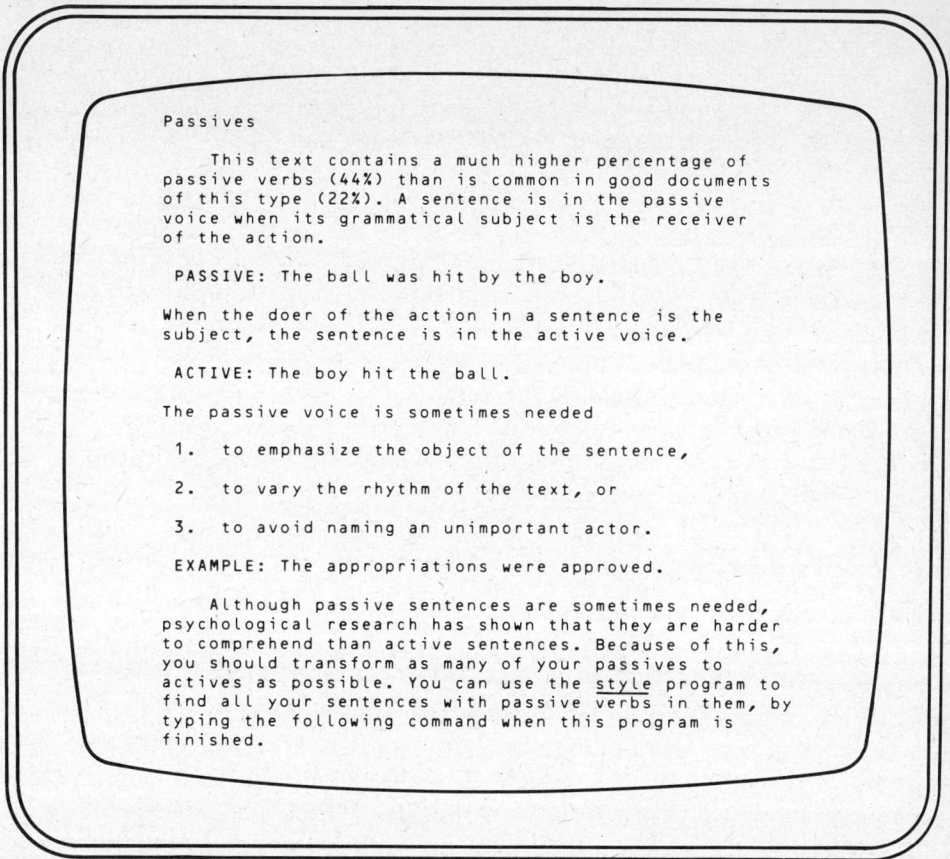

Figure 5-19. Here we see an example of the sort of tutorial material the Writer's Workbench program would present if it felt that you had made stylistic errors. It sounds a little like Miss Theiss, my favorite high school English teacher.

articles, and common typing errors such as transposition of characters or repetition of the same word twice in a row. These programs, which have also been moved over to the PC, not only locate errors, but often suggest corrections like substituting "many" for "a large number of" or "decide" for "make a decision."

Style proofreaders go beyond dictionary look-up, since they contain some ideas about good and bad writing style. Some are derived from standard texts on writing and rhetoric, and others come from experiments on comprehension. For example, writing handbooks suggest that we vary sentence length and structure, that active verbs are preferred to passive verbs, and that pronouns and adverbs be used to enhance connectivity. Stylistic guidelines like these are incorporated into the Writer's Workbench programs and their PC descendants. For instance, they will flag passive constructions, and if a document has a relatively high percentage of passive verbs, they display a short tutorial, such as that shown in Figure 5-19.

If you will be using your PC for writing fairly long, formal reports, there are other writing aids that you might be interested in. There are programs that can go through a document and generate an index or table of contents, using words that are found in headings or have been marked for inclusion. You would have to mark an index term only once, and all subsequent occurrences would be noted automatically. An alphabetic index showing the page numbers on which each term was used and a table of contents could then be printed out.

Other programs are designed to help an author maintain a bibliography. You create records with the name of a book or article, the author's name, the publisher, and so forth. References are flagged in the text, and the appropriate footnote or bibliography entry is automatically generated.

Bear in mind that these writing aids may be a standard part of a word processing program or may be sold as separate, auxiliary programs. In the latter case, you don't have to pay for a capability unless you need it.

FANCY OUTPUT

Will you be using your PC to prepare documents for reproduction? If you have a high quality printer and a flexible word processing program, you should be able to come up with camera ready copy fairly easily. As we saw in Chapter 2, precision control over printhead positioning is possible with some formed character printers. That means it is possible to vary intercharacter and interline spacing to within a small fraction of an inch. If in laying out a page to be printed you find that the copy is a little too large or too small, it is possible to shrink or stretch it by making a slight change in line or character spacing. Instead of six lines per inch, you might go to 5½ or 6½, or you might change the horizontal spacing or column width by a fraction of an inch.

Of course, getting a fancy printer is not sufficient to achieve this sort of precision control. Your word processing program (the formatting portion) must also make provision for it. You will have to run tests to make sure the software and printer are compatible and can do what you need.

If your program and printer allow it, you will be able to do even more in the way of fancy printing. Some word processing programs can manipulate multicolumnar text like that on newspaper and magazine pages. As you see in Figure 5-20, you can use columns of words or, if you prepare statistical or financial documents, columns of numbers. Some programs can even do arithmetic on the numbers.

We have already seen that type attributes such as proportional character spacing, boldface, and italics are possible with the appropriate program/printer combination. Centered lines and *justified* lines, in which both the left and right margins are straight, are possible with nearly every program and printer. If you use a quality printer with a carbon ribbon and your word processing program has the proper formatting features, you can expect printed output that looks about as good as if it had come from a

	May	June
Gross Receipts	9876.54	4567.89
Cost of Goods	1050.20	500.39
Gross Profit	8826.34	4067.50
Salaries	3000.00	2000.00
Rent	1200.00	1200.00
Interest	100.00	110.00
Depreciation	750.00	750.00
Net Income	3776.34	17.50

Figure 5-20. The formatting of this report would pose problems for some systems, whereas others would be able automatically to line up columns, move them around on the page, and even do arithmetic. The ability to handle multicolumn formats is useful for people working with text on multicolumn newsletter pages, as well as in dealing with numbers.

proportional spacing typewriter. However, it will not match the flexibility or quality of typeset material.

If you need typeset quality and produce printed material on a regular basis, for example, if you publish a periodical newsletter or catalog, it may pay off to typeset from your word processing files. Many typesetting firms are set up to accept documents from word processors, though developing a system for interfacing with a typesetting company will take time and effort.

Let's say you publish a weekly newsletter. The most common way to get text from your PC to a typesetter is to transmit it over the phone (see Chapter 8). If the typesetter happens to have compatible equipment, it may be possible for him or her to read your PC disks directly.

Unfortunately, just transferring the data to the typesetter is not enough. The typesetting equipment requires the addition of control information,

```
[P10F1M20L12] This is a sample of a
[F34] direct code conversion [F1]
file. Notice how easily fonts and
[A45P30] character [P6] sizes [P10]
can be changed. This is the most
versatile, but most difficult to use
method, because it requires knowledge
of all of the typesetter's commands.
```

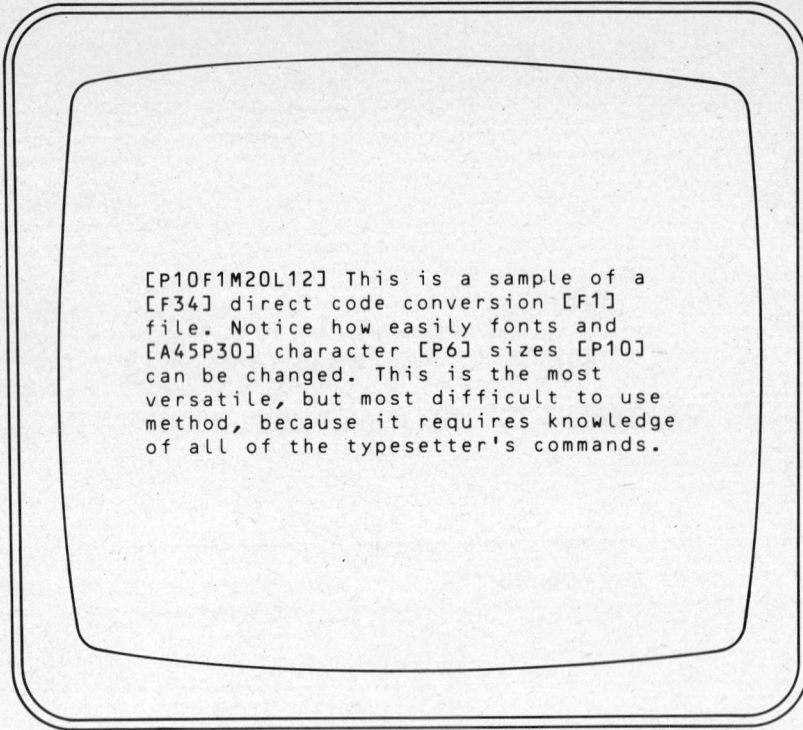

This is a sample of a direct code conversion file.
Notice how easily *fonts* and
ter sizes can be changed. This is the most versatile,
but most difficult to use method, because it requires
knowledge of all of the typesetter's commands.

charac-

A

```
     This is a sample word processing file.
Notice that there are no commands in this
file and that it is a completely normal run-of-
the-mill word processing file. Word processor
conversion techniques work best on this kind
of file, because this file has no unusual re-
quirements.
```

B

Figure 5-21. In the first example (A), which illustrates font and type size changes, control commands have been inserted by someone familiar with the typesetter. If you use relatively constant type styles and spacing (b), a program can probably be written to convert your word processing output to a typesetter file automatically.

just as we added formatting and embedded commands to our word processing files. As you see in Figure 5-21, either these commands may be entered manually, in cases in which you need the full flexibility of the typesetting equipment, or, if you have fairly uniform text, it may be possible to write a program to insert them automatically. In either case, considerable work will be involved in setting up the system for interfacing with a local typesetting firm, so you should think in these terms only if you plan to produce type on a regular basis.

CHAPTER SIX
Spreadsheet Processing Basics

Nearly everyone concerned with computers has heard of VisiCalc, the first spreadsheet processing program to be offered for a personal computer. Necessity mothered invention in the case of VisiCalc. Dan Bricklin, then an MBA student at Harvard, found he was spending more time doing arithmetic than creative analysis when working on case studies. He and Bob Frankston, a friend who had taken master's degrees in computer science and electrical engineering at MIT, wrote a program for the Apple computer that automated the calculations involved in preparing financial plans. Since the results were always visible on the display screen and the program did arithmetic calculations, they called it VisiCalc.

VisiCalc was turned over to a company that is now called VisiCorp for marketing. Since it was introduced in 1978, VisiCalc has been responsible for the sale of thousands of personal computers bought solely for the purpose of running it. People discovered that VisiCalc was easy to learn to use and that it could be used for many things in addition to making financial projections.

Given this success, VisiCalc soon had imitators and competitors. The competition may have been bad news for Dan Bricklin and Bob Frankston, but it was good news for users of personal computers. Today, the owner of an IBM PC can choose among dozens of spreadsheet processors. This competition has also forced evolution. The spreadsheet programs for today's PC are faster and easier to use and have more features than the original VisiCalc. Of course, VisiCalc has also evolved, right along with the competition.

If necessity was VisiCalc's mother, the financial planning programs that had been available on time-shared computers for many years were its grandparents. These programs did the same sorts of computations, but the results were not immediately visible. VisiCalc's innovation was that the spreadsheet was always visible on the computer's display and that whenever one part of it was changed, any other part that was affected was also changed automatically. But we are getting a little ahead of ourselves; just what is a spreadsheet?

APPLICATIONS

These are some ways you can use a spreadsheet processing program. Probably the most frequent applications have to do with filling in computerized forms that have arithmetic relationships like column totals and price extensions. Reporting systems that analyze data and compare them to projections can also be set up. Used in these applications, a spreadsheet processor can be a real time saver, perhaps justifying the price of your PC.

Decision making or evaluating alternatives is a less tangible, though possibly a more important, application. If, in your position, you make relatively quantifiable, structured decisions, spreadsheet processors can help with projecting alternative results. If you are a highly intuitive decision maker or are involved in unstructured policy decisions, they will not be as useful. Don't expect a spreadsheet program to help you decorate your building or decide whether it is worthwhile to set up a face-to-face meeting with a client.

1. Spreadsheet programs are great for filling in forms, like invoices or purchase orders. Once the variable information such as the product names, quantities, and unit prices was entered, the price extensions, discounts, and taxes would automatically be computed using formulas in your spreadsheet model, and the rest of the form would be filled in. Your weekly travel and entertainment expense report is another simple form that could be automated using a spreadsheet program.

2. Complex forms, like tax forms, could be handled in the same manner. Since so many people are interested in income tax forms, it is even possible to buy disks with prewritten templates (spreadsheet models) of the 1040 and other tax forms. You just enter your income and expense figures and the intermediate totals, and the rest of the bad news is computed for you.

3. Spreadsheets may also be used for data analysis and reporting. For instance, a sales manager might use a spreadsheet model to track the performance of each salesman or each product.

4. Models for analysis and reporting could be constructed for sports as well as for business. You might use a spreadsheet program to show how your little league baseball team and its players are doing.

5. Spreadsheet models are often used to see what would happen if things changed. You may have a business plan that depends on such factors as material, labor, and capital costs. A model could be constructed to let you see the impact of changes in these parameters on profit and cash flow. Spreadsheet programs are ideal for presenting this sort of result as *pro forma* accounting statements.

6. Reporting systems for accounting and control can be automated using a spreadsheet program. You might set up a system in which individual departments each prepare monthly budget spreadsheets, which are then consolidated into a corporate budget. The departmental spreadsheets might come in on disks or be transmitted over the phone.

If you would like to start out slowly, you could build a simple system for handling the expense reports of example 1. Each week, the individual spreadsheet forms would be consolidated into an expense summary spreadsheet. Since the information was already recorded on disk, it would be a fairly simple matter to write a short program to print the expense checks as well.

A SIMPLE EXAMPLE

The best way to get the idea of a spreadsheet is to consider a few examples. About the simplest example possible is shown in Figure 6-1. The computer display is organized into rows and columns that make up an imaginary *spreadsheet*. The rows are usually labeled numerically and the columns alphabetically. These rows and columns divide the spreadsheet into a grid in which each cell can contain either a number or more complicated *numeric formula* or a string of characters, usually called a *label* in spreadsheet jargon.

For instance, in Figure 6-1, cell A1 (column A, row 1) contains the label "FIRST SPREADSHEET," and cell B4 contains the number 25. The only cell that seems unusual is B8. Rather than a simple number, B8 contains a formula that must be evaluated in order to produce a numerical value. In this case, the numbers in cells B4, B5, and B6 are to be added together to give the value for cell B8.

But isn't that a bit awkward? The sum of 25, 50, and 30 is 105, so why not just enter the value "105" in cell B8 instead of the more complicated formula? The reason is that we might be interested in seeing what happens if one of the three numbers in column B were to be changed. What would happen if B4 were changed from 25 to 30? If we have used a formula in cell B8, the correct total would be *recalculated* and displayed as soon as the number in B4 was changed.

That is reasonable, but would you want to see the formula displayed on the screen or its current value? The formulas are of interest while you are constructing your spreadsheet, but in using it you will be more interested in results. Therefore, the current values of the formulas, not the formulas themselves, are shown on the screen. Figure 6-2 shows the actual display that would be on the screen if we had entered the spreadsheet of Figure 6-1.

	A	B
1	FIRST SPREADSHEET	
2		
3	NUMBERS:	
4	1	25
5	2	50
6	3	30
7		
8	TOTAL	105
.		
.		
.		

Figure 6-1. This is a very simple spreadsheet model in which three numbers are added together to produce a total. Some cells, like A1, contain labels, whereas others, like B4, contain numbers. Cell B8 contains a formula, which would be automatically evaluated to yield a numerical value.

```
            A                      B              . . .
1  FIRST SPREADSHEET
2
3  NUMBERS:
4        1                    25
5        2                    50
6        3                    30
7
8  TOTAL                 SUM (B4...B6)
.
.
.
```

Figure 6-2. Here we see the resultant spreadsheet that would be displayed if you entered the model in Figure 6-1. The formula has been evaluated and the resultant numerical value, 105, is shown in cell B8. If you changed any of the numbers in cells B4, B5, or B6, the formula would be automatically re-evaluated and the new total displayed.

As you see, the formula in cell B8 is not shown, but its value is. If you were to change the value of B4 from 25 to 30, the spreadsheet would be automatically recalculated and 110 would appear in B8.

Just for practice, how would you change our spreadsheet in order to show the average of the three numbers in column 1? One solution would be to put the label "AVERAGE" in cell A9 and the formula "SUM(B4. . .B6)/3" in B9. (The "/" means "divided by".) Could you have used a different formula in B9? Figure 6-3 shows another possibility.

At this point we need a term to distinguish between the resultant spreadsheet as it is displayed on the screen and the underlying spreadsheet

```
            A                      B              . . .
1  SECOND SPREADSHEET
2
3  NUMBERS:
4        1                    25
5        2                    50
6        3                    30
7
8  TOTAL                 SUM (B4...B6)
9  AVERAGE               B8/3
.
.
.
```

Figure 6-3. This spreadsheet model is similar to the first, but a ninth row has been added, showing the average of the three numbers. Note that the formula in cell B9 refers to another cell containing a formula. As long as the references are not circular, any numerical cell may be used in a formula.

that specifies our calculations. Since the underlying spreadsheet with its formulas is based on some system you are interested in, perhaps a business or a baseball team, the computerized representation of it is usually called the *spreadsheet model* or just *model*, and we will stick with that term. You may also come across the term *template*, which means a model with some cells left open for you to fill in.

ENTERING YOUR MODEL AND FORMATTING IT TO LOOK GOOD

Now that we know what a model is, how would it be entered into the computer? When the spreadsheet program is first loaded, the screen of your PC would show the row and column labels, around the edges, but the center would be blank (see Figure 6-4). The next thing you would notice would be that the cursor was expanded in size; it would fill an entire cell, and when you used the cursor control keys to move it, it would jump an entire cell at a time, not just one character space. In order to enter a label or formula into a cell, you would just move the cursor to that cell and type the label or formula.

As you typed the label or formula, it would not be entered directly into the cell, but would first appear in the *interaction area*, shown at the top of the screen in Figure 6-4. That way, you could preview it as you typed it and use editing keys like "backspace" and "delete" in case any changes had to be made before entering it.

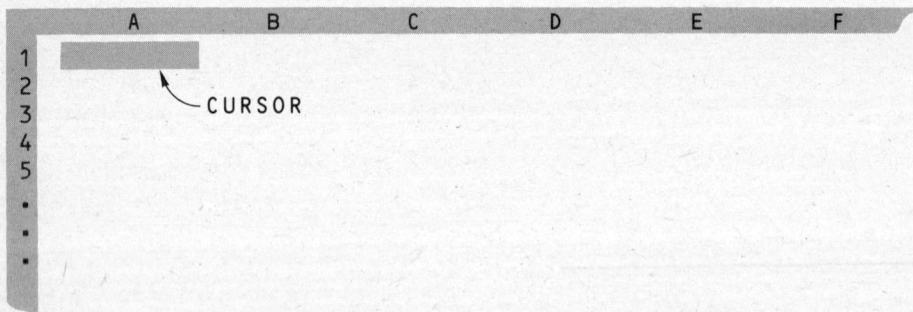

Figure 6-4. When the spreadsheet program is first loaded and run, the screen will look like this. The row and column identifiers are displayed, but the spreadsheet itself is empty. The cursor is expanded in size to fill an entire cell, and it may be moved from cell to cell using the cursor control keys. The operator interaction area at the top of the screen is used for the display of status information such as the amount of memory space remaining, for input of commands, and for editing formulas and labels before they are entered. With some programs this interaction is at the bottom of the screen, but it is always needed.

The interaction area would have other information as well; it would give you status information like the current location of the cursor, or the amount of free memory you had left, and it would be used to show your command choices, for instance, for printing the spreadsheet or saving it on disk.

Let's try a more interesting example, like using a spreadsheet processor to analyze sports data. Figure 6-5 shows a baseball team model as it would be entered. As you see, the players' names, number of times at bat, and number of hits each made are entered into columns A, B, and C. A player's batting average is computed using a formula in column D, and the team totals are shown in row 16.

Figure 6-6 shows the resultant spreadsheet display, which has a few problems. It is difficult to read: the names of the players are cut off because they are too long to fit in their cells, the decimal points clutter up the display, the column headings are at the left hand edges of their cells (they are *left justified*), and the numbers are at the right hand edges (*right justified*). Fortunately, like word processing programs, spreadsheet processors have commands for altering display formats.

Figure 6-7 shows the same spreadsheet, reformatted. For a start, the column widths were changed. The "NAME" column was expanded to 20 characters, the "AT BATS" and "HITS" columns were reduced in width, and the "BATTING AVERAGE" width left unchanged. The display formats of the numbers within columns B, C, and D were also changed to

```
         A              B            C            D
 1  BASEBALL STATISTICS, 1955 DODGERS
 2  (they finally beat the Yankees)
 3
 4  PLAYER'S AT                     BATTING
 5  NAME          BATS         HITS        AVERAGE
 6
 7  Campanell     446.00       142.00      1000 x C7/B7
 8  Hodges, G     546.00       158.00      1000 x C8/B8
 9  Gilliam,      538.00       134.00      1000 x C9/B9
10  Reese, Pe     553.00       156.00      1000 x C10/B10
11  Robinson,     317.00        81.00      1000 x C11/B11
12  Amoros, S     388.00        96.00      1000 x C12/B12
13  Snider, D     538.00       166.00      1000 x C13/B13
14  Furillo,      523.00       164.00      1000 x C14/B14
15
16  TEAM TOTA   SUM (B7...B14)  SUM (C7...C14)  1000 x C16/B16
```

Figure 6-5. This model is for the analysis of baseball players' batting statistics. The players' names, number of times at bat, and number of hits made appear in columns A, B, and C. Their batting averages are calculated using the formulas in column D. Row 16 contains the formulas for the team totals and overall batting average.

```
       A            B            C            D

 1  BASEBALL STATISTICS, 1955 DODGERS
 2  (they finally beat the Yankees)
 3
 4  PLAYER'S AT                      BATTING
 5  NAME        BATS      HITS       AVERAGE
 6
 7  Campanell   446.00    142.00   318.3856
 8  Hodges, G   546.00    158.00   289.3772
 9  Gilliam,    538.00    134.00   249.0706
10  Reese, Pe   553.00    156.00   282.0976
11  Robinson,   317.00     81.00   255.5205
12  Amoros, S   388.00     96.00   247.4226
13  Snider, D   538.00    166.00   308.5501
14  Furillo,    523.00    164.00   313.5755
15
16  TEAM TOTA  3849.00   1097.00   285.0090
```

Figure 6-6. Here we see the spreadsheet of the baseball model as it was shown in Figure 6-5. While the results are correct, they are difficult to read. Fortunately, these programs include commands for improving the format or appearance of the spreadsheet.

```
          A               B            C            D

 1  BASEBALL STATISTICS, 1955 DODGERS
 2  (they finally beat the Yankees)
 3
 4  PLAYER'S            AT                    BATTING
 5  NAME                BATS        HITS      AVERAGE
 6
 7  Campanella, Roy     446          142          318
 8  Hodges, Gil         546          158          289
 9  Gilliam, Junior     538          134          249
10  Reese, Pee Wee      553          156          282
11  Robinson, Jackie    317           81          256
12  Amoros, Sandy       388           96          247
13  Snider, Duke        538          166          309
14  Furillo, Carl       523          164          314
15
16  TEAM TOTALS        3849         1097          285
```

Figure 6-7. Here we see the baseball spreadsheet with formatting changes to improve its appearance. The "PLAYER'S NAME" column has been widened and the "AT BATS" and "HITS" columns narrowed. The headings over the columns have also been adjusted; "HITS" and "BATTING AVERAGE" have been right justified and the word "AT" has been centered. The format of the numbers has been changed to show integers in order to make them more readable.

integers; in other words, the decimal portions were dropped. The column headings were lined up over the numbers.

Some explanatory comments were also added to the spreadsheet in Figure 6-7. Textual annotations are useful for both the model builder and people reading the results. Even though the emphasis in spreadsheet processing is on calculation, commands for creating and formatting comments easily are handy.

There is one last point to be made on entering the model. Look back at the formulas in column D in our baseball team model and you will see that they are nearly identical. The basic structure is the same in each: 1000 × HITS / AT BATS. Only the row numbers vary. It was not necessary to enter each of these calculations separately. Once the first one was entered in cell D7, the *replicate* or *copy* command was used to create the others, with row numbers automatically adjusted for each copy of the formula. All spreadsheet programs have some sort of replicate command, which simplifies model entry (see Figure 6-8).

WHAT HAPPENS IF SOMETHING CHANGES, AND HOW CAN YOU SEE IT?

In the examples we have seen so far, the spreadsheet model has been used for analysis and presentation of data. Although you may not be interested in baseball, it is not difficult to imagine "serious" applications involving analysis and presentation. For example, a model that corresponded to a 1040 income tax form could be created, and once you filled in the numbers on your income, expenses, deductions, and so forth, the rest of the form

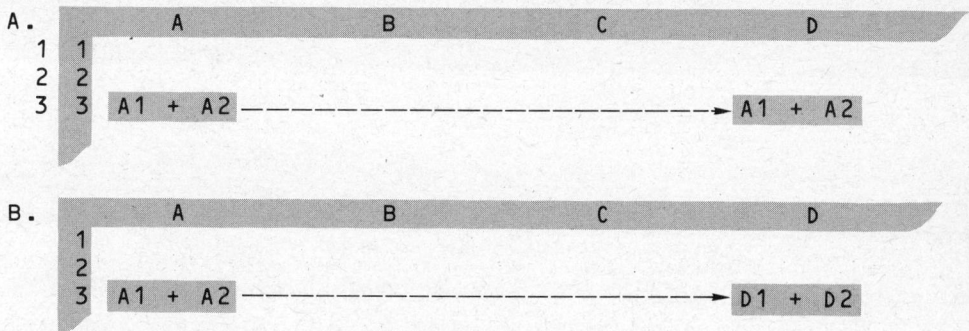

Figure 6-8. This example illustrates relative and absolute copying of spreadsheet formulas. With absolute copying (A), the cell references in the formulas remain constant; the sum of cells A1 and A2 will appear in both locations. In example B, the formulas have been adjusted to refer to the same relative cells within the new column. The value of relative copying or replication is illustrated in Figure 6-5, in which column D was created by entering a single formula in cell D7, then replicating it in cells D8 through D16 using a single relative copy command.

would be automatically computed using the appropriate formulas. Or you might use a spreadsheet to prepare monthly budget reports for a project. Once you entered the cost figures for the current month, a spreadsheet showing deviations from planned expenditures and year-to-date expenditures would be generated. Revenues and costs associated with, say, rental property could be tracked and reported in the same way.

But I'll bet you have heard of *what-if* or *sensitivity analysis*. Spreadsheet programs can be used as planning or decision making aids by altering some part of the model and seeing how another part is affected. Figure 6-9 is a model that shows what would happen to your bank balance if the interest rate or starting principal were varied. For convenience and clarity, the input *parameters* have been gathered together in one spot on the spreadsheet. As soon as either of the two input parameters was changed, the spreadsheet would be recalculated and the new results displayed.

This sort of analysis is done so commonly that some spreadsheet programs have a command for automatically stepping through a table of alternative input parameter values and generating a resultant output table.

What would happen if, instead of a five year projection, we needed a twenty year projection? The model would be roughly the same, but it would be too wide to fit on your display screen. Spreadsheet programs handle this

	A	B	C	D	E	F
1	SIMPLE "WHAT-IF" MODEL					
2						
3	Input Parameters					
4						
5	Interest Rate:	10.00%				
6	Principal:	$1,000.00				
7						
8			Balance at start of each year:			
9						
10		YEAR 1	YEAR 2	YEAR 3	YEAR 4	YEAR 5
11						
12		$1,000.00	$1,100.00	$1,210.00	$1,331.00	$1,464.10
13						
14						
15	This spreadsheet shows the effect of interest rate and your original deposit					
16	on your bank balance. To try alternative values, just enter them in cells B5					
17	and B6.					

Figure 6-9. This spreadsheet illustrates what-if or sensitivity analysis. It shows bank balances at the start of each year, given an interest rate and principal. If either cell B5 or B6 were changed, the resultant values in B13 through F13 would be recalculated. In this manner, you can answer the question, "What if interest or principal changes?"

Note that formatting commands have again been used to improve the appearance of the spreadsheet. The balances are displayed as dollar amounts with punctuation, the interest rate is displayed as a percentage, the column widths have been extended to accommodate the values, and the year labels have been centered in their columns. A textual annotation has also been added to the spreadsheet in order to explain it to the operator.

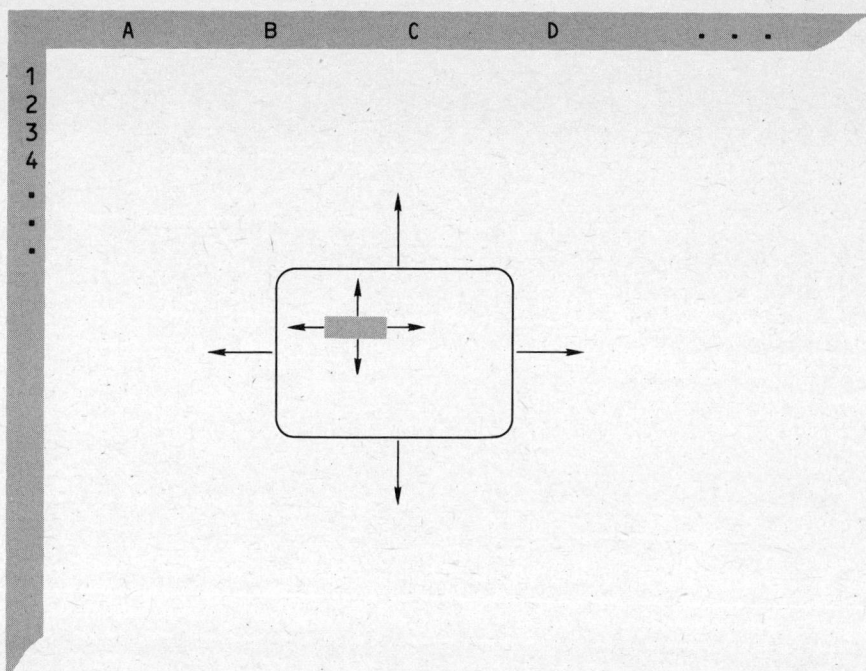

Figure 6-10. The spreadsheet in memory may be much too large to fit on the screen. Depending on the amount of memory in your PC and the program you are using, it may be more than 10,000 cells, large enough to cover a wall if it were printed out. Therefore, you need a way to view different parts of it. As in word processing, the screen may be thought of as a window that can be moved to any part of the spreadsheet using the cursor control keys. Once you have the portion of the spreadsheet you are interested in on the screen, you may move the cursor to specific cells, again using the cursor control keys.

problem in the same way as word processors do, by *scrolling* (see Figure 6-10). You can imagine that a very large spreadsheet is stored in the memory of your PC, and that only a portion of it is visible through the display screen *window.* When you try to move the cursor beyond the edge of the screen, this imaginary window simply moves, exposing a different part of the spreadsheet. Most programs also provide for jumping directly to any cell on the spreadsheet or to the corners.

Another handy feature is the ability to fix certain rows and columns on the screen so that titles, for example the column headings in our baseball example, remain on the screen even if the window is scrolled.

While scrolling would enable us to see the bank balance at the end of twenty years, it would be inconvenient if we were doing a sensitivity analysis, because the parameters are on the left side of the spreadsheet and the final balance is on the right. Fortunately, most programs allow you to break the display up into two or more windows (see Figure 6-11). Since

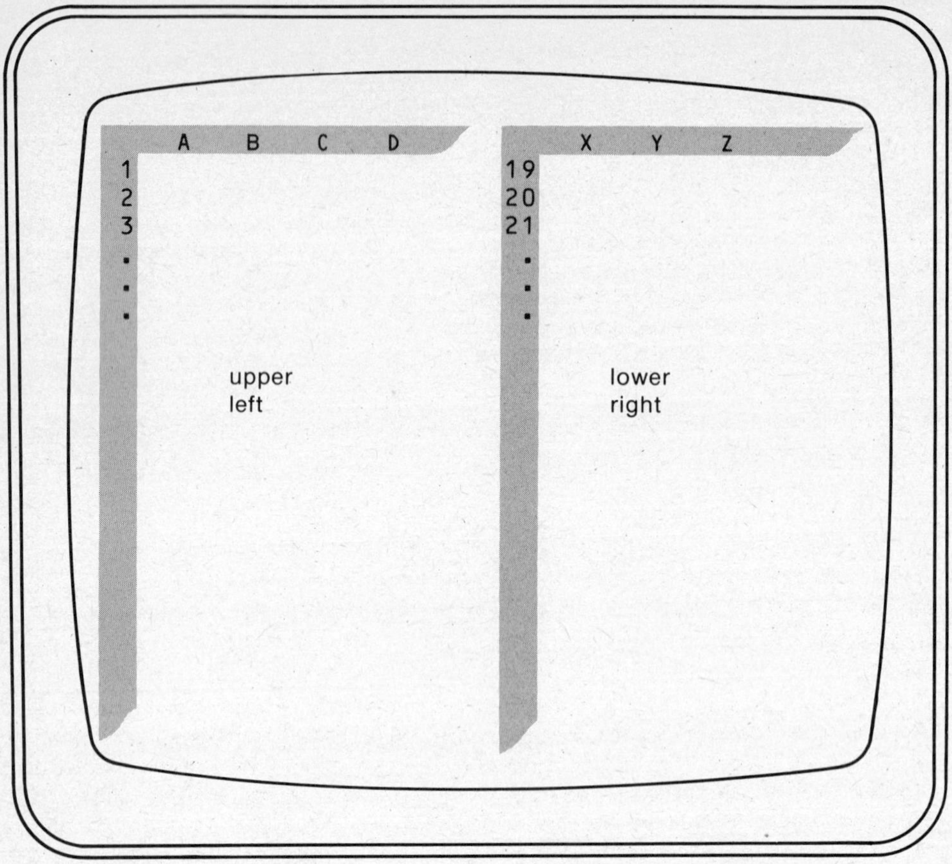

Figure 6-11. Here we see the display partitioned into two independent windows, each of which can be moved to a different part of the virtual spreadsheet in memory. In this example, the window on the left is on the upper left corner of the spreadsheet, and the window on the right is positioned down and to the right. In doing sensitivity analysis, one window can display the input parameters and the other the results. Windows can usually divide the screen horizontally or vertically, and some programs allow more than two windows.

these windows can scroll independently, we could keep one "over" the part of the spreadsheet with our parameters and another "over" the portion with the balance after twenty years, thereby seeing the results as soon as changes were made.

PRINTING REPORTS

To this point, we have entered models into memory and seen the results on the screen, but if we are going to show them to someone else, they have to be printed out. If the spreadsheet to be printed is small, it will fit on a single sheet of paper, and you can pretty well think of the screen version and the printed version as being the same. Extra wide paper and a printer that can fit a lot of characters on a line will help, but if your spreadsheet is still larger than a printed page, you will have to break it up for printing as in Figure 6-12. Some programs even figure out the page breaks automatically.

Spreadsheet programs allow you to specify a restricted area or *range* of cells to be printed. Thus, you might print only an interesting portion of the spreadsheet or you might print it on several pages. The pages could then be put together in a report or even taped together to make a single, large page. Your program will have other options such as including page numbers, headings or footings on each page, printing fixed titles along the edges of each page, and printing the row and column numbers from the spreadsheet.

If your interest is in showing someone the results of your analysis, you will want to print the resultant spreadsheet. But, in documenting your model so that someone else can study and perhaps modify it, you will want to print the formulas, not their values. Most programs allow either the model or resultant spreadsheet to be printed, although a printed model may not be formatted as a rectangle, but just listed cell by cell.

READING AND WRITING DISK FILES

If you want to save a model for future use or send it to someone else, it will have to be transferred from memory to disk. For this purpose, spreadsheet programs have commands for copying models from memory to disk and vice versa. As with printing, you may at times wish to save or load the entire model or a portion of it, and you may be interested in either the model

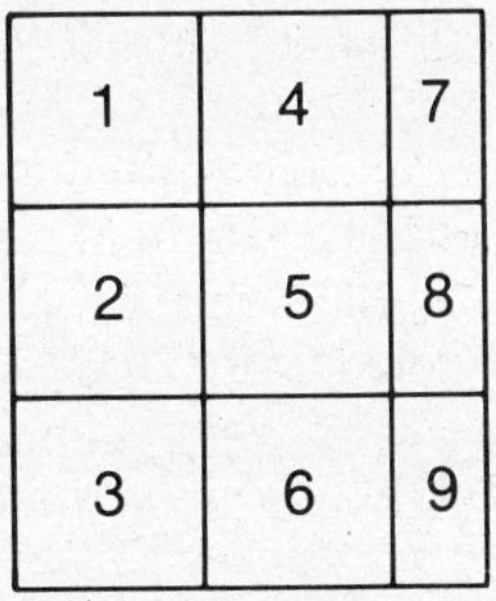

Figure 6-12. If the spreadsheet in memory is too large to fit on a single page, your program will be able to print it in pieces. In this example, the spreadsheet would be printed on nine separate pages. These could then be collated for a report or taped together. With some programs, the page breaks would be computed automatically, but with others, that would have to be done manually.

Other printing options usually include the ability to put fixed column headings or row identifiers on each sheet. These may be the row and column identifiers used on the spreadsheets, or you may specify them. In addition, it may be possible to have a heading line, footing line, page numbers, or the date printed on each page.

with its formulas or the resultant spreadsheet with the formulas evaluated.

Figure 6-13A illustrates a case in which a portion of a model would be saved or loaded. If you were interested in several baseball teams, not just the Dodgers, you could use the entire baseball model of Figure 6-5, including the headings, and statistical computation cells as a template, reading in the portion with the players' names and records from various team spreadsheets. You would set up a disk with the template in one file and smaller spreadsheets with the player data for each team.

Rather than just reading in a portion of a spreadsheet, you may want to read it from the disk and have the values added to or subtracted from those that were already in memory in the corresponding cells. This would be handy if you needed to *consolidate* several reports into one summary report, as in Figure 6-13B. In that case, figures from several departmental spreadsheets are added together to form a budget report for an entire division or company.

Consolidation can also be accomplished by moving summary results from spreadsheets into an overall model. In Figure 6-13C, the budget totals from each department's spreadsheet are brought together to form an overall summary. The departmental spreadsheets would contain detailed breakdowns of the costs and budget amounts, but only the "bottom line" would be moved to the consolidated report.

Consolidation can help you organize your thinking and reporting scheme, and it offers a way of getting around spreadsheet size limitations. Instead of one large spreadsheet, which might exceed the size of your memory or the limit of the program, you can have several smaller ones. Some programs even allow for automatic consolidation; the effects of any value change are recorded in all related spreadsheets.

Before leaving the topic of reading and writing disk files, let me say something about what actually gets written on the disk. All programs must be able to save a model with its formulas on disk, but other forms are usually possible as well.

If you plan to incorporate your spreadsheet results into a report, perhaps a business plan or an accounting statement, it is convenient to be able to direct formatted output that would normally be printed to the disk instead. Once on the disk, it may be "picked up" by your word processing program and incorporated into the complete report.

At other times you will wish to save a portion of the spreadsheet in a form suitable for further computation, perhaps for consolidation into another model, or you may plan to use a business graphics package to plot spreadsheet results. Anticipating this need for moving spreadsheet results from program to program, Bricklin and Frankston defined Data Interchange Format (*DIF*), a standard file format for interchanging evaluated spreadsheets. Since VisiCalc was first on the market and sold well, the DIF standard has caught on fairly well, and most spreadsheet, graphics, and file management programs include the capability of reading and writing files written in that format (see Figure 6-14).

A.

BASEBALL TEMPLATE

NAME   AT BATS   HITS   AVERAGE

TEAM TOTALS AND AVERAGES

B.

CONSOLIDATED BUDGET

JAN   FEB   MAR   APR   . . .

Budget
and
cost
categories

C.

ORGANIZATION BUDGET SUMMARY

JAN   FEB   MAR   APR   . . .

Departments

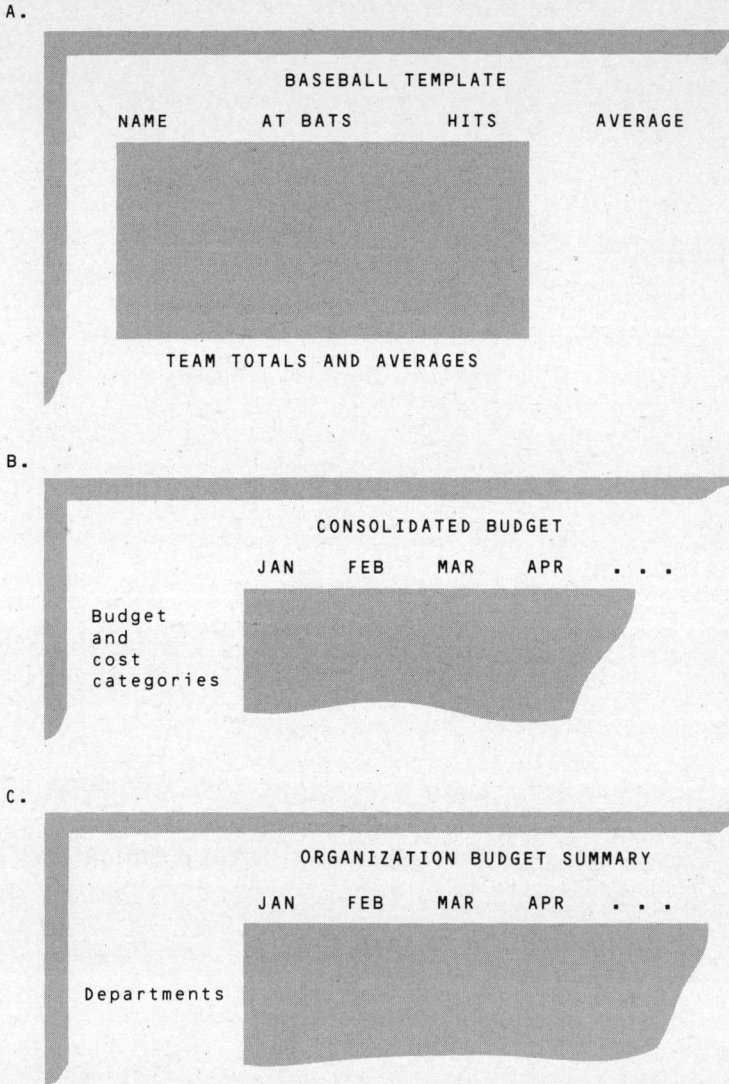

Figure 6-13. Portions of a spreadsheet may be read from or written on the disk. In our baseball example (A), the model of Figure 6-5 would be used as a template, and the player-specific data (shaded area) would be read in from spreadsheets stored on the disk. Thus, many teams, not just the 1955 Dodgers, could be analyzed using the same model.

Examples B and C illustrate consolidation. In C, each department would have a submodel in the same format as the consolidated model. The figures from the shaded portion of the submodels would be added, not merely copied in, to the consolidated model. In example C, each department would have its own budget model, with a detailed breakdown of costs into categories that were relevant for its operation. The consolidated model would read only the summary or "bottom lines" of the department models. With some systems, consolidation is performed automatically, with others it must be done manually.

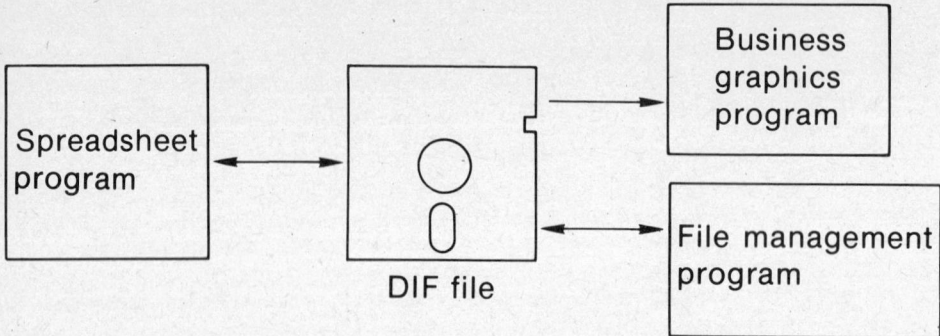

Figure 6-14. DIF, a standard format for recording spreadsheet results in a disk file, has been adopted by many software vendors. Files written in the DIF format can serve as a common interface for using a spreadsheet program in conjunction with other packages, for instance making a pie chart or bar chart of values on a spreadsheet, or moving spreadsheet results to or from a data file.

A DISCLAIMER

Spreadsheet applications can be divided into two rough categories: data analysis and presentation (budget reporting, baseball statistics, sales statistics, expense reports, tax forms, etc.) and planning, prediction and decision making tools (what-if models, sensitivity analyses). The value of the first type of application is fairly obvious and easily assessed. A spreadsheet program will save time and cost in filling in forms and implementing reporting procedures.

This disclaimer deals with the second class of application. Any decision support tool must be appropriate to your decision making style and to the kinds of decisions that you are called upon to make. If you are a highly intuitive, seat-of-the-pants decision maker, you probably won't like a spreadsheet program as a decision support tool. If you are in a position in which the decisions you make are unstructured and difficult to quantify, spreadsheets won't help. If good data is not available for your what-if model, it will not be an effective decision making tool. For instance, models that project sales using seasonal variations added to an overall trend require accurate historical data for projecting the seasonal component.

As any MBA student can tell you, there is a danger of confusing projections or extrapolations, whether made with a spreadsheet or by any other method, with forecasts. A model based on out-of-date assumptions or inaccurate data will give misleading results. There is even a danger that by "computerizing" a model you enhance its credibility. Be sure you understand any decision making model you use. If the model was constructed by someone else, be sure to study the formulas and question its assumptions. Resist the temptation to use a spreadsheet model to justify a decision that was already made on other grounds; in fact, you may use one to question such decisions.

If all of these disclaimers sound too negative, remember that a spreadsheet model will be only one of many inputs to a decision. Even if you don't place much emphasis on the results, setting it up can be a very useful exercise. It will give you a different way of looking at your problem, and thinking the problem through while formulating the model may bring previously overlooked factors to your attention.

CHAPTER SEVEN
Data Management Basics

Data management software traces its roots back to the first automatic data processing machines, which could read, sort, collate, reproduce, calculate, and print information in punched cards. In the 1880s Herman Hollerith and later James Powers designed the first punch card machines for the U.S. Census Bureau. Hollerith went on to found the company that became IBM, and Powers founded the company that, as part of Remington Rand, delivered the first commercial computer, the Univac I, to the Census Bureau in 1951.

The Univac I and its competitors soon began replacing IBM and Remington Rand punch card machines. The software that was written to ease that transition has evolved into our data management systems.

It was possible to write general purpose programs for conversion of punch card applications to computers because there were common steps and operations in many applications. Data were punched into cards, which were run through a series of machines that did things like sort the card file, select out unwanted cards, and perform computations, punching the results back into the card. There were other operations as well, but usually the final step in the process was running a card file through a machine that printed a report.

These early punch card conversion programs were called *report generators*, and they were very easy to use. You described the format of the data cards and the format of the output report, including headings and any tabulation or computation, and the report generator produced a program that would give the desired report from your data cards. Report generators and programs for sorting and merging data files were widely used in converting from punched card to computer systems, and they have continued to evolve. Report generators served as the models for the data management software that we use on our PCs, and they are still widely used in data processing departments. They also influenced the design of early data processing languages such as Commercial Translator, COBOL, and RPG.

These early report generators have evolved into sophisticated data

---

APPLICATIONS

1. Mailing lists are a common data management application; you can computerize your Rolodex file. For mass mailing, labels could be printed out in zip code order and records could be retrieved and updated by referencing the person's name. The mailing lists might be personal or business related. One file might contain both your personal and business list, as long as they were coded so that you could isolate one group or the other when you needed to do so.
2. An author or researcher might use a data management program for making bibliographical notes, simulating a file of index cards. Part of the record for a bibliographical entry would contain fixed information, like the title of the work, the author's name, and the year published. The remainder of the "index card" would hold free text, describing the book or article.
3. A data management system could be used to store data for analysis and reporting. It could be business data, for instance on sales of each product or by each salesperson, or from a totally different field. A social scientist might use a data management system to store the results of some survey research; an engineer or physical scientist might record observations on successive replications of an experiment.
4. A data management system could be used to automate a data processing function, for instance for accounts receivable. When something was shipped to customers or when they sent in payments, their customer records would be retrieved and updated to reflect the transaction.
5. More complex data processing systems require database management programs, which are capable of pulling information from several files into an integrated system. For instance, information from customer, inventory, bill of materials, and vendor files could all be pulled together in doing order entry, invoicing, payables, and receivables in a manufacturing company.

---

management systems for large computers, and now for personal computers. Although the boundaries are not clear cut, data management programs for the PC fall into three categories—*file managers, database managers,* and *index card systems.* Since they are closely related, most of the basic concepts apply to all three. We will begin our discussion with file managers, which work with one file at a time, and will point out the differentiating characteristics of the other two in the second section of the chapter. We will also come back to the history of data management software, but first let's look at an example and define a few terms.

FILE MANAGEMENT

Files, Records, and Fields

As it turns out, you already have a basic understanding of file management, even if you have never used a computer. For the time being, forget about computers, and ask yourself what the terms *file* and *record* mean. For example, if you call your auto insurance agent with a question on your policy, and he says, "Just a minute while I get your record from my file," what is he saying? He will probably walk over to a gray file cabinet, open a drawer, and pull out a manila folder with your record in it. Inside the folder is a form that has all sorts of information like your name, your address, the make and year of your car, and how much liability insurance you carry. If he were to look inside my folder instead of yours, he would see the same form, filled in with my values. In this example, the items on the insurance form are the *fields*.

The ideas of file, record, and field apply to computer data as well. The example in Figure 7-1 shows a hypothetical personnel file. There is one record in the file for each employee, and each record has five fields: EMPLOYEE NAME, AGE, SALARY, DATE HIRED, and EDUCATION LEVEL. In the old days, this information would have been punched into cards, but with our PCs it is kept on a disk.

EMPLOYEE NAME	AGE	SALARY	DATE HIRED	EDUCATION LEVEL
George Ruth	43	900	01/21/77	H
Stanley Musial	31	2300	05/05/82	B
Mildred Didrikson	48	1300	05/22/64	H
Ted Williams	53	1500	12/05/66	B
Wilma Rudolph	29	2800	01/04/70	M
Olga Fitokova	44	3100	01/31/72	B
Joseph Dimaggio	44	1400	09/22/69	B
James Thorpe	55	4700	06/09/49	H
Walter Alston	45	3400	04/30/81	D
Harold Grange	62	5000	10/04/46	H

Figure 7-1. This hypothetical personnel file contains records for ten employees. Each record is made up of five fields: name, age, salary, date hired, and education level. We will refer to this example throughout the chapter.

The file in Figure 7-1 contains only ten records, and if you had only ten employees, you would not bother computerizing your personnel file. You can begin to understand the value of using a computer by imagining that you had 500 employees instead of ten. Now, what if you needed to know which of your employees had the highest salary, or had worked for you the longest? Searching through 500 records would be tedious if they were all in manila folders in a gray filing cabinet. Even worse, what if you needed a list of employees' names and their salaries broken down by education level? If you have applications that fit this mold, you should look into file management software for your PC.

You may not be interested in personnel records, but this general paradigm, of organizing a file into records and records into fields, is useful in many contexts. An accounts receivable file would have a record for each person owing you money. Some of the fields for accounts receivable would be name, address, amount owed, date of last payment, and date of last bill. You might wish to use your PC for something closer to home, perhaps keeping track of the books in your library. In that case, there would be a record for each book you own and some of the fields would be the title, author, publisher, year published, and number of pages. There might also be a free text field, for entering an abstract or notes on the book.

I think that by now you have the idea. What are your data file applications? This would be a good time to list your files and state the fields each record will contain. While you are at it, make an estimate of the number of records in each file and the number of characters in each record.

Using a File Management System

Once you have thought through your application on paper, you will have to define your file by specifying the name, size, and type of each field, the format of the screen form that will be used during data entry and when records are updated, indices into the file for locating records quickly and in the desired order, and the formats of any reports you wish to print (see Figure 7-2).

That sounds like a lot, but it will be easy and quick. The system will guide you in defining the attributes of the fields, and default formats should be provided for the screen form and for reports. For a "quick and dirty" start, you can use the default formats; revising them should not take long if you decide you need something nicer. The system will also guide you in setting up indices, and that will take only a few minutes. The following sections explain these steps as they would be done in a typical file management system.

Setting Up a File: Field Names, Sizes, and Types

The first step in a file management application is to define the file, to describe the fields making up a record. Let's stick with the personnel file in

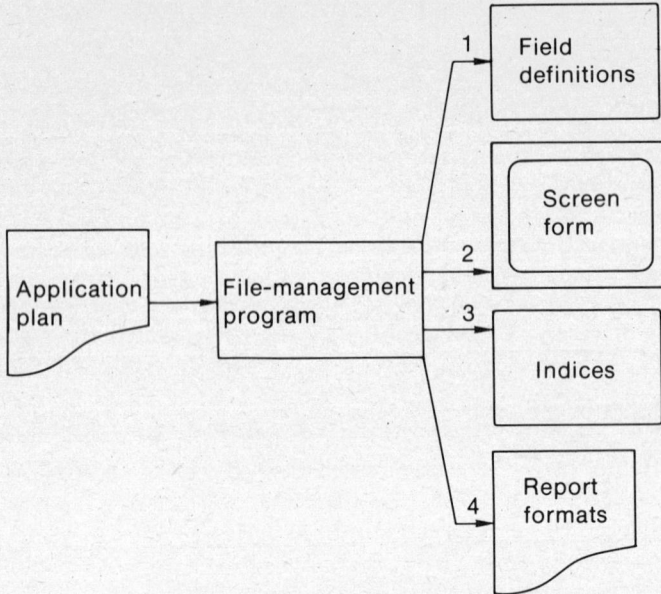

Figure 7-2. To use a file management system, you must first plan your application, then specify (1) the record description (name, size, and type for each field), (2) the format of the screen form to be used when adding new records or updating old ones, (3) any indices that will be used to locate records or sort the file, and (4) the formats and contents of reports that you will be printing. Once defined, your specifications for each of these elements will be stored on disk.

The file management program will guide you with prompts or menus so that specifying these elements will not be difficult. Default screen forms and report formats will also speed things up. Most programs will also allow you to alter the specifications after you get some operating experience with your application.

Figure 7-1. What do we have to tell the system about each of the fields? We need to specify the *field name, field size,* and *field type.* Figure 7-3 shows how this information might be specified for the EMPLOYEE NAME field and Figure 7-4 lists the specification for each field in our example.

Let's look more closely at these specifications and how they are used. The field name will be used whenever you refer to that field in future operations. For example, when you wanted to enter new information into the data file, the program would prompt you using the field name. Or if you wanted to search for people who were high school graduates, you would refer to the EDUCATION LEVEL field by its name. Some file management programs would also use the field names as default headings for report columns.

The file management program would use the field size information for error checking and for allocating disk space. If, while entering a new employee's record, you mistakenly typed an age of "435," you would get an error message, because you had exceeded the size for that field (two characters). Other size checking options might also be available, for

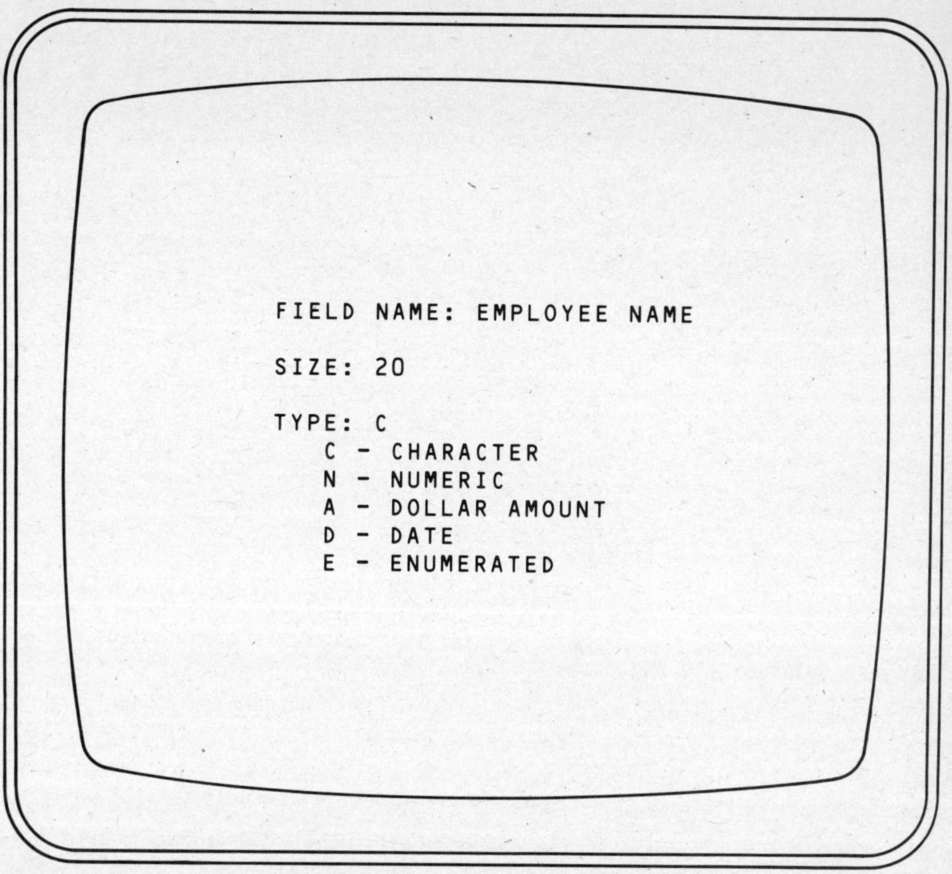

```
          FIELD NAME: EMPLOYEE NAME

          SIZE: 20

          TYPE: C
              C - CHARACTER
              N - NUMERIC
              A - DOLLAR AMOUNT
              D - DATE
              E - ENUMERATED
```

Figure 7-3. The name, size, and type of each field must be specified. Here we are defining the EMPLOYEE NAME field. The menu shows five choices for field type. Some systems may offer other choices in addition to these.

FIELD NAME	SIZE	TYPE
Employee Name	20	character
Age	2	numeric
Salary	6	dollar amount
Date Hired	8	date
Education Level	1	enumerated

Figure 7-4. This table shows the specification of each of the fields in our personnel file.

example a check to see that the input value is exactly a certain length (e.g., that a social security number is nine digits).

The field names and sizes are easily understood, but the various types may be confusing. The EMPLOYEE NAME is a *character* field, since it may contain any of the 96 printable ASCII characters. AGE is a *numerical* field, which means that it can have only a number in it.

Having specified that the AGE field is numerical has two important benefits. First, the file management program will be able to check data as they are entered and refuse to accept anything but a number. If the system asks for an employee's age and you accidentally type "4M" instead of "43," you will get an error message.* Some file management programs can do more elaborate checking on numerical values, for instance checking to see that the value is within a certain legal range.

The system also knows it is possible to do arithmetic on numerical fields. For instance, it could compute the number of years to retirement by subtracting AGE from 65. On the other hand, you would get an error message if you told it to do some arithmetic computation on a character field such as EMPLOYEE NAME.

The SALARY field is of the type *dollar amount* and the DATE HIRED field is of the type *date*. The system will know that salaries should be displayed or printed with dollar signs, commas, and decimal points, and that it is okay to do arithmetic on the values. Dates must be typed in a valid format (there would probably be several choices), and arithmetic would be outlawed in most systems. I say most, because a few let you do arithmetic on dates by storing them internally as the number of days since the turn of the century, and converting them to their printed form only when it is time to display them. In that case, arithmetic on dates, for instance computing the number of days a bill is overdue, would be possible.

The final field, EDUCATION LEVEL, can have various coded values, so its type is *enumerated*. For instance, you might decide on the following coding scheme: H: high school graduate, B: bachelor's degree, M: master's degree, and D: Ph.D. The coding scheme would be up to you, and it would save space in the file and cut down on errors, since the operator would be typing only a single letter and the system could check to be sure it was one of the legal values, H, B, M, or D. You would also have to specify the ordering you would like to see if the codes were sorted; in this case, H would be lowest because it represents the least education, then would come B, M, and D, in that order. In case you ever encounter the term, a technical person would say that H-B-M-D was the *collating sequence* for the field.

Some file management systems may offer a few more choices for field type than the five we have illustrated here. For instance, many offer a two valued type, called a *boolean* or *logical field*. These would be useful for true/false, yes/no fields, in which only two values are possible, for instance SEX.

---

*A few file management programs make an exception of the lowercase l, allowing it to be used in place of a 1, since many typists are used to that substitution.

When you sit down to define your fields, you may run into some difficulty deciding where to divide things. It we had decided to include the employee's address in the personnel record, would we set up separate fields for CITY, STATE, and ZIP CODE, or would they be grouped together as THIRD LINE OF ADDRESS? Breaking the third line of the address into three fields would mean a loss in efficiency; the system would be a little slower and the file would tie up more disk space. But it might be necessary. For example, if you planned to sort the file into zip code order for a mass mailing or knew you would have to select only employees living in a certain state for some reports, you would have to set up separate fields for STATE and ZIP CODE.

Note that we have left EMPLOYEE NAME as a single field, rather than breaking it into FIRST NAME and LAST NAME. With many systems, this would cause problems if we wanted to sort the file into alphabetical order; it would not work unless the names had been entered last name first. Other systems allow a special field type just for people's names, in which data can be entered last name first but still printed out first name last.

That is all there is to defining a data file. You specify the name, size, and type of each field. Once you have planned the file structure, specifying these characteristics for each field will take only a few minutes. This might be a good time to review by writing down the names, sizes, and types of the fields in your file management applications.

Entering Data

Once the file has been defined, you are ready to begin entering your data. Figure 7-5 shows a typical screen layout during data entry with a file management system. The screen is organized like a form, and you have the sense of filling in the blanks. The cursor jumps from one field to the next when you move it, saving time in moving about on the form. After filling in one field, you would move to the next, probably by hitting a cursor control key or perhaps one of the function keys. When the data looked good, you would enter the record into the data file, perhaps by hitting the "enter" key.

With most file management systems, you can design the layout of the form on the screen, placing the entries in a way that is logical and looks good. Once the format of the form was defined, it would be saved on disk. For "quick and dirty" applications, the system should offer a default screen layout as an option.

If you made a mistake while entering data into a field, you could fix it by backspacing and retyping, using the "insert" and "delete" keys where necessary. In addition to the mistakes that you might notice, the system would automatically check the validity of your entry, based on the field type and size. Errors that it could detect would be pointed out, perhaps in an interaction window at the bottom of the form. This window would also be used for other messages, for instance in showing a menu of the valid entries for an enumerated field along with their explanations.

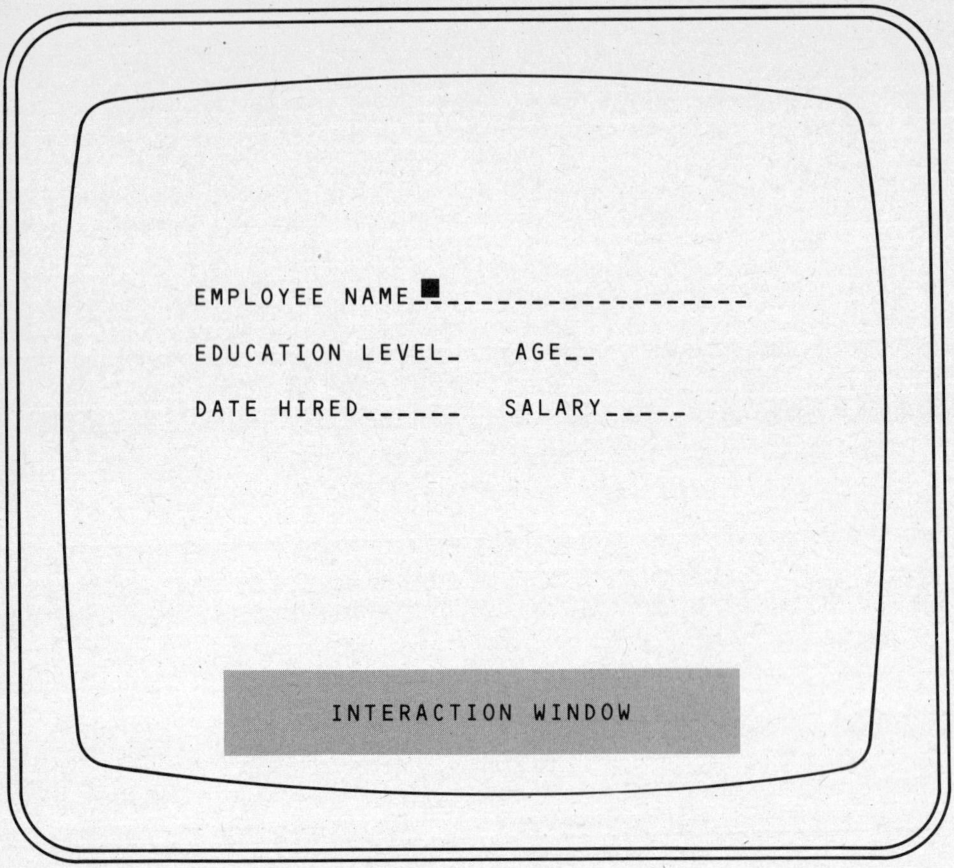

```
EMPLOYEE NAME■_____

EDUCATION LEVEL_     AGE__

DATE HIRED_____    SALARY_____
```

                        INTERACTION WINDOW

Figure 7-5. This would be the "form" on the screen during data entry. When you finished typing in the value for one field, the cursor would jump directly to the next. To correct an error, you would move the cursor back to the bad field and retype it, using the INSERT, DELETE, and cursor control keys as necessary. The system would also check the validity of your entries, for instance making sure that the salary fell within allowable limits, and would display an error message if you accidentally entered an invalid amount.

These error messages and other information (for instance, a menu showing the choices for a coded field) would be displayed in the interaction window shown at the bottom of the screen. Note that the layout of the screen "form" could be determined by the user in most file management systems, though a simple default form is handy for "quick and dirty" applications.

There are many variations on the data entry theme. Some systems speed data entry by using the values from the previous record in a field as a default. For instance, if one of the fields was CURRENT DATE, the first date you entered would automatically go into the second record, the second into the third, and so forth. An automatic serial number field, in which the default value for the serial number in a record is one more than the previous record, can also speed data entry.

Self-check digits are also used to catch data entry errors. With these, one of the digits in a field is computed from the others according to a built-in rule.* If the number the operator enters does not have the correct self-check digit, an error must have been made. A self-check digit adds one character to the field length, but it is worthwhile in situations in which errors can be costly, for instance in credit card or bank account numbers.

Searching, Retrieval, and Updating

In the opening section of this chapter, we traced a path from data processing techniques on punch card accounting machines, to report generating programs, to the file management systems we use on our PCs. People working on early systems for keeping track of and retrieving documents were also important contributors (we would call them "library scientists" today, but they probably would not have used that term). These people were interested in the problem of organizing a library so that a computer could automatically search for and retrieve all documents that were relevant to someone using the library; they wanted to automate the card catalog. They designed systems in which the user would ask for something like the titles of "all books or articles dealing with 'gerontology' and 'athletics,'" and the system would retrieve references to the relevant documents. (As we will see in Chapter 8, these document retrieval systems are now readily available to PC users through data communication.)

To see how their work on searching and retrieval has been adopted in file management systems, let's return to our personnel file. Imagine that you have entered all of the employees in the company into the file; now, what can you do? Perhaps you would like to see Ted Williams's record. A simple command (or series of menu selections) like:

`SEARCH: EMPLOYEE NAME = Ted Williams`

would do the trick. His record would be *retrieved* and displayed on the screen.

At that point, most systems would give you several options. For one, you might print Mr. Williams's record for future reference. But what if something has changed since his record was created? Maybe he has received a raise in salary since his record was created.

In that case it would be necessary to *update* his record by entering the new value in the salary field. If the file management system is well designed, that should be just like changing the value on the form during

---

*The rule for calculating the self-check digit would be something like this: sum the digits of the number, and use the units position of the result as the self-check digit. If the number in a field were 54648, the self-check digit would be 7 ($5 + 4 + 6 + 4 + 8 = 27$), so the operator would enter 546487 in the field. Although this example rule is overly simple, it illustrates the idea. As you might guess, the self-check digits used in sensitive applications such as credit card numbers are more obscure.

data entry. You would move the cursor to the salary field, type in the new amount, and hit a key telling the system that the updated record should be entered into the file. The form layout and interaction style used to update a record should be the same as when a new record is being created. That will cut confusion and make the system easier to learn.

Another variation on the search theme was developed by H. P. Luhn, one of the better known "library scientists" of the early days of computing. He grouped related documents by assigning *keywords* to them. For instance, everyone in your name and address file who is a personal friend might be assigned the keyword "friend," or books in the library dealing with the training, performance, or participation of older people in sports would have been assigned several keywords such as "athletics" or "gerontology." Luhn was more interested in the difficult problem of using the computer to assign keywords to documents automatically, than in the simple problem of retrieval. But his idea of assigning keywords to records and using them for searching and retrieval caught on, and a number of file management systems for the PC use it.

Keys and Indices

What do you suppose the PC would do when you asked it to search for Ted Williams's record? Do you think it would shuffle through all of the employee records until it came to his? That would take too long, even for a computer. More likely, you would have specified that EMPLOYEE NAME be used as a *key field*, one that would be used for subsequent searching and sorting. The file management system would then create an *index* for that field (see Figure 7-6).

The index is a cross reference, containing everyone's name and a record number or *pointer* indicating their record in the data file. It would not be necessary to search through the entire data file for Ted Williams's record; the file management program could just search the index. Once the program found Williams's name in the index, it could go straight to his record in the data file, using the pointer. Note that there is nothing to keep you from using more than one field as a key and having the system create an index for each one.

Indices speed things up considerably, but we pay a price. The biggest drawback is that they add to the conceptual complexity of the system for the user. They also tie up disk space. And what happens when you add a new record to the file, for instance when a new employee is hired? The record would be added using the familiar screen form shown in Figure 7-5, but the system would have to take the time to update the indices as well as the data file. Most file management systems will let you add data in batches and require that you update the indices only once, when all of the new records are in. That would be a time saver if, say, twenty new employees were hired on the same day.

From time to time you will also want to delete records from a file, for

```
EMPLOYEE NAME           RECORD POINTER

Alston, Walter               9
Didrikson, Mildred           3
Dimaggio, Joseph             7
Olga Fitokova                6
Grange, Harold              10
Musial, Stanley              2
Rudolph, Wilma               5
Ruth, George                 1
Thorpe, James                8
Williams, Ted                4
```

Figure 7-6. This index enables the file management system to locate and retrieve a record quickly, given the EMPLOYEE NAME. In searching for *Ted Williams*, the system could quickly determine that his record was number four in the data file, read it into memory, and display it on the screen or print it.

instance when an employee leaves the company. Again, both the data file and the indices would have to be updated.

Seeing More Than One Record at a Time

What would have happened if, instead of searching for Ted Williams's record (EMPLOYEE NAME = *Ted Williams*), we had given the following command?

SEARCH: EDUCATION LEVEL = H

Instead of finding just one record that matched our *search condition*, the system would have turned up four. In other words, there are four records in

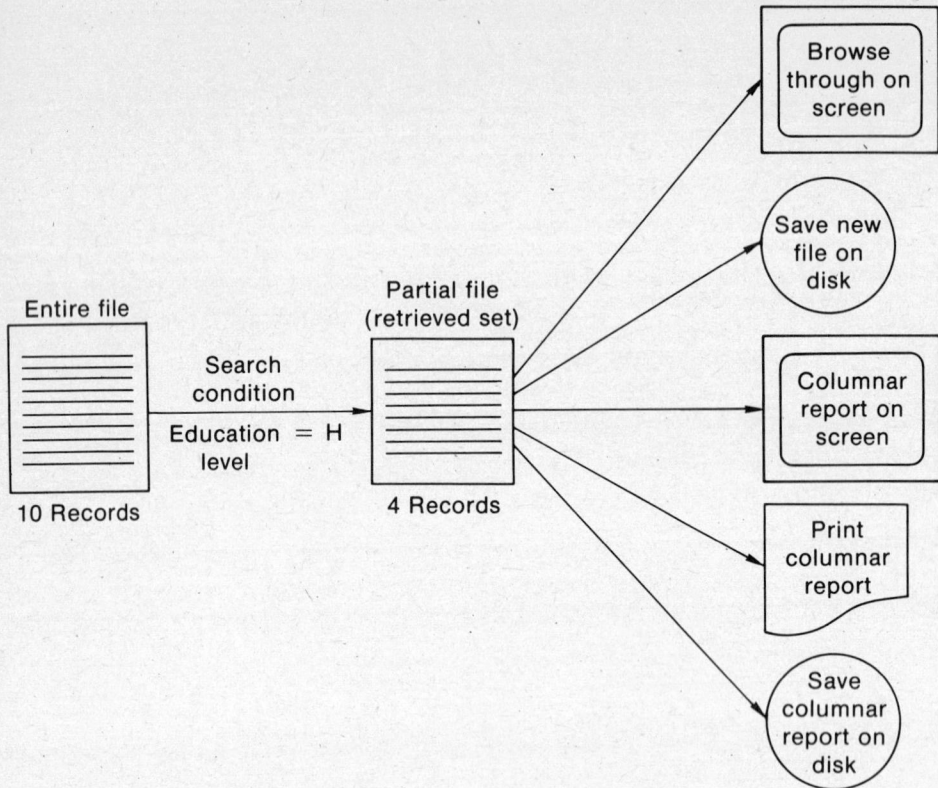

Figure 7-7. Generally speaking, when you search on some condition, several records will satisfy it. In this example, we asked for all high school graduates, and four of the ten records in the personnel file were retrieved. They can be thought of as constituting a new, smaller file that is a subset of the original file.

As the drawing suggests, you would then have several options. You could browse through the set of retrieved records one at a time, you could save them on the disk as a new file, or you could put them into a columar report. The columnar report might be displayed on the screen, printed, or written on the disk for further processing using another program, perhaps a word processor or communication package.

the *retrieved set.** At this point, depending on the system, we might be presented with several options (see Figure 7-7).

A typical system would display the record of the first high school graduate on the screen (in this case, George Ruth) and inform you that there were three others. You could then browse through the other high school graduates by asking to see the "next" or "previous" record. Whenever you

---

*In the first example, the retrieved set contained only one record (Ted Williams's). If we had searched for *Donald Budge,* there would have been no matches; the retrieved set would have been empty.

found an interesting record, you could give the command to print it or update it.

With some file managers, a new data file containing only high school graduates could be created. It could be a temporary file that would be erased when you were finished with it, or it could become a new, permanent file.

Another option is to generate a *columnar report*. The problem of displaying a record in the format of a form (like Figure 7-5) is that you can only see one record at a time. A report enables you to see a group of records. The report in Figure 7-8 shows the EMPLOYEE NAME, SALARY, and DATE HIRED for all of the high school graduates together, not just one of them at a time. Note that we decided not to show all of the fields in our report, just the ones of interest.

Several other common features are illustrated in the sample report. The system has put a title, page number, and date on the report, in places we would have specified. We also asked for some arithmetic; the system has totaled the salary column and calculated the average salary. The column spacing and headings might have been determined by default (the system

```
January 21, 1984                          Page 1 of 1

                        MITTY, INC.
                   HIGH SCHOOL GRADUATES

   EMPLOYEE NAME            SALARY     DATE HIRED

   George Ruth             $900.00     01/21/77
   Mildred Didrikson     $1,300.00     05/22/64
   James Thorpe          $4,700.00     06/09/49
   Harold Grange         $5,000.00     10/04/46

   TOTAL                $11,900.00
   AVERAGE               $2,975.00
   RECORD COUNT 4
```

Figure 7-8. This columnar report shows only the high school graduates. A file management system lets us control the report format in many ways, some of which are illustrated here. The date, page number, and title have been put at the top of the page, the column and heading spacing was chosen to make the report look good, we selected only the fields we were interested in for this report (EDUCATION LEVEL, SALARY, and DATE HIRED), the dates hired and salaries were printed in the proper formats, and the record count, total, and average salary were automatically computed.

would figure them out using the size, type, and name we had given for each field), or we might have specified them ourselves.

As you see, a file management system might offer many options for controlling the format of columnar reports, and each program will have its own report formatting features. You might be able to create new columns by doing arithmetic, for instance multiplying PRICE by QUANTITY to get a VALUE column, even though there was no VALUE field in the data file. Some systems can compute other statistics, like standard deviation or correlation coefficients. The ability to get subtotals is also common; for instance, some systems give the total sales for each department within a company, with a grand total at the end. Some systems give you the option of printing the full report or a summary report, in which only the totals are shown.

A final point to make concerning reports is that they may be displayed on the screen, printed, or written out as disk files. Even if you plan to print a report, it is convenient to be able to preview it on the screen, since that would not take as much time as printing, would be quieter, and would save paper. Previewing on the display is particularly handy when you are trying to work out the final content and appearance of a report. When you get the report the way you want it, you print it out and save the report specification on disk for future use.

At times, you might also want to "print" a report on the disk. Once it was saved on disk, you could use a word processing program to make changes in it for final presentation or for inclusion within another document or transmission over phone lines to another computer.

More Complicated Searches

Let's try another search and retrieval example. If you wanted to search for everyone making over $2,500, the command would be:

SEARCH: SALARY > 2500

This is the same format as the earlier examples, except that we have used ">," the symbol for "greater than." File management systems typically let you search for values that are "equal," "less than," "greater than," "not equal," "less than or equal," or "greater than or equal" to other values.

What would the command:

SEARCH: EMPLOYEE NAME < Ruth

mean? This might be a little confusing because we are comparing characters (Ruth) instead of numbers. In the case of character comparisons, the computer will use alphabetical order, so this command would search for everyone whose name is before "Ruth" in the alphabet.

Practice a little. Can you write a command to search for everyone hired after June 1970 or everyone who is not a high school graduate? These tasks are not difficult, but how about searching for high school graduates earning over $1,200? This request is tougher because it involves two fields, SALARY and EDUCATION LEVEL. Don't worry, file management systems handle multiple field searches in a simple, natural way.

The command to search for high school graduates earning more than $1,200 would be:

```
SEARCH: SALARY > 1200 AND EDUCATION LEVEL = H
```

The two search conditions were simply joined together with the word "AND," which expresses what we were looking for. You can also use the word "OR" in searching. For example, the command

```
SEARCH: SALARY > 3000 OR EDUCATION LEVEL = D
```

would find everyone who was either well paid or well educated. Do you see how it works? One last variation on the theme would be to add parentheses to your search request, for example:

```
SEARCH: SALARY > 3000 OR (EDUCATION LEVEL = B AND AGE > 50)
```

That search would retrieve Williams, Fitokova, Thorpe, Alston, and Grange from our personnel file. If we switched the parentheses around, like this:

```
SEARCH: (SALARY > 3000 OR EDUCATION LEVEL = B) AND AGE > 50
```

the search would retrieve three records. Can you say which three?*

Some systems offer another variation on the search theme, searches for patterns within fields. Instead of searching for an exact match on the entire field, for instance *George Ruth*, you could give a command to search for the occurrence of the characters *George* anywhere within the name field. In this manner, you could retrieve the records of everyone named *George*. If the personnel file had contained the employee's addresses, a search of this type could have been used to find anyone living on a certain street, for instance anyone with the string *Park Avenue* or *Park Av* in their address. These pattern searches, in which an exact match for the entire field is not necessary, are sometimes called *wildcard* searches. These same alternatives for character search patterns will turn up in Chapter 11, which discusses word processing.

Just in case you run across them, let me give you a couple of terms. The kind of searches we have been talking about here are called *Boolean searches*, and the comparison symbols (greater than, less than, etc.) are called *relational operators*. They are called Boolean because in mathematics

---

*Williams, Thorpe, and Grange.

Boolean algebra deals with variables that can be only true or false, like our search conditions, which are either met or not met by each record. It is not particularly important to know those words, but they are used in articles and advertisements, and you should not be thrown by them.

Sorting

Now let's pay some attention to the order in which records are retrieved. The file in Figure 7-1 is stored in the order that the records happen to have been typed; it is not *sorted*. What would happen if we wanted an employee report in alphabetical order so that we could easily look up someone's record? A file management system should be able to handle that for us.

Sorting is handled in two ways. The first is literally rearranging the order in which the records are physically stored on the disk. This can take a lot of computer time and there may be limits on the size of the file to be sorted. A poorly designed program might even lose some data if it runs out of disk space during the sorting process.

While physically rearranging the records may sometimes be necessary, sorting the file is usually done by creating and then sorting an index, leaving the records themselves in their original order. Refer back to Figure 7-6. The index shown there is sorted on the EMPLOYEE NAME field. Note that the system was clever enough to sort by last name, not first. Sorting on another field could be accomplished by creating and sorting another index. Once the file is sorted on a particular field, the system would be able to retrieve records in that order, for instance for browsing, or to print a sorted report.

Look at the report in Figure 7-9 for a more complex example of a sorted report. Can you see the order in which that file has been sorted? It is sorted on SALARY within EDUCATION LEVEL. Or, to put it in computerese, the *major* sort was on EDUCATION LEVEL and the *minor* sort on SALARY. Note that subtotals are shown every time the EDUCATION LEVEL changes.

Of course, in your situation you might need more total levels; for example, a marketing manager might divide the country into regions, the regions into districts, and the districts into branch offices. A report showing each salesperson's sales quota and performance would be ordered on name, within office, within district, within region. There would be intermediate totals at every *control break,* in other words, whenever the office, district, or region changed. A final, grand total would summarize the sales for the entire nation. Would multilevel reports be useful to you? If so, how many levels do you require? (Most systems limit the number of levels.)

Changes

Throughout this chapter, I have been suggesting that you stop for a while and think about your file management applications; that you plan them. But

```
January 21, 1984                              Page 1 of 1

                        MITTY, INC
              PERSONNEL BY EDUCATION LEVEL

EDUCATION
LEVEL           EMPLOYEE NAME        DATE HIRED       SALARY

   H            George Ruth          01/21/77        $900.00
   H            Mildred Didrikson    05/22/64      $1,300.00
   H            James Thorpe         06/09/49      $4,700.00
   H            Harold Grange        10/04/46      $5,000.00

HIGH SCHOOL TOTAL                                 $11,900.00

   B            Joseph Dimaggio      09/22/69      $1,400.00
   B            Ted Williams         12/05/66      $1,500.00
   B            Stanley Musial       05/05/82      $2,300.00
   B            Olga Fitokova        01/31/72      $3,100.00

BACHELORS TOTAL                                    $8,300.00

   M            Wilma Rudolph        01/04/70      $2,800.00

MASTERS TOTAL                                      $2,800.00

   D            Walter Alston        04/30/81      $3,400.00

DOCTORATE TOTAL                                    $3,400.00

GRAND TOTAL                                       $26,400.00
```

Figure 7-9. This report is more complicated than that shown in Figure 7-8. It is sorted by SALARY within EDUCATION LEVEL. Note that EDUCATION LEVEL is not sorted alphabetically. If it were, a bachelor's degree (B) would come before a high school degree (H). Instead of alphabetical order, the collating sequence we specified earlier (H-B-M-D) has been used.

Intermediate totals are printed whenever there is a control break, in other words, when the value of EDUCATION LEVEL changes. The final total summarizes the entire report. A file management system will usually accommodate at least three levels of totals, and some allow an unlimited number.

no matter how thorough your plan, you will probably overlook something or something will change after you have defined your files and entered your data. What then?

With most file management systems, some restructuring of data files is possible. It should be possible to add a new field or drop an old one without losing the rest of the data. This will not be necessary too often, but when you need to do it, you will be glad it can be done, even if it takes a few hours and it requires studying the manual or getting help. Restructuring a file is one of those complex things that should at least be possible, even if it can't be simple.

Bear in mind that adding or deleting a field will require redefining the format of the screen form used for data entry and displaying or updating records. Furthermore, the formats of some of your reports will be affected, and these will also have to be changed.

DATABASE MANAGEMENT AND INDEX CARD SYSTEMS

So far, we have used a single personnel file for most of our examples, and my guess is that most of your work with file management systems will be with single files. However, what happens if you have an application involving several related files?

With many of the file management systems for the PC, the answer to that question is "forget it," but others are designed to work with more than one file at a time. You have probably seen the term *database management system* or *DMBS* used in ads for programs and may have noticed that I have been using the term "file management system" throughout this chapter. I have done so in order to distinguish between programs that work with only one file at a time and those designed to work with several. If a database contains several related files, then you need a database management system.

Can you think of examples in which it would be handy to use several related files? What about invoicing? In preparing an invoice, you need information about the customer you are shipping goods to, which would be found in the customer file, and other information about goods you are shipping, which would be found in the product file (see Figure 7-10). When the operator keyed in the customer's name, address, credit standing, and so forth, they would be pulled from the customer file, and when the product number was entered, the description and cost would be pulled from the product file.

To shed a little more light on this topic, let's extend the personnel example to two files. We are no longer dealing with a small company with ten employees; Mitty, Inc., a sporting goods concern, has prospered and now employs thousands. Of course, the organizational structure has become more complex. The company has been organized into several divisions, football, baseball, boxing, tennis, and so forth. The divisions are separate entities from the employees, so in addition to the employee file, the personnel manager has created a second file, the division file (see Figure 7-11).

The division file contains a record for each division in the company, and the fields correspond to the attributes or dimensions of divisions, things like the name of the division manager, its annual sales, the number of

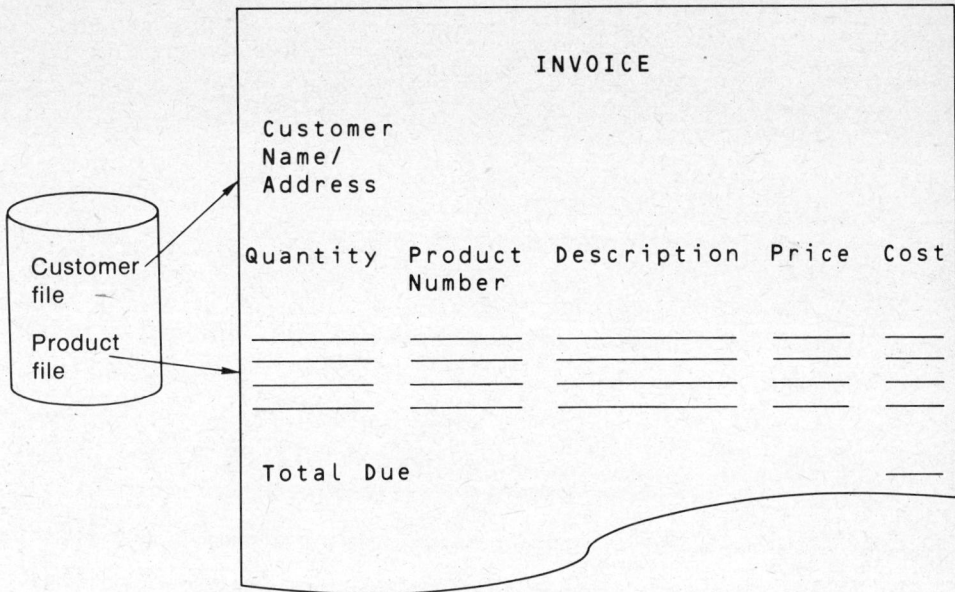

```
                        INVOICE

        Customer
        Name/
        Address

        Quantity   Product    Description   Price   Cost
                    Number
        _____  _____  _____  _____  _____
        _____  _____  _____  _____  _____
        _____  _____  _____  _____  _____

        Total Due                                    _____
```

Figure 7-10. Information from two files would have to be combined to print an invoice. The customer's name, address, credit rating, and so forth would come from the customer file, whereas product oriented information such as the description of the item and its unit price would come from the product file. Since this application requires multiple files, a database management system would have to be used; a file management program would not suffice.

products it manufactures, or the corporate group it belongs to (Mitty, Inc. has really gotten bureaucratic). Note that in order to tie the employee and division files together, they must have a common field, so a DIVISION NAME field would have to be added to each employee record as well. This field would link an employee record to the corresponding division record, and if it did not establish a unique relationship, there would have to be more than one common field.

Now, if we are using a DBMS, we can search across file boundaries. An employee oriented report could be generated that showed the names of the employees' division managers or their corporate groups, even though that information was in the division file. Or the personnel manager might query the system to see who the highest paid employee was in a given corporate group or how many people worked for a given division manager.

At this point, you might consider your own situation. Do you have any applications requiring the multifile capability of a DBMS? What are they?

Truth in Advertising: A Few Terms

A few terms that are widely used in advertisements should be discussed, so that they won't intimidate you. For a start, we should return to the term

DIVISION NAME	MANAGER	ANNUAL SALES ($ MILLION)	NUMBER PRODUCTS	CORPORATE GROUP
Baseball	Charles Stengal	17	32	major
Football	Knute Rockne	21	29	major
Tennis	Jack Kramer	29	16	consumer
Track and Field	James Elliot	9	47	consumer
Boxing	Burgess Meredith	8	18	consumer
Basketball	John Wooden	18	8	team
Soccer	John Carroll	7	6	team
Swimming	John Weissmuller	11	12	consumer
Wrestling	Aleksandr Medved	6	4	team
Golf	Samuel Snead	24	17	consumer

Figure 7-11. In our personal example, we might have a second file with a record for each division in the company. The fields shown here correspond to attributes or dimensions of corporate divisions, not employees. We might even have a third file with information on the corporate groups.

DBMS, since some software vendors take liberty with it. Many programs advertised as DBMS can deal with only one file at a time, they are what I have been calling "file management" systems. This is not to imply that those software vendors are dishonest; DBMS is a common buzzword, and it is not well defined.

You will also see ads for *hierarchical* and *network* DBMSs. In a hierarchical DBMS, you must specify the relationship between the entities in the database. In the case of our personnel example, we would have had to state explicitly that each employee belonged to only one division, and to find an employee record, we might have had to know what division he is in first. But what happens if an employee can be working for two divisions at once? Network systems are more general in that, if an employee were a "member" of two divisions, you could "navigate" from employee to division or division to employee, but the relationships would still have to be spelled out.

Explicitly describing the structure of the database in this manner makes it possible for the DBMS to save time in retrieval and space for the storage of records, but a price is paid in terms of conceptual complexity for the user and in a loss of flexibility if the database structure has to be modified. In an effort to simplify things, E. F. Codd began publishing a rigorous description of databases and retrieval operations in 1969. Codd's work has evolved into what are called *relational DBMSs*.

The goal of these systems is to simplify the user's view of the database so that retrieval from various files can be accomplished without the user's having to understand the hierarchical relationships among them. You could find the average salary of people in the consumer sports group without knowing anything about the structure of the database. Codd and his followers have also made a systematic study of various cases of re-dundancy and ambiguity in databases, leading to improvement in the art of database design.

You will see more ads for relational systems than any others, but the term has become diluted in the process. When you see an ad for a "relational" DBMS, you are probably safe in assuming that it can handle multiple files, and that it is not necessary to specify any sort of hierarchical or network relationship among records. As such, you will find that they are easier to understand and to use, though generally less efficient than hierarchical systems. How much less efficient, and whether or not that matters to you, depends upon your application.

Before closing the book on DBMSs, we need to discuss whether you need to be a programmer to use one. The theme of this book is "what you can do with your IBM PC without being a programmer," but in order to use a DBMS fully, programming is involved. The hierarchical and network systems require a programmer for setting up the database, though it can be used by anyone once set up.

With a relational system, you should be able to do quite a bit without the help of a programmer, since you can ignore the fact that it is a DBMS and use it as a simple file management system. A programmer will still be needed to help with multiple file applications or with generating complex reports and file manipulations. Experience with database design and such things as Codd's study of redundancy and ambiguity will also be welcome in setting up a complex data management system. You can do it yourself, but you should plan on spending time to become proficient or perhaps take a course.

Index Card Systems

In addition to file and database management systems, a number of software companies have packages built around the metaphor of a file of index cards. Figure 7-12 shows a typical record from an index card file. As you see, there

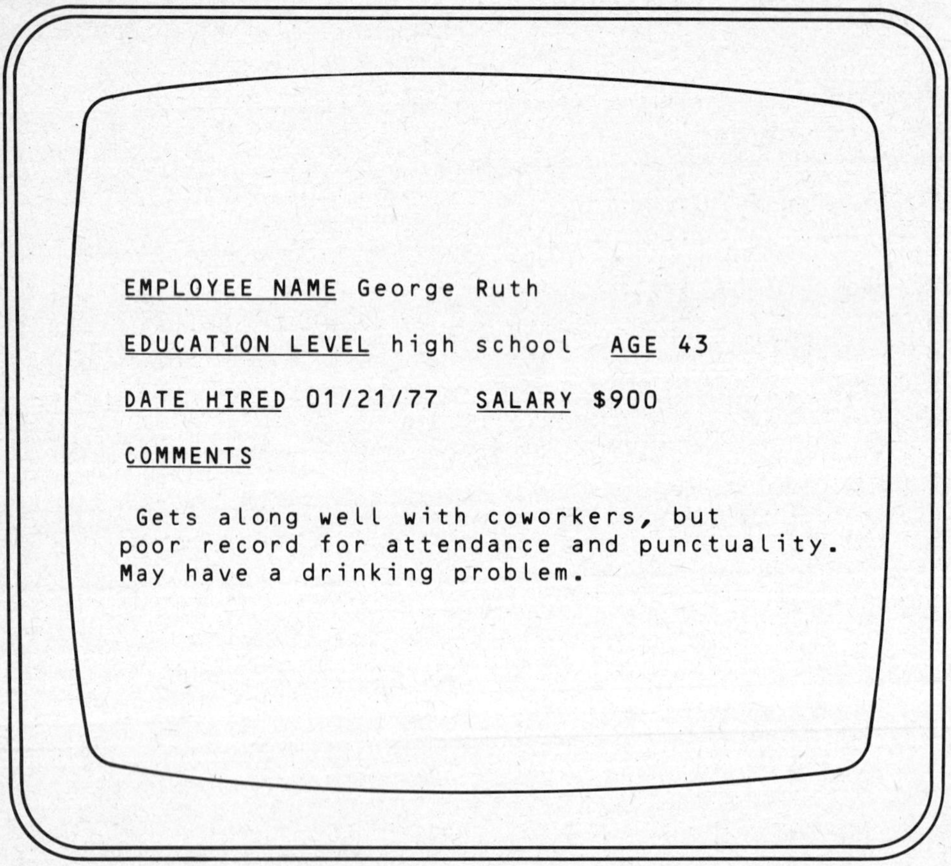

```
EMPLOYEE NAME George Ruth

EDUCATION LEVEL high school   AGE 43

DATE HIRED 01/21/77   SALARY $900

COMMENTS

 Gets along well with coworkers, but
poor record for attendance and punctuality.
May have a drinking problem.
```

Figure 7-12. With an index card system, you could set up records like this one. The usual sort of fixed fields are used, and there is also an area for free text. The free text area in this example is used for comments about the employee. Since the free text can be fairly long, the speed and convenience of the editor is critical. Many index card systems also allow you to assign keywords to a record for retrieval.

is a free text area in addition to the usual fixed fields. Depending upon the system, this free text area may be limited to one screen full of data or may be more open ended.

While index card systems may seem unique, they are really just a variation on the file management theme. The free text area is merely a field of type character with a relatively large, or perhaps unlimited, size. Since the free text field can be large, the editing commands, those that are used for making new entries and revising old ones, must be powerful and easy to use. In fact, the same sorts of commands that are used in a word processor are needed. One of the most important things to look at in an index card system is the editor. It should use the function keys on the PC, and it would cut down on training problems if it worked like your word processor.

Index card systems are really just file managers with souped-up editors for free text. Most of them also provide for keyword retrieval and searches for patterns (like *Park Avenue* in the earlier example) within the free text area, as well as searching for specified field values. A final distinction is that, in order to speed up retrieval, some index card systems restrict you to a single file per disk.

CHAPTER EIGHT
Remote Communication Basics

Communications has the most distinguished heritage of any of our computer applications; it is the oldest and in many ways the most important. It is important because teletypewriters, developed for communications, have evolved into our keyboards and video displays, and, even more fundamentally, because the data encoding schemes used in our personal computers were developed for communications. The invention of electrical telegraphy, of the idea of using electrical currents to encode information for transmission or transformation, was in essence the invention of electronics.

The roots of computer communications are in telegraphy. When I was in grammar school, I was told that Samuel F. B. Morse invented the telegraph in 1837. But check the *Encyclopaedia Britannica* and you will learn that the term "telegraph" (from the Greek words for "far" and "write") was coined by a Frenchman named Claude Chappe around 1792. In fact, Chappe and others in France and England had been at work on telegraph systems using electricity since before Morse was born.

But telegraphy really goes back to the first person who was too lazy to go over to the neighboring village to deliver a message, and got the idea of beating on a hollow log instead: "five drumbeats means there is a saber-toothed tiger heading your way." Perhaps Morse drew his inspiration from stories of Indian smoke signals.

Many people in Europe and the United States were working on electrical telegraph systems when Morse applied for a patent in 1837. But let's not sell Morse short. His system was practical; he got government support, built a 37 mile line between Washington and Baltimore, and on May 24, 1844, public service was inaugurated with "what hath God wrought," the message we all learned about in grade school. Morse and his partner Alfred Vail were entrepreneurs as well as inventors.

As a computer buff would say, Morse's system became a de facto standard. In 1848 the Associated Press was established in order to pool telegraphic expenses for journalists, and in Europe, Reuters News Service

APPLICATIONS

1. Electronic mail is the most common communication application, remote or local. An electronic mail message might be a short memo asking someone to set a date for a meeting or a long report that you wish to share with a coauthor or your boss. You could even "broadcast" it to everyone in your department. When you connect your PC to an electronic mail system, you are informed of any new messages, and given the opportunity to read them, save them on disk, print them, reply to them, or throw them away. The central computer, where the mail is saved while waiting to be read, might be another personal computer (even a PC), a large computer in your organization's data processing department, or a large computer belonging to a company that offers electronic mail service on a billed, utility basis.

2. Using your PC as an intelligent terminal, you could access a database on a remote computer belonging to a company selling information services to the general public. It could be a stock quote, a movie review, financial background data on a company, the box score of last night's Dodgers-Cardinals game, an encyclopedia entry, or all of the New York Times articles mentioning the Pope during the month of August.

3. Perhaps there are specialized databases for members of your profession or industry, for instance a database for doctors, lawyers, or engineers specializing in aircraft design and failure.

4. You might post an electronic want-ad on a computer bulletin board in order to sell a car, to get help interfacing a printer to your PC, or to find a date for next Saturday night. The bulletin board may be local to your city or on a large computer that services the entire country.

5. PCs in each of your company's branch sales offices could be used to call a central computer (perhaps another PC) and transfer data files containing the day's orders to the main office. This might even happen automatically, late at night, when the phone rates are lower.

6. You could carry on a teleconference with a group of people interested in the same topic. It might be a group brainstorming on the specifications for a new product or a discussion of a research topic among a group of professors.

converted from carrier pigeons to telegraphy. Before the invention of the telephone, intracity telegraph networks were quite common. Many local telegraph companies sprang up using Morse's system, and soon those local companies began to merge. In 1856 they formed the Western Union Telegraph Company.

Telegraph equipment was not all that Morse gave us. Just as important was his alphabetic code, based on dots and dashes. Again, the original conception was not his. The Greeks had devised a system for encoding their 24-letter alphabet by 300 BC, and what about all those guys in medieval prison movies who tapped messages to each other through thick dungeon walls? But Morse's code was efficient, was picked up by other entrepreneurs, and became another de facto standard (there were European and U.S. versions).

Morse was just the start. In 1846 Royal E. House invented the first printing telegraph. By 1867 stock tickers were printing 40 words per minute (remember ticker-tape parades)? The histories of telegraphic printers and typewriters commingle to set the stage for the keyboard and the printer on your PC.

The French inventor Jean Maurice Emile Baudot also stands out in the history of telegraphy. He engineered improved transmission schemes and made basic contributions to the design of printers, which were still being used in the Teletype machine, the most common computer terminal until the 1970s. Like Morse, Baudot invented an alphabetic code that was appropriate to his transmission and printing scheme. His original five level code was later permuted by Donald Murray to minimize the number of holes punched in a paper tape, based on the frequency of occurrence of the various letters. Murray's "Baudot" code was still in wide use in 1966, when the seven level ASCII code used in the PC and most other computers was adopted as a standard.

The first instance I am familiar with of electronic communication involving a computer was in 1940. George Stibitz, Thornton Fry, and Samuel Williams, employees of Bell Laboratories, used a Teletype terminal to demonstrate their Complex Computer, which was located in New York, at a meeting of the Mathematical Association of America, held at Dartmouth College in New Hampshire. Ten years later, a demonstration of remote communication with an electronic computer, the National Bureau of Standards's SEAL, took place in Washington, D.C., and the Whirlwind computer, built at MIT, was processing telemetry data from radar equipment.

Batches of data and programs began to be moved between computer centers in the 1950s. These early "teleprocessing" systems emulated existing systems for sending telegraphic messages. For example, when I was at UCLA we had a large computer center (the Western Data Processing Center) which supported researchers at 89 universities in the western states, and, on a regular daily schedule, we received programs to be run from these schools. The first sending and receiving units read and punched paper tape at rates of 500 or more characters per second. Soon these gave way to machines that read and wrote magnetic tape.

However, it was not until the 1960s, when time-shared computers became widespread, that the interactive, on-line computer communications we do with our PCs really began. A time-sharing system made no distinction between a user sitting at a terminal in the same building or one who dialed in over phone lines from somewhere else, and in the early 1960s the first "portable" terminals began to appear (see Figure 8-1).

Commercial projects also helped develop the technology for remote access to a single computer by many users. Probably the most important of these was a joint venture between IBM and American Airlines to put reservation clerks on-line to a central computer. The system, called SABRE,

Figure 8-1. This is what a portable terminal looked like in the early days of interactive computing on time-sharing systems. (Courtesy of Anderson Jacobson)

began operation in 1963. There were huge cost overruns and it performed below specification at first, but a lot was learned building SABRE and the feasibility of such applications was established.

At about the same time, the visionary people who gave us time-sharing realized that remote access was not limited to a single computer. In 1960, Joseph Licklider, at MIT, envisioned a network of many time-sharing computers, tied together with high-speed communication lines. With a local call or direct connection to any computer on the network, it would be possible to reach any other. In this manner, remote colleagues could work collaboratively and share resources (see Figure 8-2).

By 1962 basic techniques for moving data *packets* (data plus addressing

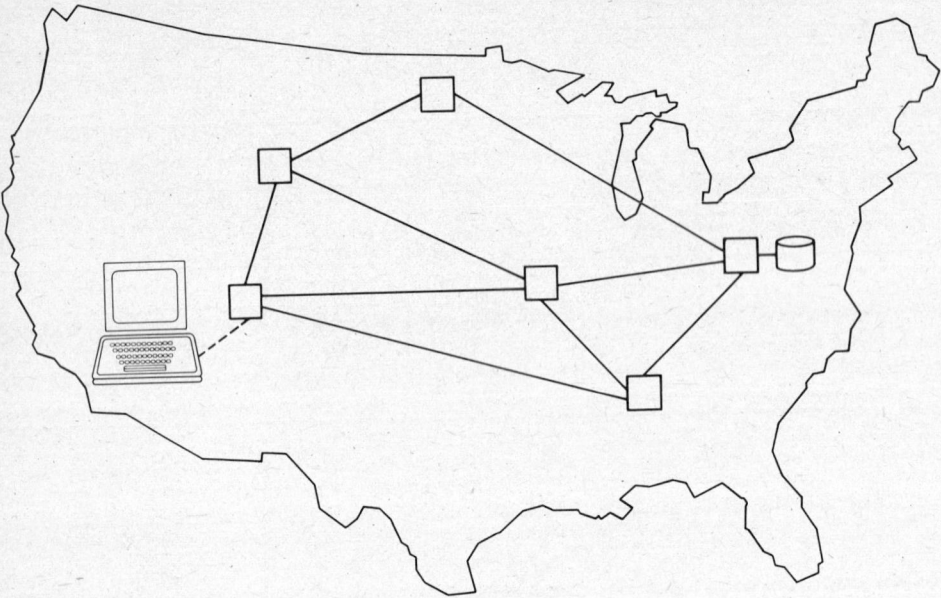

Figure 8-2. With a computer network, mainframe time-sharing computers may be spread around the country or even located on other continents. They communicate with each other using high speed transmission channels (perhaps a combination of satellites, lines, and microwave connections). Data are sent in blocks or packets, and, since there are many possible paths between each pair of machines, a packet will almost assuredly find a path to its destination, even if one computer is out of service.

If you are in Southern California and want to examine information in a database on a network computer in New York, all that is necessary is a local call (dotted line) to a Southern California computer. Once the connection was made, it would ask which network computer you wanted to use, and establish a connection. The remote computer would then ask for your password in order to identify you, and as far as you were concerned, it would be just as if you were in New York from that point on. You would interact directly with the New York computer to examine the database on its disk.

information) through a network were worked out under the direction of Paul Baran at the Rand Corporation. In 1966, Thomas Marill and Lawrence Roberts reported on a cross-country link between the System Development Corporation in California and MIT. Just as Licklider was influential in having ARPA (Advanced Research Projects Agency) fund the development of the first major time-sharing systems, he was instrumental in ARPA's decision to fund development of the first general purpose computer network, the ARPA Net.

The ARPA Net, using packet switching, was implemented by Lawrence Roberts and his colleagues, and in December of 1969, the first four computers went on-line. Today, there are over 75 nodes in the continental U.S., Hawaii, and Europe, and the network handles roughly 14 million packets of information each day. As Roberts predicted in a paper published in 1970, the ARPA Net has created a community of geographically dispersed colleagues, sharing hardware, programs, and data.

Even before the ARPA Net went on-line, similar commercial ventures were planned. The first company to try it commercially, Packet Communications, Inc., spent all of their capital getting the appropriate regulatory permissions and went broke. However, others, including Telenet, founded by Lawrence Roberts, have prospered. When you connect your PC to a remote computing service such as the Source in Virginia or Compuserve in Ohio, quite possibly you do so over Telenet.

The idea of computer communication among people in their homes has had an even longer run than the idea of computer communication among knowledge workers. My favorite fictional account is a short story written by E. M. Forster in 1928. It is called "The Machine Stops," and as you can guess from the title, it does not paint a very optimistic picture of widespread computer communication. In Forster's science fiction, all communication becomes electronic, people seldom leave their quarters, and their basic natures are changed for the worse. The society is totally dependent upon electronic communication, the system is too complex to be understood (it is worshiped instead), and, when the "machine" stops, society perishes.

A much more upbeat view has been put forth in the computer science community. In the United States, the most important statement of the case in favor of "information utilities" was made by Hal Sackman and Barry Boehm in 1972. In their book *Planning Community Information Utilities*, they projected the technology, applications, likely costs, and benefits of systems similar to The Source and Compuserve. There were similar publications and advocates in Europe, Canada, and Japan at the time.

In the early 1970s, when these ideas were being formulated, they were predicated upon the assumption that the people using the systems would have simple terminals in their homes and offices, and that the computing "intelligence" would all be centralized in large time-shared computers. At that time, I wrote several papers that were sharply critical of these proposals on a number of grounds; however, I also overlooked the possibility that a personal computer might be used instead of a simple terminal, and that changes things significantly. If we really do all end up with computers on our desks and in our homes, computer communication might turn out to be as important as men like Sackman and Boehm predicted. We'll have to wait to see whether or not the emperor is wearing clothes.

Let us break PC communications into two general cases, remote and local. Local communication refers to relatively high-speed connections, usually within a single building or a building complex, whereas remote communication generally occurs between your PC and a distant computer. The remote computer might be across town, across the continent, or across an ocean.

These distinctions may blur at times. For example, the remote communication techniques used to dial a computer in another state might be used to dial a computer within your building. Some people also predict that we will eventually have three important levels of communication between computers. They believe that remote communication will be handled differently for connections within an urban area than outside of it; that, as in the early days of telegraphy, we will have metropolitan area networks. But, for now, the distinction between local and remote communication applications and techniques is a useful one. This chapter covers remote communication; the next covers local communication.

The remote computer you communicate with may be a large time-shared machine or another personal computer. You might be using an electronic mail service to send a memo to your boss, retrieving information on a specific topic, or looking up the box score on yesterday's Dodger-Giant game. In any case, you will begin by making a connection with the remote computer.

MAKING THE CONNECTION: MODEM BASICS

The connection begins with your telephone. The first step is connecting your PC to the telephone, and that requires some special hardware, called a modem. A modem is needed because PC data is *digital*—it is made up of ones and zeroes—and must be converted to *analog* tones before the telephone system can transmit it. Similarly, when tones are received from the remote computer, they must be converted into digital data that your PC can store. This two way conversion, from digital to analog and back, is handled by the modem. You will need one on your PC, and, of course, the remote computer will need a compatible modem at the other end (see Figure 8-3).

The modem is placed between the computer and the phone line, and, as you see in Figure 8-4, there are three basic ways to plug them together. In the first illustration, the modem is built on a regular PC circuit card and plugged into an expansion slot, just like a memory board or any other accessory board. In this case, a telephone cord attaches to the modem card at one end and plugs into the wall jack at the other. A modem like this one,

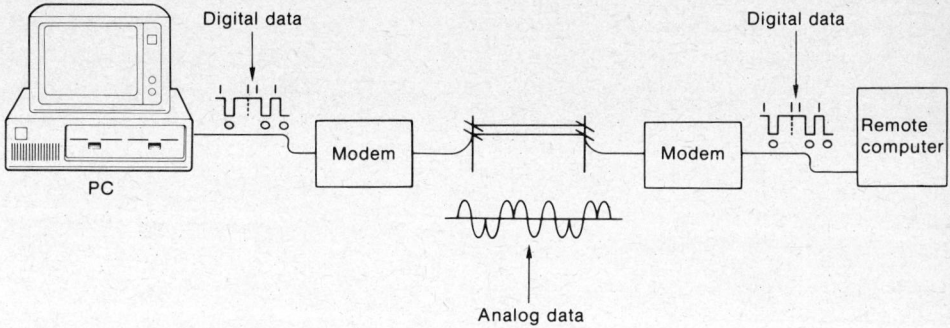

Figure 8-3. The telephone network is designed to transmit analog signals and computer data are stored in digital form. Modems are used to bridge this communication gap. Digital 0s and 1s from the computer are converted to analog signals and transmitted to the remote modem, which converts them back to digital data for the remote computer to read. The modems at both ends must be compatible.

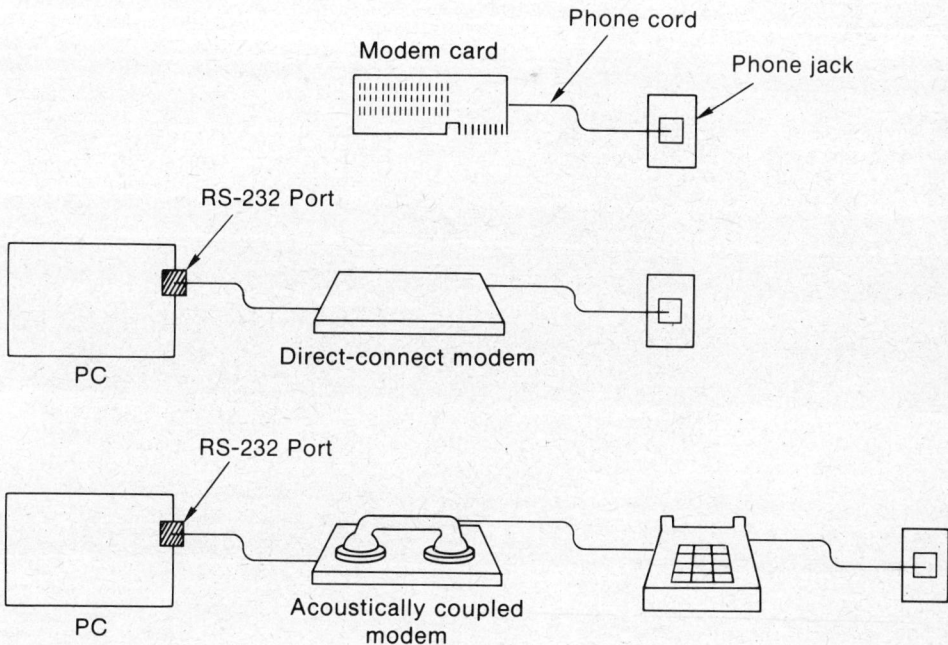

Figure 8-4. There are three basic ways of connecting a PC, modem, and phone line together. The simplest is to plug a modem card directly into one of the PC expansion slots and run a standard phone cord from there to the wall jack. In the second example, the modem plugs directly into the wall jack, but connects to the PC through a serial port, the RS-232. Finally, you can connect a modem to the phone line acoustically, by placing the phone handset in a pair of rubber cups on top of the modem. The first two are examples of direct-connect modems and the third is an acoustic coupler.

which plugs straight into the telephone jack, is called a *direct-connect modem*. In the second illustration, a direct-connect modem interfaces with the PC through an asynchronous communication (RS-232) port, just as if it were a printer. (If you are a little rusty on the ideas of ports and circuit boards, take a second to refer back to Chapter 3.) The last illustration shows an *acoustically coupled modem* (or simply an *acoustic coupler*), where the connection is made by placing the telephone handset on a pair of rubber cups (see Figure 8-5).

MAKING THE CONNECTION: THE DATA LINK

Once the PC is connected by means of the modem to the phone system, you have to establish a link to the remote computer. The simplest way to do this is to dial its number directly, just as if it were a person. If you have never done so, find out the phone number of a remote computer (ask a friend or someone in a computer store), and call it using your regular telephone. The number will ring as usual, but when the computer at the other end answers, you will hear a high-pitched tone instead of a pleasant "hello." That is its way of telling your modem that a connection has been made.

Figure 8-5. This is an acoustic modem or acoustic coupler. It connects to the phone network through the telephone handset, which is placed in the rubber cups on the top. Connection to a PC would be through the RS-232 connector on the right-hand side.

An acoustic coupler is more flexible than a direct-connect modem, since it can work with nearly any phone (except a Princess), even in a phone booth. However, the connection is less efficient. For that reason, acoustic couplers are almost always limited to 300 baud transmission rates. (Courtesy of Novation Inc.)

Dialing directly is fine if the computer you wish to connect to is close by, but what if it is far away and the toll charges begin to mount up? There are several alternatives. If you make heavy use of one remote computer, for instance, if your company has two branch offices in the same city, you might look into leasing a line between the two locations from the phone company. Depending upon local rates and the distance between your two branches, the break-even point may be reached in a few hours of connect time each day. If you can justify the fixed cost of a leased line, you will get a bonus—a less "noisy" line with fewer transmission errors. By the way, you might hear someone speaking of the *switched network*; this is just telephone company jargon for the standard dial-up lines we use with telephones, (as opposed to leased lines).

What happens if the remote computer is across the country instead of across town? Again, for heavy users, the telephone company has various leased line and unlimited-call services, such as WATS. If you do a lot of computer communication, check into your alternatives with the phone company. Also, check into the companies competing with the phone company for voice communication, like Sprint or MCI. Your PC is as happy talking over a Sprint line as you are; just be sure that the remote computer is in an area served by the communication vendor.

Another possibility is that the remote computer you will be using is on a network such as the one in Figure 8-2. Most of the services selling access to their computers on a "utility" basis, for instance Dow Jones, The Source, Compuserve, or Dialog, can be reached over one or more networks. In that case, a call to the nearest network node will get you connected. You may be billed directly for line charges by the network company (often called a *value-added carrier*), or the communication cost may be absorbed by the company offering access to the remote computer. If you wish to use one of these networks for communication between computers within your organization, the value-added carriers will also be happy to provide you with access to their networks for a fee.

You might be wondering how fast data zips around over these various links. Figure 8-6 shows the typical transmission or rates for various media. As you see, the dial-up phone lines are the slowest, with typical speeds of 30 or 120 characters per second (CPS). With relatively expensive modems, you can push that up as high as 960, but few if any remote computer services will have compatible modems at their end of the line. Since they are less noisy, communication can go faster with a given error rate over a leased line, if you have fast enough modems. Communication between the computers on a network typically takes place at about 5,000 CPS, but the link between you and the network is probably just a 30 or 120 CPS phone line.

In reading ads, you will often see speeds measured in bits per second (*BPS*). Since in most cases each character requires 10 bits (see Figure 8-7), the character rates quoted above correspond to 300 to 9,600 BPS. You will also come across the term *Baud rate*, another measure of speed named in honor of Jean Baudot. Although the Baud rate is related to BPS, they are not

	Typical CPS	Maximum BPS
Dial-up telephone	30 or 120	2400
Leased telephone	120 or 240	9600
Network	5100	51000

Figure 8-6. This table shows typical remote communication speeds. Speeds are usually measured in bits per second (BPS). Using a typical value of ten bits per character (it may actually vary, depending upon the communication system), we get the character rates that are shown. As you see, leased lines are reliable at faster rates than dial-up lines, assuming you have the proper modems.

The network speed is for transmission between network computers, but the link between your PC and the network would probably operate at 300 or 1200 BPS. Note also that acoustic couplers are almost always limited to 300 BPS transmission.

always the same, even though many people mistakenly use them as if they were.

To put these speeds in perspective, 30 characters per second is about 300 words per minute, and we typically speak at a rate of around 120 words per minute. A message that has been stored in a disk file can be transmitted over the phone faster than it can be read, if you have a 120 CPS connection.

TALKING TO THE REMOTE COMPUTER

Let's say you liked your PC so well that you decided to buy some IBM stock. Being a nervous person, you like to keep tabs on the stock price, so you decide to check it out using Dow Jones's computer service. The Dow Jones

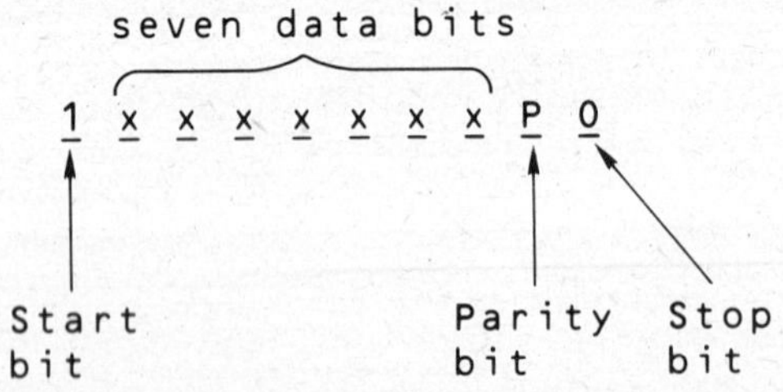

Figure 8-7. In asynchronous communication, data are transmitted one character at a time. The typical character frame consists of ten bits. The start bit is necessary to mark the beginning of the character, since the time between characters is not fixed i.e., the transmission is not synchronized. After the start bit come the seven bit, ASCII code for the character being transmitted. The parity bit, used for error detection, is explained in Figure 8-13, and the character terminates with a stop bit. Nearly every remote system you use will conform to this pattern.

computer is on the Tymnet, Telenet, and Datapac (Canadian) value-added networks. Since you are in a city served by Telenet, you call a local number and connect to the network.

The Telenet computer in your city will prompt you, essentially asking "which computer on the network do you wish to connect to?" Your reply would be the code for the Dow Jones Computer, which happens to be located in Princeton, New Jersey. Within a few seconds, you would be switched through to their computer (unless it was temporarily out of service). From that point on, it would be as if you were directly wired into the Dow Jones machine; the network would be *transparent*.

The Dow Jones computer would then ask you for your account number and your secret password, for billing purposes and to keep someone else from using your account. Once it accepted these as valid (i.e., once you were *logged on*), you would be ready to inquire about the price of IBM stock. That would involve just two commands, first selecting "current stock quotes," then asking for the price of IBM. At that point, you could jot down the stock price, log off the system, hang up the phone, and go back to using your PC for something else (see Figure 8-8).

You would be billed for the time you spent looking up IBM's price, and each service has its own formula for determining charges. Two of the factors that might be used in figuring your bill are *connect time*, the number of seconds between your logging on and logging off, and *CPU time*, the number of seconds the remote computer actually spends working on your job, as opposed to the jobs of the other folks who are logged in at the same time you are. If you decided to store some data on the disk file of the remote computer, perhaps some old electronic mail, you would also be charged for that. Finally, you might be charged for each time you used a certain program or access a certain data base; for instance, although they don't do so, Dow Jones could decide to charge you a small fee for each stock quote you requested. There are many variations on the billing theme, and many services also charge a minimum fee each month just to have access to their computers.

STORING DATA ON YOUR DISK

Okay, so we got a stock quote, but was a personal computer necessary for that transaction? No, a simple *dumb terminal*, consisting of just a keyboard and a video display or a keyboard and a printer, would have been sufficient. In fact, most remote services are designed so that they can be used by someone with a lowest-common-denominator dumb terminal. But as long as we have a PC, can't we do more?

What would have happened if, instead of simply wanting the price of IBM stock, you had wanted the prices of several stocks, or perhaps some historical data on IBM stock (see Figure 8-9)? If you requested that information and it was displayed on your video screen, you would spend a

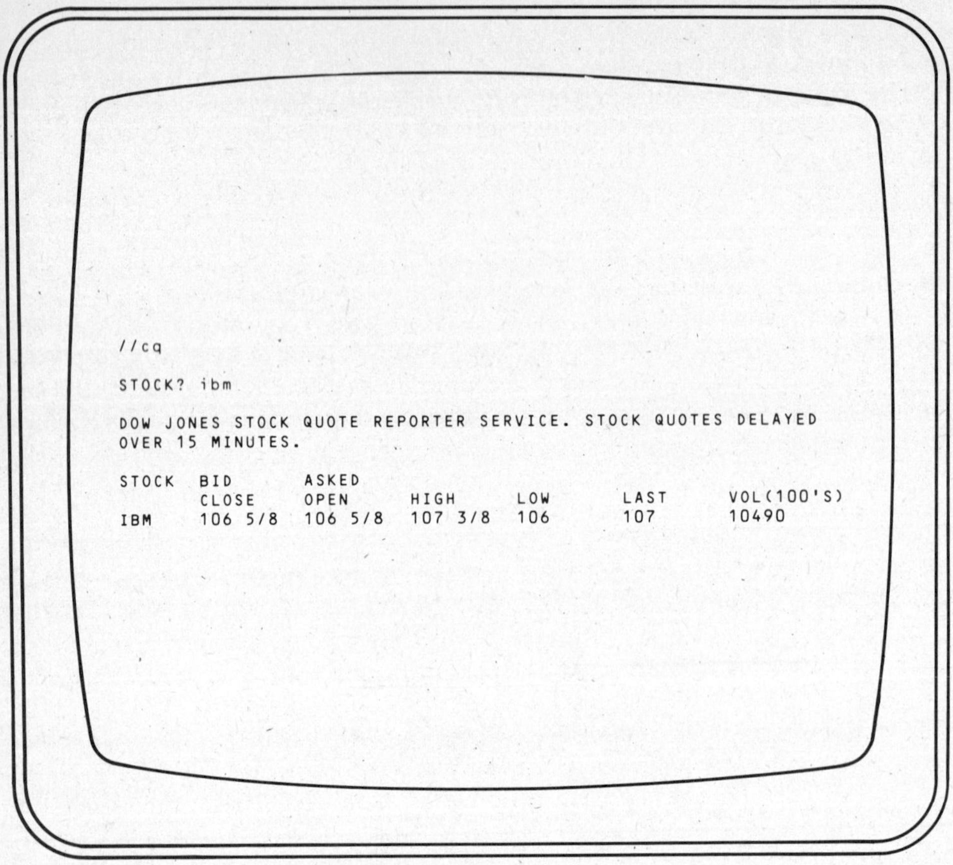

```
//cq

STOCK? ibm

DOW JONES STOCK QUOTE REPORTER SERVICE. STOCK QUOTES DELAYED
OVER 15 MINUTES.

STOCK  BID      ASKED
       CLOSE    OPEN     HIGH      LOW     LAST     VOL(100'S)
IBM    106 5/8  106 5/8  107 3/8   106     107      10490
```

Figure 8-8. A simple stock market price inquiry can be made with only two commands. The user's input is shown in lowercase letters. The "//cq" is the command for current quotes and the "ibm" indicates that you want the price of a share of IBM. The uppercase letters are from the remote computer. This example is very similar to an inquiry on the Dow Jones remote computer service.

good deal of time copying it down. Luckily, that would not be necessary.

For starters, most communication programs for the PC will let you turn the printer on, so that everything that is displayed on the screen is simultaneously printed. If you turn your printer on, the stock data will be printed out as it is received, and when you are finished, you can log off and read it over at your leisure. It isn't even necessary to sit and watch it as it comes in.

That's better, but what if you would like to analyze that stock data using a spreadsheet model or add it to a data file that you are saving on floppy disk in your office? It would be tedious to sit down with the printout and key the data back in to your spreadsheet or data file. But that won't be necessary either, because your PC communication program should also let you *capture* data as it is received in a disk file (see Figure 8-10). When you

```
STOCK? ibm dec txn aapl

STOCK   BID       ASKED
        CLOSE     OPEN        HIGH      LOW        LAST      VOL(100'S)
  IBM   106 5/8   106 5/8     107 3/8   106        107       10490
  DEC   120 3/8   120 1/4     121 5/8   118 7/8    121       4637
  TXN   159 1/2   159 3/4     163 1/4   158 1/2    163 1/8   1636
  AAPL  42 1/2    42 5/8                                     7770

//hq

DOW JONES HISTORICAL STOCK QUOTE REPORTER SERVICE

STOCK  ibm 80 m

   1980 MONTHLY SUMMARY

  DATE    HIGH      LOW       CLOSE     VOL(100/S)
  01/80   72        61 3/4    68 5/8    109420
  02/80   70 1/2    62 1/8    63 3/8    85645
  03/80   63 1/2    51 3/8    55 5/8    107779
  04/80   56        50 5/8    54 7/8    88474
  05/80   56 5/8    52        55 3/8    87499
  06/80   60 3/8    55 1/4    58 3/4    89637
  07/80   66 1/8    58 3/8    65 1/8    86682
  08/80   69 1/8    64        65 1/2    80707
  09/80   69        63 1/2    64 1/4    88549
  10/80   71 1/2    63 5/8    66 5/8    115969
  11/80   72 3/4    66 1/4    68 1/2    94674
  12/80   69 1/2    63 1/4    67 7/8    100020
```

Figure 8-9. If you want quotes on more than one stock or on the history of a stock, a few commands will do the trick. Here "ibm dec txn aapl" got us the prices of IBM, Digital Equipment, Texas Instruments, and Apple Computer stocks. The second example is a historical quote ("//hq") giving the monthly prices of IBM stock during 1980.

It would be tedious to have to copy this much information from the display by hand. When you retrieve a lot of data, it is convenient either to print it as it comes in or to capture it on a disk for future analysis or editing. With a dumb terminal, this would not be possible.

finished transferring the stock data and logged off the remote computer, the data would be in a disk file, ready for subsequent processing.

Before going on to the next topic, let me just mention that the we have only spoken of incoming data. With most communication programs, you also have the ability to capture the commands and anything else that you type on the keyboard or send, thereby creating a complete log of both incoming and outgoing messages. Also, during transmission, the computers might exchange a few funny control codes that you don't even see on the screen, and these can be erased while browsing with your word processor.

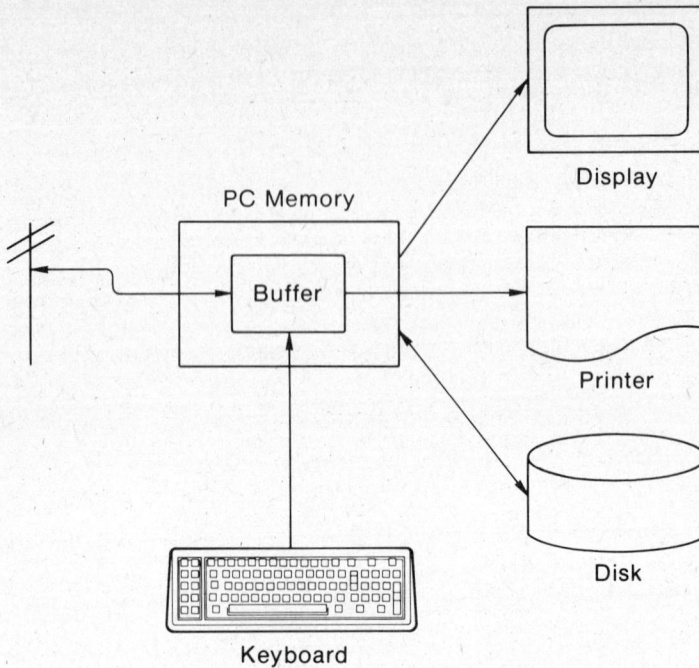

Figure 8-10. As data is received from the remote computer, it goes into a buffer in the PC's memory. From there it can be routed to the display, the printer, or the disk. Data to be transmitted can come from either the keyboard or a disk file.

MAIL

Electronic mail is the most common communication application, so let's look at a typical mail system that might be offered as a service and accessed over a value-added network. Figure 8-11a shows a typical screen display at the time you log on. A brief title, the date received, and author of each new message are shown. You could either read, discard, or temporarily save each message.

If you decided to read message number 3, you would see something like Figure 8-11b. The subject, author, date, and copy list are shown in addition to the text of the message. Note that this message was automatically sent to everyone on the "manager list," not just to you. After displaying the message, you would be given a choice of erasing it, filing it away on the remote system's disk, sending it to your PC, where it would be displayed and you could print it or capture it in a disk file, or replying immediately.

Your reply would be written by filling in a few blank fields (subject, address, and copy list), as in Figure 8-11c. (If it was an immediate reply to a message you had just read, the system could automatically fill in the address.) Note that as you were typing the text of your reply, you would need the same sorts of capabilities as are found in a word processing editor. You would need to enter the message, format it, and correct any errors. In some cases you would use your own word processor to write electronic messages, and in others you would use an editing program on the computer running the mail service. Once it was written, you would issue a "send" command, putting the message in Lew Whitaker's file. He would see it the next time he logged onto the system.

But what would happen if instead of three messages, you found, say, 50? You would not want to read them one at a time; instead, you would capture all of the mail in one local disk file on your PC.

As an example, I get about 50 messages averaging 900 characters in length per week. A little arithmetic translates that into 45,000 characters per week. At a transmission rate of 30 characters per second, transferring a week's mail takes 25 minutes. Instead of reading the messages as they come in, I capture them on disk, while I do something else.

Once the mail transfer is finished, I log off and browse through the mail file using a word processing program, just as if it were a document. As I go through the week's mail with the word processor, it is a simple matter to delete the messages that I don't wish to save (using the block-delete command) and to compose replies to any that I wish to answer. When finished browsing, I print out the messages that I saved.

A little careful reading between the lines of the last example points out the biggest problem with electronic mail. It is so quick and convenient that people use it a lot. That means you can be swamped with mail if you are not careful. Electronic mail is fun, especially at first, and there is some danger of overusing it. Maybe you could send your competitors into bankruptcy by giving them electronic mail systems to play with as a distraction.

HANDSHAKING

Suppose you were transferring a large file from a remote computer and printing it as it was received. What would happen if the printer ran out of paper halfway through the transfer? If the remote computer did not know what had happened, it would continue transmitting data, at the rate of 30 or more characters per second. By the time you put new paper in the printer, a lot of the file would have been lost. Or what if you were reading a message as it was displayed on your video screen, and found that you couldn't read fast enough to keep up with the computer? The message would just scroll off your display and be lost, unless you could ask for a transmission pause.

Problems like these call for *handshaking* conventions. Handshaking is simply a means for the receiving computer, in this case your PC, to signal that it is temporarily tied up, so the remote computer can suspend transmission. Your PC communication program would monitor the system for problems like being out of paper (or a disk being full, the communication buffer in memory being full, the disk drive door being open, the operator

A

```
YOU HAVE 3 NEW MESSAGES:

1.   DRAFT OF NCC PAPER        4-29-84   NATE HORWITZ
2.   TUSCON ITINERARY          4-30-84   ROBERT MYAVSKOVSKY
3.   NEW YORK MEETING AGENDA   4-30-84   LEW WHITAKER

READ
ERASE
FILE
```

B

```
SUBJECT:  NEW YORK MEETING AGENDA
FROM:  LEW WHITAKER
DATE:  4-30-84
CC:  MANAGER-LIST

    The branch managers from each region will meet at
corporate headquarters from June 6 to June 9, 1984. The
following topics will be considered ...


PRINT
ERASE
FILE
LOCAL COPY
REPLY
```

C

```
SUBJECT:  New York Meeting Agenda
TO:  Lew Whitaker
COPY:

TEXT OF MESSAGE:

Lew,

     Got the agenda for the meeting, but wouldn't Hawaii be a
more efficient location for the meeting since ...

SEND
```

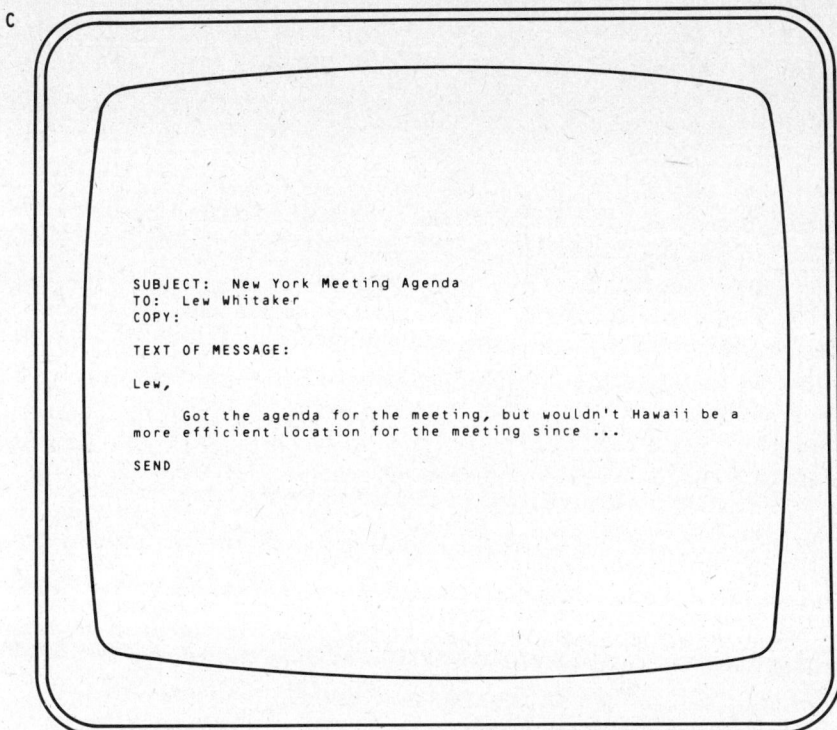

Figure 8-11. These frames illustrate an electronic mail system. When you first log on, the system lets you know how many messages are waiting in your electronic "mailbox" and tells you a little bit about each, so you can decide whether to read them immediately, erase them unseen, or file them away for future reference.

If you had asked to read message number 3, you would see a display similar to that in the center panel. Having read the message as displayed, you would have the option of printing it, erasing it, filing it away in the mail system, making a copy on your disk, or writing a reply.

Writing a reply is similar to using a word processing editor. After filling in the subject, address, and copy fields, you would enter and correct the text of your message. When you were finished, you would send it. In other words, it would be put in Lew Whitaker's incoming mail file.

asking for a pause in order to read the screen, and so forth) and send a "suspend transmission" code to the remote computer as soon as some problem was detected. Once the problem was fixed, it would send a "resume transmission" code, and things would carry on.

Simple, right? The only hitch is that for some inexplicable reason, everyone has not agreed to use the same codes for "suspend transmission" and "resume transmission." I know of four different handshaking conventions or *protocols* that are used on various remote computers. Many PC communication programs offer a choice of several popular handshaking protocols. This is not to say that there is no uniformity. One protocol, called XON/XOFF, is far more common than the others, but it is not universal. In selecting a communication program for your PC, be sure that it is compatible with the handshaking protocols used on every remote computer you plan to be using.*

TRANSFERRING FILES IN THE OTHER DIRECTION

We have seen that it is possible to transfer files from a remote computer to your PC, to *download* them, by capturing information that the remote computer transmits to your display. But what about *uploading* files, transferring them from your PC to a remote computer? What if you have written a long report you wish to share with a colleague? The process would be reversed. First, the report would be composed using your word processing program. You would revise it, make corrections, and print it out, as usual. When it was finally complete, it would be saved in a disk file and transferred to the remote system using your communication program.

That sounds simple, doesn't it? It will often be just that simple, but depending upon the communication program you are using in your PC and the program on the remote computer that is receiving the file, there could be some software incompatibility. Again, you have to worry about hand-shaking, but in the other direction.

Even if the two systems agree on handshaking conventions, there could be a problem with the data file itself. Recall that you used a word processing program to prepare the file to send to the remote computer. Now some, but not all, word processing programs put special control characters in the text file, to signal such things as shifting to boldface characters, ending a line or paragraph, tabbing, and so forth. In other words, they use more than just standard ASCII printing characters. This may cause problems at the receiving end.

This is not to scare you away from transferring files from your PC to remote computers, it is just to let you know that there may be problems. The problems, if they do arise, will be soluble by a moderately skilled technician, but you should run some tests or get a guarantee of compati-bility before you pay for a PC communication program.

ERROR CHECKING

Even if you have no handshaking problems, there might be transmission errors. Remember that you are using the telephone system, and sometimes there will be bad connections. Extraneous noise or static on the line or even

*Just out of curiosity, you might be interested to know that the code for "suspend transmission" is 0010011 and the code for "resume transmission" is 0010001 with the XON/XOFF protocol. These are examples of ASCII codes that don't correspond to printed characters but are used to control the system.

noise in the room can cause a transmission error. The likelihood of this happening is less if you are using a direct-connect modem that plugs into the wall instead of an acoustic coupler, but in either case it will happen sometimes.

Several techniques are used to catch errors during remote communication. The first is visual checking. If I get a message that begins "Dear Larty," I can figure out that it is a garbled version of "Dear Larry." But what about characters sent from your PC to the remote computer—who can visually check those?

Surprisingly enough, you can also check outgoing characters. Can you guess how? Remember that in the discussion of handshaking we saw that the receiving computer could send a "pause" code whenever it needed time to attend to something? If it could send a pause while receiving data from the other end, there must be simultaneous two way transmission. Or, to use the proper jargon, there must be *full-duplex communication* (see Figure 8-12). Full-duplex communication is the key to visual error checking, since the character you see displayed on your screen is not put there by the PC when you hit the key; it is transmitted to the remote computer and then echoed back for visual verification. A character can be incorrect on your display and still have gotten through correctly to the remote computer (it would have been garbled on the return leg), but the odds of a bad character coming back correct are small indeed.

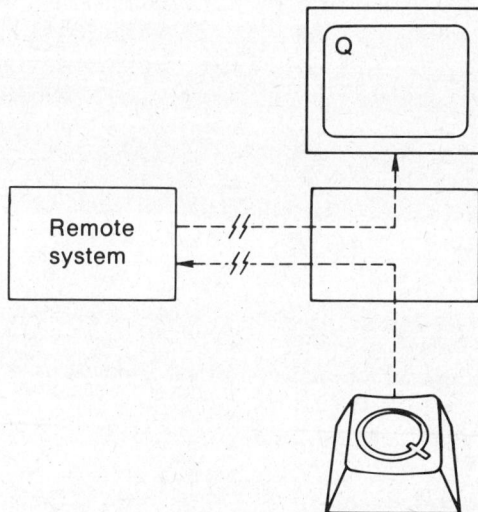

Figure 8-12. With a full duplex system, there is simultaneous two-way transmission. When you type a "Q" on your keyboard, it is sent to the remote computer, echoed back to your PC, and displayed on the video screen. That seems like a lot of trouble, but it enables you to inspect the character visually to see whether it was received correctly. If you notice a lot of garbled characters, you can hang up the phone and dial again to make a better connection.

In many cases, for instance in sending and receiving interoffice memos, visual verification of transmission is good enough. But, in more critical cases, *parity checking* may be worthwhile (see Figure 8-13). Parity checking requires adding an extra bit to each character sent from either computer. The trick is always to be sure there are an odd number of 1 bits in each character sent from either computer. This means that if the ASCII code for a character has an even number of 1 bits, the parity bit would be set to 1, and if the character already has an odd number of 1 bits, the parity bit would be set to 0. As long as both computers have been programmed to test for odd parity, many transmission errors will be caught.

Of course, people being what they are, some of the remote computers you use will want even parity instead of odd. In order to cope with this problem, your PC communication program will probably offer several choices: no parity bit, odd parity, even parity, or ignore the parity bit, even if it is there.*

But even with parity checking some errors might slip by undetected, right? Can you think of an example? What happens if two bits are accidentally changed from 1 to 0 during transmission? Parity is unchanged, and the error goes undetected. That is not the sort of thing you would like to have happen if you were transmitting payroll data.

For even more sensitive data you want a *block checked* file transfer. What happens in this case is that the data are broken into blocks of, say, 128 characters (with some programs you can choose the block size). As each block is transmitted, a *checksum* (see Figure 8-14) is computed and sent along with it. The receiving computer recalculates the checksum when the data arrive and makes sure that it is the same as the checksum that came with the data. If it is the same, the program acknowledges receipt, and gets ready to receive the next block, but if it does not match, it signals for a retransmission. The program would keep track of the number of retrans-

---

*A parity bit is also associated with each byte of memory in your PC, and whenever data is transferred between the CPU or an input/output device and memory, parity is checked. This checking is done automatically whenever information is transferred to the memory from any source, so you don't have to worry about it.

Letter	ASCII code							Parity bit (odd)
A	1	0	0	0	0	0	1	1
B	1	0	0	0	0	1	0	1
C	1	0	0	0	0	1	1	0
D	1	0	0	0	1	0	0	?

Figure 8-13. A parity bit is an extra (eighth) bit, used for error detection. If the remote computer you are communicating with uses odd parity, your PC must do the same. Odd parity means each character must have an odd number of bits; even parity means each character should have an even number. Since the ASCII codes for "A" for "B" have an even number of bits (two each) the parity bit must be set to "1" to make it odd. The "C" already has an odd number of bits (three), so the parity bit is 0. What would the parity bit be for the letter "D"?

A.

Data   Checksum

| DEAR FRED . . . | |

B.

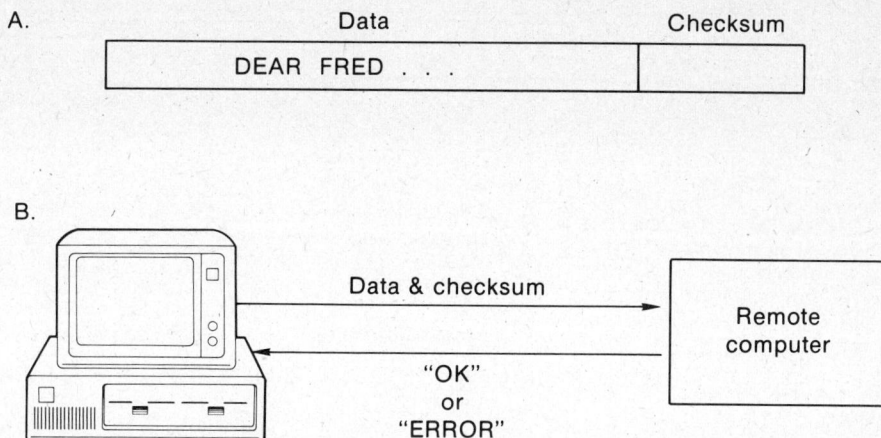

Data & checksum →

Remote computer

"OK"
or
"ERROR"

Figure 8-14. Parity checking will fail to detect two-bit errors, but if data are transmitted in blocks, error detection checksums may also be used. The checksum would be computed from the data portion of the block in some well defined way and sent along with the data. At the other end of the line, the receiving computer would recompute the checksum using the same formula. If it got the same result, it would send back an "OK" signal, and get ready to receive the next block. If it got a different checksum, it would send back an "error" message, and the block would be retransmitted. The system would be programmed to keep track of the number of retries and to give up after, say, five.

missions necessary, to let you know if there were a lot of problems. The PC would also be programmed to give up after a specified number of retries had failed.

There is no single standard for checksum calculation or for the protocol used to acknowledge receipt of a valid block or to ask for a retransmission. If you are planning to do block checked transfers, be sure the program in your PC and the program in the remote computer are compatible. You may need the services of a programmer here.

AT THE OTHER END OF THE LINE

How do you imagine the "remote computer" that we have been speaking of? What do you think the Dow Jones computer in New Jersey or the ARPA Net computer in London look like? I'll bet you see them as mainframe computers in large, glassed-in, air-conditioned rooms, surrounded by programmers and operators. That is often the case, but might the remote computer not be just another PC?

Let's consider a few examples in which that might happen. One is local electronic bulletin boards. I can connect to The Source computer in Virginia (using Tymnet or Telenet) and get reviews of current movies (see Figure 8-15). Alternatively, I can call a local number, connect to a PC and get re-

```
                    CASABLANCA
                     (GREAT)
                  MICHAEL CURTIZ
                  102 MINUTES B&W
                      (1943)

        CRACKLING INTRIGUE, TINGLING ROMANCE, AND A SUPURB MOODY
    ATMOSPHERE MAKE THIS TAUT MELODRAMA ONE OF THE BEST WORLD WAR
    II FILMS. HUMPHREY BOGART, IN A MEMORABLE PERFORMANCE, IS IN
    TOP FORM AS THE OWNER OF A DINGY CASABLANCA NIGHTCLUB. HE
    HELPS AN OLD FLAME, PLAYED BY INGRID BERGMAN, AND HER
    UNDERGROUND LEADER-HUSBAND, PLAYED BY PAUL HENREID, ESCAPE
    THE NAZIS.

        THIS CLASSIC, WITTY THRILLER SEEMS TO EARN MORE
    APPRECIATION AS TIME GOES BY. ALSO WITH CLAUDE RAINS, CONRAD
    VEIDT, S.Z. SAKALL, PETER LORRE, AND SYDNEY GREENSTREET.

        ACADEMY AWARDS -- BEST PICTURE; CURTIZ, BEST DIRECTOR;
    JULIUS J. EPSTEIN, PHILIP G. EPSTEIN AND HOWARD KOCH, BEST
    WRITING (SCREENPLAY). NOMINATIONS -- BOGART, BEST ACTOR;
    RAINS, BEST SUPPORTING ACTOR; ARTHUR EDESON, CINEMATOGRAPHY
    (BLACK AND WHITE).
```

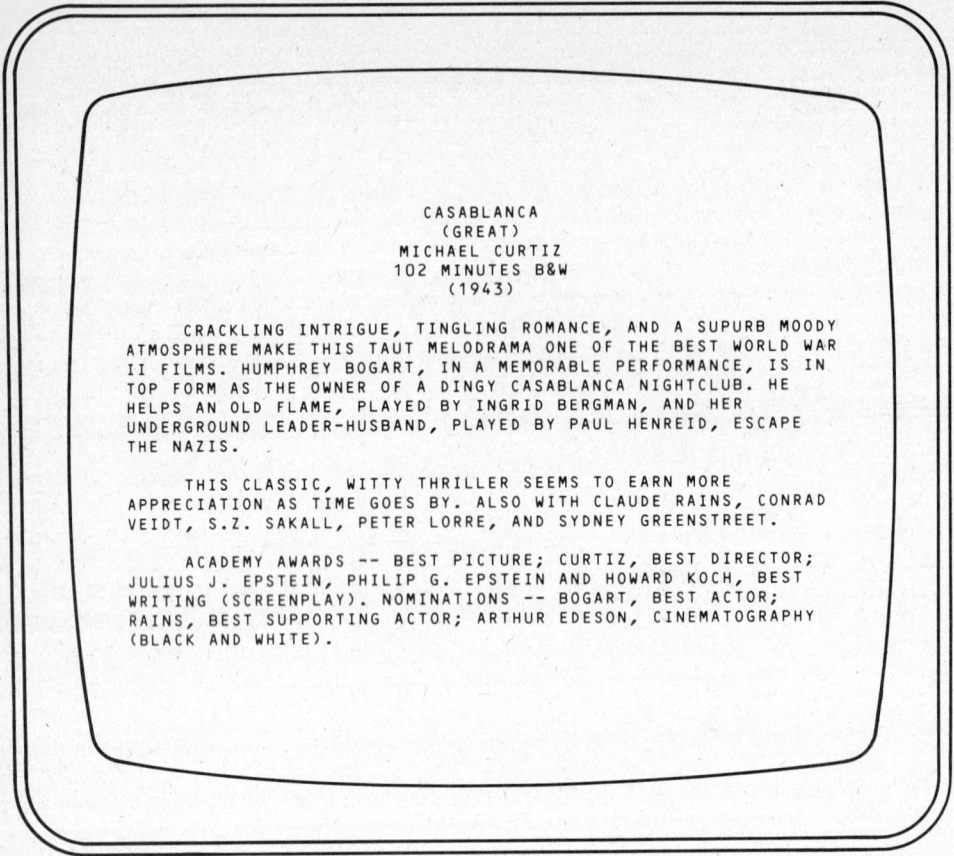

Figure 8-15. This movie review was retrieved using a centralized information utility over a network. A local system could have given more information, for instance the address of the theater where it was playing, the showtimes, and admission prices. Not only that, the communication cost would have been less, since it would not have been necessary to use the network. For many applications, decentralized communication, perhaps confined to a metropolitan area or even a neighborhood, makes more sense than large, centralized computers.

Furthermore, the review is succinct, but it certainly doesn't convey as much information as, and lacks the style of, a review written for a newspaper or magazine. You can feel the pressure of writing for a slow and expensive medium. The value of remote communication for many business and professional applications seems pretty well established, but the jury is still out on personal information services.

views of the movies that happen to be playing in theaters on the west side of Los Angeles. Not only that, I get the admission price, the showtimes, and the address of the theater along with the review. There are literally hundreds of local bulletin boards using personal computers in Los Angeles, and thousands around the country. Decentralized systems like this may turn out to be more desirable than centralized systems for many services.

The movie review bulletin board is a one way street; you get information but don't leave any (though it could be modified to allow callers to leave their comments on a given movie). There are also a lot of two way bulletin boards in operation. If run for the general public, they often deal with a specific topic like computer dating, science fiction, or want ads. Others let you choose your topic from a menu.

PC based bulletin boards are also used in business. A store or manufacturer might use one to answer customer questions, to announce new products, or even to accept orders. For instance, a computer store in my area has a bulletin board with their prices, specials, and other announcements on it. Or, if you have trouble with CP/M-86 or any other PC software you bought from Digital Research, you can leave a problem report on their bulletin board and rest assured that a technician will see it. Novation, a modem manufacturer, has technical specifications and pricing information for their products on a bulletin board.

There is nothing to stop you from using your PC as the "central" computer in an electronic mail system, set up just for your company. It is partially a matter of comparative cost. Which is cheaper—using your own computer and paying the telephone line costs yourself, or using a centralized electronic mail system and paying for the service at their rates? Convenience also comes into play. Which system has the easiest-to-use software for composing, editing, saving, and replying to messages?

Another application for PC-to-PC communication is unattended file transfer, which is often done late at night in order to take advantage of reduced phone rates. You might transfer files containing the day's orders from each of your branch offices every evening. If time is not of the essence, you could transfer your electronic mail in late night batches as well.

All of these applications, in which your PC becomes the "remote" computer, the one that answers the phone, require a little extra hardware and a lot of extra software. At the very least, you will need an *answer/originate* modem, one that can detect a "ring" on the phone line, "answer" the call, and send out that high pitched tone that says "okay, I'm here." If you have just one dial-in line, one modem will suffice, but if a second person calls in, he or she will get a busy signal. Multiple lines, each with a modem, are possible, but, just as with business phones, you will have to shop around for the communication system.

The software part is tougher. A number of communication packages have been designed for handling dial-up communication, but some customization will doubtless be necessary on your part. If you will be handling multiple incoming lines, you have a small time-sharing system on your PC, and that will require further software expertise. Plan on getting programmer assistance if your PC will be answering the phone.

CHAPTER NINE
Local Communication Basics

Whereas the last chapter covered remote communication, this one covers local communication—using your PC to talk to other computers within the same building or building complex. Local communication has a shorter history in the computing world, not really getting underway until people began installing time-sharing systems. When that happened, it was necessary to string cables around to the terminals throughout the building, and the well seasoned Teletype terminal and its cabling were used for years. High speed communication between terminals and mainframe computers just evolved out of the protocols that had been developed for data transmission between early mainframes.

The development of value-added networking was also important to local communications. These networking techniques were brought indoors by researchers at the Xerox Palo Alto Research Center, when they hooked a cluster of experimental personal computers together in the early 1970s to form the first local network. Our history of local communication is brief since, in the main, local communication has the same ancestry as remote communication, which was discussed in the last chapter.

Let's break the discussion of local communication into two cases, communicating with the mainframe or minicomputer that might already be installed in the data processing department of your organization, and communicating with other distributed computing devices like personal computers or word processors. Let's start with the larger machines.

COMMUNICATING WITH THE COMPUTER CENTER

Does your organization already use computers for data processing or administrative support? If so, you might want to access those computers using your PC as an intelligent terminal. For instance, if sales data from your dealers is kept on a central computer in the data processing department, you might like to transfer it to your PC on a weekly basis for

APPLICATIONS

1. You could transfer sales data from the mainframe computer in your company data processing department. You might simply use your PC as a local terminal to look up a few current figures once in a while, or you could set up a system in which the complete records of each sale were transferred into a data file on your PC once a week. In the latter case, you might use a spreadsheet program and word processor to make a regular weekly and year-to-date sales analysis and report. The company data processing people would have to help you get started.
2. Your PC could be used as a terminal to update the files in the central computer. You could update the personnel files as new people resigned or were hired, fired, or promoted. Again, the data processing staff would have to be involved, primarily for control purposes, to establish safeguards against your inadvertently making errors in changing the central files. They would also have to make sure you couldn't read confidential records.
3. Does your company already have a central computer, perhaps operated by the word processing department, for administrative support? If so, you could work on a spreadsheet model at home over the weekend, bring it in on Monday, and transfer it to the administrative computer so your secretary could edit it and incorporate it into a report.
4. If the PCs in your department are all connected together on a local area network, you could conduct a local teleconference, perhaps brainstorming about themes for the new advertising campaign. This would be similar to a teleconference on a remote system, but it would be confined to people in your building. You would be impressed by how much faster it would be to retrieve and display the entries in the conference transcript.
5. Perhaps you would use the local network to distribute a memo to everyone on a certain electronic mail list. The list might include all top management people or everyone on the company soccer team.
6. If you have an IBM PC, and the person in the office next to yours has an Apple, you cannot read each other's disks. However, it would be a simple matter to transmit a file from one machine to the other over a local network. As with most local network applications, this could be done using a remote computer as the intermediary, but the transfer would take much longer and the chances for a transmission error would be much greater.

analysis using a spreadsheet program. Or perhaps you have been working at home on a report, and you would like to transfer it to the office administrative computer so that it could be revised by your secretary and distributed through the electronic mail system that already runs on the administrative computer. Do you already have a terminal that is connected to the central computer? If you are getting a PC, you don't want both it and the terminal on your desk; you want to use the PC in place of the terminal at times and use it as a PC at other times.

These things are all possible, but extra hardware and software will be needed, as well as some programming and technical expertise. For that reason, we will present a quick overview in this section, but bear in mind that the departments operating the central computers will have to be involved in getting your PC to communicate with their machines.

Synchronous and Asynchronous Communication

In the last chapter, dealing with remote computers, the PC communicated over phone lines using a modem. By computer standards, that communication takes place at relatively low speeds, typically, though not always, 30 or 120 characters per second. Although the term wasn't introduced there, that communication was *asynchronous*, which means that the time between characters is free to vary, that is, they do not have to be synchronized. It is easy to build machines for asynchronous communication (the telegraph world has been doing it for years), but it is inefficient, because each character must be preceded by a character start signal and followed by a character end signal. *Synchronous* communication is more common in the world of large computers. They typically transmit blocks of data, along with error detection information, in a lockstep mode. Once the block starts coming, it must all come at a fixed rate.

Assuming that your organization's large computers are also from IBM, you will have heard people speaking of *Bisync (BSC)* or *SDLC* communications. These terms also turn up a lot in ads. These are simply protocols that IBM has established for synchronous communication. They establish the wiring and the handshaking and error checking conventions necessary for data transmission. Older products use the BSC protocol and newer products use SDLC. *HDLC* is another synchronous communication protocol that was set up by a standards organization. Don't lose any sleep over these terms; they are standard protocols, and it is not necessary to know their technical specifications.

In some cases, your large computers may already be set up to accept asynchronous communication from people using terminals. If this is the case, the asynchronous communication techniques described in Chapter 8 will work fine, as long as you have a modem and a communication program. In most cases, however, there will be few or no asynchronous ports on the large computer, and you will have to emulate a synchronous terminal with your PC.

Making a Synchronous Connection

Figure 9-1 shows a typical synchronous communication configuration. The central or *host* computer is a large machine that contains the data and programs used for reporting and for controlling the entire organization. It

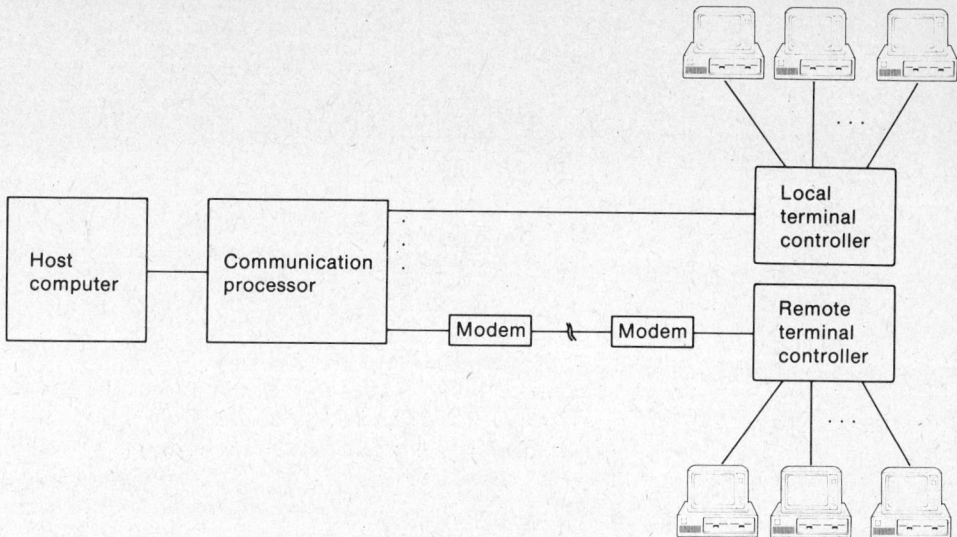

Figure 9-1. The mainframe computer in your data processing department might be serving as a host to hundreds or even thousands of terminals in the building or throughout the country. A second, special-purpose computer, the communications processor, is often used to handle communication tasks such as assembling messages from remote terminals before passing them on to the host for processing. The host and the communication processor would be in the same room, and the transfer rate between them would be very high.

The communication processor could interface to many terminal controllers, say 32 of them, each of which might interface to many terminals. Some of the terminal controllers might be in the building and others at remote sites.

could have billions of bytes of disk space, millions of bytes of memory, high speed printers, magnetic tape units, and already be connected to hundreds of terminals. The communication processor is itself a computer that has been designed and programmed for controlling a communication network. It would be in the same location as the host, and would handle communication-oriented tasks, in order to take a load off the host. The connection between the host and the communication processor would be a very high speed cable. The communication processor would in turn be connected to a number of terminal controllers. The terminal controllers could be either in remote locations, connected with the central system over relatively high speed lines, using synchronous modems, or in the same building as the communication processor, connected with cables.

In order to connect up to this sort of system with your PC, you have two choices. Either you make your PC seem to the network as if it were a terminal controller with just one terminal attached to it or you make it seem

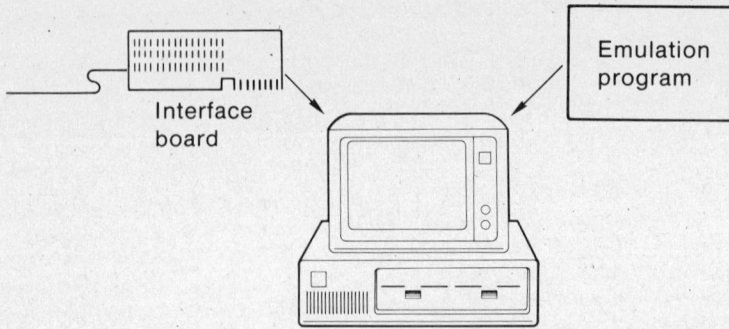

Figure 9-2. If you are going to use your PC to access the files in a central system, like the one in Figure 9-1, you will have to trick the communication processor into thinking your PC is a standard terminal. In order to emulate a terminal, you will need a synchronous communication board in one of your PC expansion slots and a terminal emulation program. The program will do its best to make your PC behave exactly as the terminal would.

like one of the synchronous terminals. In other words, the PC must *emulate* either a synchronous terminal or a terminal controller (see Figure 9-2).

In order to emulate a terminal or controller, you will need both hardware and software. The hardware will come in the form of a board that plugs into a PC expansion slot and should have the appropriate coaxial cable along with it. The software will have to be clever enough to fool both the terminal controller or communication processor and the user into thinking your PC is a garden variety synchronous device. The easy part is emulating the "back end" of a synchronous terminal, since the communication protocols between a terminal and its controller are well defined. Emulating the terminal's operator interface may be more difficult.

To see some of the sorts of problems that arise in emulating the operator interface, let's consider an example. Perhaps your organization has an IBM 5520 computer for the administrative workers. The 5520 is an office automation system that can accommodate up to 24 display stations, so there may be a synchronous terminal on every secretary's desk. The 5520 comes with software for office tasks such as word processing, checking spelling, suggesting synonyms, maintaining data files, and communicating with other computers, for example large IBM hosts.

The 5520 uses IBM 5253 terminals, so the trick is to make your PC act just like a 5253 terminal. Emulating the "back end" of the 5253 is fairly easy, since the data communication protocol is well defined. But a quick look at the keyboards of the PC and the 5253 reveals problems with the operator interface. The keyboard layouts and the meanings assigned the various keys are all different. In order to use your PC as if it were a 5253, you would need a template showing how the emulation program had assigned the 5253 functions.

The author of the terminal emulation program tries to make sure that the PC-turned-5253 behaves just as a real 5253 would in all circumstances. The screen must clear when a 5253 screen clearing code is received, codes for underscoring, blinking characters, intensified characters, and so forth must all be interpreted as they would be by a 5253. It turns out that, using the emulation program supplied by IBM, a PC could do almost everything a true 5253 could, but not quite everything. One option on the 5253 is emulation of a different IBM terminal, and that is not possible with IBM's emulation program.

There will often be problems with data coding and format also. As one example, the 5520 uses the code "5" (00000101) to signal a tab in a document. Great, but what if the document is a word processing file that you created using IBM's EasyWriter program? The "5" must be converted to a string of five spaces to be compatible with EasyWriter. Okay, that's not hard, but what if the file you want to transfer to the 5520 is a VisiCalc spreadsheet, where the tab code is "9" (00001001)? Problems of this sort are surmountable, but some technical background will be needed. And let's not get so caught up in the possible bumps in the road that we forget that the PC offers significant advantages over the standard 5253 terminal. Without the disks available on the PC we could not even be considering file transfers in the first place.

If your company uses an IBM mainframe computer, the code translation problem goes further, since it won't even use the ASCII code to represent the standard printing characters. The computers that IBM's current mainframes evolved from used a code called BCD (binary coded decimal), and the mainframes now use a code called EBCDIC (extended BCD interchange code).

Emulation of the 5253 on a PC is relatively easy and the program supplied by IBM does a fairly complete job, but in other cases it might be tougher. For instance, what happens if you want to use your PC to emulate a terminal that has more keys on its keyboard or can display more lines of information than the PC? For instance, certain models of the popular IBM 3270 series terminals have 43 line displays. That would be a problem. In general, be skeptical about claims that your PC can be connected to a given host computer. Make sure you try out the hardware and the software. Don't count on just buying a circuit board, loading in an emulation program, and starting right up; you will have to work closely with the technical people in your data processing department.

This discussion of the 5253 is meant as an illustration and does not imply that it is the only terminal that IBM (and other vendors) support. Indeed, IBM offers broad support for their 3270 terminals. Using the appropriate circuit board and IBM's 3270-PC control program, you can emulate many (but not all) 3270 functions.

In fact, this hardware/software package, called the 3270-PC (see Figure 9-3), goes beyond simple 3270 emulation. The control program is really a cross between an operating system and a terminal emulator. It enables you to be doing as many as seven things concurrently. You could be running up

Figure 9-3. The PC-3270 can work as a PC or emulate a 3270 terminal connected to a central computer. In fact, you can connect to as many as four separate remote computers simultaneously. Each job uses a different window on the display. Switching from one window to another requires only a single keystroke. You could also be using DOS in another PC-3270 window. If you already have a 3270 terminal on your desk, check the PC-3270 out. (Courtesy of IBM Corporation)

to four separate jobs on a mainframe computer (which would treat your PC as if it were just another 3270 terminal), working with information in two electronic "notepads," and running a separate program under DOS (although there are restrictions on what the program running under DOS can do). To help you keep track of all of this, the control program would divide the display screen into windows, associating one with each of your seven jobs. As you see, the 3270-PC control program performs many operating system functions.

The 3270-PC comes with a nicer keyboard than the standard PC. It has more keys, in order to be more compatible with the 3270 terminals, along with the oversize shift and return keys that you are used to on Selectric typewriters. There is also an optional high resolution color display. Since the original 3270 terminal family is now about eight years old, it would seem that the 3270-PC might be IBM's answer to replacing it. With the 3270-PC you have a computer, not just a terminal, and are using modern components.

Approaching It from the Other Side

Thus far, we have spoken as if you had a PC and then got the idea to use it to access your organization's database. What if, instead, you already have a synchronous terminal on your desk? If the terminal happens to be a member of the IBM 3270 family (and it turns out that about 40% of the terminals in the world are), you are in luck. IBM will sell you a box that looks like the system unit from a PC without the keyboard and display (see Figure 9-4). You can connect this package up to your 3270 and use it as a stand-alone PC when it is not being used as a terminal to the central computer. Of course, you will run into the difficulties of keyboard and other differences mentioned above, but this is another way to get a personal computer and access to your central computer without having two machines on your already overcrowded desk.

The Role of the Data Processing Staff

As we have seen, programmer assistance will be necessary to set up many applications involving communication with a central computer. Technical skill will be required to interface the hardware and the basic terminal emulation software. Additionally, programs for your specific application will probably have to be written. Don't forget that, for the most part, the programs running on your central computer were written under the assumption that they would be used by people with relatively simple terminals. In order to take advantage of the local storage and processing capability of your PC, systems will have to be redesigned and new programs written for both the mainframe computer and the PCs.

IBM and a number of prominent mainframe software companies are working on mainframe and PC programs, designed together for these

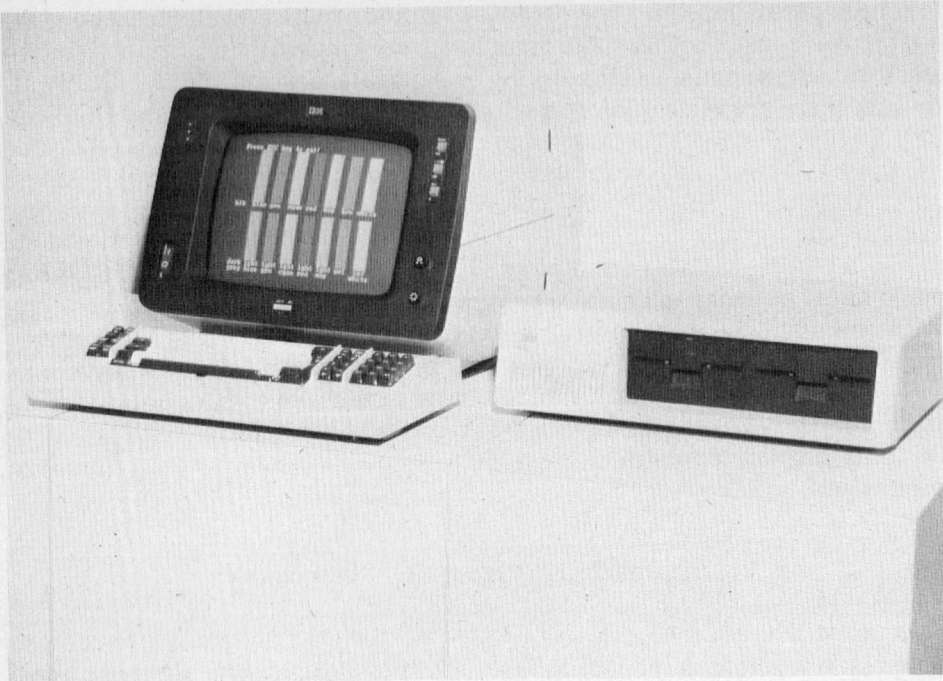

Figure 9-4. If you already have an IBM terminal on your desk, you can turn the tables and use it to emulate the PC, by adding a conversion unit. The unit contains a PC system board and disks, but uses the terminal's keyboard and display. (Courtesy of IBM Corporation)

communication tasks (see Figure 9-5). These range from very simple packages, in which the PC can store information on the mainframe disk as if it were another floppy disk (a *virtual* floppy disk), to file transfer programs, to sophisticated programs that enable the user to transfer information from many mainframe files, bringing it to the PC in a format that makes it ready to be used immediately by, say, a spreadsheet, word processing, or file management program. Note that these programs involve both the main-frame computer and your PC and that they are quite sophisticated, so actual evaluation and selection will be done by the people in the data processing department.

Your in-house staff will probably also be involved in training people to use these programs once they are operational. The data processing people should be involved from the planning stages on if you plan to use PCs to communicate with their systems.

Maintaining control over data integrity and security might prove to be an even tougher problem for the data processing staff than developing new systems and software. Think about the things that can go wrong. As more and more people gain access to the data files, there is more and more

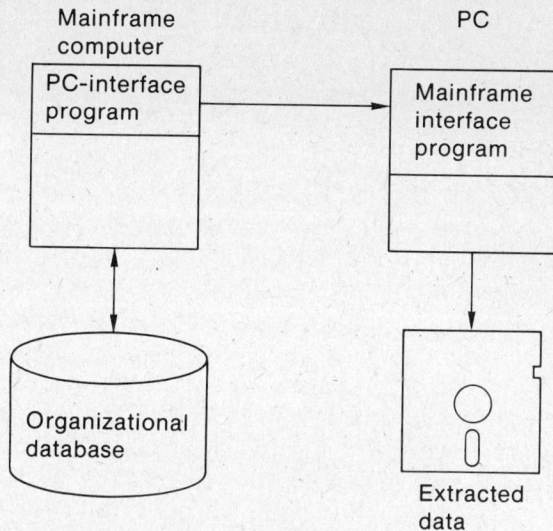

Figure 9-5. In order to move data between the PC and mainframe databases, sophisticated interface software is needed in both machines. For this reason, the responsibility for evaluating, selecting, and installing that software belongs in the data processing department. It is beyond the scope of any individual PC user.

opportunity to make mistakes. What if, on your first day with access to the company database, you accidentally delete your personnel record, while browsing through it? What if you accidentally enter inaccurate data while updating a file? There is also the problem of having multiple, inconsistent copies of records floating around the company. What happens if you are using a copy of a file that you transferred from the central computer last week, someone else is using a month-old copy, and a third person is using the current file on the mainframe?

Even if no one has "permission" to update central files, problems can occur. A well intentioned executive might make an information request that consumes many hours of mainframe time, without realizing the cost. The first major on-line system, the American Airlines SABRE reservation system, ran into significant problems at first, partly because people at terminals requested many more complete flight rosters than anyone had anticipated.

What if someone who is trying to step on your fingers on the way up the corporate ladder not-so-accidentally looks at or modifies your personnel record? As more and more people in the organization get passwords and learn how to access the central computers, the chance of a competitor or prankster getting in and doing malicious damage grows.

The central data processing staff have responsibility for building in safeguards against this sort of thing, and your PC access will have to work within the context of those safeguards. There will be a system of passwords. You will have permission to read some files, but not write on them. You may be allowed to read or write others, and there may be some that you are not even allowed to read. Even if you have legal access to a file, you might be allowed to look at it on your display, but not transfer it to your PC disk, since it would be easier for it to fall into unauthorized hands.

LOCAL NETWORKS OF DISTRIBUTED COMPUTERS

Now let's look at the second type of local communication, using your PC in conjunction with other distributed machines, often other PCs. This idea, called *local area networking*, is a hot one these days; everyone predicts a bright future for the concept. For instance, Strategic Inc., a market research firm, projects 110,000 local networks by 1987 with 920,000 personal computers connected to them. That works out to a predicted average of about eight computers on each local network. If you work in an organization with more than a half-dozen or so administrative or professional workers, you very well may be hooked to a local network sooner than you think. With that in mind, let's see what they are like.

Sharing Hardware, Software, and Data and Communicating

Figure 9-6 illustrates the idea of a local network. PCs on workers' desks, often referred to as *workstations* in networking circles, are able to communicate over the network with other PCs and with shared resources such as a large disk file or one or more fancy printers. The network also has one or more *resource controllers* or *servers*. A resource controller is in fact another computer that has been programmed to control the shared disks, printers, or other common resources. With some manufacturers' systems, it would be another IBM PC, programmed to interface with the network. Let's use the term *node* to describe any of the computers on the network, whether they are workstations or resource servers.

Both the technology and the motivation for local area networks come from their big brothers, the value-added networks. Local networks were developed for the same reason as the ARPA Network: to enable people at personal computers to share expensive hardware, programs, and databases and to communicate with each other.

How might that work? The simplest view of the local network is that the workstations are independent of each other but can use the common resources. In that case, you would use your PC as if it were a stand-alone computer, but you could save some of your larger files on the shared hard disk or print a report using the shared printer. The primary motivation in this case would be to save money. Perhaps there would have to be only one floppy disk drive in each of the workstation PCs, and maybe none of them would need a printer. If, say, ten PCs shared a 50 million byte disk, that would be 5 million bytes for each. Along the same lines, the workstations might share an expensive laser printer for high quality, high speed output.

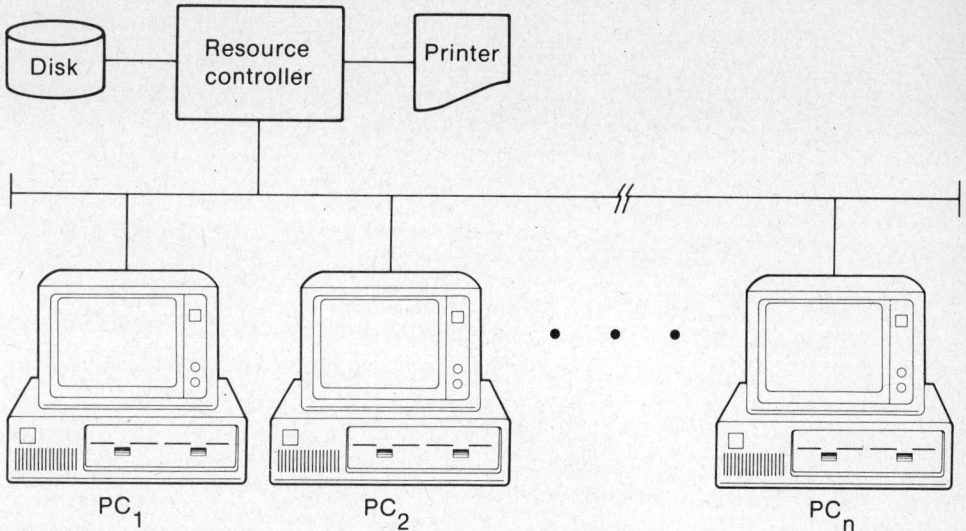

Figure 9-6. Here we see a simple local area network. The PC workstations are located in people's offices. By connecting to a network cable, they can communicate with each other and gain access to the shared resources on the network. The resource controller is a computer (perhaps even another PC) that has been programmed to keep track of the shared resources and enable the people at their workstations to access them. Shared resources might include hardware, data, or programs.

Local networks of personal computers started out in just this way, as an attempt to economize, but as hardware prices have fallen and as they continue to do so, the motivation will come more and more from the desire to share files and facilitate communication among the workstations.

The simplest form of file sharing would be to keep a single copy of a commonly used program on the shared disk, for example a word processor that everyone used. Instead of each person having his or her own copy on floppy disk, there would be a single master copy, and when you wanted to use the word processing program, you would load it from the shared disk into your PC. That would save disks and ensure that everyone was using the latest version of the software, but do you see a problem? The problem is not technical, but legal. If the software were purchased from an outside firm, it would be copyrighted, and copying it from the shared disk to the workstations would be illegal. One of my consulting clients, a college, would have established a local network of 32 personal computers if it were not for this roadblock. Instead, they installed a time-sharing system. Software companies will have to come up with policies to cover these situations, if local networking is to thrive.

Another form of file sharing occurs when two or more workstations can read and write the same file at the same time. This would be most common in an administrative application. For example, in a wholesale firm, several operators might be updating an inventory file, or in a college, they could be working with a student registration file. This sort of thing is common on time-sharing computers, but not all local networks support it today, since software must be written to ensure that two operators do not both try to update the same record at the same time. This *record lock* capability may or may not be possible with a given local network, so be cautious if you have this kind of application.

Software Is the Hard Part (Where Have You Heard That Before?)

Software is actually the key ingredient in a local network, not hardware. Take the simple example of sharing a printer. What happens if you want to print a report and the shared printer is tied up printing something for someone else? Your report must be transferred to the disk of the resource controller, where it can wait until the printer becomes free. If there are several print jobs ahead of it, it will have to wait in line, or in a *queue* as byte-headed people say, until its turn (see Figure 9-7). That is all fair and democratic, but it requires software to keep track of the jobs in the queue, to send a high priority job to the front of the queue, to let you know the status of your pending print job, to start one job when another finishes, and so forth. You will recognize all of this as similar in function to the spooling software we discussed in Chapter 4.

A more critical example is electronic mail software. Articles in computer magazines paint glib scenarios of people eliminating "telephone tag" by leaving electronic messages on the shared disks of local networks, routing reports to everyone in their departments, replying to questions as soon as they arrive in the electronic mail, filing important electronic messages away on the shared disk, and so forth. That all sounds great, but it requires a lot of sophisticated software.

Recall our discussion of electronic mail in Chapter 8. When you receive an electronic memo, you might print it, erase it, file it on the central disk for future reference, write a reply to it, forward it or your reply to others, or transmit it to a floppy disk on your PC, among other choices. If you decide to write a snappy reply, you will need an editing program. If you decide to file it away for future reference, a program to categorize it and find a place for it in your old mail file will be needed. To recall it later, you will need a program to retrieve and read through old mail. If you plan to send it on to others, there will have to be a program for creating and maintaining distribution lists, for instance of all the people working on a certain project.

When you stop to think about it, a complete electronic mail system encompasses a file manager, a word processor, and a lot of other software that is geared strictly to mail processing. That's not simple, and few vendors of local networks can deliver such software.

I think you get the picture. As local networks move from passively allowing independent PCs to share a disk or printer for economic reasons to

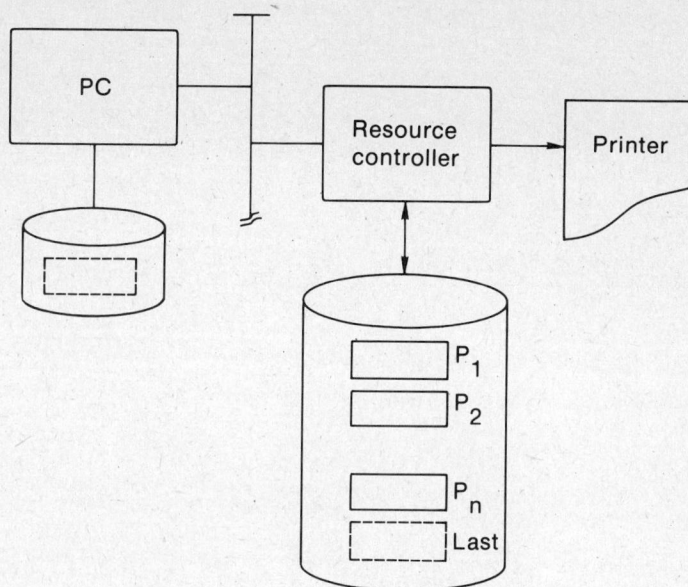

Figure 9-7. This example illustrates the sort of thing the resource controller must be programmed to do. If you wish to print a file that has been created at your workstation (dotted square), it must be transmitted over the network to a disk file on the resource controller. If the printer you need was not in use, the resource controller would start printing your file immediately (assuming that the proper paper was in the printer). If it was busy, your job would be put at the end of a queue, and activated in its turn. Of course, if you are the boss and you need it in a hurry, your job could be given high priority and pushed to the head of the queue. This sounds simple, but a good deal of software would be needed.

coordinated systems in which information is shared and there is a lot of communication between workstations, a lot of software is needed. Be careful, because not many vendors have it (yet).

Extending the Network

Figure 9-8 shows our local network, extended a bit. One or more special devices might be added to it, for instance a publishing company might have a typesetting machine on its local network. If you do engineering design it might be a larger computer with sophisticated hardware and software for doing three dimensional graphics. In one organization where I consult, a special purpose computer for monitoring telemetry data is one node on a network.

Even if you have no special devices like these, you might have *gateways* to other networks and communication links. The gateway might, for example, be a high speed modem that allows the workstations on your local network to communicate with the mainframe computer in the data

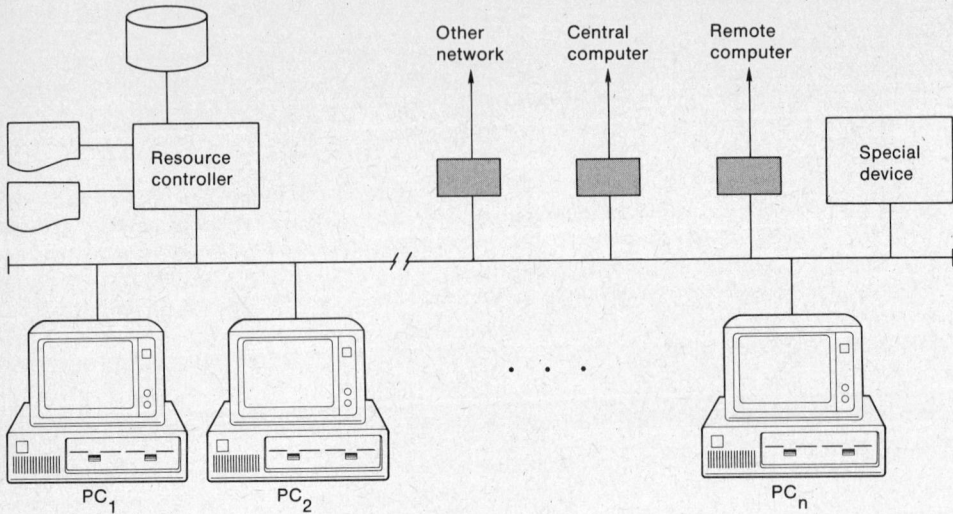

Figure 9-8. Here we see an augmented network. A second printer has been added to the resource controller. Perhaps it is relatively slow, but does color printing, whereas the first one is faster, but black and white. In addition, there may be special-purpose devices like a typesetter or high speed plotter. There are also gateways to another local network (perhaps in an adjoining building or another floor), the central computer in the data processing department, and the remote, dial-up world.

processing department, or a low speed modem for remote communication such as that discussed in the last chapter.

It might even be a gateway to another local network on another floor or in a nearby building. In fact, many people envision hierarchies of networks being common (see Figure 9-9). Perhaps each project or floor will have its own network. Most of your transactions would be within your own area, but you would be able to communicate with colleagues in other departments when necessary. If you hear someone refer to the 80-20 rule, he or she is speaking of a rough rule of thumb that says 80% of your communication is within your own department or area and 20% outside of it. If this is the case, a hierarchic network makes sense.

To be successful, network software will have to be clever enough to hide these levels of network hierarchy, so that it will seem the same whether you are sending a message to someone on your local network or to someone outside of it. The procedure for creating and sending mail to someone in your department should be the same as for someone on another floor of your building, across town, or across the country.

Don't expect to see this sort of transparency in every network system you see advertised for the PC. Again, we must be careful to distinguish between what is possible to imagine, and what you can buy today. If I convinced you

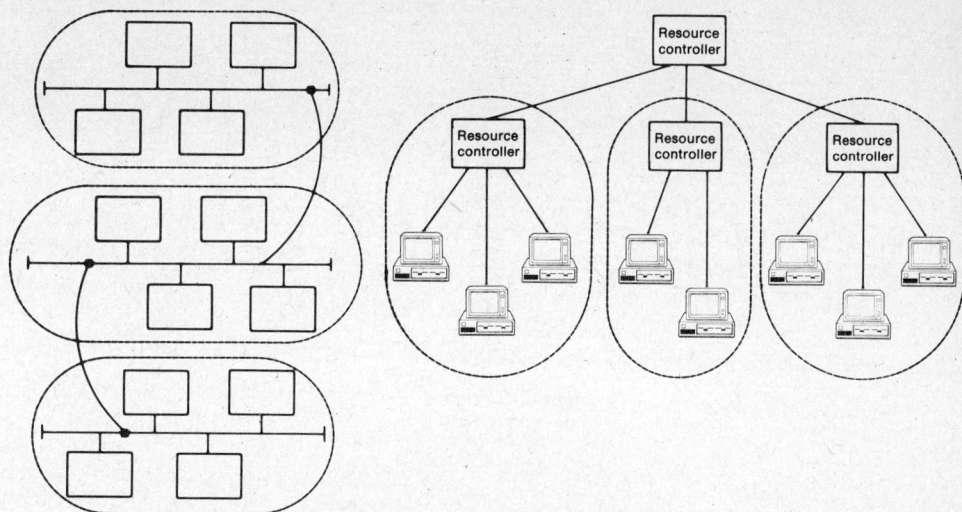

Figure 9-9. Local networks can be connected together to form hierarchies. The subnetworks inside the dotted lines might be located on separate floors or in adjoining buildings, or they might belong to people in different organizational units. For instance, a department or project group might have its own subnetwork. Although the majority of your communication would be within the subnetwork, it would still be possible to communicate with the others. Ideally, that communication would be handled in the same way as communication within your local group. Note that a hierarchy can be achieved with either a bus network (*left*) or a star network, in which the resource controllers are at the center of the star.

that the software requirements for communication and data sharing were tough for an isolated local network, imagine the software problems in a hierarchy of networks and outside communications. We have a lot of work to do in developing operating standards and supporting software.

Hooking Up to a Network

Figure 9-10 shows two of the ways in which a network might be configured and PC workstations connected to it. In both cases, a network interface board is installed in one of the PC expansion slots, and a cable from that board connects the workstation to the network. Depending on the system, these cables may be flat or round, and their cost per foot will vary significantly. The cable seems mundane, but things like its cost, flexibility, and sturdiness will affect the cost of installing your network, maintaining it, and changing it around if people's offices move or are reconfigured.

In Figure 9-10a, the cables from the workstations connect directly onto the network bus or main cable. Again, mundane things like how difficult it is to make a connection, what the connector costs, and what happens to the network if someone's connector comes loose are important considerations.

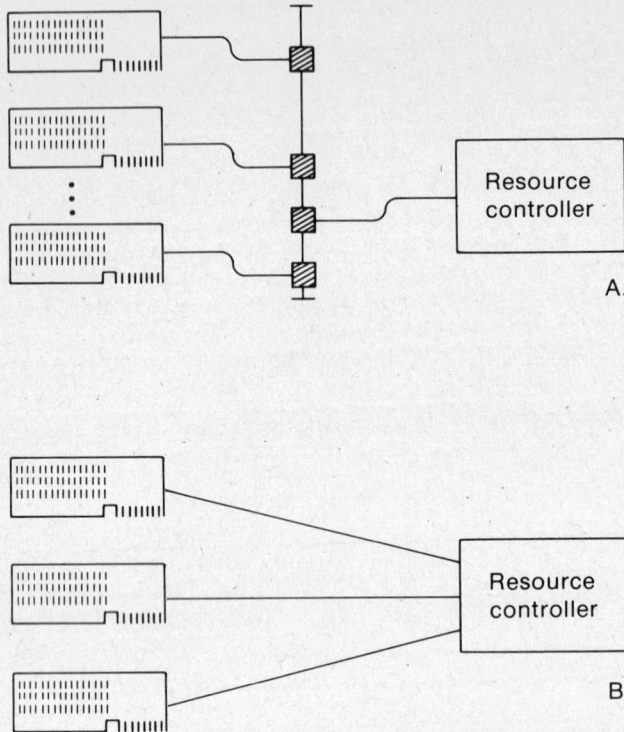

Figure 9-10. Regardless of the specifics of the technology, all networks are constructed by connecting your PC to a cable using a special network interface card in one of the expansion slots. This card takes care of basic data transfer and error checking and makes sure that data addressed to your workstation gets there.

A resource controller is also shown connected to the bus, and it may or may not use the same kind of connector. Depending upon the lengths of the cables and the bus, extra hardware might be required to amplify the signals between one node and another.

Figure 9-10b shows a *star* configuration, in which the resource controller is at the center of the network. Again, the individual workstations would have network interface cards; this time the cables run to the resource controller. Either a star network or a bus network could be extended to hierarchy, as we saw in Figure 9-9. In that case, different cabling or amplifiers might be necessary to connect the subnetworks.

Every vendor's network system will have its own constraints on the lengths of cables and number of connectors. For instance, with the 3Com Ethernet system for the PC, the maximum distance between any two computers is 2,500 meters, and there could be no more than 1,000 computers in the entire network.

What Is the Network Made of?

There are a number of competing technologies in the local area network world today, and we should review them briefly. Figure 9-11 shows some of the possibilities.

For reference, the table includes RS-232 cables (sometimes called *twisted pairs*), like those used between a PC and a modem or printer. Twisted pairs are used for local data communication at times, but there are significant limitations in terms of speed and cable length. Even though RS-232 theoretically goes up to 19,200 bits per second, with the electrical problems inherent in, say, a 100 foot cable, 1,200 would be more realistic. But even 19,200 is far too slow for many of the functions we have been speaking of in this chapter.

Perhaps you have read of *broadband* and *baseband* networks. These terms refer to the way in which data are encoded for transmission over the network, but for us the fundamental differences are the rate at which data move through the network and the number of simultaneous transmissions or *channels* possible. Baseband networks are slower, single channel affairs, but they are cheaper, and at least for now much more common. Broadband proponents want a multimedia office, with video, voice, facsimile, and data all transmitted simultaneously over the same network.

Baseband networks are for digitial data only; however, with the proper

Media/Device	Typical Transfer Rate (bits per second)
(RS-232)	1,200
PBX	56,000
Baseband	1-10 million
Broadband	400-500 million
Optical	3 billion

Floppy disk	250,000
Hard disk	5 million

Figure 9-11. There are a number of basic interconnection options for local networks, and their data transfer speeds are shown in this table. The RS—232 option is too slow for many of the applications we have been discussing in this chapter, and optical connections are fairly far in the future. Nearly all local networks available for your PC at this time are baseband systems in the 1 million to 10 million bit per second range. For purposes of comparison, the speeds at which data are transferred between your PC and its disks are shown. As you see, transferring a file from a shared disk on the network might be about as fast as reading it in from your own hard disk.

hardware and software, this could include digitized voice and even *slow scan video*, in which just a few frames are sent each second, and facsimile transmission. Digitized voice is in fact starting to become fairly common. A device called a *Codec* (coder/decoder) is used to convert the sound of your voice to digital data and back again. It is like a digital tape recorder. Instead of recording your voice on tape, it is recorded in computer memory. Once encoded, a message can be saved on disk for future replay. (Voice recording is also discussed in Chapter 3.)

If digitizing your voice requires, say, 1,500 bytes of memory per second, a 30 second phone message would require 45,000 bytes of disk storage. Such messages can be sent over baseband networks. The same goes for slow scan video and facsimile transmission.

However, don't go out this afternoon looking for a baseband network for your data, voice, and slow scan video communication. Today's products are strictly for data communication and will remain so until PCs start coming with built-in telephones and Codecs. A few personal computer companies are offering these as options today, but IBM isn't one of them.

Baseband or broadband networks require stringing some extra cables around the building. Can you think of an alternative that wouldn't? If there is a phone system already installed in your building, couldn't the phone wires be used for data communication? Couldn't connections between PCs be made through the in-house switchboard or as they are called these days the PBX (private branch exchange) or the CBX (computerized branch exchange)? The answer is "yes, but."

What happens if you are at your desk in a large building and want to use your PC for remote communication over the phone lines? The first step in making a connection would be to dial 9 to get an outside line, then call the remote computer. Obviously, your data connection would be made through the in-house PBX. There is no reason why you couldn't establish a data connection to a local computer in the same manner.

That is the "yes" part; now for the "but." Although a lot of people predict a rosy future for PBX-based data communication, the data rates are quite limited compared to even the slowest baseband networks. To make matters worse, if a line is tied up by your computer, you cannot be speaking over it, which is presumably why the PBX was installed in the first place. However, if your data loads are small, the PBX might be a candidate for your local network. It is also worth noting that IBM is a major investor in ROLM corporation, a major PBX manufacturer, so they may very well have some PBX-based products waiting in the wings for the PC.

Telephone companies in the U.S. and abroad are beginning to use optical fibers in place of copper within and between cities, but they have not yet found their way into local area data communications. Today, there are no optical networks for your PC, but at least one minicomputer company offers an optical link between their CPU and a high speed terminal. Optical communication has left the laboratory, manufacturing costs are dropping, and standards are developing. I would not be surprised if optical networks were available for the PC fairly soon.

To put these communication rates in perspective, Figure 9-11 lists the rates at which information is transferred between a PC and its disk. At the present time, almost all local networks available for the PC are baseband networks, with transfer rates in the same ballpark as those of a hard disk.

Moving Data Through the Network

What actually happens when one node transmits something to another? Recall that synchronous data are transmitted in blocks or packets (see Figure 9-12). A good deal of electronic "bookkeeping" is needed to send a packet from one node to another. Each packet has a destination address as part of its header. In most systems, the sending node just broadcasts the packet over the network leaving it up to the other nodes to check the address as it "goes by." Only the node that the packet is addressed to reads it; the others ignore it. Once it is received, an error detection checksum is computed, and if everything is okay, the sending node is so informed; otherwise, a request for retransmission is sent.

Sounds simple, but what happens if two nodes try to send a packet at the same time? Various schemes have been worked out to keep that from happening. Just so the terms won't throw you, I will outline the two most common conventions, token passing and CSMA.

The *CSMA* (carrier sense, multiple access) approach works like an old-fashioned party line telephone. When a workstation or resource controller is ready to transmit a packet of information, it "listens" to see if any other computer is already using the network. If the network is free, it will transmit its packet, and if the network is busy, it will wait a while (a random amount of time) then try again.

If you come across *CSMA/CD*, this is just CSMA with the addition of *collision detection*. Collision detection handles cases in which two nodes

Header	Data	Trailer
Address block-length	Fixed or variable length	Checksum

Figure 9-12. Data are sent over the network in blocks or packets. The first part of the packet, the header, contains things like the destination address, the packet length, and codes necessary to synchronize the transmission. The data packets that follow could be either fixed or variable in length, depending upon the system. The trailer would contain a checksum that would be recomputed by the receiving node to check for transmission errors.

For example, with the Ethernet, the header is 14 bytes long, the data field may vary in length from a minimum of 46 to a maximum of 1,500 bytes, and the trailer is four bytes. The minimum length of a block is 64 bytes (14 + 46 + 4), in order to make collision detection possible.

mistakenly start transmitting at the same time because they both checked for a busy signal at the same time. Collisions are detected by having the node "listen" while it is transmitting, to make sure no other station is also on the line. If a data collision is detected, both nodes pause for a random time before trying again.

Token passing is another approach to the same problem. In this case, an imaginary "token" or permission to use the network is passed electronically from one node to the next. The token represents permission to transmit, so if a station has a packet ready to send, it will hold the token and send the packet. Once the receiving station acknowledges that it got the packet, the token is passed on. If there is nothing to transmit, the token is passed on immediately.

As you see, there is a lot of bookkeeping to be done, but as a user, that will all be hidden from you, just as you are unaware of the sparkplugs in your car. In order to enable many vendors to tie their personal computers onto a network, standards are being sought for these bookkeeping and hand-shaking activities.

Standards

Since local area networks appear to be yet another wave of the future, many companies are offering them, and there are many incompatible products. They use different cables, different hardware for connecting cables, and, most important, different software approaches.

The International Standards Organization has taken an important step toward sorting this out, by establishing seven functional "layers" of network architecture. By dividing the problem up this way, standards at a given level become manageable. The lowest level deals with the physical connections between nodes, things like cable lengths and characteristics and connector sizes, so that the network will plug together. As you move up from that level, questions involving things like packet format, addressing, error detection, and collision detection come into focus. At higher levels, issues dealing with the operating system on the PC come up. The highest levels are concerned with the sorts of thing you actually see at your PC, how received data is presented on your video display, how you transfer a file from a central server to your workstation, how to send an electronic mail message, or update a data file, and so forth.

As you might guess, standards are coming along faster at the lower end of the hierarchy than the top. Some have been underwritten by standards organizations, and others are just commercial standards used by more than one vendor. The most important is the Ethernet standard for the lower communication levels.

Ethernet began, as we stated earlier, at Xerox. The first Ethernet connected a cluster of experimental personal computer prototypes, called the Alto. Many of the hardware and software developments that are at the forefront of personal computing and office automation came out of that project, and the Ethernet is one of them. When Xerox made Ethernet a product, they enlisted two other companies, Digital Equipment Corporation and Intel, to join them in publishing a standard for the physical links and protocols for passing data packets around on the network. Since that time, many companies have jumped on the Ethernet bandwagon, and basic communication links may now be established among dissimilar computers with Ethernet interfaces.

Because of this standardization, several companies have begun manufacturing LSI chips that take care of the low level Ethernet connection and communication. This will have the effect of driving the cost per connection of Ethernet nodes down dramatically, say to $100.00 by the mid-1980s.

There are other low level network standards; Datapoint Corporation's ARCNET for example, has been picked up by several manufacturers, but Ethernet is most important today. Whatever IBM does also tends to become a standard in the computer field, and they have not yet come out with a local network system. Many industry crystal ball gazers expect IBM to define its own local network architecture and eventually to offer it with Ethernet as an option. I would not be surprised to see IBM announce a broadband network for the PC either. We shall see.

Ethernet notwithstanding, we are far from being able to plug our PCs into any old office network, the way a telephone can be. Someday, competing brands of personal computer might just plug into a standard network and work just fine, but that is going to take a good long time.

PART THREE
Software and Hardware Selection

Part III, like Part II, is organized by applications, but by now I assume you are familiar with the terms and how the software may be used, have some experience using the software, and are ready to purchase a program and set your final hardware specifications.

Don't be overwhelmed by the number of programs on the market. You won't have time to evaluate all of them, and whichever you get will be useful. If you have been writing and revising handwritten reports or using a pencil and calculator to compute spreadsheets, any word processing or spreadsheet program will be a big help. Furthermore, you will learn from any program you acquire. After two weeks of using a program on real applications, you will have a much better understanding of that application, your requirements, and the strengths and deficiencies of the program than can be gleaned from this or any other book. After using a program for a while, I would recommend rereading the chapters dealing with that application.

Adapt your evaluation effort to your situation. If you will use a program only occasionally, it does not make sense to spend hundreds of hours selecting it. On the other hand, if you are thinking of buying 100 copies and entering into an ongoing business relationship with the vendor, the time would be well spent. As you read these chapters, keep your specific applications in mind, since certain features will be irrelevant and others critical. Also, contact the software vendors, asking for literature, demonstration disks, copies of magazine reviews, and so forth. Appendix E lists vendors you can start with.

Since software choices are more complex than hardware choices, Part III concentrates on software evaluation. However, there are hardware implications for each application, and these are covered at the end of each chapter. Remember, the more hands-on experience you have with your own applications, the better off you will be reading these chapters. As in Part II, the chapters are independent of each other, so, if you wish, you can read Chapter 10 first, then skip directly to your primary application.

CHAPTER TEN
Software Selection:
General Considerations

Someday, personal computers may be fully standardized and packaged. You might just order the Model T from IBM or the phone company, plug it in and turn it on. Whether or not that day ever comes, it is not the way things are now. You have many decisions to make in selecting software for your PC.

Many software questions are specific to the type of software you are looking at. In choosing word processing software, things like justification of text and proportional spacing of characters would be important considerations, but they are unimportant in a discussion of spreadsheet processors.

These application specific issues are discussed in the following chapters, each of which deals with a separate application. This chapter covers software issues that apply to all programs, regardless of the application. Surprisingly enough, software selection begins with you, not the characteristics of the programs (see cartoon).

YOU, YOUR ORGANIZATION, AND YOUR RESOURCES

Know Your Applications

The most important step in selecting a software package is to understand how you will be using it, to know your applications. If you were to ask me a question like "which is the best word processing program for the PC" or "which communication program do you use," I would answer that the best program for me may not be best for you. I use my word processor to write long documents, but you might be interested in mass mailing or correspondence. I communicate with a wide variety of remote computers, but you may be planning to connect to the same one all the time.

SOFTWARE SELECTION: QUESTIONS TO ASK

You

1. How will you be using your PC? Pin your applications down in as much detail as possible. Write a list of your applications and their specifications.
2. What is your background and what resources are available?
3. What are your goals? Do you see the PC as a mere tool, or are you looking forward to really building some expertise, to "getting into it"?
4. How large is your organization, who will be using the programs, and how many copies of each program will you buy?
5. Where can you "test drive" programs? Where can you get references and others' opinions?

The Program

1. How hard will the program be to install, and will you need help?
2. How difficult will it be to learn to use the program? Although no one likes something that is tough to learn, you won't mind spending the time if you plan to use it for years to come; however, you may begrudge the time if you will only be a casual user or if there is a lot of turnover in your organization.
3. Is the screen layout clear and consistent? Can you easily distinguish status and program control information from your data?
4. Is the program controlled primarily by commands or menus? Menus tend to be preferred by beginners and casual users. Are the prompts and menu choices clear and appropriate for the person who will be using the program?
5. Is it possible to construct macro commands, combining several built-in commands into an automatically executed sequence? Macros are helpful if a program will be used regularly as part of a data processing or reporting system.
6. Is context dependent help available? Is it more helpful than confusing?
7. Are defaults used to simplify program operation for standard situations? If so, can they be easily overridden (temporarily or permanently) when necessary?
8. Are the manual and reference materials clear and well organized, and do they show care? Remember, they must serve as both tutorial and reference documents.
9. Are there provisions for recovery from machine and operator errors? Does the program use warnings and other messages to protect you from yourself? Make mistakes on purpose and see what happens.
10. Can the program be copied?
11. Is the program compatible with your hardware and operating system? Remember that there are several operating systems and several versions of each. Peripherals, particularly printers and hard disks, can cause problems as well.
12. Can the operating system commands be invoked from within the program?

13. Are data files produced by the program compatible with other software that might want to read or write them?
14. What language was the program written in, and is the source program available?
15. Is auxiliary software needed to run the program?
16. Is the program efficient in terms of speed, memory, and disk requirements?

The Company

1. Does the software company have a well articulated plan for enhancement of its present products and integrating them with new ones? What sort of software does it plan to offer for the personal computers that will be around in five years?
2. Does the company allocate significant resources to user support?
3. How is the rest of the "iceberg"? Has the company's software been popular enough to attract an active user community? Are there publications, auxiliary programs, and so forth devoted to its products?

Software selection is the complicated part of configuring your PC. These are general questions that should be raised in choosing any software package, regardless of the application. Each of them is discussed in this chapter. The following chapters raise questions that are specific to particular applications.

The better you understand your applications and think through the sorts of reports and documents you need to produce, the better your software choice will be. Even if you plan to work with a consultant or have other help, you will save your time and the consultant's by preparing yourself.

This and the other points in this chapter refer to reading this book as well as selecting software. You will get more out of the book if you stop reading for a while and think through your PC applications. List them, describe each, and think about their relative importance. Is one of them sufficiently important to justify a personal computer all by itself? Which application will you computerize first? How much time will you spend every day on each of them? When you begin looking at actual programs, you should have concrete examples of your usage in mind so that you can guide tests and demonstrations. Finally, be sure to think about the future. How will your applications change over the next two or three years?

Know Your Capabilities and Resources

Your software should match your background and interest in learning. If you are a beginner, a relatively simple, though less powerful package might be best. Distinguish between the technical background necessary to set up a program for use and the background needed to operate it once it is installed. For example, a complex communication program might be difficult to

SOFTWARE SELECTION
STARTS WITH YOU!

configure for the remote systems that you plan to use, but easy to operate once it is set up.

Even if you are a beginner, a consultant, someone in your corporate data processing department, the technical staff at a computer store, or a member of a local PC user's club may be able to help you. In choosing software you will be able to visit stores for demonstrations, go to trade shows, read magazine reviews, and so forth. Consider all of your resources. You might list them before reading on.

Know Your Degree of Involvement

How much do you want to learn about computers? Do you see yourself using them as a mere tool with no interest in learning about computers per se, or are you really curious to get deeper into things? In the latter case, you will be willing to put out the effort to learn to use more powerful, though complicated application programs. It might turn out that you end up buying a second program after using your original choice for a while, discovering its limitations, and building your skills and confidence.

Will your usage be peripheral to your profession, or will the PC play a central role in your work? Are you thinking of using it once a month to prepare a sales report or department budget or will you be using it daily in writing memos, developing plans, communicating with colleagues, and keeping track of your personal and company data files? In the former case, you will settle for simple, easily learned software that can do your job; whereas in the latter case, you will want relatively comprehensive software, even if it takes more effort to learn. Ask yourself how many hours per day you expect to be using your PC and how much time you have for learning.

Don't underestimate the commitment you are making. Even if you see your PC as peripheral and plan to use it infrequently, you have some learning to do. Plan to spend time training with, reading about, and experimenting with whatever programs you obtain. By the way, don't be surprised if you get involved with your PC and end up spending more time than you thought you would. Computer widows are as common as Monday Night Football widows these days.

Large Organizations

Are you buying one copy of a program for your own use or 1,000 copies for use by every middle manager in your corporation? In the latter case, you are obviously making a much more important decision and will want to spend time and money investigating alternatives. Perhaps you will want a consultant to help with the selection. In keeping with the theme of knowing your needs, spend more time with the 1,000 people who will be using the software than you do with potential vendors. Their attitudes and desires should guide the selection.

The business parameters also change if you are making a large purchase. Most obviously, you will get a substantial discount. All sorts of arrangements, including licenses to make unlimited copies of a program and its documentation, have been worked out between software vendors and large customers. Don't forget that software often filters through two middle men, a distributor and store, before reaching the end user.

If you are a very large customer, go to the source for a quantity purchase. Your contract should cover software maintenance and updates; what happens when errors are discovered and enhancements are made to the program? You should be entitled to updates, if necessary, when new versions of the operating system come out. Who is responsible for reproducing and distributing new versions of the program? You might also negotiate for other special services such as training, ongoing access to a support person for consultation and assistance, or modifications to the program to better adapt it to your organization or hardware.

You will not simply be negotiating for the right to so many copies of the program; you will be entering into a long term business arrangement. By making a commitment to a vendor, you will to some extent have standardized on their products. People in your organization will learn to use the program, arrangements will be made for training classes and materials, hardware decisions will be made, and procedures will be established around the software. It will be difficult and costly to change, so look at the vendor carefully.

If you are a major customer, you may be able to be briefed on the vendor's future plans and become a test site for (and hence a limited codesigner of) its future products. As in any other business relationship, you should feel good working with the people.

Get Hands-On Experience

Once you know how you will be using programs, try a few out. You might do this at a computer store, your corporate data processing department, or a friend's home. If you are considering a quantity purchase, you can probably get an evaluation copy of a program. If possible, see demonstrations that are tailored to your plans. If you will be using a data management program to keep track of your clients, try it out using some real client data. Don't test it with just a few records; test it with as many as you plan to have. See the program do what you will use it for, not what a salesman wants you to see. The following chapters suggest specific tests and questions to ask in trying the various types of software.

Don't try only one program, try a few. If you have been preparing pro forma accounting statements with a pencil and hand calculator, the first spreadsheet program you see will seem terrific, but they are not all the same. You need some perspective.

Of course, you have to balance the amount of effort you put into evaluating programs against the payoff. If word processing is a secondary application, you should not spend weeks testing every program on the market. Instead, you might try one out to gain perspective, read some magazine reviews, and look over a few vendors' sales literature. At that point, test the one or two that seem best and pick one. If you stick to well known programs from reputable companies, you won't get a terrible program, even if you don't get the "best." Appendix E lists some of those well known programs from reputable companies, programs that are serious contenders. It would be nice if we could simply tell you which program is best for each application and be done with it, but of course the question is more complex than that. Use Appendix E as a starting point.

THE PROGRAM

The most important steps in selecting software have to do with understanding your needs and resources, but there are questions to ask about a program as well.

How Difficult Is Installing the Program?

Some programs come ready to use. You take them out of the package, put the disk in drive A, turn the power on, and begin using the software. In most cases, however, you will need to do a little more, making a backup copy of the *distribution disk*, which is then put away in a safe place (see Figure 10-1).

These steps are easy, but sometimes installing a program requires more work. It might be necessary to go through a step in which you "tell" the program about your hardware, for instance your printer. If you have a relatively common printer, answering a single question may suffice to initialize the software for it, but less common printers may be more complicated. Getting a program running with a hard disk may also be tricky. If you are using data communication, some initialization will be necessary to set some parameters. If you like a program, but have some

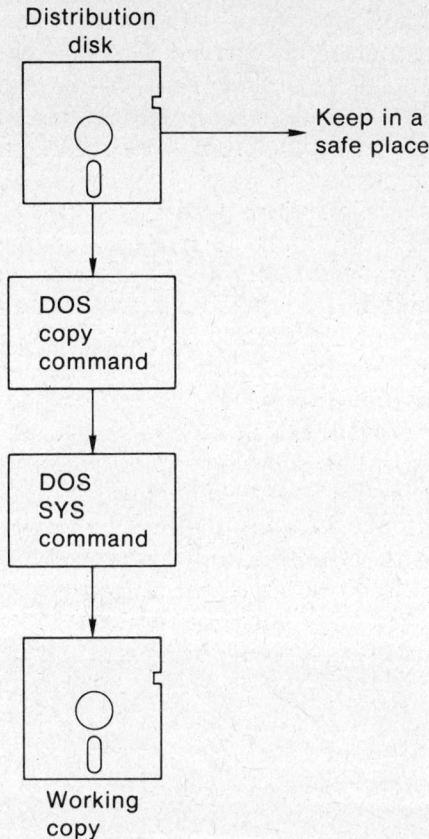

Figure 10-1. Making a backup copy is simple. After using the DOS FORMAT command to prepare a new disk, the distribution disk is copied to it using the DOS COPY command. Note that the distribution disk is write protected, so that it cannot inadvertently be erased. It should be kept in a safe place for a backup, if needed. In some cases, this procedure will be a little different, but it is always simple and is explained in the instructions. In some cases, the software vendor modifies the program so that only one backup copy can be created, in order to make unauthorized duplication more difficult.

doubts about your ability to set it up to operate in your environment, line up some help (ideally, from your dealer, before paying).

Ease of Learning

Once the program is operating, you will have to learn the ins and outs of using it. But don't worry. There is no doubt in my mind that anyone reading this book would be able to learn to use any of the programs we are discussing. The question is how long will it take, and once learned, will you be using it often enough that you don't forget how to use it?

Remember that it may not be necessary to learn all of it at first. Jack McGrath, editor of a newsletter on VisiCalc, estimates that you learn 80% of what the program can do in the first four to five hours and 15% in the next four to five weeks; you may never learn the rest. The word processing program I am using to write this book has commands to prepare form letters for mass mailing, but I have never bothered to learn to use them. It also has an integral spelling corrector, which I learned to use once, decided it was not very good, and have now forgotten.

Be skeptical of programs that claim to be so easy to learn that you won't even have to read the manual. There is no such thing as a free lunch. One way to make a program easy to learn is to be sure that it is not capable of doing much. A word processor with only ten editing commands would be much easier to learn than one with fifty, but it might not be very useful.

What you want is a program designed so that it is easy to learn to do simple, commonly done things. However, it should still be possible to do more complex things, even if it is more difficult to learn to do them. In other words, it should be simple to do simple things and possible to do complex things. For instance, your communication software should make it quick and easy to connect to a remote time-sharing service and send someone a short electronic note, but you may be willing to put up with some complexity in setting up the system for something a little trickier, like sending or receiving electronic mail at night, without your having to be there to operate it.

Screen Layouts

If two programs have roughly the same capability, one may still be easier to learn than the other. If you watch a demonstration and the screen appears cluttered and poorly organized and the program converses in computer jargon, plan on extra learning time.

A common way to avoid confusing the operator is to set aside a portion of the display as an interaction area or *interaction window* (see Figure 10-2). The window might be the top few lines of the display, at the bottom, off to the side, or even in the middle. In some programs, you can control the size and placement of the interaction window, perhaps shrinking it or eliminating it once you become an expert. Pull-down windows are a variation on this theme. When you need temporary explanations, they unfurl like window shades on the screen, and roll back up when you have read their contents. With one program, Wordstar, the interaction window appears automatically when you pause in the middle of a command, shows you your options, then disappears when you make your selection.

An interaction window may be used to show the status of the program or system, to give you feedback if you make a mistake, or to let you see your operating options. Status information might be the time of day or the date, the name of the document you are working on with your word processor, or the amount of memory remaining in your spreadsheet program. When you make an error, it should be explained in the interaction window. Even if you

```
Interaction window


        Data area
```

```


        Data area



    Interaction window
```

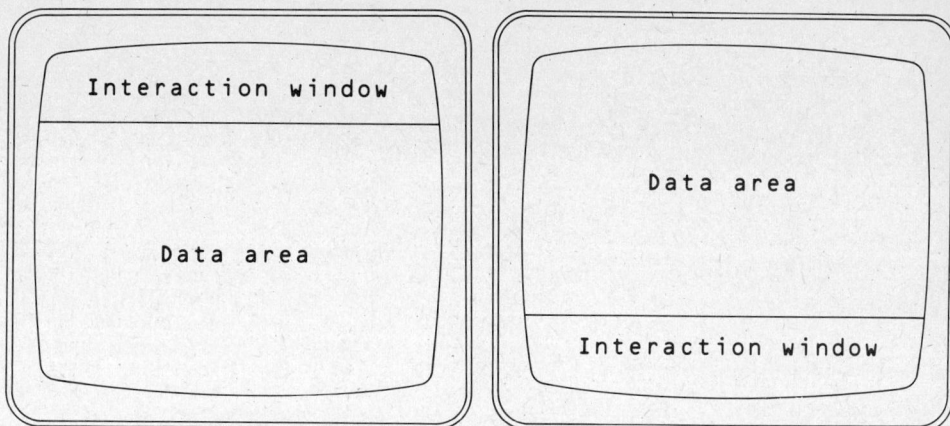

Figure 10-2. Programs often reserve a portion of the display as an interaction area or window. This window can be used to show status information (for instance the time of day or amount of memory remaining free), to give an explanation if you make a mistake, or for inputting commands and selecting options. In this example, the top lines of the display are used for the interaction window, but it might be at the bottom, off to one side, or even movable at your discretion. In some cases, you can eliminate it or reduce its size once you have learned the program and no longer need it.

are a computer expert, you will appreciate a program that gives clear, jargon-free error explanations. A third use of the interaction window is to let you tell the computer what you want it to do next, to issue *commands*.

What Next? Commands, Menus, and Function Keys

Figure 10-3 illustrates several alternative command styles. The top two examples use *menus* to show your options. In the first, both the command and its explanation are shown in the menu. You would choose a command either by typing the first letter of its name (e.g., "L" for "load") or by pointing to it with the cursor and then hitting the "enter" key. The second example is similar but uses a smaller interaction window, since only one command explanation is shown at a time. The smaller the interaction window the more space there is on the screen for the data you are working on, perhaps a spreadsheet or letter you are writing.

In the third example of Figure 10-3, no menu is shown. In that case, you would have memorized the available commands and would simply key in your selection. This mode of control is sometimes referred to as *command-oriented* as opposed to *menu-oriented*. If you are using the cursor control keys to point to menu entries, you will find that command-oriented systems are harder to learn to use, but faster to operate once you are trained. If your PC has a mouse for pointing, menu selection can be sped up.

It might seem as though memorizing all these command choices would be

A.
```
LOAD FILE FROM DISK
SAVE FILE ON DISK
ERASE FILE FROM DISK
RENAME FILE
COPY FILE TO ANOTHER DISK
DISPLAY NAMES OF ALL FILES ON DISK
```

B.
```
LOAD SAVE ERASE RENAME COPY DISPLAY
TRANSFER INFORMATION IN MEMORY TO DISK
```

C.
```
READY (L,S,E,R,C,D)
```

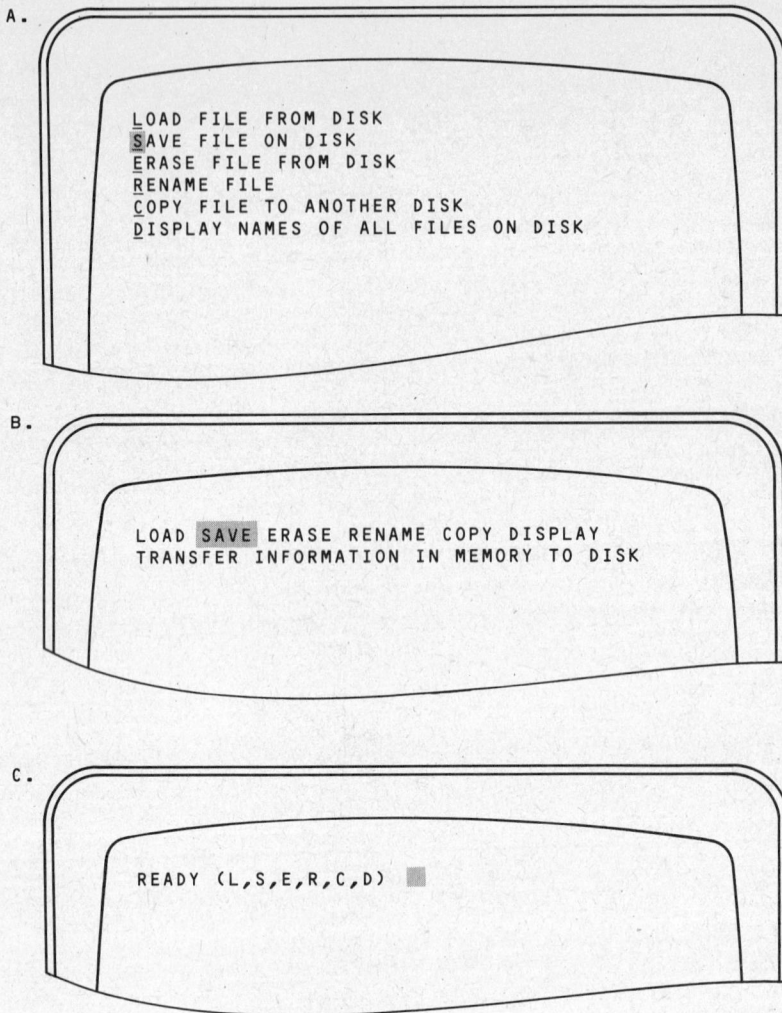

Figure 10-3. This figure illustrates three command style alternatives. In example A, a menu of command choices and their explanations are displayed. You would select one either by typing its first letter or by pointing to it with the cursor and hitting the ENTER key. Example B is also menu oriented, but in order to reduce the size of the interaction window, one line is used for the command names and one for their explanations. As the cursor is moved from one command to the next, the explanation changes.

Example C illustrates a command-driven approach, rather than a menu. It is assumed that you have memorized the options at a particular point, so you just key in the appropriate code. Cryptic programs might not even present the prompt ("L,S,E,R,C,D"). Once you have learned a command-driven program, you will be able to operate it rapidly, but it will be harder to learn than a menu-oriented program and you will forget the commands if you don't use it fairly frequently. Having a pointing device such as a mouse may cut the speed advantage of a command-driven program by speeding up menu selection.

very difficult, but it isn't. If you use a program regularly, the commands become second nature with surprising ease. On the other hand, if you expect to use it infrequently or if it will be used by relatively untrained (or insecure) people, the menu-oriented approach is better. In the latter cases, look for self-explanatory choices, with understandable English explanations and prompts.

Command selection may also be made using the soft function keys on the left side of the PC keyboard. Since the meanings of these keys vary from program to program, you may have some problem memorizing their functions. To help with this problem, the program might explain the function key meanings in an interaction window, or might come with a template with the meanings printed on it (see Figure 10-4).

Macro Commands

Many programs can be customized by allowing the user to string together several commands to form *macro* (long or large) commands or instructions. When the macro was *evoked*, the sequence of commands would be executed

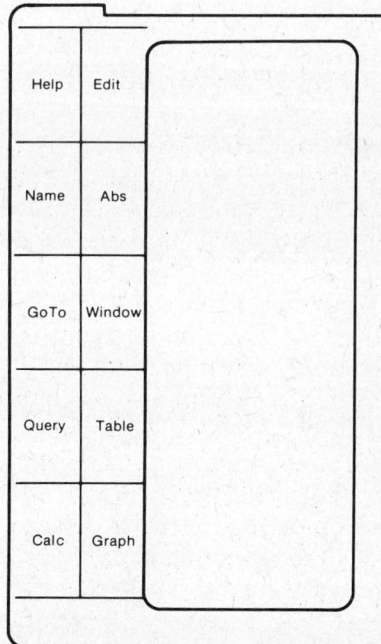

Figure 10-4. A template may be used to remind the operator how the soft function keys are being used by a particular program. The alternative is to memorize the key meanings or to display them in an interaction window on the screen.

automatically. In this manner, it is possible to extend the basic program to define new commands that are tailored to your application.

Macros can be a little tricky to set up, but they can save time and simplify operation for someone who is a beginning computer user. For instance, a macro command might be defined to execute the series of commands necessary to initialize a communication program for use with a certain remote system. When you wanted to use that remote system, you would evoke only the single macro and would not have to think about the constituent commands. A beginner would not even have to know what they were.

Once defined, evoking a macro should be the same as evoking any other command. If the program uses menus, then the macro should become a new menu choice, if it uses function keys, then the macro should be assigned a function key, and so forth. The operator should not experience any difference between macros and built-in commands.

Difficulty in setting macros up is less important than difficulty in using them, because you go through the setup process only once. Some skill will be required, and you may find defining macros confusing at first, particularly if you are not familiar with the program. But once you learn to use the built-in commands, you will begin to see how to put them together to form macros. You may be able to construct them by yourself, or you may wish to get a few hours' help from a programmer, but in either case no special skill will be necessary to use them once they are set up.

Program Modes

If a program offers many options, there will be too many commands for a simple menu. In that case, the commands may be arranged hierarchically. Figure 10-5 shows a hypothetical command hierarchy for word processing. When a selection is made at the top level, the program shifts to the next level or *mode* where a new set of command choices becomes available. The example of Figure 10-5 shows a two level hierarchy, with five different modes, but some programs may have many more levels and modes.

Programs with multiple command modes can be confusing and difficult to learn if they are not carefully designed. It is easy to become lost if the program does not let you know which mode you are in. It can get even more confusing if the program allows you to move horizontally in the command hierarchy, as in the case of the dotted line in Figure 10-5. Look for a program in which moving from one mode to another is always done in a consistent manner, perhaps using one of the function keys to move up in the hierarchy.

Don't worry if this seems confusing. If the program is well designed, it won't take long to learn how to navigate from one mode to another. As an example, the command hierarchy in the 1-2-3 program, from Lotus Software, goes down five levels at some points, but is easily learned. Making a reference diagram like Figure 10-5 will also help you while learning a program.

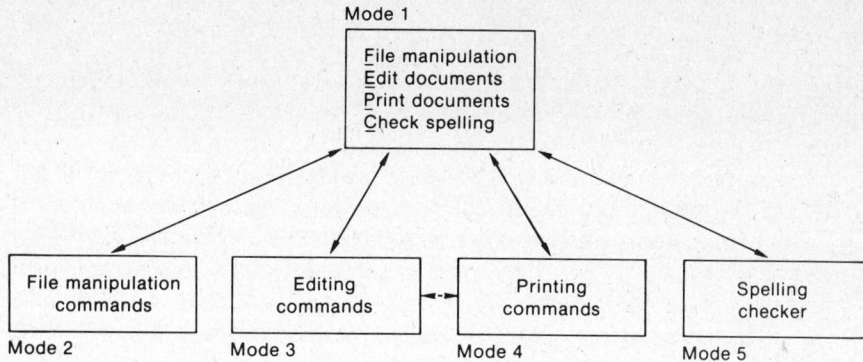

Figure 10-5. If a program is fairly complex and there are many commands, they may be broken up into related groups and organized hierarchically. Here we see a two level hierarchy with five groups of commands or modes. Some programs may allow you only to move up and down in the hierarchy (along the solid lines), whereas with others you can move horizontally (dotted line). You should look for a program that makes it easy to know where you are in the command hierarchy and is consistent in the manner of moving from one mode to another.

You may encounter one other variation on this theme. The program might automatically switch modes, depending upon the position of the cursor. For instance, if the cursor is pointing at a spreadsheet on the screen, the spreadsheet commands are available, and if it is pointing to text the text editing commands are available.

Help Screens

If a short command explanation is insufficient, some programs use *help screens* to show your options. These screens of explanatory text appear when requested (probably by hitting a certain function key). Since they do not appear unless you ask for them, they will not slow an expert user down. Instead of confining the explanation to a small window, the entire display, or at least a large, temporary window, is used for the help. When you finished reading the explanation, you would leave the help system and the normal operating display would reappear.

Help screens are something like having the program manual on disk, ready to be read whenever a question arises. In fact, they often refer you back to the manual page on the same topic. In some cases, you must select the help topic from a menu, but the better programs automatically call up explanations for the commands that are relevant to what you are doing when you request help. As an example of this *context-dependent help*, if you were trying to sort records in a data management system when you requested help, the explanation of sorting would be displayed. In addition to tutorial help, you should be able to get very specific information, for instance explanations of errors and when they occur, or an augmented menu of command choices at a given spot.

Although it is nearly mandatory for a software developer to include some sort of help system with software these days, it may not always be helpful. Be a little skeptical in deciding whether the help facility in a particular program will help or confuse you. I often find help screens most useful for refreshing my memory when I have not used a program for some time, and not as helpful as a general tutorial. The best way to learn to use a program is to have someone show you how or to read about it in a book or manual. Also, be aware that the help text may consume a significant amount of disk space, so once you are thoroughly familiar with a program, you might want to erase the help files.

Defaults

Generality increases complexity and learning time. If your word processing program always puts page numbers in the upper left corner, you don't have to learn anything about how to make choices. However, if it is flexible enough to put page numbers on the bottom, in the center, on alternate corners depending upon whether it is an odd or even page, to print the page number in various formats, and so forth, you need to learn how to control it.

Defaults are a commonly used technique for hiding this sort of complexity. In the page numbering example, you would specify that your favorite format, perhaps putting the number in the center at the bottom, be used by default if no page numbering command were given. You would have to give a command only when you wanted to deviate from that format. A program that makes clever use of defaults can be simple to operate in most situations without sacrificing flexibility.

Look for a lot of defaults. It should be easy to override them temporarily (during a given session) or to change their values on the program disk. In addition to being able to change defaults, be sure it is possible to see what their current settings are. This will help you when setting default values by trial and error.

Manuals, Reference Cards, and Tutorial Programs

Look carefully at the documentation that comes with a program. The quality and style of the program manual can give a clue as to the standards of the software company, and it should be a very useful tutorial and reference document.

Some software vendors downplay written documentation since they feel that users of their programs won't go to the trouble of reading a manual. I may be old fashioned, but I find manuals very helpful. Manuals serve first as teaching aids and later as references. In fact, one thing to look for is a manual with separate tutorial and reference sections.

As a teaching aid, it should be well organized, giving an overview of the purpose and operation of the program before launching into details on its operation. It should also show you how to install the program and set defaults. Beware of manuals that are organized alphabetically, rather than logically; they may be great for references, but are terrible for learning. Look for clear illustrations and lots of examples. If the language is too technical for you, the manual will be of no value. The programs we are talking about are not highly technical, and if you cannot understand the manual, that means the author is insensitive, not that the subject is above your head.

Some software comes with tutorial programs and data files designed to teach you to use the program, with your PC acting as a programmed teaching machine. These can be valuable if they are well done. The Select and Volkswriter word processing programs and 1-2-3 and Multiplan spreadsheet processors do a good job with tutorial programs. But even in these cases, they complement, but do not replace, the manual.

For reference purposes, look at the index and appendices. Try finding a few terms in the index, using names that seem reasonable to you. Look for appendices explaining error conditions and program options. If the program has many command modes, look for a diagram showing the command hierarchy. Fold-out reference cards are particularly useful. No matter how long I have used a word processing program, I keep the reference card handy.

Be skeptical of a program with poor documentation, and don't believe the salesman that tells you it isn't important. If you really like a program, but not the manual, check to see if someone has written a book on it. For instance, there are many good books available on the Wordstar word processor. In the case of a popular package, there may also be tutorial programs on the market to help you learn to use it.

Handling Errors

Rest assured, you will make mistakes; everyone does. You might forget to close the door after inserting a disk in a drive or fail to remove the write-protect tab from a disk. Perhaps you will try to print a report without first turning the printer on, or the printer will run out of paper in the middle of a job. What happens if part of a disk goes bad? Even if you never make mistakes, things will go awry at times. Can the rest of the file be read?

These things sound silly, but some programs cannot even recover from simple errors. I am writing this book with a word processing program that cannot recover if I forget to close the door on the disk drive. Other problems can cause more trouble. What if you type a long manuscript into your word processor, only to find the disk is full when you give the command to save it? If your program is not able to recover from such errors, for instance by letting you insert a new disk or erase some unwanted files from the old one, you will lose your work.

When testing a program, try to make it fail. Leave the drive door open and the printer off on purpose. See what happens. Try overflowing memory, hanging up the phone in the middle of a communication session, saving a file on a full disk. A good program will let you recover from any of these conditions.

The program should also protect you from yourself. One technique is asking for *confirmation* of drastic commands. For instance, the DOS operating system will not let you erase all of the files on a disk without asking if you are certain that you mean to do so. In addition to having you confirm drastic actions, the program commands should be designed with some sensitivity to inadvertent errors; you do not want a program in which function key 4 means "edit text" in one mode and "delete file" in another, and reaching the control key combination for deleting a paragraph or page should actually be an awkward movement, forcing you to look at the keyboard for a second. This sort of consideration is less important with menu-oriented programs.

Regardless of how hard a program tries to protect you from yourself, it will not always succeed. When it doesn't, you will be thankful if the program has an *undo* command, which reverses the last thing you did no matter what it was. I'll bet you can't find an experienced computer user who has never erased a file accidentally or deleted a section of a word processing document when he or she meant to move it. An undo command will save you in that situation.

Another way in which a program can protect you from yourself is by automatically making backup copies whenever a file is changed. For instance, the word processor I am using to write this chapter automatically keeps the old version on disk when I revise the draft. If something goes wrong while the revised chapter is being written from memory to the disk, or the file becomes unreadable, I can fall back to the last version, even though my revision will have been lost.

Copy Protection

In discussing initial program setup, the first step was to copy the program onto a working disk, saving the original for backup. But you should know that some software companies *copy protect* their programs. In order to protect themselves against people who would make copies for friends or even for resale, they distribute their programs on disks that cannot be copied or can be copied only once. It is easy to understand why they do this, but unfortunately there are legitimate reasons for copying a program you have purchased.

The most obvious one is backup. What happens if a program disk goes bad after repeated use or someone accidentally leaves it in the sun or spills coffee on it? Some software vendors give you two copies of the program when you buy it or else enable you to make one extra copy, but both might become damaged. If you have two PCs, say one at home and one at the office, you would want to be able to make second copies. (Although that would be a violation of the licensing agreement for many programs.)

Similarly, if several people use the PC at the office, each might want his or her own program disk, perhaps each with different default values. Computer dealers with several demonstration units in their stores have these problems.

Copy-protected software is particularly troublesome for people using a hard disk, a local network, or an electronic disk simulator, since you cannot move the program from its floppy disk, severely cutting its utility. Being able to copy a program is desirable, since it gives you operational flexibility. Find out whether or not it is copy protected.

There are a number of companies that make utility programs designed to get around the copy protection schemes, and in many cases, they are able to copy a copy-protected disk. Using these programs in violation of software licensing agreements is illegal, particularly if you give the copies you make to others. But when used for legitimate purposes, copying utilities are valuable.

Hardware and Operating System Compatibility

There may be compatibility problems in using a program with your hardware or operating system. It might seem as though any program written for the IBM PC would work with your IBM PC, but that isn't always the case. You must know the memory, disk capacity, and number of drives required by a program. Some programs require the Color/ Graphics Display while others can use either it or the Monochrome. If you have bought any non-IBM hardware, there may be problems. A given program may not be compatible with your hard disk or printer.

As we have noted, some programs may be available for one operating system and not the others. Be sure your software is compatible with your operating system. Also, beware of different versions of the same operating system. I have a number of programs that work fine with Version 1 of DOS, but will not work with Version 2. Although there probably will not be any problems, there may be, so be a little paranoid on the issue of compatibility. Make sure your dealer knows which version you will be using, and find out what the software vendor's policy is on compatibility with future versions. They should guarantee compatibility or at least make updates available at a nominal cost.

Access to the Operating System Commands

You should be able to use operating system commands from within an application program. For example, what would happen if you had just received a communication file from a remote computer, and upon trying to save it on disk, you discovered the disk was full? You would need to delete some files from the disk in order to make space. But which file should you delete? To decide that, you would want to display the names of the files on the disk. Displaying file names and deleting a file can be done using the directory display and delete commands in the operating system, as long as you can use them from within the program.

In some cases, the program will allow you to use the operating system commands directly and in others they will be simulated, using commands or a menu that is part of the application program. Regardless of how it's done, look for the ability to perform the operating system functions that were listed in Figure 4-2. At a minimum, you should be able to delete, copy, and examine files and the disk directory from within an application program.

Programming Language and Source Program Availability

If there is a chance that you or someone in your organization might want to modify a program someday, you will want to know what language it was written in and in what form it is available. As we saw in Chapter 4, programs are written in a higher level language and then either compiled (translated) into machine language so they can be executed directly or interpreted instruction by instruction as they are executing.

When you buy application software, you generally get only the object program, the machine-language version. Modifying a machine-language program to a significant extent is a difficult, if not impossible, task. Even if you buy a program that is distributed in its source language, to be interpreted, there are ways of protecting the program (both legally and technically) so that it cannot be read or modified.

What you need in order to modify a program is the right to the source version, so you can change it, then recompile it into a new, modified object program. However, most companies refuse to sell the source versions of their programs, or if they do, the price may be high. If you think you may eventually want to modify a program, check into the availability of the source program before committing yourself. For the major applications we are concerned with in this book, it is unlikely that you will be involved with modification, but for other applications, for instance accounting, it is more likely to become an issue.

Of course, you will want the program to be written in a higher level language that you or someone in your organization knows. If it is written in, say COBOL, and all you know is Pascal or BASIC, you will have to spend some time learning COBOL. The implementation language also affects speed of execution. Generally speaking, a program that has been compiled into machine language will execute much faster than one that is being interpreted as it is executed. But that gets us into the topic of the next section, efficiency.

Efficiency

Efficiency will mean different things in every application, and in some cases there will be tradeoffs between ease of learning and operation, on the one hand, and efficiency on the other. However, all things being equal, you want a program that is efficient in three ways: it should execute rapidly, use little memory, and tie up little space on the disk.

Do not be fooled into thinking that computers are so fast that speed is not important. In a computer store demonstration, using contrived data, any program will seem lightning fast. Even after you get it back to your office, a program might seem speedy, but once you are accustomed to it, you may find it frustratingly slow. There may be significant differences in speed among programs that do much the same thing. Programs written in assembly language are the fastest, those compiled into machine language from a higher level language are second, and interpreted programs are much slower. We will see several examples of speed differences in Part III, but for now remember that, if possible, it is a good idea to time programs using your own data and applications.

As we have seen, the cost of memory is dropping, and software is being written to use more and more. Still, some programs are more efficient than others. Differentiate between minimum and desired memory requirements for a program. Don't buy a word processing program to use on your 64KB PC only to get home and find out that you only have enough memory to write one page memos, or that it slows down to a crawl because of constant delays while transferring program segments and parts of your document between memory and the disk. Again, testing on your application, not a contrived computer store demonstration, will show up problems.

The other side of the coin is that you should find out how much memory a program is capable of addressing. Many of the PC programs on the market were originally written for eight bit computers, then converted. That means that they were designed for computers with 64KB memories. Furthermore, some characteristics of the architecture of the PC CPU, the Intel 8088, make using all of the memory a somewhat tricky proposition. For both of these reasons, a program might have an upper limit on the amount of memory it can use, just ignoring any over that limit. In that case, the only way to exploit the speed advantage that your large memory should give is to use an electronic disk simulator.

Disk requirements may also be a problem. A program that uses disk space inefficiently may force you to add capacity unnecessarily or may slow operations down. This might be a particular problem in file management if you have many records. Again, a computer store demonstration using a sample data file with ten records won't tax the disk capacity of any program, but your application may. By now, I'll bet you have discovered the theme of this section: test speed, memory, and disk performance using your applications.

APPLICATION INTEGRATION

Everyone claims that their application software is "integrated," but what do they mean? Different things. Integration between two application programs should cover two levels: (1) the programs should have similar user interfaces and command structures, so that skills picked up in learning to operate one help with the other, and (2) it should be possible to move data freely between them. In many cases, people claim integration without satisfying these goals. Let's put integration in perspective by considering its varying degrees.

Shared Files

The most common form of software integration is where two programs "communicate" by sharing data files. Let's consider an example, and see where pitfalls might occur. Let's say you have created a budget spreadsheet that you would like to include as part of a larger budget report. Since the spreadsheet was stored on a disk, it might seem as if you could easily include it in the full budget report, using your word processing program to read it (see Figure 10-6). In other words, the spreadsheet program would *export* the file to the word processing program and the word processing program would *import* it. Now, where might we run into problems with this form of shared-file integration?

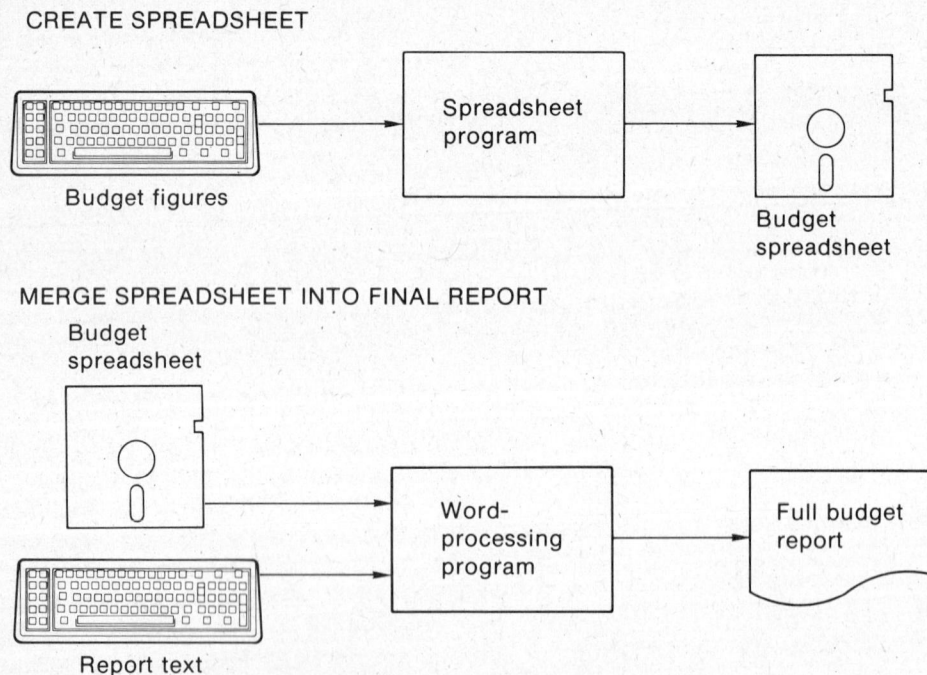

CREATE SPREADSHEET

Budget figures → Spreadsheet program → Budget spreadsheet

MERGE SPREADSHEET INTO FINAL REPORT

Budget spreadsheet

Report text → Word-processing program → Full budget report

Figure 10-6. The most common form of application integration is when two programs communicate through common data files. In this example, the budget spreadsheet is written to the disk, where it may be read by the word processor and incorporated into the full budget report. If you plan to integrate applications in this manner, watch out for incompatibilities in file structure and data format.

Most obvious would be the case in which the word processing and spreadsheet programs ran under different operating systems, for instance DOS and CP/M-86. In that case, the file written by one program could not be read by the other without first using a special file copy program to translate from one disk format and operating system to the other. Although such programs are available, the extra step would slow you down and add operating confusion, particularly if you're a beginner, so they should be relied upon only in exceptional cases.

But even if both application programs share the same operating system, there can be problems. Some programs, particularly file managers, build their own disk file structure, organizing the data within a single, very large conventional file. These programs must provide utility commands for copying their files into the standard operating system format, just as if there were an entirely different operating system.

Even if both programs use the standard operating system file structure, data recording and formatting may be incompatible. For example, a word processing program might put special (non-ASCII) format control characters in a text file or a file management program might encode multiple choice or numeric values in order to save disk space. It doesn't really matter why it might have been done, but you should be on the lookout for incompatibilities in data formats within files; program A will not always be able to make sense of a file written by program B even if it is able to find it on the disk and read it.

In order to get around this sort of incompatibility, application programs often include utility routines that copy the files into a format that can be read by other programs. These might be designed for compatibility with a specific program that is very popular or they might create files in a standard format. One proposed standard that is making some headway as an inter-program data format is the data interchange format (DIF). Again, however, writing a DIF file or running a utility program that "filters" out control characters is an extra step, complicating operations and taking time.

Program Families

The next step up the ladder of levels of integration is a family of programs designed to work together from the start. That means that they create fully compatible data files, avoiding the problem of translating from one format to the other, and their user interfaces are consistent. For instance, the editing commands used to alter text in a word processing document would be the same as those used for altering the contents of record in a data management file, so that if you had learned to use one program, you could easily learn the other. To be compatible in this sense, the programs should present the same interface to the user, including such things as menu styles, command and function key meanings, and even the style and format of manuals, tutorial programs, or help facilities.

A number of companies have developed compatible software families with programs for all of the applications covered in this book. You should give serious thought to picking a single vendor and using their complete family of programs.

Multiple Application Packages

Going a step further, *multiple application* packages do away with the concept of two (or more) separate programs communicating by exporting and importing files. Instead, the user perceives just one program that treats all text, data, and perhaps graphic images in a coherent, homogeneous manner. Everything is seen as being stored in a homogeneous memory and being accessed and operated on by one set of operators (see Figure 10-7). For instance, the entire memory might seem like a large spreadsheet, with a budget in one corner, a graph below it, and a memo to be communicated somewhere else on the sheet. Moving data from, say the budget to the memo, might involve the sort of reformatting we discussed above, but that would be hidden from the user.

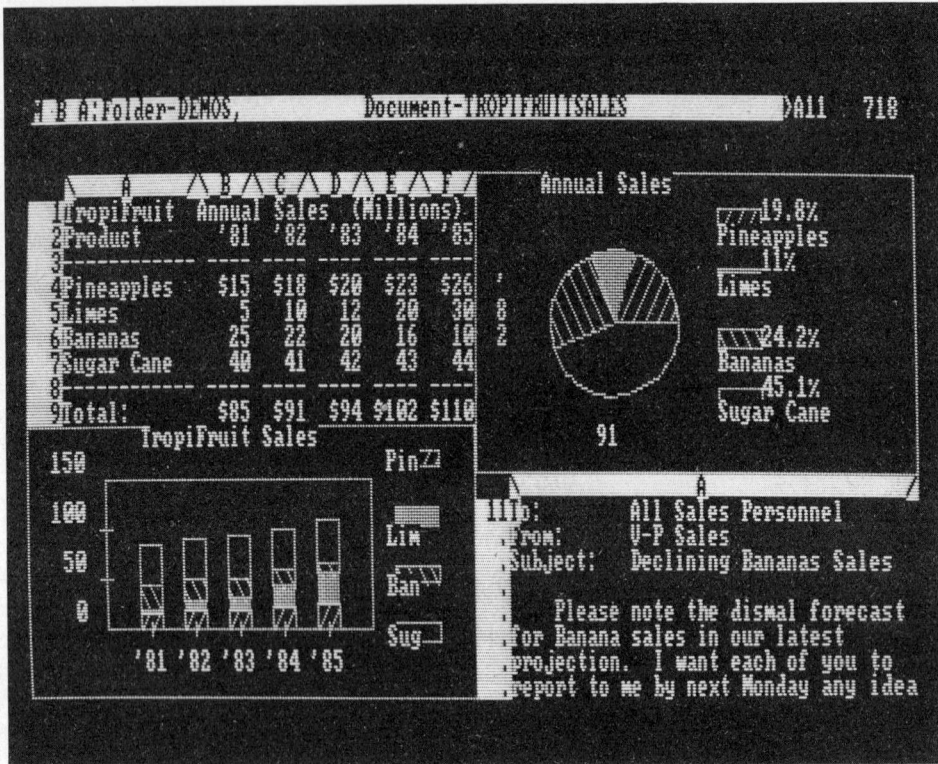

Figure 10-7. The Context MBA program shown here is a multiple application package. The graph, memo, and spreadsheet all appear to the user to be on a single, homogeneous spreadsheet. There is no need to move information from one file to another. (Courtesy of Context Management Systems)

Several of the multiple application packages for the PC combine all of the applications we are concerned with in this book, and for many users the problem of choosing application software may be reduced to choosing one of them. There are compelling reasons to do so. Compatibility between applications is fairly well guaranteed, as is the transfer of training from one application to the next. One of these packages will probably even cost less than the constituent components would if purchased individually. But, of course, there are tradeoffs.

The crux of the problem is that you are confined to what the software vendor decides to offer. If you like the word processing component but are not crazy about the spreadsheet program, you are stuck. Or perhaps there is still another application that you would like to see added to the basic package, perhaps a project scheduling module or even Pacman. Again, you are confined to what the vendor offers; other people's programs won't work within the highly integrated structure.

While multiple application packages are very important today, I would expect to see their role decline in the long run, as operating systems become more powerful. A major advantage of multiple application packages, the common user interface for each application component, will disappear as sophisticated user interface facilities are incorporated into operating systems. If all application programs use the interface provided by the operating system, they will be uniform. The problems of data compatibility are somewhat tougher to handle, but with a multitasking operating system, programs that filter out differences in format can be run automatically as data are moved from one application to another. Finally, each multiple application package has a dominant application, generally the spreadsheet processor, which may be inappropriate to other applications.

Regardless of their long-run prospects, you should certainly consider both program families and multiple application packages. In deciding whether any component is too weak a link, evaluate it as if it were a stand-alone program. If each component is satisfactory, you will be able to eliminate compatibility problems, have only one vendor to deal with, and probably save some money as well.

THE REST OF THE ICEBERG

The Software Company

You should also be aware of the past record and policies of the company you are buying your software from. This is particularly true if you are from a large organization that will be buying large numbers of packages. You want to deal with a company that will be around in the future and will continue to enhance their software and develop new, compatible programs. They should have a well articulated technical direction and philosophy that makes sense to you. If you are a major customer, the software company should be willing to spend some time discussing their plans with you, and you should at least make the effort to become well informed by reading about them in the trade press and working with consultants.

Hopefully, the software vendor also has the resources and desire to support its customers and dealers. For instance, you might ask whether it has a hotline with a toll-free phone number for answering technical and operating questions. Newsletters are another form of communication and some software vendors have electronic mail systems that can be used when you have questions. Find out about new versions. Will you be advised when errors are discovered in the program, and what is the charge for updates? For instance, problems were found in the first versions of the word processing and spreadsheet programs IBM offered with the PC. People who had purchased the spreadsheet program were automatically sent a new copy in the mail and those who had the word processor were given a free update if they brought the old one to a dealer. You can't ask for better support than that; however, it would be unrealistic to expect that level of support for small-quantity purchasers. The distribution costs are simply too high.

The User Community

Ads for programs stress their features: "our spreadsheet has ten functions not found in VisiCalc" or "with our data management system, records can contain 1,024 fields." They often show checklists comparing their product to someone else's. Program features, speeds, and capacities are important, but they are far from the whole story.

When you decided to purchase an IBM computer, you got more than a certain amount of memory, an Intel 8088 CPU, a printer, and some disk storage. You got membership in a community of IBM PC users, which meant that you would be able to use thousands of programs and hardware add-ons for the PC, to read a half dozen or more magazines and hundreds of books about it, to find someone to service your computer in most large cities, to attend PC trade shows where you could see the latest products, to find programmers, hardware technicians, consultants, and friends who could help you with your PC, and so forth. The machine was only the tip of the iceberg, and as IBM understands very well, most people buy computers for the bottom of the iceberg, not the tip.

Software packages are also tips of icebergs (see Figure 10-8). User communities grow up around popular programs, and they become quasi standards. People know how to use them, and other programs are written to be compatible with them.

Let me give a few examples. One of the operating systems available for the PC is CP/M. There is an annual trade show devoted to CP/M, there are dozens of books explaining how to use it and how it is structured internally, there are at least three magazines devoted to CP/M, and there are several directories of software that are compatible with it. The Wordstar word processing program serves as another example. Since it has sold well, there

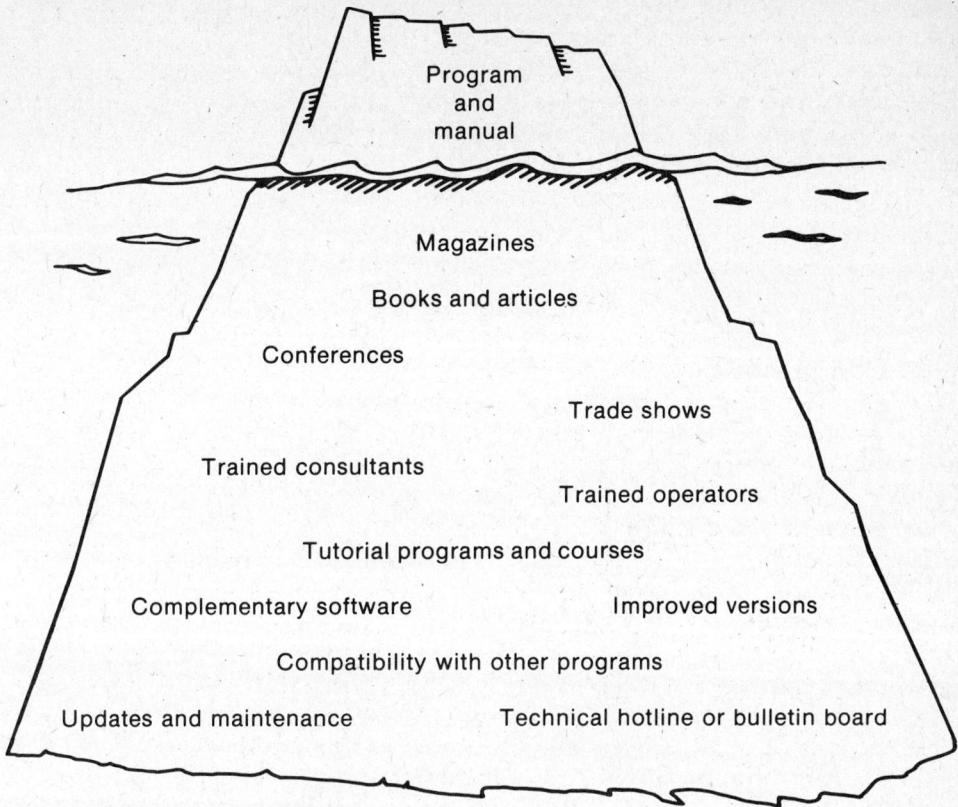

Figure 10-8. Buying an IBM PC makes you a member of a large user community, and so does buying a popular software package. As this "iceberg" shows, you get more than just the disk and manual.

are books and tutorial programs on the market to teach you to use Wordstar, there are reference cards summarizing its operation, and there are auxiliary programs like spelling checkers, thesaurus programs, and index and table of contents generators designed to work with and complement it. Several computer stores and a storefront school near my office offer classes on the VisiCalc spreadsheet program. The school offers classes either at its location or at the customer's site. Prewritten VisiCalc models are available for many applications, and most graphics, file management, and communication programs are compatible with it. Dbase II is a popular data management program, which has encouraged a number of companies to produce utility software to make it easy to use, and many consultants and programmers are familiar with it and can help you in applying it.

These are just examples. Many others, competitors of these programs, could have been cited, but they illustrate the point that there is more to a program than the disk and manual that you get when you buy it. This ancillary material may mean even more to you if you are part of a large organization, in which many people will be using the same program, than if you are an individual user. It will be possible to get training materials and find people to run classes for you. How-to books will often be better than the program manual, and they will certainly be cheaper if you are buying a number of copies.

Free Software

There is no such thing as a free lunch, but there is free software from two sources, the *public domain* and *freeware*. A number of clubs and universities produce and distribute software that is in the public domain. This is done on a volunteer basis, and only a handling fee is charged for public domain software.

Freeware is similar to public domain software, but is generally offered with the hope of returning a profit. Freeware authors send out copies of their programs for the same nominal handling fee, but they suggest that the user submit a modest fee (typically $35) if the program proves useful. They also encourage those receiving the program to copy it for friends, again with the hope that all who find it useful will remit the voluntary fee. A cynic might feel that no one would ever remit the suggested fee, but people offering freeware tell me that they receive a significant number of payments. The program sells itself and the user's conscience does the rest.

What is the catch? The catch is that public domain and freeware programs are sold as is. There is no support, no commitment to fix errors, no one to call for help. In other words, the program is the iceberg; there is nothing below the tip.

Still, in certain circumstances, you might want to take advantage of this software. For instance, let's say that your primary, bread-and-butter PC application is word processing, but you would like to learn something about communication. In that case, you should select a supported, commercial word processing program using the guidelines suggested in Chapter 11. However, you might pick up a public domain or freeware communication program to experiment with. If, after using it for a while, you decide to purchase a supported communication program, you will have a much better idea of what features you need. You might even find that the free program is sufficient for your applications or that communication does not really interest you. Sources of free software are included in the Appendices, along with sources of supported software.

CHAPTER ELEVEN
Word Processing

Open almost any magazine on personal computers and you will find several ads for word processing programs for your PC. But which program is best for you? This chapter covers the questions to ask and tests to try in evaluating a word processing program. We will also look at writing aids like spelling checkers and report formatters. The hardware implications of word processing applications are also covered at the end.

WORD PROCESSING SOFTWARE

While reading this section, keep the general comments of Chapter 10 in mind, particularly the part about considering your needs in evaluating a word processor. It may even turn out that word processing is inappropriate for you. If your typing load consists of letters or other short documents and you seldom make errors or revisions, you are better off with a typewriter. But for almost any other typing application, you will be better off using your PC as a word processor. There are more word processing programs on the market than any other kind of program. That competition makes for good programs, but makes choosing tougher. On the other hand, relax as you evaluate the alternatives; you cannot go too far wrong because any of the better known programs will be a big help.

Basic Editing Speed

Most likely, the majority of your word processing time is spent entering and revising text, so the speed of basic operations such as scrolling, cursor movement, searches for simple patterns, and insertion and deletion is critical. One way to get a handle on editor speed is to create a test document that is, say, 10,000 characters long and try a few experiments.

You won't have to key in all 10,000 characters to create the test document; the word processing program will help. Just key in a few sentences or a paragraph, then use the "block copy" command to duplicate it, leaving you with two paragraphs. Use the "block copy" again, giving four paragraphs, etc. Do this a few times, and you will have a test document and will have gotten a feel for using the program.

Once you have created the test document, use a watch to see how long it takes to perform the following common operations:

Scroll from the beginning to the end, one line at a time.
Scroll from the beginning to the end, one page at a time.
Jump directly from the beginning of the document to the end and back.
Move the cursor 200 characters to the right.
Search through the entire document for a specified word.

If you can't find the time or place for an exact timing, at least form a subjective opinion of the program's speed. Some programs are much faster than others, and speed is an important consideration. A fast program will save you time, and less obviously, it will be easier on your eyes. With slower programs, an inordinate amount of time is spent changing the display, and in my experience, watching the screen during rewriting leads to eyestrain.

Basic Editing Convenience

Convenience, the number and design of simple editing functions, may be more important than speed. Does the cursor always stay on the text instead of going off into the "white" space in the margins? If it does, editing may be a little faster, although perhaps confusing to a beginner. Is word wrap handled properly when you insert or delete text? When you move (or backspace) the cursor beyond the left or right side of a line, it should move to the adjacent line automatically. If it doesn't, that will slow you down. In correcting typos, you make constant use of the simple search for a pattern, but how many keystrokes does it take to give the search command? I know of one program that requires seven keystrokes to start a simple search for a pattern. That is clearly inconvenient.

Table 11-1 lists editing commands that would be used frequently by all word processing users. Make up a table showing the number of keystrokes it takes to issue each of them. You can probably do so using the manual, but again, doing it on the machine will add to your familiarity with the program.

In making these comparisons, remember that not all keystrokes are equal; some commands might require the control key plus another one, whereas others would use a single function key. The most convenient may be a matter of personal taste. The best way to get a handle on convenience is to spend some time using the program. After a half hour you will know where the frustrations are hidden. Make sure your test document is fairly long, since nearly any system will seem quick when working on a single paragraph.

Table 11-1. You will use these basic editing functions in every word processing job. If cursor movement is awkward or a few key commands are missing, it will cost you a lot of time. The simple search commands are used to search for typos when correcting text that has been proofread, filling in the blanks in forms, or making systematic changes. Specifying the characters to search for and initiating the search should be as simple as possible. Revision consists mainly of inserting and deleting text, so that should also be quick. The best reformatting (assuming that the program does on-screen formatting) is automatic, but if it isn't, it should at least be easy.

Move the cursor to the top left of the screen.
Move the cursor to the bottom left of the screen.
Move the cursor to the left of the current line.
Move the cursor to the end of the current line.
Move the cursor to the end of the current screen.
Initiate a simple search for a pattern.
Continue searching for the next matching string.
Delete a character, word, or line.
Delete from the cursor to the end of the current line.
Reformat the entire current paragraph.
Reformat from the cursor to the end of the current paragraph.

Complex Editing Functions

The simple functions are used in everything you do. The more complex functions like block operations and complex searching and replacement are used less frequently, so you may be willing to put up with less convenience in these. Remember the guideline from Chapter 10 that "it should be simple to do simple things and possible to do complex things." Some people, for instance those who write only short, unique letters, will seldom need these features and should put little emphasis on them.

What can the program do? All word processing programs can move and copy blocks, but can the one you're considering make multiple copies, print a block, write it to the disk, or erase it? In searching for patterns, can you specify such things as searching for whole words only and matching and replacing uppercase letters at the start of a sentence properly? Do you work with columnar reports? If so, look for a program that can line up columns of figures, do arithmetic, and move columns without disturbing the rest of the page.

Speed and convenience are also factors here. How many keystrokes are required to mark and copy a block? If you mark a block and then scroll to another part of the text, how difficult is it to find it again or to delete the block markers? Again, test the program.

Document Assembly

A word processor is often used to assemble documents from prewritten, boilerplate material. If you have this sort of application, look at document assembly features such as the ability to include text from master files on the disk.

Nearly all word processors let you read an entire file, but can you read a portion of a file and create menus to guide the operator in selecting paragraphs for insertion? Figure 5-15 showed an example in which it was possible to set up a menu letting the operator select sections of a file for insertion in the document. But with many word processing programs, you would be restricted to reading in entire files, with no ability to generate custom menus like the one in the illustration. In either case, you want a program that is able to read in boilerplate material simply and quickly. In comparing programs, try them out on one of your own document assembly jobs.

Command Structure Consistency

Consistency is also important. If the control key is used to "amplify" one command, for example turning a word delete into a line delete, the control key should be used to amplify all commands. Consistent conventions should also be used in moving from one mode or menu to another, for instance, if function key 10 gets you from the print mode to the main menu, it should also be used to get you from the margin setting mode to the main menu.

In using an editor for a while, you will discover its inconsistencies. Making a diagram showing the various modes and the keys used to move between them will also highlight inconsistencies. Check back to Figure 10-5 for a general example of such a diagram.

Memory Management

Simple systems work only with documents that fit entirely in memory. If you are writing short documents, this will not matter, but with long documents it would be an important restriction.

Assuming that a system can handle documents that are larger than memory, does it read them automatically from the disk or must you give an explicit command to read or write? The former case is conceptually simpler, but probably slower. An expert user might actually prefer a system that does not rewrite automatically, but leaves it under his or her control.

If documents larger than memory are not allowed, the program may still allow you to print several together. For example, each chapter in a book could be a separate, small document, but they could all be printed in a single batch, with consistent page numbering and formatting. This would help, but it would still be awkward to edit. For instance, searches and block operations could take place only within a chapter.

How Large a Document Fits in Memory Without Causing Disk Access?

This question is related to the one above. Even if the system handles oversize documents automatically, it will slow down when disk access is necessary. If you work with large documents, one of your first experiments should be to see how large a document will fit in memory. Then build an oversize file and try a few more scroll timing experiments such as those suggested above. Check to see how long it takes to jump from the start of the document to the end when disk access is involved.

If you like a system, but the document space is too small, it may be possible to increase it by adding memory to the computer, but some programs place a modest upper limit on the size of the document buffer regardless of the amount of memory installed. You may have a 512K system and still find that the document space is limited to, say, 30KB. If you will be writing long documents and need a large buffer area, make sure the program you buy will use all of your memory.

But what if you have or like a word processing program that is suitable in every way but this; if its only flaw is that it reads and writes the disk too frequently? Can you think of a way around the problem? An operating system with an electronic disk emulator (see Chapter 4) would eliminate most of the disk access time delay, even though the word processing program required many transfers to and from disk.

Multiple Documents

Several word processing programs allow you to work on two or more documents at one time (Figure 11-1). There are separate windows on the screen for each one, and either you have a special command for moving from one to the other or you simply move the cursor.

But would you want to edit more than one document at a time? Although you might not, it is sometimes convenient to be able to read or copy from one document while editing another. An author working from an outline or a set of notes might find it convenient to have them available in a separate window. If you do document assembly, or are extracting material from one document for inclusion in another, a second window could also come in handy.

Including multiple windows in a word processor creates the appearance of simultaneously working on two independent tasks. As we have seen, multitasking operating systems will eventually provide this sort of

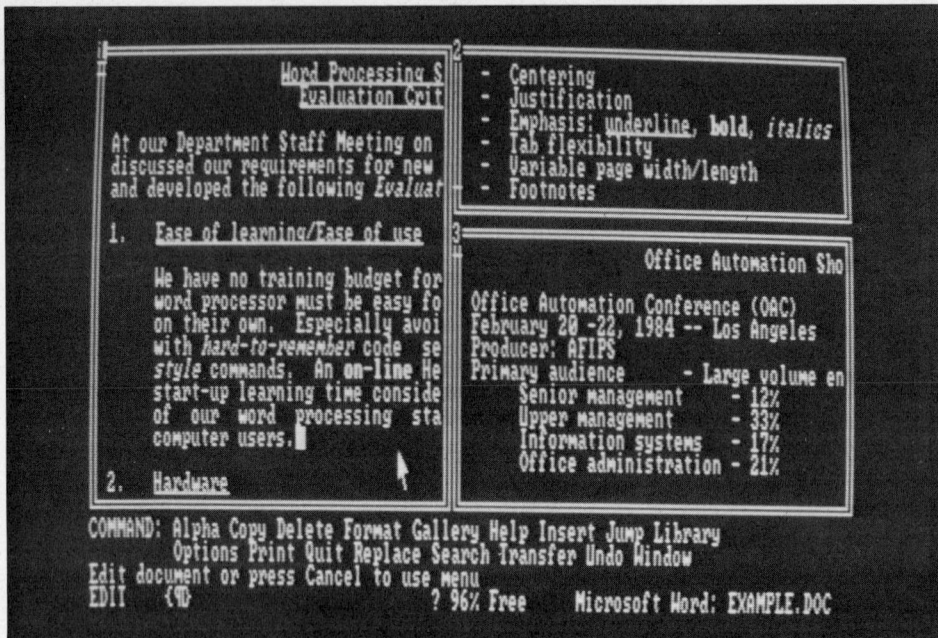

Figure 11-1. As you see here, some word processors allow you to work on several documents at once. That would be handy if, for instance, one was an outline and the other a report you were writing from it. In some cases, the same effect can be achieved using a multitasking operating system. (Courtesy of Microsoft Corporation)

capability without building it into an individual application program like a word processor.

Transitions Between Editing and Printing

Once you have created a document, you will want to print it. With some systems, the editing and printing programs are kept in memory at all times so moving to print mode takes only a few keystrokes. In others, the document being edited must first be saved on the disk and a separate printing program must be loaded. (These steps might be partially automated, but they still take time.) Some systems even return control to the operating system between these phases. Between these extremes are systems in which the document remains in memory, but the new printing program must be read in from the disk.

The faster transitions of the first case sound great, but if the printing program is always kept in memory, there will be less space for other things. Either document size will be limited or functions will have to be cut out. A nice compromise is a system in which the editing program has a built-in capability for simple printing without loading the full print program or, alternatively, in which the printing program has routines for simple editing.

How important are these transitions in your particular case? Do you usually work on many short documents or a few long ones? In the former case, you would tend to favor a system in which the editor and print programs are both in memory, since you don't need a large document area and you go through the edit/print cycle often. If you work with long documents, edit/print transitions are infrequent, so it is okay if they are a bit slow and clumsy.

Simple Print Formatting

All word processors provide for control over the basic format of the page (see Figure 11-2), and most of your printing will be done using standard default values for such things as margin sizes, page numbering options,

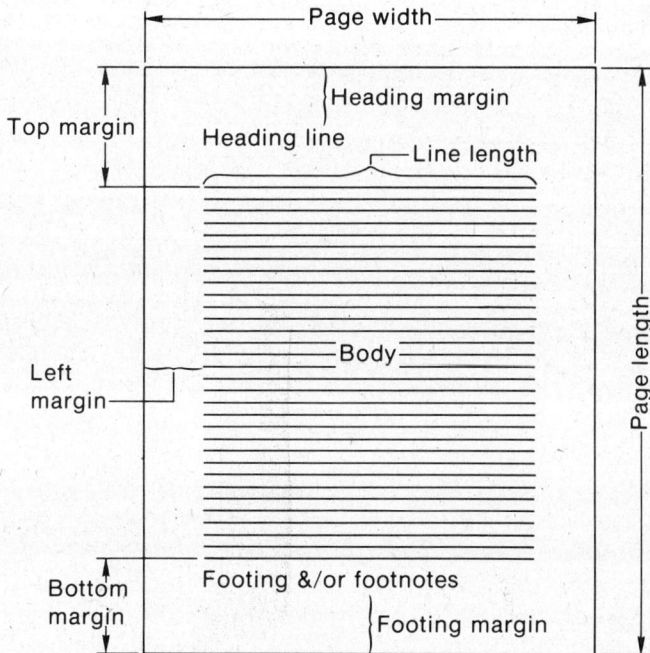

Figure 11-2. All word processing programs enable you to control the size of the page and the four main margins. Heading and footing areas may also be designated on most systems. The system should use default values for these common parameters, and they should be easily changed and reset. If the lengths are specified in inches instead of numbers of characters or lines, you will have less trouble getting things lined up when working with proportionally spaced characters.

justification, and line spacing. How many keystrokes are necessary to start printing when you use the standard default values? How hard is it to temporarily override defaults? For example, check to see what you have to do to change from single to double spacing and back. In case you forget them, can you display the current print-parameter values, or do you have to print a page to see what they are? How hard is it to change the default values permanently?

On-Screen Formatting Versus Embedded Commands

As we saw in Chapter 5, there are two basic approaches to controlling the format of printed output: using the editor to shape the document the way you want to print it or inserting using special format control commands at appropriate places in the text.

The first sounds best at first blush; it is conceptually simpler because what you see on the screen is close to what will be printed. There will be no big surprises like a letter in which the second page says nothing but "Sincerely yours."

However, there are problems with on-screen formatting. For one thing, there are many effects that cannot be shown exactly (using today's PC displays), so, in reality, all word processors use some embedded commands to control the format of the printed page. Furthermore, on-screen formatting will slow you down while you are creating and revising your document. It takes time to reformat paragraphs after they have been modified or to mark special portions of the text, for instance tables, so that they will not be reformatted to look like paragraphs. Something as simple as changing margins or switching from single to double spacing may require reformatting the entire document.

The value of on-screen formatting will vary with your applications. An author who does a lot of editing and then prints out a rough draft will not want to make the sacrifice in editing speed, whereas a secretary who types many short letters will.

If you look at a system with on-screen formatting, time it to see how long it takes to format your entire test document. Also, pay attention to the formatting commands, since you will use them constantly. Check to see if you can format a single paragraph with one command and the entire document with another, since both will be useful. If the program requires that the cursor be at the start of a paragraph in order to reformat it entirely, look for a single-keystroke command that will move it there, since reformatting the entire current paragraph is a common operation. Some programs give you the option of inserting hyphens when long words end lines during formatting; they even suggest the places where the words might break. Hyphenating will slow you down, but may help improve the appearance of your documents.

Some programs automatically reformat paragraphs after every change.

That is a significant convenience, but pay attention to how much time it takes.

Repetitive Documents

Will you be using your word processor to prepare repetitive documents, for instance for mass mailing? If so, you want a system that lets you create a template document with blank spaces that can be filled in either automatically, using values from a file on the disk, or manually, using values entered by an operator, at the time the letters are being printed.

If you will be automatically merging values from a data file, the most important consideration is compatibility between your word processing software and the program that creates the data file. If the file is small, you may be able to create and maintain it using the word processing program itself, but if it contains more than 100 or 200 records, you will probably choose to use a separate file management program. Be very careful of compatibility problems between it and your word processor.

With most programs, manual insertions in a repetitive document are made using the search command. Look back to Figure 5-15 again, and you see that the "@" character has been used to mark the blank spaces that must be filled in. Since the search command is used in document assembly jobs, check again to be sure that searching is fast and that a search can be repeated with a single keystroke (in moving from one blank to the next).

If you will be doing a lot of manual entry into repetitive documents, it might pay to look for a system that allows you to set up custom prompt screens to guide the operator. Some programs can even capture data in a file as it is being entered into a template.

Regardless of whether you merge values in from a data file or enter them manually, repetitive documents require some programming features like condition testing. You want to be able to print somewhat different documents depending upon the value of the data.

Formatting Reports

Do you write formal reports with section headings and footings, fancy page numbering schemes, footnotes, indices, and tables of contents? If so, check to see whether these things are possible on the program you're considering. They are somewhat specialized capabilities, so you might be willing to put up with some complexity in order to get flexibility. Be sure to try the system using the report format you like to use. If you want footnotes that fall across adjacent pages and are separated from the body of the text with a row of five hyphens, make sure that sort of flexibility is offered. If you like the editing portion of a word processor, and the formatter is satisfactory for your simple work, but not for complex reports, you might consider buying the program and getting a separate auxiliary formatter for report writing. These are discussed in the section on auxiliary programs.

Fancy Printing

As we saw in Chapter 2, many printers have the capability for fancy things like boldface, underlining, super- and subscripts, overstriking, proportional character spacing, and precision control over line and character spacing (see Figures 2-12, 2-13, and 2-14). Proportional spacing and precision control over spacing are particularly useful if you prepare formal documents or final copy to be pasted up and printed. If these effects are important to you, check to be sure that the software supports them and is compatible with your hardware. Don't just read the manual or ads; try the program out with your printer. Again, if your favorite word processing package meets most of your requirements, but falls short in fancy printing, you might look into a stand-alone formatter for use on complex jobs.

Simultaneous Editing and Printing

Several programs allow you to save a finished document on the disk, start it printing, then go on to edit another one while the first is still printing. This, like editing several documents in separate windows, is a special case of something that could also be done with a multitasking operating system or a simple system that had been augmented with a print spooler.

At first, this feature sounds good, but be sure you try it out. The editor will slow down while a second document is printing. If you do a lot of printing and really need to save time by overlapping it with editing, you should consider adding a memory buffer to your printer. As we saw in Chapter 2, a print buffer that is large enough to hold the entire document will free the PC completely while printing goes on.

Compatibility with Other Programs

The question of compatibility was raised in Chapter 10 when we discussed the characteristics of all programs, including word processors, but it bears repeating here because you are likely to use your word processor in conjunction with nearly all other programs. You may use it to edit documents to be transmitted over communication lines, to incorporate a spreadsheet or report from a data manager into a written report, or in conjunction with spelling checkers, report formatters, and other auxiliary programs for writing.

Compatibility can break down if the word processor or the program it is interfacing with uses special characters in the files they create or use other techniques, even "tab" characters instead of blanks, to compress data. If you are planning to use your word processing program with other software, run tests to make sure they are compatible or get a guarantee from your dealer.

Don't forget the other general issues mentioned in Chapter 10. If you have a hard disk, and therefore a lot of documents, be sure your operating system allows a hierarchic file directory, like the one available under DOS Version

2. For instance, you might store personal letters, business letters, and templates of legal forms in different subdirectories. Pay attention to copy protection, documentation, tutorial material to help you learn to use the program, and the other general issues.

No program will be best in each dimension outlined; indeed, there are design tradeoffs making that goal impossible. You will be most satisfied selecting a package that meets your needs, but doesn't provide extraneous capability. A less sophisticated package designed for light typing might be cheaper, easier to learn to operate, and even faster than a full featured system. Table 11-2 lists the points mentioned in this section along with the people that might be most interested in them.

AUXILIARY WRITING AIDS

As we saw in Chapter 5, spelling checkers, report formatters, and other auxiliary writing aids are available to supplement basic word processing packages. In some cases, these auxiliary capabilities are bundled in with a word processing program, and in others you have to purchase them separately (see Figure 11-3). In fact, the availability of a wide range of compatible, well integrated auxiliary software might be a significant factor in choosing one word processing program over another. The bundled packages can save you money, and of course all of the programs are compatible, but you might find some weak links in the bundle or pay for something you really do not need.

If you plan to use an auxiliary program, it must work with your word processor. The files must be compatible and the command styles should be consistent. Obviously, they must both use the same operating system and basic file structure. You should be able to run the auxiliary program without leaving the word processor. For instance, you would like to be able to edit a document, print it using a report formatter, then return to editing without returning to the operating system between each step.

Spelling Checkers

Your spelling checker and word processing program must work well together. For example, if the word processor uses embedded commands to control print formatting, the spelling checker should ignore them. If ".NP" is the command to begin a new page, you don't want the spelling checker to flag it as a misspelled word. Similarly, many word processors use nonprinting characters in the text to control such things as font changes or the ends of lines, and the spelling checker should also ignore those characters.

Even if your spelling checker can read the word processor files and ignores irrelevant commands, it may still be loosely integrated. Writing and correcting spelling is typically a three step process (see Figure 11-4). You

Table 11-2.   Who needs what? No word processing program is going to be best for everyone. This table shows who should pay particular attention to each of the factors discussed in the section on word processing software.

Basic Editing Speed
  All users
Basic Editing Convenience
  All users
Complex Editing
  Those writing relatively long documents requiring frequent revision and polishing
Document Assembly
  Those with this class application, who assemble documents from prewritten material
Consistency of Command Structure
  All users, particularly those with little prior experience
Memory Management
  Those with relatively large documents
Buffer Size
  Those with relatively large documents
Multiple Windows
  Look for them only if you have an application in which they can be used.
Edit/Format Transitions
  All users, but particularly those preparing many relatively short documents
Simple, Default Formatting
  All users
On-Screen/Embedded Commands
  On-screen formatting for those with relatively little prior experience and those working with many relatively short documents
Repetitive Documents
  Those with this class of application, for instance in mailing or billing
Augmented Formatting for Reports
  Those with this class of application, students, and authors of formal reports and papers
Precision Control over Printing
  Those preparing documents for reproduction or documents in which appearance is very important, for instance in formal correspondence
Simultaneous Printing and Editing
  May save some time if you do a lot of printing
Compatibility
  Important to those using other software in addition to word processing

create a document using the editor, then it is saved on the disk, where it can be read by the spelling checker. The spelling corrector flags the misspelled words (under your guidance), then you use the editor a second time to correct them. In some systems, it is necessary to execute the editor, then the spelling corrector, then the editor again, as three separate steps; whereas,

Basic Formatter	Augmented formatter
	Index-contents generator
	Bibliography file manager
Editor	Grammar checker
	Thesaurus program
	Spelling checker

Figure 11-3. You can buy a separate word processing package (editor and basic formatter) and choose various writing aids to go with it, or you can buy a package that bundles one or more auxiliary functions with the word processing program. The most commonly bundled modules are spelling checkers and augmented formatters, which may be tailored for either formal reports or merging data files with a template to produce repetitive documents such as mass mailings. Buying individual components gives more flexibility, but a bundled package will probably cost less and there should be no question of incompatibility.

with others you move from step to step without leaving the word processing program.

Others carry integration a step further, allowing you to see words in context at the time the spelling corrector discovers that they are not in its dictionary (see Figure 11-5). This can help with deciding whether or not a word is spelled correctly, but it may slow you down if the system stops to show you every occurrence of a correct word that happened not to be in its dictionary, for instance a common proper noun. The best compromise may be a program that shows you a word in context only if you are in doubt and ask to see it, so be a little skeptical of this "feature" until you see how well it is designed in a given program.

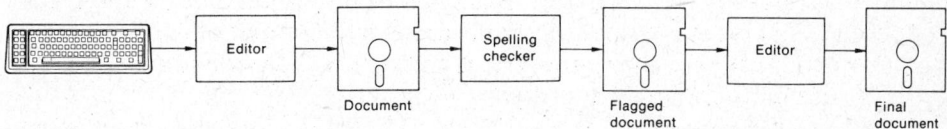

Figure 11-4. Spelling correction is usually a three step process. First you create the file to be checked using the editor, then the spelling checker reads through it, creating a version in which the misspelled words are flagged, and finally you correct the bad words, using the editor for the second time. If the transitions between the phases are awkward, for example, forcing you to run three separate programs, you will waste a lot of time.

```
B:JIMRESEA.DOC  PAGE 3 LINE 9 COL 53            Action(F/B/I/D/S)?

F - Fix word       D - Add to dictionary
B - Bypass word    S - Add to supplemental dictionary
I - Ignore word



L----!----!----!----!----!----!----!----!----!----!--------R
.pn 2
     As a result of the logical structure and organization of the

practice of medicine, medical superstition was vanquished in

Rome.  One of the first steps in developing an organizational

structure is to dispel superstition because an organizational

structure for medicine and medical superstition are incompatable.
```

Figure 11-5. This spelling checker shows you suspect words in context. That is sometimes a help in deciding whether a word is indeed misspelled or not, but it can slow you down.

Finally, some spelling checkers can be used to look a word up while you are writing or editing. If the word was not in the dictionary, the program would suggest likely alternative spellings. This would be handy while writing, but only if it was possible to look the word up quckly, without exiting from the word processing program. If a spelling corrector has a lookup command, time it to see how long it takes, and note how many keystrokes are needed to look up a word while you are editing a document.

Spelling Checker Evaluation

As with any software, you should test a spelling checker using a typical document if possible. In doing so, pay attention to questions of speed and convenience. For a start, time the program on a document of typical length. Some are much slower than others in scanning through a document to come up with the list of suspect words.

A test of scanning speed is a good start, but it isn't even half the story, because the majority of your time with a spelling corrector is spent in deciding whether the words it turns up are truly misspelled. It will help if unmatched words are presented in alphabetic order, since, unless you are a confident speller, you will be looking many of them up in a dictionary. The ability to query the program for closely spelled words that are in its dictionary, or to see the words in context also helps at this stage. Some programs take the initiative and suggest what the correct spelling might be without being asked.

Pay attention to the number of correctly spelled words that are not found in the dictionary. A high proportion of correct words being flagged can be due to a small dictionary or, if the program works with roots, prefixes, and suffixes rather than whole words, an inefficient matching routine. In either case, it wastes your time, but as you add words to the dictionary, the problem will diminish. Over the years, I have added about 500 words to my spelling dictionary, which has reduced the number of false "misspellings" significantly.

The other side of the coin is incorrectly spelled words that are not flagged. This could also be due to a bug in a root + suffix program or to a dictionary that contained misspelled words. To test for the former, see if the spelling corrector catches nonsense words like "exspell" or "despell."

The Dictionary

Each program is distributed with an initial dictionary, and they all make provision for the addition of new words during proofreading. Some programs also allow the addition of entire batches of words, perhaps from another specialized dictionary, in one operation. Conversely, if you mistakenly add a bad word, it should be possible to delete it from the dictionary.

You may also be able to set up multiple dictionaries. For instance, there might be one with computer terms, which would be used (in addition to the main dictionary) with documents about computers. If several different people use the program, they might each have separate dictionaries of words they use commonly.

Multiple dictionaries can save a little time and storage. The space required by the dictionary is also a concern, particularly if your system uses floppy disk. A large dictionary may result in fewer spuriously flagged words, but may use more disk space and slow things down. On the other hand, clever encoding can compress many words into a tight space, so don't jump to the conclusion that a program with many words in its dictionary necessarily wastes disk space; check it out (one of the operating system commands, for instance DIR in DOS or STAT in CP/M-86, will tell you the total number of bytes in a file).

Report Formatters

Although all word processing programs have print formatting modules, students, researchers, and others who produce relatively large, formal reports or people who need a lot of control over the physical appearance of the final document (for pasteup and printing) might wish to obtain an auxiliary formatter that provides more functions than the formatting portion of their basic word processing program.

Stand-alone formatters read document files that have been prepared with a word processor and produce a printed report. They are controlled by commands that are embedded in the text file when it is created. In addition, some provide a specialized programming language in which a series of formatting commands is evoked whenever a certain event occurs. For example, you could program the formatter to print an extended heading at the start of every even numbered page or a complex footing at the end of each page. That sort of programming can be a little tricky, and you might need help in setting it up.

Print formatters duplicate the functions of the printing portions of word processing packages, and the questions raised about printing in the word processing software section apply to them as well. Table 11-3 lists the sorts of things a print formatter can do for you. The features are listed to give a feel for your options; no program has all of them. In selecting a print formatter, you should be certain that it is sufficiently flexible to produce reports in the style you require.

However, capability is not the entire story. Some programs might be more convenient than others as well. For example, it should be possible to print relatively standard documents, quick reports and rough drafts, with few or no formatting commands. In order to do that, the formatter should offer easily changed default values for common formatting options such as page and margin sizes, paragraph handling, header format, and page numbering. As usual with defaults, be sure it is easy to examine the current values as well as to change them.

Since formatters rely heavily on embedded commands, the ability to preview the final output on the screen is a convenient option (see Figure 11-6). Many systems also let you store it on the disk. When you see the output, but it is not exactly what you want, it is important to be able to change various parameters without reediting the text.

For example, what happens if you print a document and it comes out ½ inch too long. With an inconvenient system, you would have to reenter the word processing editor and change a formatting command. Perhaps you would change the spacing between lines from ⅙ to ⅐ inches. Although this would work, it would be time consuming, particularly if the second time it still wasn't quite right, and you had to repeat the cycle again. With a better designed formatter, you have the option of changing parameters like horizontal line spacing while executing the formatting program. You would simply change the parameter and rerun the format program.

Other Writing Aids

There are a number of less popular writing aids, which you should consider if you will be doing a lot of original writing on your PC. Keep the time

Table 11-3. This is a list of the sorts of things that special report formatting programs can do. You won't find this much flexibility in most word processing programs; so if you need it, look for a stand-alone formatter.

The ability to specify margins in inches rather than numbers of characters

Left and right justification and ragged left columns

Automatic preparation of multicolumn pages

Placement of text within boxed areas

The availability of custom type fonts using graphics mode on dot-matrix printers

The ability to use all of the font options available on the system printer in character mode (compressed and extended print, boldface, italic, subscript and superscript)

The suppression of widows and orphans by automatically shortening pages if necessary

Breaking pages whenever certain conditions are met (for instance not starting a certain paragraph unless it fits completely on the current page)

Various paragraph format options, including automatic spacing, indenting, outdenting, bulleting, and numbering

Automatic maintenance of chapter and section numbers

Arabic and Roman numerals in page, chapter, and section numbering

Multiple line page headers and footers

The inclusion of chapter or section names, page numbers, or dates as part of page headers or footers

The ability to place headers and footers at any point on the page

The ability to treat headings, footings, page numbers, margins, and footnotes differently for odd and even pages

The ability to set footnotes off in a number of ways or to continue them on the adjoining page

The ability to select numbering schemes for designating footnotes

The ability to defer footnotes to the end of the document, with a variety of symbols and conventions for designating them

The ability to hold marked terms and terms occurring in headings for inclusion in an index

The ability to generate a table of contents using the headings in the document

needed to learn to use a program in mind when deciding whether it is worthwhile. Don't try to "computerize" things just for the sake of doing so. If you are not sure whether one of these programs is worthwhile, try getting along without it at first. You can always pick it up after you are thoroughly used to your word processor.

If the print formatting portion of your word processor is sufficient for your needs, but cannot generate indices and tables of contents, there are independent programs for doing just that. As you write, you flag the terms to be indexed and the chapter and section headings. The program then reads the text file, and notes the pages on which the flagged words occur. Once the

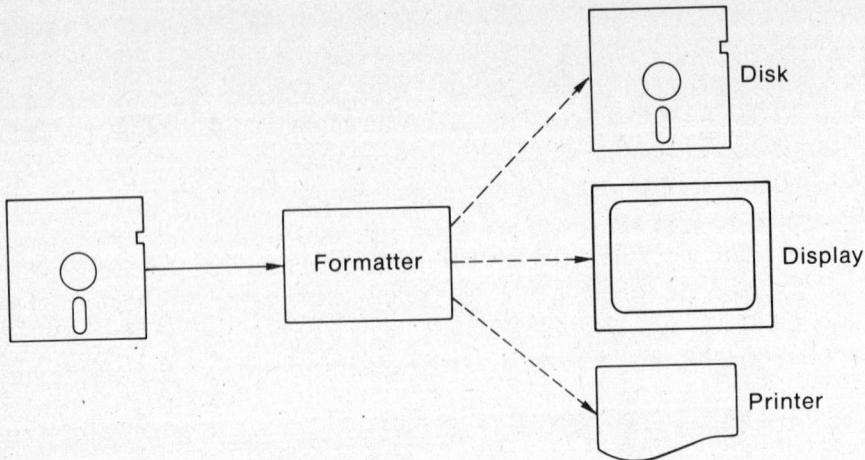

Figure 11-6. Using a formatting program that relys on embedded commands to control printing gives you more flexibility in shaping the output, but because you don't see a formatted version on the screen while you are editing, it may take several edit/print cycles to get a document the way you want to see it.

For that reason, a formatter that lets you "print" the document on the screen or disk as well as on paper can be useful. You can make trial runs without using paper. The ability to change printing parameters like margins, character spacing, and line spacing without returning to the editor will also save you a lot of time.

entire document is printed, an alphabetized index and a table of contents with page number references is generated.*

If you buy a stand-alone index and contents package, be sure it is compatible with your word processor. It must not only be able to read the same files, but also accurately simulate pagination, so that it can predict which pages of the document the various terms and headings will fall on.

There are also programs designed to help with your bibliography. They are specialized file managers, designed to maintain a file of bibliographic entries, for example author's name, title, publisher, publication date, and city. References are flagged in the text and the appropriate citations may either be inserted as footnotes or collected into a formatted bibliography at the end of the document. In selecting such a package, you should make sure it is flexible enough to produce footnotes and bibliography entries in the style and format you commonly use. It must also, obviously, be compatible with your word processor. Pay attention to convenience. It will not pay to automate your bibliography maintenance if you end up spending excessive time moving back and forth between the bibliography program to the word processor, trying to get them to work together.

As was mentioned in Chapter 5, there are programs for checking

*Beware of the fact that some programs might sort the index into the standard ASCII order, which would put all capital letters ahead of lowercase letters.

grammar and writing style as well as spelling. They do limited syntactic analysis and rely heavily on dictionaries of "suspicious" phrases and terms. For example, you can expect to see dictionaries of sexist, wordy, or trite phrases. Punctuation errors, like an unmatched parenthesis, would also be caught by some programs.

If you do a lot of writing, you may want to look at one of these programs. The best test would be to run it with a chapter or article you considered a finished product, and see what sorts of errors it turned up and what you thought of its corrections. The program may turn up passive constructions, sentences that are unusually long or short, overly complex sentences, or too many sentences of the same length and complexity. They also make statistical summaries of factors relating to style, for example, average sentence length, the degree of variation in length, or the number of passive sentences. If you try the program on something you consider finished and it gives you useful suggestions, get it.

As mentioned above, some spelling checkers can be used for looking words up while you are writing, as well as for after-the-fact proofreading. There are also thesaurus packages for looking up synonyms while you are writing. As with spelling checkers that can look words up, pay close attention to how well a thesaurus program is integrated with your word processing editor. How many keystrokes are required to look a word up and get back to entering your document, and how much time does it take? If the thesaurus program cannot be called from within your editor, and it doesn't respond quickly, you won't find it very helpful in writing. Also, be aware of the disk space required for the dictionary and synonym files, since they must be on-line at the same time as your word processor.

HARDWARE

Software choices are the toughest, but word processing has some implications for your hardware as well. Let's look at each of the PC components with word processing in mind.

The Keyboard

IBM offers only one keyboard, so it doesn't seem that you have much choice here, but a few comments are in order. As we saw in Chapter 2, a touch typist who is used to a standard Selectric keyboard might want to get a set of oversize keytops or even to replace the keyboard. If you don't feel replacing the keyboard is justifiable, you might at least look at a software package that lets you redefine some key meanings, perhaps switching the backslash and backspace keys. The same key reassignment program will let you assign entire sequences of keystrokes to a single key. Being able to type a commonly used word or phrase or give a control command with a single keystroke is very handy in word processing.

The Display

If you're an occasional user of word processing, either the Color/Graphics Display or the Monochrome Display will do. However, if you will be spending a lot of time editing text, either writing or doing production typing, the Monochrome Display is probably a better bet, since it uses more dots to form each character and they are therefore sharper. Furthermore, the green phosphor is easy on your eyes, and some word processing programs actually change the screen faster on the Monochrome display than the Color/Graphics Display. That all adds up to less eyestrain. If you are not sure how important this factor is in your case, check the Monochrome Display and a high quality color monitor side by side in a dealer's showroom.

If you end up choosing the color monitor because you need the graphic capability for other applications, look for a word processing program that takes advantage of the color capability, since certain color combinations are easier on your eyes than others. A program that cannot use color will display white characters on a black background, but since white requires precise focusing of the red, green, and blue colors, the characters are more likely to be a little blurry, whereas black characters on a white background would be sharp. Furthermore, human factors studies have shown dark characters on a light background to be easier on your eyes because pupil dilation is relatively constant. My eyes tell me the same thing after a few hours in front of a color monitor, so look for a program that allows black characters on a white background, and be sure that your color monitor has an adjustable brightness control.

If you must have graphics and the character quality of the Monochrome Display, you have two somewhat unsatisfactory choices. One is to purchase both displays. That will cost a lot of money, take up a lot of space on your desk, and tie up two expansion slots for displays rather than just one. To add insult to injury, a little technical help might be needed to get your software to switch smoothly from one display to the other.

The second option is to purchase a non-IBM display board. There are boards on the market that give you the best of both worlds, high resolution for sharp characters as well as graphics. That sounds like such a terrific idea that you might be wondering how IBM is able to sell any of their own boards. The most important reason people stick with IBM is software compatibility. If you decide to purchase a non-IBM display board, be sure that it is software-compatible with the standard PC display boards. You don't want to discover that some of your programs won't work with it. If you can't get a guarantee from your dealer or the board manufacturer, at least test it with the software you plan to be using. For a tough test, try it with a program that uses the display heavily, perhaps Microsoft's Flight Simulation or a game.

Printer

The printer is the biggest hardware choice you have to make in configuring a PC for word processing, but luckily it is relatively obvious. Begin by considering your quality requirements. The output of some printers is about as good as that of a carbon ribbon typewriter, whereas others are decidedly inferior. In addition to general appearance of the type, ask yourself which special features such as boldface, subscripts, justification, precision control over line and character spacing, and so forth are important. Remember that both the printer and software must be capable of fulfilling your requirements.

If your application requires the highest quality character appearance, a formed-character printer is still the lowest cost answer today, even though you will pay a premium in price, speed, and mechanical complexity compared to a dot-matrix printer. As we saw in Chapter 2, rapid progress is being made in dot-matrix printers, so keep an eye on them. A multipass, dot-matrix printer with lots of dots per character really might fill the bill. Before long, I would expect nonimpact dot-matrix printers, for instance ink-jet or laser printers, to dominate the market. Also, times are changing along with technology. Perhaps people are starting to be impressed by, or at least accepting of, something that looks like a computer printed it.

After narrowing your choice to printers that meet your requirements for character quality and special effects, pay attention to things like the size of the printer, how much noise it makes while operating, and its cost. Decide whether you need oversize paper or whether standard 8½ inch sheets are sufficient.

Pay attention to forms handling. Will you be using single sheets of paper, perhaps printing letters on your company stationery, or continuous forms? For feeding single sheets, you will want a friction feed printer, whereas a forms tractor will be better for continuous forms. If you will be preparing repetitive documents like mass letters, special continuous forms made of your stationery might be handy. Check with a supplies vendor for them.

Speed is another consideration. Remember that advertised rates of printing can be misleading. A printer that types rapidly but moves paper slowly can be very slow. If you do very little printing, speed may not be a problem, but if you will be printing a lot, make an estimate of the time you will spend printing each day. If you have a fairly even balance between printing and editing, for instance in typing short correspondence, you might be able to compensate for the slow speed of a formed-character printer by adding a buffer, to free the PC for editing one letter while the previous one prints.

Finally, be paranoid about compatibility. IBM does not offer much choice in printers, so you are likely to end up with one from another manufacturer. Your printer must work properly with your other hardware and with your software. If you add a memory buffer between the PC and the printer, you have still another chance for a compatibility breakdown. Make compatibility your dealer's responsibility.

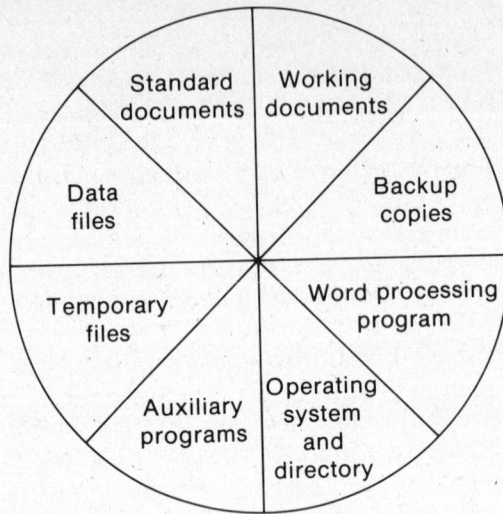

Figure 11-7. This figure shows the sorts of things that might be stored on disk. You might think that disk capacities sound high, but remember that you will be storing more than just the documents you are working on.

Memory

More is better. The more memory you have, the faster the system should be. You will have more space for documents and more of your software will fit in memory. All that means reading and writing the disk less frequently and, therefore, faster operation. Of course, if your software does not make use of all the memory you have, it won't help you, so choose software that does. Think about your future requirements here as well. Memory prices are constantly falling, and software designers will be using more memory to improve their products. This goes for all software, not just word processors.

Disk

Again, more is better. In estimating your disk requirements, the documents you write are just the tip of the iceberg (see Figure 11-7). In addition to working documents, you will need space for backup copies, your word processing software, a copy of the operating system and disk directory, auxiliary programs for things like data management or checking spelling, data files if you are doing any sort of mass mailing or other repetitive document applications, and standard documents that you use frequently. The following space requirements are typical:

Drive A

Word processing program (90KB)
Spelling corrector (30KB)
Spelling dictionary (90KB)
Standard documents and templates (10KB)
Operating system (50KB)

Drive B

Document files (150KB)
Backup copies (150KB)
Temporary files

(Plan on temporary files space of about the size of your largest single document.)

Even if you have many small documents, having space for many on one disk cuts down on filing problems and helps you organize yourself. It is nice to be able to keep all correspondence on one disk, all work on a given project on another, and so forth. Therefore, for word processing you will want at least two double sided floppy disk drives, and, particularly if you will be preparing repetitive documents or merging values from data files, think about a hard disk.

CHAPTER TWELVE
Spreadsheet Processing

This chapter looks at spreadsheet software, from the standpoints of efficiency, ease of entering and manipulating a model, data representation and calculation facilities, flexibility in viewing results, and printer and disk power. The great majority of spreadsheet programs are interactive, the screen being updated as soon as a change is made, but there are also noninteractive packages, and they are discussed as well. The final section of the chapter covers the hardware implications of your spreadsheet applications.

MEMORY, STORAGE, AND SPEED

Will you be constructing fairly large, complex spreadsheets? If so, the capacity and speed of the program, its efficiency, will be important. You will want a program that uses memory and disk storage efficiently and calculates quickly. Spreadsheet programs seem similar at first encounter, so it is surprising to learn how much variation there is in speed, memory, and disk storage. If you run some of the benchmark tests suggested in Table 12-1 and illustrated in Table 12-2, you will find that the programs vary by a factor of at least two to one on all dimensions, and it goes much higher on some.

Each program has a published maximum number of spreadsheet rows and columns, but in most cases, a maximum sized model will not fit in memory. For instance, one program features spreadsheets of "255 rows by 63" columns (theoretically 16,065 cells), but testing it on a PC with a 576KB memory, we found the maximum model size to be 3,500 cells. You will also discover that some programs can use as much memory as you care to install in your PC, whereas others will not use anything over a certain upper limit. A few programs are able automatically to page the model onto the disk when memory becomes full, but the majority cannot. If you plan to build large models, look for a program that handles consolidation of submodels

Table 12-1. Experiments for comparing speed and capacity. The speeds and capacities of spreadsheet programs vary over surprisingly wide ranges, so if you will be making heavy use of spreadsheets, you might want to conduct some comparative experiments or benchmark tests. With relatively little effort you can compare speed of execution, memory requirements, storage requirements, storage input/output time, and print time. The time spent on the tests will pay off in two ways: you will learn which programs are most efficient, and in setting up the tests you will gain familiarity with the operation of the program.

Constructing a benchmark spreadsheet for making comparisons is easy, because you can use the program's own copy command. Place a formula to be replicated in the corner of the spreadsheet, then use the copy or replicate command to fill an entire column, then copy the column to fill in a rectangular range of cells. With just a few commands you can fill a spreadsheet with a given number of cells for speed comparisons, or fill memory to see what the program's maximum capacity is.

You can try experiments to compare the following:

Capacities

The maximum model size, given the installed memory

The maximum amount of memory the program is capable of using

The maximum numeric precision, which may cause problems if you work with large numbers

The amount of disk storage required to store a certain spreadsheet in each of the available storage modes (as a model with formulas, internal form with formulas evaluated, DIF, and any other external representations that would be used for interfacing with other software)

Speed

The time it takes to recalculate a given model (for instance, build a model in which each of 500 cells is evaluated by adding the values in two adjacent cells)

The time to scroll horizontally and vertically, one row or column at a time

The time to scroll horizontally and vertically, one screen at a time

The time to go to the corners of the spreadsheet

The time to add, delete, or blank a row or column

The time to read/save a spreadsheet in each available mode (see above)

The time to load the spreadsheet program after the computer is powered up

The time to print a model of a given size

Convenience

The number of keystrokes needed to change a single letter in the middle of a label or formula in a cell

The number of keystrokes to copy a single cell relatively or absolutely

The number of keystrokes to copy a row or column relatively or absolutely

The number of keystrokes to place a one paragraph comment on the spreadsheet

The number of keystrokes to print a multipage, formatted spreadsheet using default values for the print formatting parameters

Table 12-2. Spreadsheet benchmark examples. These six tests illustrate the kinds of benchmark comparisons you might make of speed, memory, and storage use. The first test timed recalculation in a 10 by 256 cell spreadsheet. The next two tests involved memory use. A simple formula was copied throughout the worksheet until the system ran out of memory, and as you see, only 1-2-3 made use of memory above 320K, so it could accommodate the largest model with the memory set at 576K; however, at 320K VisiCalc had more room. The final three tests deal with disk input and output. The times are for reading and writing a 10 by 254 cell model, with recalculation suspended. By the time you read this, there will be new versions of all three programs on the market, so do not place too much emphasis on the actual results, but use these examples as a model for your own experimentation.

	VisiCalc v 1.1	1-2-3 v 1.0	MultiPlan v 1.0
Recalculation time (in seconds) for 10 × 254 cells using multiplication and addition	45.9	13.6	41.7
Spreadsheet size (numbers of cells) with a 320KB memory	8,147	5,685	3,500
Spreadsheet size (number of cells) with a 576KB memory	*	10,928	3,500
Time (seconds) to load 10 × 254 cell model	177	55.9	20.4
Time (seconds) to save 10 × 254 cell model	71	42.3	20.5
File size (bytes) for 10 × 254 model	40,960	89,856	41,242

*Due to an apparent bug in this version of the program, VisiCalc would not run with the larger memory.

well. Dividing your large model into submodels essentially extends your memory capacity and may also help to clarify your thinking.

Program speeds also vary considerably. I have worked with many spreadsheet programs, and can cite horror stories in which one program might be 40 times slower than another, and three-to-one speed differences are common. With small models, computation lags might not bother you, but if you are building large models, they will. Being able to continue typing during recalculation is some help, but since you don't see what you are typing, it still is not satisfactory. The ability to suspend recalculation of the spreadsheet while a model is being built or a number of values are being entered is a necessity, particularly with a slow program. Don't buy a program without this feature.

Times for disk transfers also vary significantly from program to program. We have found eight-to-one differences in the time to read or store the same model. Even the time it takes to load the spreadsheet program itself can be quite long. Not only do disk times vary, but also you may find a given model taking up twice as much disk space with one program as with another.

Some differences in efficiency are due to careless programming or the language that was used to write the program. There is no consolation for these deficiencies, but some are a result of design tradeoffs. The most important concerns *precision*, the maximum number of significant digits in a number. Longer numbers take up more space in memory and doing arithmetic on them is slower, but some applications require a high degree of accuracy. If this is so in your case, you might have to stay with a certain program even if it is slow.

MODEL ENTRY AND MANIPULATION

VisiCalc and the other early spreadsheet programs were command oriented, with little on-line help. Still, they were relatively easy to learn to use, because the idea of a paper spreadsheet was familiar and it was represented directly on the video display. Furthermore, the programs had relatively few commands, making it possible to learn much of what they could do in just a day or two.

As spreadsheet programs have evolved, they have gotten more complex. There are more commands with more options, and several have grown into multifunction programs with modules for limited word processing, simple file management, communications, and business graphics. These more complex programs are generally menu oriented, with extensive context-dependent, on-line help. They are slower to operate, but easier for a beginner or casual user who tends to forget commands between sessions.

As we saw in Figure 6-4, all spreadsheet programs have an interaction area for showing status information, selecting commands, and editing the contents of the current cell. An important bit of status information is the amount of memory remaining.

Pay particular attention to the ease of editing the contents of the current cell. As a formula or character string is keyed in, it goes into the edit area. The program should use the cursor move, insert, delete, and other special function keys at the righthand side of the PC keyboard for altering this information. Check to see how many keystrokes it takes to change a single character in the middle of a complex formula or to move the cursor to the first or last character.

Once the formula or character string in the edit area is correct, it can be entered into the spreadsheet by hitting the "enter" key. Some programs also have the option of entering it whenever the cursor is moved out of the current cell, which speeds things up when you have a long list of numbers to enter. Using the numeric keypad at the right of the PC keyboard can also speed the entry of numbers, but since those keys double as cursor-control keys, some programs will not be able to use them (others will). If you will be entering a lot of numeric data, pay attention to these features.

Spreadsheet Area Designation

With many spreadsheet programs, the only way to refer to a cell or group of cells in a command or formula is by giving their coordinates. However, other programs give you the option of naming a cell or group of cells, so a formula like "SUM (K1...K12)" might become "SUM (Monthly-Cost)." Named areas will simplify moving the cursor around on the spreadsheet ("GOTO Total Expense" instead of "GOTO N44"), but more important, they provide better documentation, in case you or someone else has to study a model after it is created.

In entering formulas or giving commands, you frequently need to designate a group of cells on the spreadsheet, and there are three basic methods of designating an area. With a few programs, an area is assumed to begin with the current cell, and you have to input the number of cells in the area. This method is confusing and error prone. Most programs allow you to specify an area by giving the coordinates of its corners (for example A11...C11 would be a row and A11...C15 a rectangular area). This is better, but it is still awkward. The most convenient method of designating a group of cells is to point to its corners, an option with many programs. Programs offering this option should use a consistent style for pointing to the corners of designated areas, and it is most helpful if they are identified by highlighting, reverse video, or color changes as you move the cursor, so that you can easily see the limits of the area.

Manipulating Areas

Commands for inserting, deleting, blanking, moving, or copying rows or columns are found in nearly all spreadsheet programs, but their execution times may vary by a factor of up to eight to one, so you might want to try a few benchmark comparisons. Speed of copying will be of some concern, but convenience and simplicity is more important. As we saw in Figure 6-8, when you copy a cell or group of cells, the formulas in them may either be held constant or changed relative to the new cell location. You will do a lot of copying in constructing models, so pay attention to what is involved. Designating the cell(s) to be copied and the destination is fairly simple (again it is nice to be able to point to the destination), but telling the program whether the addresses of the formulas should be absolute or relative can be a bother, depending upon how it is handled by the program.

At least one program requires that you answer the question "absolute or relative?" for every reference in the receiving area, a very tedious process. With others you tell the program once for each cell reference in the formula being copied whether it should be handled absolutely or relatively. Still other programs assume that all references should be relative unless the cell being referred to is marked as an absolute cell. The latter method has two advantages. First, since most copying is done with relative references, it is simpler. You don't have to answer any "absolute or relative?" questions. Second, it provides better documentation because you can see which cells are referred to absolutely by examining the spreadsheet. Some people prefer the third method, in which relative references are the default, and others find the second method less confusing. I doubt if anyone would prefer the first appraoch.

Macro Commands

Macro commands, which are described in Chapter 10, are useful if you are setting up reporting and analysis systems in which a spreadsheet program is used on a regular basis. The command sequences associated with a macro would be given a command name associated with a function key, or a custom menu, depending upon the command structure of the program.

These preprogrammed sequences could be used for something simple, for instance entering a certain formula or label at several points on the spreadsheet, or something complex, like setting up your own menu of commands to simplify operations for a relatively unskilled user. For example, you could set up a menu with four choices: READ, CONSOLIDATE, PRINT, and SAVE. You would then associate a series of commands with each choice. When the operator evoked the new menu, these commands would take care of specifying file names, printer setup commands, and so forth. Setting up macros requires a bit of expertise, but they enable novice users to run custom applications easily.

Making the menu generation facility available to the user in this manner is important. It enables you to set up reporting systems in which command choices that are tailored to your application seem just like they were a built-in part of the system. If you plan to use a spreadsheet program for regular reporting, make sure it has good macro capabilities, even if a programmer will be called in to set the system up.

DATA AND CALCULATION

Data Types and Operations

The basic idea of a spreadsheet program is that each cell contains either a number (or rather a formula that, when evaluated, boils down to a single number or value), or a character string used for headings or comments. As a computer person would say, numbers and character strings are two possible *data types*. Computer people also speak of the sorts of *operations* that are reasonable to perform on a given type of data. For instance, arithmetic operations like addition and subtraction make sense when dealing with numeric data, but not when dealing with character strings; multiplying "Larry" times "Press" makes no sense. On the other hand, an operation like deleting a character or word from a string does. You might recognize the idea of data types from Chapter 7, where field types in data management are discussed.

In addition to strings and numbers, some spreadsheet programs provide other data types like integers (whole numbers, without decimal points), percentages, dollar amounts, and dates. You can easily understand the idea of doing arithmetic on data such as numbers or dollar amounts, but what about dates? All spreadsheet programs allow you to display dates, probably offering several format choices (like "8/14/82" or "August 14,

1982), and with a few you can do arithmetic on dates, for instance computing the number of days between two dates. Programs that allow arithmetic on dates store them internally as the number of days since, say, the turn of the century.

Labels

The treatment of strings also varies considerably between programs. Although the heart of a spreadsheet application is computational, dealing with numbers, a good deal of your time in constructing a model will be spent working with strings. You will add titles, headings, and descriptive comments to make the spreadsheet readable, and it should be easy to create and revise them.

For a start, the maximum string length allowed will vary among programs, and, all things being equal, longer is better. The way in which they are displayed also varies considerably. The more primitive programs have *hard cell boundaries*, displaying only as much of a string as will fit within the current cell; anything that will not fit is merely truncated. As you might imagine, that makes writing titles and other annotations very difficult, and if the spreadsheet format is changed (for instance widening a column), the strings must be redone.

If a program has *soft cell boundaries*, it displays as much of a string as possible, continuing into adjacent cells if they are empty. Better yet are programs that treat a text area of the spreadsheet in a manner similar to a word processor, with the ability to edit text and reformat paragraphs. Although they do not provide full word processing capability, they are adequate for spreadsheet annotation.

Numbers

Table 12-3 lists the sorts of numeric operations that are found in spreadsheet programs. There is a lot of overlap in function between programs, so the unusual operations are separated from the common ones. With a few hours' practice with a spreadsheet program, you will be able to master most of these operations, so I won't explain each of them here.

Use the table as a checklist, keeping your applications in mind. Don't be intimidated if some of the functions sound too mathematical. Generally speaking, the more complex math functions will be used in applications in which forecasting is involved. If you are not trained in that area, someone else, perhaps a staff econometrician will be building the models, and of course they should compare the available functions.

A few programs allow for automatic *iterative*, or repeated, computation. For an example, refer back to Figure 8-9. In that example, we computed the effect of changing interest rates on a bank balance. When we changed the value of the interest-rate parameter in cell B5, we saw what happened to the rest of the model. If we wanted to test the effects of, say, five different

Table 12-3. Spreadsheet operations. This table shows the operations that can occur in a spreadsheet model formula. The first group under each heading are almost universally available, whereas the second are not. You or a staff person who will be building forecasting models should review this checklist against your requirements.

Arithmetic
1. $+, -, \times, /$, exponentiation, sum, count, max, min, table lookup, absolute value, natural log, common log, exponential, trigonometric, square root, integer, modulo, conditional evaluation of expressions
2. Percentage, inverse trigonometric, round off, remainder, random number, arithmetic on dates

Financial
1. Net present value, internal rate of return
2. Depreciation by various methods, present value of an annuity, mortgage payment amount

Statistical
1. Mean, standard deviation
2. Variance, correlation coefficient, linear regression coefficents, moving average

Data Generation
1. Simple growth, compound growth
2. Seasonally adjusted growth

---

interest rates, we would have had to type in five values and write or print the results of each trial. With at least one program, "1-2-3," it would be possible to put the five optional interest rates in a table on the spreadsheet, and generate the corresponding table of final bank balances with a single command. In other words, all five iterations would have been accomplished with one command.

Another program, MultiPlan, allows you to make iterative computations in which a value is determined by successive approximation, for instance in finding the roots of an equation. Again, this sort of thing would be used in complex forecasting or even engineering models, and if you are not already familiar with these techniques, they will be of little interest.

LOOKING AT YOUR MODEL

Cursor Movement and Scrolling

Since spreadsheet models are invariably larger than the display, you will make a lot of use of commands for cursor movement and scrolling (refer back to Figure 8-10). As such, look for a program in which the display changes rapidly, with relatively few keystrokes. Most programs will use the cursor control keys for up, down, left, and right movement, but some may have more commands, for instance for moving a screenful at a time or for moving diagonally or to the edges of the screen or the spreadsheet (see Figure 12-1). There should also be a single-key command for moving directly to a certain cell or named area on the spreadsheet. If you take the time to run a few tests with a stopwatch, you will see that cursor movement and scrolling times vary considerably among programs, and extra commands might help compensate for a slow program.

Pay attention to the consistency and human factors design of the cursor movement and scrolling commands. Little things, like a program positioning the screen so that it is full when you go to the right side of the spreadsheet instead of leaving it off the edge will save time and aggravation.

All programs have some provision for designating areas within the spreadsheet as *protected*. It is not possible to move the cursor into those

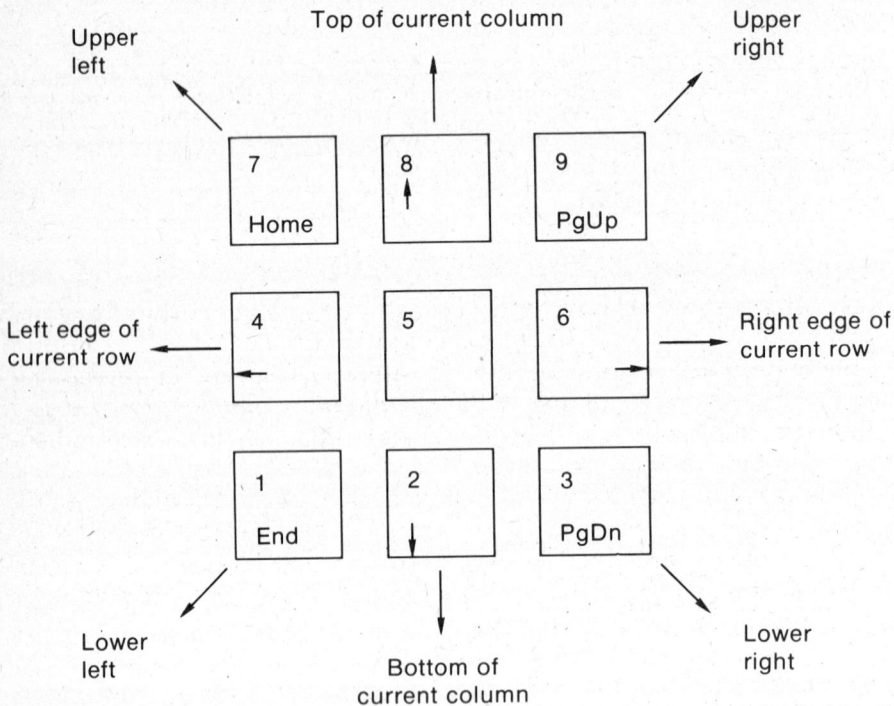

Figure 12-1. This illustration shows how the numeric keypad could be used to move the cursor within the screen window or, when shifted with ALT key, to scroll the window over the spreadsheet (*arrows*). Shifting with the CTRL key, rather than the ALT key, could cause the window to scroll a screenful at a time.

In addition to looking for a full complement of cursor control and scrolling commands, make sure they are executed rapidly; scrolling by single rows or columns can be quite slow with some programs. Also watch for small conveniences like temporarily being able to use the numeric keypad for entering numbers instead of cursor control or always being left with a full screen after scrolling to the right-hand edge of the spreadsheet.

areas, which keeps a user from inadvertently changing them. For instance, you might want to protect the areas around the edges of the spreadsheet that are used for headings. Some programs have a command for protecting all cells that contain formulas, which is handy because the user may have the need to change numeric input, but will seldom have reason to change the computations. It is also useful to be able to fix certain areas of the spreadsheet so they remain on the screen even when the rest of the display scrolls. Again, this would be most handy for headings.

Formatting the Display

Programs offer varying degrees of control over the format of the spreadsheet. They all allow you to change the widths of the cells. The earliest programs required that all cells be the same width, but today most programs allow you to have variable column widths, and I would consider that a minimal formatting requirement. Other formatting options may include control over the number of digits displayed within a cell, rounding and justification options (left, right, and centered), and the manner in which dollar (floating dollar signs, credit signs, and commas), date, and percentage data are displayed.

It should be possible to change global format defaults and to override them temporarily, for instance widening a particular column, while leaving the others at the default width. Although not possible with all programs, it is convenient to be able to associate display format specifications with individual cells or arbitrary areas on the spreadsheet.

With some programs you can sort a portion of the spreadsheet after making computations. For instance, our baseball team spreadsheet in Chapter 6 could have been set up always to display the players in alphabetic order or sorted according to batting average.

Several programs allow cells to be formatted as entries in simple bar graphs (histograms), and the multiple application packages allow the construction of complete business graphs from data stored in a designated area on the spreadsheet. With these you can get pie charts, line graphs, or bar charts of data that have been computed on the spreadsheet.

Windowing

Since the display is small relative to the entire spreadsheet, most programs enable the user to split the screen into two or more independent windows (horizontally or vertically). Several programs allow for eight or even more windows.

Multiple windows are particularly useful in modeling applications. You leave one window over the parameters that you wish to change and move the other to the affected variables, in order to see what happens when you make the changes. If a system allows for multiple windows, all cursor movement and scrolling commands should operate in the same manner within a window as they do when the entire screen is displayed. It should be possible to protect and fix designated areas within a window in the same manner as it is done on the full screen, and an option whereby two windows scroll in synchronized fashion is also convenient when you are experimenting with a model. Of course, the cursor would be located within only one window at any given time, and a single keystroke or movement of a mouse should be all it takes to switch it to another window.

DISK AND PRINTER INPUT AND OUTPUT

Disk Options

As we saw in Chapter 6, either complete models or parts of models may be saved on disk. Most programs have commands for saving either the model with its formulas, or the results of the evaluation. Evaluated results are either saved in the standard DIF format or in a format that is unique to the program. Every program allows you to save the entire model with its formulas, but the time and storage requirements may differ significantly.

Every user will be affected by the efficiency of storing entire models, but flexibility in storing and loading partial models will be relevant only if you are planning to build consolidated models. If so, pay attention to the flexibility and degree of difficulty in designating areas. Most programs have the ability to save a partial spreadsheet and later copy it into a different one. With others, it is possible to add or subtract the values on the subsidiary spreadsheets from the values in the corresponding cells when they are loaded in from disk. With still others, it is possible to set up automatic links between the master and subsidiary spreadsheets, so that the effects of changes are always reflected in the entire system. Setting these compound spreadsheets up may be a little tricky, but after you have had some time to become familiar with the program, it will not be difficult to learn to use the more esoteric capabilities like automatic consolidation.

Some programs will use the DIF format for saving partial spreadsheets for consolidation, but this format was actually designed for moving spreadsheet data between programs. If you can write spreadsheet data out in DIF format, many file management and business graphics programs will be able to read it. For this reason, the ability to read and write DIF files should be a high priority feature. In some cases, a spreadsheet program will even have built-in commands for reading and writing files that are directly compatible with some other program, for instance a graphics package, file manager, or statistical analysis program. If you plan to use your spreadsheet program in conjunction with one of these, look into file compatibility.

You will also want to be able to write output that has been formatted for printing on the disk, in order to have the capability of using a word processing program with it, for instance to incorporate the results of a spreadsheet analysis into a report or proposal without having to key them back in.

Several multiple application packages have the ability to treat a portion of the spreadsheet as a simple, record-oriented file. The same types of search, retrieval, and sort operations as are discussed in Chapter 7 are provided, and in some cases, these files can be larger than the spreadsheet and spill over onto the disk. However, these programs are not designed primarily for record processing, and among other problems, disk input and output may be quite slow.

Printed Output

As when writing to the disk, it is possible to print either the model with its formulas or the evaluated results. The model would be printed for purposes of documentation, but with most programs, it is printed out as a long list, one line per cell. If it can be printed in something close to the usual rectangular format, it might make better documentation.

The evaluated model would, of course, be printed in order to present the results. Since nearly all spreadsheets are too large to fit on a single page, every program provides for printing only designated areas, which can either be kept as separate pages or taped together to form a single sheet. With some programs, you have to decide explicitly where the page breaks should fall, but others offer a default option that decides the page breaks within the printed area for you, a major convenience.

Each program offers various formatting options within the printed pages, including margin setting, page titles, page numbering, optional printing of row and column designations or titles on each page, and footnotes. In addition, italic type, boldface, compressed print, expanded print, underlining, double underlining, and other formatting options might exist for the printed version even though they are not possible on the display screen. The more such features a program has, the more polished the reports you will be able to generate. On the other hand, be aware of operating convenience; you do not want to have to specify many parameters just to print a simple spreadsheet. A program that offers easily overridden default options will be convenient, as will one in which you can store print control information as part of the spreadsheet. If the print control information is stored on the spreadsheet, you can set it up once, and in the future it can be printed without operator action.

It is also convenient to be able to give a few printer commands manually, for direct execution while you are printing results. Look for the ability to skip the paper to the top of a new page, and to pause temporarily during printing or abort the print command.

COMPLEMENTARY MATERIALS

VisiCalc is unique among the spreadsheet programs in that it was first. For that reason, many complementary products have been developed to enhance it, and to a lesser extent other popular spreadsheet programs. For instance, there are several VisiCalc user newsletters, including one published by Software Arts (Bricklin and Frankston's company). In addition, "how-to" books have been written for several of the popular programs. These might be better training guides than the program manuals, and they are certainly cheaper if you have several users and only one copy of the program and manual. Other training materials include audio and video tape courses, interactive teaching programs, and lessons built around sample spreadsheets that are included on a disk. Spreadsheet courses are also standard fare on the curricula of computer schools, community colleges, and other adult education schools.

In addition to training aids, there are many "canned" applications for the popular spreadsheet programs. Instructional books often contain a number of models that you can key in and use. More extensive models, or templates, are usually sold on disk. You can buy tax forms, investment analysis models, and many others on ready-to-use disks. Be careful, though; you don't want to use a model you do not understand. I would not make a real estate investment on the basis of an analysis performed using a spreadsheet model that I had picked up in a store without studying the model very carefully (see the Disclaimers section in Chapter 6).

There are also utility programs available, which can extend the power of a spreadsheet program. These are generally post-processors that read the spreadsheet from disk to produce specially formatted reports, sorted output, graphic displays, and so forth, and they are widely available for the more popular spreadsheet programs.

NONINTERACTIVE PROGRAMS

As we saw in Chapter 6, VisiCalc and the spreadsheet processors that followed it were descendants of financial planning languages that ran on time-shared computers. PC spreadsheet processors were a significant departure because of the way in which the user interacted with the program. With a PC, the display is connected directly to the memory, so the screen can be changed quite rapidly. The time-sharing systems used slow terminals, and interactions were generally limited to single-line input and output. In using a financial planning language, you would key in your model one line at a time, using statements similar to the formulas and labels in an interactive spreadsheet. When the model was complete, it would be run and a printed report, perhaps in the form of a spreadsheet, produced. If an error was discovered or you wanted to change a parameter, it was necessary to enter the correction and rerun the model. As you can imagine, this was a slow process (four to eight times slower when building a relatively small model using an interactive spreadsheet program, according to one study).

On the other hand, it was possible to create larger, more complex spreadsheets, the listing of the model gave clearer documentation than a typical spreadsheet printout, and systems involving complicated hierarchic levels of consolidation were possible. These programs were used primarily by staff people to implement complex forecasting models or reporting systems.

There are noninteractive modeling systems available for the PC, and you should consider them if you need very large, complex models and automated systems. Setting up a simple model will take much longer using one of these programs, but you might ultimately be able to do more.

In evaluating a financial planning language, bear in mind the same sorts of features and considerations listed above for interactive programs. Also, look for a program with a built-in editor. If you have to use a separate program for creating or modifying your model, you will waste a lot of time moving between the editor and spreadsheet program. The output should not only be available on the disk or printer, but also you should be able to display it, scrolling the screen as if it were an interactive spreadsheet. Also look for a program that enables you to do some limited "what if" analysis, once the model has been run and the output produced.

HARDWARE

Input

Of all of the applications covered in this book, spreadsheet modeling would seem to be best suited to a mouse or other pointing device. Many of the newer spreadsheet programs have menu-oriented command structures, and some even provide a means by which a somewhat technically oriented user can extend the command set by defining new menus. Menu orientation lends itself to control through pointing at alternative choices. Furthermore, in building a spreadsheet model you often designate areas on the screen by pointing to their corners, and there is relatively little textual input (compared to word processing, for example). All of these factors make pointing devices seem useful for building and reviewing spreadsheets.

Display

You will have to make a compromise in choosing between the PC displays for spreadsheet applications. The speed and good character quality of the Monochrome Display would seem best at first because the spreadsheet is made up of character data. However, spreadsheet programs are often used in conjunction with business graphics packages, which of course require the Color/Graphics Display. (With some graphics packages, you can define a graph using the Monochrome Display and output it on a printer or plotter, but this is very time consuming, since it usually takes several trials to get the graph to look the way you want it to and without the Color/Graphics Display there is no way of previewing it.)

Furthermore, some of the spreadsheet programs can make use of color if it is available, for instance displaying black characters on a white background (which, as we mentioned in Chapter 2, is easy on your eyes), showing negative numbers in red, or using a different color for protected areas of the spreadsheet. However, these are secondary considerations, and if graphics is not a concern, you will be happy using a Monochrome Display for your spreadsheets.

Memory

Spreadsheet programs can use a good deal of memory, especially the multiapplication packages. Even if you cannot imagine making up a spreadsheet that covers thousands of cells, you may surprise yourself. As you become more familiar with the program, you will find new uses for it. Furthermore, your models will tend to grow as you revise them; as your understanding of the situation evolves you will elaborate your spreadsheets, creating more detailed submodels. So even if you initially envision relatively simple spreadsheet calculations, the value of a generous amount of memory will soon become apparent.

CPU

Execution speed is a consideration, since recalculation can take many seconds with a large model. Multiple application packages with graphic and data management components can also be compute-bound. If you like a program, but it is too slow, find out whether there is a version available that uses the 8087 math coprocessor. The 8087 should have a significant effect on the speed of spreadsheet computations.

Disk

Even though a number of spreadsheet programs can work with just one disk drive (you load in the program then remove the disk and insert a new disk with your spreadsheets on it), you will always be better off with a two drive system. In estimating disk requirements, bear in mind that it is often desirable to store several related models on one disk (they may be submodels to be consolidated into a summary), and that a spreadsheet package is often used in conjunction with a word processor, file management program, or graphics package, so disk space for these must also be considered.

Printer

If you plan to be graphing your spreadsheet results, you will need either a graphics (bit-addressable) printer or a plotter. Compatibility between a graphics package and a particular printer or plotter is often a problem, so be sure to test them out together before committing yourself. Again, speed differences between plotting programs can be significant, so take a stopwatch along as well.

Since spreadsheets, which often model processes that flow through time, can become quite wide (the theoretical maximum spreadsheet size of some programs is as big as a billboard), you might consider getting a printer that can handle 15 inch paper. It will cost more and take up more desk space than a smaller printer, but the wider output might compensate for those costs. Also, look for a printer that is able to print in a compressed mode (say 16 characters per inch). This will give you more spreadsheet per page, but, again, beware of compatibility problems. You don't want to get to your office and discover your program is incapable of putting the printer in compressed print mode, and having a printer that can put 200 characters on a line will not do you much good if the maximum line width allowed by your spreadsheet program is 132 characters.

CHAPTER THIRTEEN
Data Management

As usual, you should keep your own requirements in mind as you read this chapter and evaluate data management software. In thinking about your applications, recall that we discussed three types of program in Chapter 7: file managers, database managers, and index card systems. There is a good deal of overlap in the applicability of the three, but file managers can usually handle relatively large files and are useful in applications in which data may be entered in batches and columnar reports are needed. Database managers are more powerful than file managers since they are capable of doing the same sorts of things, but can work with two or more files in the same application. You will have to seek the help of a programmer or make your spouse a computer widow(er), if you plan to exploit the multiple file capabilities of a DBMS fully. Index card systems typically deal with single files and are oriented toward applications like a Rolodex file, in which you usually add, display, update, delete, or print single records. They often have good facilities for editing free text fields and for keyword retrieval. Index card systems usually offer fewer options than the others, but on the other hand, they are generally the easiest to use.

Have you planned your data management applications yet? Before looking at any candidate programs, decide what your files will look like—how many records will they have, how many fields per record, how many characters per field; are there free text fields? Remember to estimate your future requirements as well as today's. What will your reports look like, will updates be made singly or in batches, do you need multiple files for any application? Even if your ideas are tentative and incomplete, put some effort into this step. Once you have an idea of how you will be using your data management program, read on.

If data management is a major application, or if you will be purchasing many copies of a program for use throughout your organization, you should construct a test file and run some comparative benchmark experiments. Since the test file will have to be generated outside of the data management system, you may need some technical assistance, but it will pay off if this is a critical application. Table 13-1 suggests some quantitative tests and comparisons.

Table 13-1. Experiments for comparing speed and capacity. The speeds and capacities of data management programs can vary over wide ranges. If you plan to make heavy use of your data management software or your applications involve large files, the effort of conducting benchmark experiments measuring speed of execution, memory and storage requirements, storage input/output time, and print time may be justifiable.

Unfortunately, creating test files for data managers is somewhat more difficult than for spreadsheet or word processors, since the copy commands within the latter may be used to create the test cases. For data management benchmarks, the test files will have to be created by another program, and then imported into the data management file structure. That will require some technical skill and time (a few hours).

The test file to be imported will have to be in the format required by the data management program (commas between fields, quotes around fields, etc.). You can create the test file using a word processing program or by writing a simple BASIC program to generate it. The latter is preferable, since it would be possible to vary the records in a controlled manner, for example creating a serial number field or a randomly ordered field to test sorting and indexing times. In designing your test files, bear in mind that the file size, the number of index fields, the order of the file, the type and length of index fields, and so forth will affect performance. Of course, the test file should approximate a real application, and, if you have some actual data already on disk, that should be used for the benchmark tests. Don't forget to see to it that the tests are run on similar or identical hardware systems. .

Regardless of who generates the test files or how they do it, the following comparisons can be made:

Capacities

Maximum numeric precision

Maximum number of characters per field

Maximum number of records per character

Maximum number of records per file

Maximum number of files per disk

Maximum number of index fields per file

Maximum number of sort keys per file

Availability of multidisk files

Maximum number of screen definitions per disk

Maximum number of report definitions per disk

Maximum number of search specifications per disk

Storage space required for a data file

Storage space required for overhead files (see Table 13-7)

Storage space required per index

Maximum size for a file that will be sorted

Speed

Time required to create an index for a file using numeric/alphabetic key fields assigned at random

Time required to physically sort a given file using numeric/alphabetic fields
continued

Table 13-1. *continued*

Time required to search for a randomly selected record by index key, keyword, partial key, or record number

Time to retrieve a given percentage of the file based on index key, keyword, or partial key

Time to step from one record to the next within a retrieved set, ordered on an index value

Time to step from one record to the next within a retrieved set, in physical order

Time to update an index after deleting a single record

Time to update an index after deleting a set of records

Time to update an index after adding a single record

Time to update an index after adding a set of records

Time to redefine a file, adding or dropping a single field

Time to import a given number of records from another program

Time to print a given report

SELECTING SOFTWARE

In evaluating any data management software, you will be interested in its capabilities in file definition, data entry, indexing and sorting, searching, updating and retrieval, report generation, and interfacing with other programs. They will each be relevant, regardless of which type program you get, so we will cover each. Database managers bring up a few other questions, so we also have a brief section on them, followed by the usual discussion of hardware implications.

File Definition

Capacity Limits

Each program has its built-in limits on the maximum number of characters per field, fields per record, records per file, and files per disk, and these can be compared to your requirements. As with spreadsheet programs, the maximum numeric precision may also be a factor, so check it out if you work with large numbers.

Of course, if you read that a program allows files of up to 64KB records, each of which can have up to 256 fields of 256 characters, don't jump to the conclusion that you can have a 4MB file. You may not have the hardware to support it, and even if you do, operations on a file that size would be extremely slow on a PC. If you do have large files, benchmarks such as those suggested in Table 13-1 will be most valuable. They may very well lead you to a minicomputer.

Regardless of your file sizes, storage requirements will vary among programs since they employ different data compression strategies and require differing amounts of overhead space for file and report definitions and indices. We will return to the topic of storage requirements in the section on "Hardware Implications" in this chapter, but, again, consider taking the time for some benchmark tests if you have doubts.

Data Types Supported

An informal survey reveals that all programs allow for numeric, character, and date fields. If those are not sufficient for your application, you should look for a program that offers more of the choices listed in Table 13-2. Bear

Table 13-2. Data types. These data types are found on various PC data management systems, although no one system offers all of them as far as I know. The field type governs data validity checking, determines which operations are legal, and the way in which the data will be displayed or printed. Which of these would be required in your data management applications?

Numeric: the only valid entries are numbers, which can contain signs and decimal points. The minimum and maximum legal values will be fixed by the system, as will the number of significant digits. Arithmetic operations are legal on numbers, and options for displaying them cover things like rounding, the number of decimal places, and the treatment of commas and the sign.

Character: any of the 96 printable ASCII characters are allowed. In many cases, there will be a maximum length limit for character fields, but in some systems, unlimited (free text) fields are allowed. Editing operations are critical when dealing with long character or free text fields.

Inverted names: the name is automatically stored and sorted last name first, but printed or displayed first name first.

Self-checked numbers or characters: an extra, error checking character is added to the field, and every time a value is keyed in that character is checked to make sure it is correct.

Logical fields: only two values are allowed, true or false. The system need only tie up one bit (0 or 1) to store a logical value.

Dollar amounts: similar to a number, but always displayed or printed with two decimal places, with optional dollar signs, credit signs, and commas.

Integers: also similar to a number, but without a decimal point, a whole number. Computation with integers is faster than with decimal numbers, dollar amounts, or dates, and they will generally have a lower maximum value than numbers.

Dates: only legal dates are allowed, and several alternative display formats are usually available. Some systems permit dates to be displayed or printed only as if they were character data, whereas others allow arithmetic operations on dates, for instance subtracting the current date from the date a payment became due.

Enumerated: the legal values are explicitly enumerated by the user, for instance, the legal values for the variable DAY would be *Sunday, Monday, . . . , Saturday.* In this case, the values would be ordered for sorting and comparison, but in others, for instance COLOR (*red, blue,* etc.), they would not.

User defined: a programmer supplies the routine for checking the validity of the data.

in mind that alternative data types serve three general purposes; they give error checking information (for example, no alphabetic characters in a numeric field), they determine which operations are legal (for example, no arithmetic on character data), and they govern the manner in which the data will be displayed or printed.

Specification and Respecification

In setting up an application, you must specify the name, type, length, and any other relevant attributes of each field. You might also be required to specify at the time a field is defined whether it will be used as a key for sorting or indexing. Systems that let you make this determination while you are using them rather than while you are specifying the file are more flexible.

The specification process should be simple, and with most systems it is. Menus or prompts usually control it fully, and I have found that with most programs it is possible to specify a file without even referring to the manual. Correcting errors made during specification should be easy. You should be able to review the specification on the screen, and edit it until it is correct. Once it is complete, it will be stored on disk. The system should also allow you to print a copy of the final specification (along the lines of Figure 7-4), for the purpose of documenting the application. Even if the specification process is a little clumsy, you do it only once per file, so it may not cause a problem.

It may not matter much whether it takes 10 minutes or 30 minutes to define a file in the first place, but it is important that you have the ability to go back and change the definition after you have been using the file for a while. No matter how carefully you plan, you will want to make some changes after using a system for some time, perhaps to add, widen, or drop a field or two.

Changing the structure of a file not only means changing its specification; the data will also have to be rearranged. A utility program must be provided for copying the data from the old format into a format that is compatible with the revised file definition. Since this will not happen often, it is okay if that utility program runs slowly or is somewhat difficult to use; in a pinch you can get someone to help you out, but make sure file structure changes are allowed by the program you buy.

Security

Some data management programs include passwords for keeping unauthorized people from seeing or changing data. Security is a more important concern in multi-user systems than with personal computers, so password protection has not gotten much attention in PC programs. Larger systems often have multiple levels of password protection, with the ability to selectively designate fields, records, or files as read-only or no-access. Data encryption techniques are also employed to render sensitive data unreadable, even if it is somehow tapped.

Some PC-based systems allow you to specify a password at the time a file is defined, but most do not even offer that option. Even in those cases, it is not very difficult for a programmer to circumvent the protection scheme. As things stand today, your best bet is probably to protect sensitive data by keeping it on a disk that is safely locked up. But as hard disks with large files become more prevalent, data management systems will probably begin incorporating more security features.

Data Entry

Screen Orientation

Data entry may either be *field-oriented* or *form-oriented*. In a field-oriented system, you are prompted (the field name would be the default prompt) and enter values for each field. The value entered is checked to be sure it is valid, and if it is, the system moves on to the next field. If it is invalid, you are given an error message and asked to key in a new value. Thus, data entry is like a question and answer session. The problem with field-oriented data entry is that seeing and correcting your errors is clumsy, involving prompts like "is the record correct now (yes/no)?" and "which field would you like to change?" For that reason, a form-oriented system would be faster and less confusing for an untrained operator.

In the form-oriented approach, a blank form is displayed on the screen, and you have the sense of filling in the blanks on a form, a well-known point of reference for everyone (check back to Figure 7-5 for an example). A well designed system will have simple means of allowing you to move among fields and going back to edit entries if you see that you have made an error.

Look for a system that can generate a default screen format using the field names and lengths as a guide. That will save you time in setting up a "quick and dirty" application; however, for ongoing applications you also want the ability to define custom screen forms that are laid out in a manner that looks good, with titles and arbitrary field designations. Again, it will not matter much if creating custom screen forms is a little awkward, because you do it only once per application, but it should be possible. Also, be sure that you can print the screen form out for documentation and that it is easily revised if you decide you don't like it.

Field Editing

As I stated above, the ability to make corrections when you see a mistake in a field is important. When dealing with relatively short fields, you might be satisfied with a program that forces you to retype the entire entry, but when the field is long, you want to be able to change parts of it and leave the others alone.

For fixed-length fields, any system that uses the PC's "insert," "delete," and cursor control keys properly will suffice, but field editing becomes particularly critical in systems that allow for relatively long or free text fields. In these cases, the requirements for correcting and reformatting are the same as for a word processing editor. Pay careful attention to the power and convenience of the field editor if you have long character or free text fields. Use the checklists suggested in Chapter 11 (on word processing) as a guide. All things being equal, pick a system with field editing commands similar to those on your word processing program, in order to avoid confusion.

Error Checking

As we have seen, data should be checked for validity when they are entered. All systems do minimal checking, making sure field lengths are not exceeded and that numbers do not contain any alphabetic characters. Other things to look for are the ability to specify an exact (as well as a maximum) field length, a minimum field length, maximum and minimum numeric values, self-check digits on fields, or enumerated allowable values (Table 13-2 describes the latter two). A few systems even allow a programmer to write a subroutine that is evoked for error checking whenever data are entered into a certain field. For example, a user-defined error checking routine might look for inconsistencies between fields, like a high salary for a low paying job category.

Partially Automated Evaluation

Some systems simplify data entry, particularly when it is done in batches, by automatically supplying default values for some of the fields in a record. For instance, you may have the option of designating a field as a serial number, so it is automatically given a default value one greater than the value entered in the prior record; or a program might be able automatically to calculate a field value that depends upon others, for instance multiplying HOURS times RATE to supply a default value for the GROSS PAY field.

Another possibility is always to use the value entered into a certain field in the prior record as the default value for that field in the current record. For instance, in a billing application, each record might have a date field. You would have to key in the date only for the first record on a given day; it would automatically be carried forward into all subsequent records (this was called "gang punching" in the punch card days).

A final consideration is that it is usually necessary to designate fields for automatic evaluation at the time the file is defined, which is not as flexible as if it can be done at data entry time. Regardless, it should be possible to override automatic evaluation during data entry.

These features will be of most interest to those who enter data in batches, although they can save anyone time.

Batch Entry

Will you be entering records whenever something comes up during the day or are your data management applications such that you can gather a batch of *transactions* and enter them all at once? In the former case, your files are always up to date, but the latter may be more efficient if your system provides for entering batches of data. If you have batch-oriented applications, look for a system that cuts down on index building time by allowing you to key a group of entries into a temporary *transaction file*, later merging all of the transactions into the *master file*. The merging might take a while, but it is automatic, so you can do something else while it goes on.

Indexing and Sorting

As we saw in Chapter 7, data management programs are capable of sorting files into various orders, either by physically rearranging the records or by creating a sorted index to the file. The index would also be used for searching and retrieval. Although all programs are able to do these things, they vary significantly in terms of flexibility and speed. We will save our discussion of indexing and sorting disk requirements for the hardware section.

In planning your applications, think about which fields will be used as indices and sort keys. For instance, in a mailing list application, it is likely that you will want to retrieve records by NAME, STATE, or ZIP CODE, but unlikely that you would do so on SECOND LINE OF ADDRESS. Many programs limit the number of fields that can be used as indices or sort keys, so be sure to check your requirements against the specification.

Also check to see if hierarchic sorts are possible and, if so, how many levels are allowed. This will be important if you plan to generate columnar reports with several summary levels, for instance employees within departments within divisions.

If your files will be very large, even in the 100 record range, you will find significant speed differences among programs, and a slow program might be either a minor inconvenience or a total disaster. Tables 13-3 and 13-4 show the sorts of speed differences you can expect to find between programs and the effect of file size on speed, respectively. They are included less for the actual figures than to convince you of the necessity of really running some tests if you plan to have large files or have a lot of data management applications.

Searching

As we saw in Chapter 7, searches may be based on an explicit record number, on the entire contents of the field, on the partial contents of the field, or on a keyword value. Most systems allow for two or three modes, and in evaluating searching power, you can begin by asking which modes are allowed.

Explicit Record Number

Every system can retrieve a record if you know its explicit number, its relative position in the file. Searches on record numbers will be fastest, but

Table 13-3. Speed variation among programs. Jack Abbott compared the speed of five data management programs in a Byte Magazine article. He constructed a standard test file of 1,007 records of 128 characters (15 fields), and ran a number of tests. The times show the spread between the slowest and fastest programs. Note that Abbott also recorded the file sizes, finding overhead files requiring from 9% to 19% more disk space.

Although not run on an IBM PC, the hardware configuration was comparable to a floppy disk PC, and the programs he tested are available for the PC. In looking at the times, don't pay as much attention to the absolute times (some programs are faster, others are slower than these five) as to the wide ranges. You really should benchmark time sensitive applications.

Task	Time Range for Five Programs
Merge in a batch of 50 records	1–15 minutes
Delete 50 records	1 minute 20 seconds–1 hour 21 minutes
Physically sort the file on one alphabetic field	3 minutes–14 minutes 30 seconds
Build a one field index	3 minutes–4 minutes
Retrieve one record	3 seconds
Extract a retrieved set of 50 records, spaced equidistantly throughout the file	20 seconds–6 minutes 30 seconds
Total storage required	135–155K

obviously are troublesome in many applications. In order to search on record number, you must keep an index outside of the system. If no new records are ever added or deleted, that might be feasible, but even then you would have to make constant reference to the printed index. At least one other mode is required to complement this one, so a system that offers only record-number retrieval (a few do) should not be considered.

Field Content

Nearly all systems allow boolean searches based on the contents of a field. You should expect the command format for searches to be very simple; there is no reason for it to be complicated. Some programs attempt to "simplify" search specification by leading you through a series of questions or a set of menus, but they are more confusing and slower than the simple command-directed searches illustrated in Chapter 7.

All six relational operators should be available, as well as AND, OR, and parentheses. You will also appreciate the ability to store a frequently used search command away in a library, so that you do not have to think it through and key it in every time it is used. Finally, pay some attention to search time; as we have seen, it may vary by a factor of 10, which can be frustrating.

You might also come across the term *soundex* in a discussion of matching

Table 13-4. Effects of varying file size on speed. These tests show the effect of file size on speed. The times for some operations, like retrieving one record, are relatively insensitive to file size, others go up in rough proportion to the length of the file, and others, for example sorts, go up at an even faster rate.

Again, do not place much emphasis on the absolute times, since this is a very slow program.

	Number of Records in the File		
Task	12	100	500
Import a file into the internal data format of the program	45 seconds	5 minutes 51 seconds	29 minutes 9 seconds
Restructure the file after eliminating one field	57 seconds	7 minutes 3 seconds	37 minutes 33 seconds
Merge a single record into the file and update the index	57 seconds	1 minute 51 seconds	4 minutes 34 seconds
Build an index on a single four digit field consisting of random numbers between 0 and 9999	19 seconds	1 minute 59 seconds	22 minutes (1 minute 7 seconds)
Retrieve one record based on the four digit random field	7-9 seconds	10-15 seconds	15-19 seconds (5-6 seconds)
Extract a retrieved set of ⅓ of the file based on a one character random field	54 seconds	3 minutes 49 seconds	17 minutes 55 seconds
Copy the entire file, including its definition, indices, and data to another disk	57 seconds	2 minutes 10 seconds	7 minutes

and searching. This refers to systems that treat names as special cases, and try to find close matches, for instance matching on Siegal even though you searched for Seigel.

Partial Field Content

The ability to search for partial matches is handy, but is not provided on all systems. The command format would be the same as when searching for full fields, but the search uses patterns or templates that can match many values. For instance, you might search for any record with *Williams* in the name field or *Park* in the address field. Partial field search capability adds considerable flexibility to a system; the only drawback is that such searches are slower than full field searches, particularly in free text fields.

Keywords

Keyword searching is often used with index card systems because the free text field often conveys as much relevant information as the fixed fields, and you need a retrieval method that can take that information into account. Be skeptical in evaluating an index file system that does not allow for keywords.

If a system does allow keyboard retrieval, associating a keyword with a record should be simple and fast. It should be possible to see a record's keywords and edit them, adding new ones or deleting old ones at any time. In assigning keywords, it is helpful to be able to get a display or printout of all currently assigned words, along with their frequencies. Although I don't know of any PC programs that do so, a program that provided some of the early aids for automatic assignment of keywords developed by H. P. Luhn and his colleagues would be helpful. They included things like compiling word frequency tallies (concordances) and giving extra weight to words found in the first and last sentences of paragraphs. A program that automatically suggested keywords might turn out to be a time saver.

Operations on the Retrieved Records

Regardless of how it is specified, a search will retrieve a set of records that match the condition called for. There may be either no matching records (the retrieved set is empty), one, or several. If there are none, the system will simply inform you of that fact and wait for another search command. If one or more records are found to match the search condition, the system tells you how many and gives you the chance to work on the retrieved records.

Single Record Operations

Most data management systems display the first record in the retrieved set on the screen. The display should be in the same format as the screen form used during data entry, since that is familiar. If the first record was not the one you were interested in, the system should have commands to step to the next record (in either direction), or jump straight to the start or end of the retrieved set. The records might be presented in their physical order or ordered on some sorted index field. The speed with which programs move from one record to the next while browsing varies considerably, so keep a stopwatch handy while you try them out.

Once on the screen, it should be possible to update the record, write it to disk, or print it. The updating process should be exactly like creating the record in the first place, so you only have to learn one procedure. Also, since it can take a long time to update the indices after you change an index field, be sure the program offers the option of doing so in batches, rather than automatically updating the indices each time a change is made.

Deletion is even more time consuming because not only does it require that the indices be changed; some programs also physically move the records on the file to fill in the unused space (although there are better techniques for reclaiming space). At any rate, the program should offer the option of merely marking a record as "deleted," but not actually changing the file until you give a command to do so, at which time all deleted records would be expunged. Note that this approach also allows you to restore a record, if you discover that it should not have been deleted.

Operations on Sets of Records

In addition to updating, printing, storing, or deleting the single current record, it is often possible to operate upon the entire retrieved set. Options to look for include storing the retrieved set on disk (temporarily or permanently), listing the records on the display or printer, sending a formatted columnar report to the display or printer, and deleting the entire set of records.

Report Generation

Nearly all data management systems provide some means of printing formatted columnar reports. In order to define a report, it is necessary to specify things like which fields are to be included in it, which records are to be printed, what the headings, column spacings, margins, titles, and so forth are to be, and what additional columns and totals, if any, should be calculated. Table 13-5 shows the options you can look for in selecting the report generation features that your applications require. Although no program offers all of them, you can use the table as a checklist.

Regardless of what is possible, each report you print will have to be defined. Doing so should be simple, and it usually is, but because it is more complex than defining a screen form, the system will probably use a series of menus and prompts, and therefore report definition may be somewhat time consuming. For that reason, you should look for a system that is able to produce reports in a fairly standard default format with a minimum of specification on your part. You will particularly appreciate this capability if you need to produce a variety of ad hoc reports rather than a few reports that are repeated periodically as part of a data processing system.

Of course, there must be a means of naming report definitions and storing them in a library once they have been set up. From that point on, they can be evoked by simply giving the command to print the specific report. It should also be possible to recall a specification from that library and edit it in order to alter the appearance or content of the report if you decide it needs to be changed.

It should be possible to direct the report output to the display screen or the disk as well as the printer. Directing it to the display will be useful while you are designing the report, trying to get its layout and contents the way you want them. Design or "debugging" of the reports will go much faster if you can preview them on the screen.

The ability to output a formatted report to the disk is of course useful for postprocessing, for example, if it is to be included as part of a word processing document. Be sure that the output produced by the data management program is compatible with your word processing program. If it uses non-ASCII control codes, it may not be.

Table 13-5.   Report generation options. This table lists the features that you can look for in specifying columnar reports. Although most systems are capable of printing selected columns, typically with three levels of control break, many give relatively little control over the appearance of the report.

Report Content

The ability to specify which fields will be included in a report

The selection of records using Boolean search criteria (in some systems, the selection will have to have been made by first retrieving the records to be included and then giving the command to print the report)

Printing the report with the records sorted (in most systems, the file would have to be sorted before giving the command to print the report)

Multiple control break (subtotal) levels (the file would first have to be sorted into proper order with most systems)

The option of full reports, like the one illustrated in Figure 7-9, or summary reports with only the intermediate and final totals shown

The ability to compute fields that are not included in the input file, for instance multiplying length by width to list an area, even though there was no area field

The ability to compute total fields that are not included in the input file, in the same way as new columns are computed

Calculation of averages, standard deviations, and other descriptive statistics in addition to totals and record counts

Report Appearance

Headings and footings that are repeated on every page

Headings that are repeated at control breaks

The ability to force a new page when control breaks occur

Page numbering, dating, and margin setting

The availability of special effects such as underlining, double underlining, boldface, overstriking, italics, compressed and expanded print, and so forth

The ability to specify the spacing of the columns

The ability to specify the field headings, including multi-line headings, and to position them (left, right, or centered) within the column

Interfacing with Other Software

The previous paragraph mentioned the possibility of "printing" a formatted report on the disk, where it could be read by a word processing program, if their data formats were compatible. A data management system may be able to export or import data in other formats as well.

If you need to produce reports that are beyond the capability of your data management system, there is another alternative. Most programs are able to write an unformatted file to the disk, with a record on each line and the fields separated by some character, usually a comma. A relatively unskilled programmer would be able to write a program that read this data and produced a report in any format desired. Of course, you would have to get some help with this (or else learn a little BASIC programming yourself). If you plan this sort of postprocessing, have a programmer check the candidate systems to be sure they are capable of generating output that is compatible with the BASIC interpreter.

Many data management programs can also write DIF files, which can be read into a spreadsheet or alternatively picked up by a business graphics program to produce charts and graphs. If you have only a few rows and columns to transfer from the data management system, it is probably easier to key the data back into the spreadsheet or graphics program, but if you transfer large amounts of data on a systematized basis, look for the capability of writing DIF files. If the data management program you pick is a highly popular one, you might even be able to find postprocessors that can read its files directly, without the need to go through the intermediate DIF format. The converse is also true; many data management programs have special commands for reading files written by popular spreadsheet programs.

You may also need to import files from other applications, so your data management program should be capable of reading DIF files as well as the sort of unformatted record-per-line ASCII files referred to above. Again, a little knowledge of programming, typically in BASIC, may be needed to prepare an unformatted file that is compatible with your data manager, but not much.

DATABASE MANAGEMENT SYSTEMS (DBMS)

As we saw in Chapter 7, a DBMS may be thought of informally as a file management system that is able to work with more than one file at a time. We do not need to spend a lot of space on DBMSs because the factors discussed above, in the context of single file management, are applicable.

If you are certain that all of your applications will involve single files, the added expense of a DBMS would not be justified. If you will be doing a few multifile applications, you should get a relational system, which you can use as a simple file manager, and get some programming help when it is time to set up the multifile applications. If you plan to use your PC for substantial data processing applications, you should also consider DBMSs based on a network model, but in that case you will definitely need help from a programmer. It will probably pay off to get a second, file management program for your own personal applications, and leave the network based applications to the programmer.

There were two aspects of the DBMS that were not covered as part of simpler file management programs, the *data manipulation language* and its editor. In order to produce complex reports, bringing together information from several files, a DBMS will either incorporate its own programming language or rely on an external language processor, perhaps a PL/1 or COBOL compiler. In either case, the capability and power of the data manipulation language will be a significant factor in selecting a system. It should provide the usual control and assignment statements, and internal data types such as variables, arrays, and records (with sufficient numbers of each). In addition, the data manipulation language should provide access to all of the DBMS commands for data entry, searching, report generation, and so forth. None of this should be familiar to you at this point, so the programmer who will be working with this facet of the DBMS should be called in to help select the system. If the data manipulation language is interpreted rather than compiled, execution times might turn out to be quite slow, so you might also have the programmer try out a few benchmark tests if your applications involve many or large files or complex retrieval sequences.

The time required to develop a DBMS application will also be cut down if the system includes an integral editor for writing programs in the data manipulation language. If it does not, you have to use a word processing editor to write and change programs, and constantly moving back and forth between the DBMS and the word processor wastes time.

HARDWARE IMPLICATIONS

CPU

CPU speed will be a constraint on your data management tasks, but there may not be much you can do about it. The 8087 arithmetic coprocessor will not help as much with data management as with, say, spreadsheet processing because there are not many complex computations involved. Data management is more concerned with character manipulation, particularly in activities that are likely to bog down, like sorting and index building. The language in which the system is written will have more effect on speed than the 8087. We have run tests comparing the speeds of interpreted and compiled versions of the same data management program* that show that the compiled version is anywhere from three to 20 times faster, depending upon the operation.

Memory

A large memory will speed sorting, indexing, searching, and so forth because less disk input and output are required, *if* the program has been written to use all of the memory. However, many of the data management programs on the market for the PC were converted from eight bit systems with small memories, so they do not use all of the available memory. If you generally like a program, but discover that it slows down because it does not use all of your memory, consider electronic disk emulation (Chapter 4). Table 13-6 shows the sorts of improvement you might expect.

*TIM from Innovative Software

Table 13-6. Effects of electronic disk. An electronic disk emulator will speed data management significantly, even if the program was not written to take advantage of the full PC memory address space. This comparison was run using the TIM program, from Innovative Software, and it gives you an idea of the improvement you can expect if you use electronic disk to emulate floppy drives. Of course, the improvement will not be as dramatic when comparing an electronic disk to a hard disk.

Task	With Electronic Disk	With Floppy Disk
Sort a 500 record file	34 seconds	1 minute 7 seconds
Search on a four character field	2.4 seconds	5–6 seconds
Merge one record, updating the indices	4.4 seconds	16 seconds

Disk

The starting point for making an estimate of disk requirements is to multiply the expected number of records by the number of characters per record, but there are several other factors to consider.

First, each system will store the data in different ways, some taking more space and others compressing data to save space (but slowing access down). For instance, if numeric data is stored as ASCII characters, each digit in the number requires a byte of disk space, but if they are stored as binary numbers or in other space-efficient formats, they take up fewer bytes. The cost is that numbers must be converted back and forth between the two representations, which may slow the program down. Similar encoding can be used to save space for logical or enumerated fields.

Even larger space savings may be achieved if the system stores data in variable-length records. If you define a NAME field as having a length of 25 characters, some systems will set aside 25 bytes per record whether the person's name is *Mark Twain* or *Samuel Langhorne Clemens*. Unless your records have many short fields, a system with variable length records will save you some disk space.*

You must also add the space of several overhead files to your estimate of the space required for a data file (see Table 13-7). This will amount to a 10% to 25% addition, depending upon the system and the number of indices, reports, screen forms, and search specifications you create. As you see, it might be rather difficult to get a precise estimate of the space your files will take up, so if space is a critical concern, some benchmarks might be in order.

Sorting a file will also require temporary working space on a disk. If you anticipate physical sorts of large files, run tests to see both how long they take and how much space the working files require.

*If there are many short fields, space may actually be lost because of the overhead bytes needed to delimit each field, either with a separating character or by some other means.

Table 13-7. Overhead files. There will be several overhead files associated with each data file. For this reason, an overhead factor of 10% to 25% should be added to your estimate of disk space required for the file.

The definition of the file (field names, sizes, types, etc.)
The library of screen form(s) for data entry and display
The library of report definition(s)
The library of commonly used search specification(s)
The index(ices) used for file access and sorting

In addition to the space used up by your files, you must plan disk space for the data management program, which may be quite large. In fact, several are so large that the entire program cannot fit on one disk, requiring that you swap program disks during operation, which wastes time and can cause errors, confusion, and even damage to disks that are carelessly thrown on the desk.

If you have a multidisk program or will be working with relatively large files, give serious thought to a hard disk. A hard disk would simplify your operating procedures and be signficantly faster, since many data management operations require disk access.

Printer

If you will be using your data management system to produce columnar reports, rather than just printouts of single records, you are a good candidate for a printer that can handle wide (15 inch) paper. If it has a compressed print mode and your program can use it, you can get still wider columnar reports. However, a wide printer will cost more and have a large footprint, so think through the contents and format of your reports before deciding that you need one; try to devise a way of getting by with narrow paper.

For printing long reports, or printing on special forms such as carbon sets or gummed labels for mailing, a tractor feed mechanism will be superior to friction feed. Long reports will also be quite time consuming, so make some estimates of how long your reports will be and how long it will take to print them. If you decide that it is necessary to go to a faster printer than the standard IBM printer, be sure to test the software and printer together. If the printer is rated in excess of 120 characters per second and you are using an interpreted program or have a multifile application, you may discover that the program, not the printer, is the limiting factor.

CHAPTER FOURTEEN
Communication

The most important step in getting set up for remote communication is selecting a software package, so this chapter opens with a consideration of the factors to consider and questions to ask in evaluating these programs. Since all of the factors we discuss will not be relevant to every user, use Table 14-1 to spot the ones you should pay particular attention to. Of course, you will need a modem and your communication requirements will affect the other components of your PC, so we will also cover hardware in this chapter. Finally, there are many remote services available, and we present a few tips for finding and evaluating them.

This chapter is devoted to the selection and evaluation of software and hardware for remote communication, but it does not cover local communication, for two reasons. The first is that product offerings are quite primitive at this writing. Much of what I could say would doubtless be out of date by the time it was published. The second reason is that, unlike the other applications we have discussed, the typical reader of this book really cannot do the necessary evaluation and make an intelligent decision about what to buy. Consultants, technical people, and the people from your organization's data processing department must really be called in. You can review Chapter 9, which summarizes the issues and points out a number of pitfalls and questions to raise, but you should have expert help in evaluating and selecting local communication software and hardware.

SOFTWARE

As with any software, the considerations of Chapter 10 come into play with a communication package. Most important, you need to understand your applications before proceeding, because standardization among remote services is lacking, and you may run into compatibility problems. It is as if you needed a different sort of telephone for each long distance area code. So, begin by deciding which remote services you will be using. If you will be using a remote system for electronic mail, which one? Will you be accessing

Table 14-1. Summary of software characteristics. In selecting a communication program, there are many questions to ask and features to look for. This table summarizes the relevance of each. You will not find a single program that is great in every dimension, so concentrate on the features that are important in your operation.

Convenience of Configuring and Reconfiguring the Software: Important for all users, particularly those who use more than one remote system. Technical help may be necessary in setting up the configurations initially.

Convenience in Making the Connection: Saves time for frequent users, but not essential to system operation.

Character Format Options: For ASCII data, parity bit options compatible with all remote systems must be provided. Block checked file transfers may be necessary for binary data.

Control Characters and Transliteration: Your system must be able to transmit all of the control characters required by any remote system you plan to use. In addition, it must be possible to filter out unwanted control characters. Full transliteration capability will be needed only for communication with computers that do not use the ASCII code.

Logging Transcript on the Printer: Only necessary if logging on disk is not possible.

Logging Transcript on the Disk: Necessary for all users involved in interaction with remote systems.

Handshaking: PC communication software should be compatible with the hand-shaking protocols of each remote system you plan to use.

Buffer Manipulation: Convenient, but not essential for users involved with interactive applications.

File Transmission: Useful for all users transmitting files longer than, say, one paragraph, with any degree of frequency. Compatibility with the remote systems may be a problem, and it should be checked out for each of them.

Editing: Useful for those transmitting many relatively short files, composed during an interactive session. If not available, the remote system editor will have to be used, reducing convenience and increasing cost.

Block Checked File Transfer: Parity checking and visual inspection suffice for interactive applications, but block checking is desirable for batch transmission of sensitive data or for applications where binary files are transmitted.

Unattended Operation: Unattended operation, either handling incoming calls or dialing out, is useful if you plan to use your PC as a remote resource, serving those calling in, or if late night file transfer is desired.

Terminal Emulation: Those using remote programs that assume a certain model intelligent terminal will require a special communication program that emulates that terminal.

a specialized data base? Which one? Once the services are pinned down, you can look for a program that is compatible with all of them.

Keep the rest of the factors raised in Chapter 10 in mind as you look over communication programs. Look for good documentation, easy access to the operating system commands (you would be unhappy if after receiving a long file you needed to delete something from the disk to make space for it but couldn't), and program speed. All of the general factors are relevant, but now let's look at others that are specific to selecting a communication program, beginning with ease of installation.

Convenience of Configuring and Reconfiguring the Software

Once you have chosen a communication program, it will have to be installed and adapted to your particular PC and the service(s) you will be using. If you aren't 100% sure that you can install the program properly, don't worry, because someone can probably do that for you, and from that point on, learning to operate the program will be easy. Just remember that if you will be using more than one remote service, the program may have to be set up differently for each, and you will want one that can easily switch from one setup to another.

Regardless of whether you or someone else has to set the software up, it would be nice to get a program that was easy to install. There are all sorts of minor differences between one remote computer and another, so it is necessary to specify values for a dozen or so communication-related parameters, including:

Transmission rate	Handshaking option
Parity checking option	Buffering option
Number of data bits	Number of stop bits
Remote echoing (yes/no)	Handling of carriage returns and line feeds

You certainly don't want to begin each communication session by answering questions like these, so be sure that once you (or a technician) has figured out the correct values, they can be installed as the defaults. That way, once the program is initialized properly, you can forget these parameters.

Will you be using more than one remote system? If so, you want a program that provides a library of alternate configurations. The most commonly used parameter values should be set as the defaults, but a single command or menu selection should be all it takes to switch to another one of the configurations in the library.

Whether you or someone else does it, figuring out the correct communication parameters for a given remote system might take some trial and error, and there are a few program features that can make that task a little easier. Look for a program that lets you change the configuration without losing the telephone connection. Installation will also be easier if you can see abbreviations for nonprinting characters as they are received (though once the setup is finished, you will want to turn that feature off). These features will help if some difficulty is encountered in setting the program up, but even if they are not present, installation should not take more than an hour or two of experimentation.

It may also be necessary to configure the program for operation on your particular PC. For example, if both your printer and the communication program expect to use the same RS-232 port, you have a problem. Again, you may need a little one time technical assistance.

Convenience in Making the Connection

To connect with a remote computer, you have to dial its number and then give some commands to identify yourself as a valid user, in order to *log in*. It's a simple process, but it can get tedious. It may be as simple as just dialing the number of a friend down the street, or you may have to get an outside line through your switchboard, connect to a voice network like Sprint and key in your ID code and the computer's phone number, or use a data network with its own phone number and computer ID code. None of this is difficult, but it can easily require dialing over 20 digits, only to get a busy signal and have to try again. Once the computer connection is established, another 20 keystrokes might be needed to log in and give a beginning command to start your session.

Simple programs require that you do all of this manually, but others automate some or all of the steps involved in making a remote connection. A program might maintain a library file with the telephone number, communication parameters, and log in and other commands for several remote systems. In these cases, a single keystroke could suffice to complete a connection or retry if the line was busy.

Many of the programs that automate the connection process are designed to work with a specific brand auto-dial modem, so if you want this convenience, your modem choice may be made for you. Also, be aware that problems may be encountered when connecting through a switchboard or value-added network. They may require extra characters and pauses, switching between pulse and tone dialing, etc. If you can't test the program in your own environment, make sure the dealer understands the conditions and guarantees that it will work.

Character Format Options

As we saw in Chapter 2, a byte consists of eight bits, and an ASCII character uses only seven of them. If you are transmitting ASCII data, the eighth bit may be either ignored or used as a parity bit for error detection (recall Figure 8-13). If you have non-ASCII or *binary* data, in which all eight bits are meaningful, some other provision would have to be made for error detection (see the section on block checked transmission, below), and it may turn out that transmission is not even possible.

As we saw, remote computers differ in the ways in which they treat the parity bit. Some systems use odd parity, some even, some ignore it, and others always set it to one or zero. Regardless, your communication program won't work unless it offers a consistent option. Odd and even parity are nearly standard choices, but watch for the others; they may not be possible.

The parity bit causes more problems if you have to transfer binary data, in which the eighth bit is significant. For instance, the output of a word processing program may use the eighth bit in some characters to control document format, or if you are attempting to transmit an object program, all eight bits will be used. Note that these cases occur in the transmission of files that have been prepared off-line, not in the conversational mode. With many communication programs and with many remote computers, binary (eight bit) file transmission may not be possible without some programming, so look before you leap.

If you have an eight bit file to transmit, and compatibility problems are discovered, there is a common but inefficient way around the problem. If your communication program comes with a utility program for converting each of the eight bit bytes into two four bit *nibbles*, the new file can be transmitted (see Figure 14-1). Of course, it will take twice the time to transmit, and a utility program will have to be run at the other end to put the bytes back together again. In a pinch, however, this will do.

There are also utility programs that compress ASCII files, by taking advantage of the fact that certain characters (like "a" or "e") are much more common than others (like "Q" or "@"). Compressed files can save some transmission time, but because of the time taken and added complexity in running a data compression program, you won't be interested in one unless you really plan to transmit a lot of data.

Control Characters and Transliteration

All communication programs work the same when dealing with the 96 printing ASCII characters; they are displayed when received and trans-

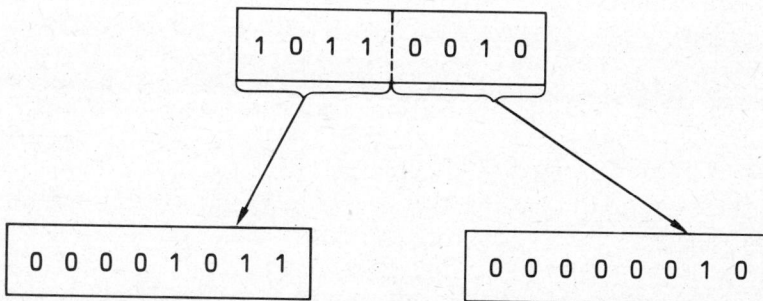

Figure 14-1. If a communication program is incapable of transmitting eight bit data directly, a utility command may be provided for breaking each byte into two four bit nibbles. These may be transmitted to the remote machine, where a corresponding utility is needed to "reassemble" the bytes. This technique will do in a pinch, but it adds complication and doubles transmission time.

mitted when typed, but you can run into problems with the nonprinting codes. Many remote computers use nonprinting characters for control commands. For instance, most remote systems will interpret a ctrl-c (the code that is transmitted when you hold the control key down and type a "c") as a command to stop running whatever program is being used. If your communication program were not able to transmit a ctrl-c, you couldn't use a remote system that used it as a command character. Other commonly used command characters include a *break* signal $\frac{1}{10}$ second of steady 0 bits), Esc (on the PC keyboard), and various other control key combinations. Be sure your communication package can transmit these codes.

Nonprinting characters must also be handled properly when they are received. While you are first setting your system up, it helps to be able to see abbreviations displayed whenever one is received (e.g., "∧C" for a ctrl-c), but it should also be possible to ignore them during normal use. For instance, remote computers may transmit several null characters (0000000) after each carriage return, under the assumption that you are printing the information being received and your printer needs a time delay while the carriage returns and the paper advances. If you are not printing the incoming text, you want your software to ignore these null characters, to filter them out.

With nearly every program, you can selectively cause certain characters to be ignored or filtered out, but the most flexible programs let you set up tables showing how each of the 256 possible character combinations should be handled (one table for incoming characters, another for outgoing). In addition to ignoring a certain character, it is possible to substitute another code (computer folks call that *transliteration* instead of substitution). A program with full transliteration capability would enable you to communicate with large IBM computers that used the *EBCDIC* character code instead of ASCII.

Unless your company has large IBM computers in-house, you probably won't need to handle codes other than ASCII, but flexibility in handling the nonprinting characters will still be helpful. Setting up these character substitution tables might require some technical assistance, but once it is done, you can forget it.

Logging the Communication Transcript on the Printer

Incoming data and the characters you type will usually be displayed on the screen, but you might also want to keep a printed log of a communication session. Most programs offer this capability as an option, but make sure that printing can easily be switched on and off. That way, you can get a printed record of only the important parts of a "conversation" with a remote computer. With some programs, you can even suspend printing of outgoing characters while continuing to print everything that is received (or vice versa).

If your communication program prints characters directly as they are received, the remote system must be capable of inserting null characters in the data stream to allow time for carriage returns and line and page feeds. As we saw above, the null characters are included as time delays, and should be filtered out and not displayed. If your software buffers incoming characters before printing them, it avoids this problem.

Logging the Communication Transcript on the Disk

Logging the transcript on the disk is much handier than logging it on the printer because you can process the received information after the telephone connection is broken, so be sure your communication program can do it. If you receive a memo from a colleague or some historical data on a company you are analyzing, and they are stored on disk, you may be able to move them directly to some other report. Disk logging is also a time saver. If you had lots of information coming in, say, all of the electronic mail you received during your two week vacation, you could log it on the disk, not even reading it as it was received, then browse through the log file on the disk using your word processing program.

As with printer logging, look for a program that lets you toggle disk logging on and off, and offers the option of only recording incoming or outgoing information. You want the same sort of flexibility in character filtering and substitution for information going into a disk file as you do for information that is being displayed.

Before it is written to the disk, the transcript of a communication session is accumulated in a buffer area in memory (look back at Figure 8-10). In most cases, the buffer will be large enough to hold many minutes' log, and when it becomes full, it will automatically be written to the disk. All things being equal, a program with a large buffer will be a little faster than one with a small buffer, but as long as handshaking is allowed, buffer size is not a critical factor.

Handshaking

At various points in the communication process, it is necessary to suspend transmission temporarily. The suspension might be requested by the operator at the keyboard (for instance if it is difficult to read information as fast as it is arriving), or by the program (for instance if the printer runs out of paper or the disk buffer becomes full).

As we saw in Chapter 8, the most common convention for transmission suspension is the XON/XOFF protocol. If your PC sends an XOFF to the remote computer, it suspends transmission until an XON is received and transmission is resumed. If all computers used this convention, the world would be a happier place. Unfortunately, other protocols exist as well, so it is imperative that your PC communication software is compatible with the conventions used by each of the remote computers you will be using. In addition to XON/XOFF there are several less common protocols such as break/return characters or sending one line at a time. If you will be using several remote systems, you may need a program that offers several protocol choices. The great majority of cases will be handled by one of those standard choices, but some communication packages are open ended, allowing programmers to supply their own handshaking subprogram.

But what happens if the remote computer doesn't support any form of handshaking? That would be uncommon, but if it were the case, you would need a PC communication package with a double buffer option. When one buffer fills up, its contents would be written to the disk, and incoming characters would be routed to the second buffer. This sort of operation is time sensitive, and it probably will cause you to lose some data if the remote computer cannot insert null characters for time delays between lines.

Buffer Manipulation

As we have seen, the communication transcript is generally stored in a buffer before being written on disk. Many systems enable the operator to pause and manipulate the transcript while it is still in the buffer. It may be possible to examine information in the buffer, clear the buffer if it is found to be irrelevant, force the contents to be written to the disk even though the buffer is not yet full, and see how much buffer space is still available.

While these capabilities may be of some use, the ability to edit information in the buffer is more useful. The same sorts of operations as are performed by a word processing editor are desirable—scrolling and cursor movement, insertion and deletion, searching and replacing, and so forth.

While it may be useful to be able to edit incoming material before it is saved, it is even more important if the system is able to transmit data from the buffer. In that case, you can compose messages (perhaps electronic mail) during a communication session and transmit them without using a word processing program.

File Transmission

That brings us to file transmission. Up to this point we have concentrated on conversational applications, in which you type a few commands to the remote computer and it responds with an answer, perhaps a fairly large amount of information, which is captured in a buffer and printed, or more likely written, on disk. But what if you have a lot of information to send, perhaps a long memo or a list of all of the sales you made during the day?

You could type it in at the keyboard, but that would be inefficient for many reasons. Your phone bill and remote computer charges would mount up as you typed in the data. Furthermore, it would go much slower because a word processing or data entry program running on your PC would be much quicker and more convenient to use than one running on a remote computer. If the information to be transmitted—a spreadsheet, say, or some accounting data—were already on disk, it would be very wasteful to retype it.

Transferring a file to a remote computer, uploading, is generally trickier than downloading; there is a better chance that you will run into problems. With nearly any communication program, you will be able to transmit a file as a steady stream of characters. As far as the remote computer is concerned, it just seems as if a super-fast typist is keying them in. But what if the remote computer cannot keep up with the transmission? Some programs allow you to slow or *throttle* the transmission intentionally. In other circumstances, the PC might have to implement XON/XOFF or some other handshaking protocol (in the other direction now). Another possibility is that the remote computer will send a prompt back to the PC after each line is received, and the PC will have to be programmed to wait for that prompt before sending the next line.

Even if these sorts of synchronization problems are solved, you may still have trouble. The remote computer might expect the PC to send or not send a line feed character after each line. Or certain characters coming from the PC might be inadvertently treated as commands by the remote computer, and have to be filtered out. As you see, uploading files can be tricky, so make sure your communication software is compatible with the remote systems to which you are planning to send files. If it isn't, someone may be able to bail you out by writing an appropriate program for the remote computer, but that will take time and trouble.

Editing

The previous section dealt with uploading files that were created before the communication session began, but what happens if you decide to compose a message during a communication session, for instance a reply to an electronic memo?

With many communication packages, you would be out of luck. Others might provide one of two solutions. With some programs, you can give a command to load in your word processing program temporarily, use it to write the reply on disk, then return to the communication program to upload the file from the disk. That would be confusing to a beginner and time consuming, but it is better than nothing.

If you will be sending a lot of electronic mail and conducting teleconferences, activities in which spontaneous replies are often needed, you are better off looking for a communication program with a built-in editor. These programs enable you to create and edit a memo right in the communication buffer area in memory. Once it is correct, it is transmitted, without ever having been saved on the disk. With some programs, you could even edit one message while another was being sent or received.

If your communication package offers neither of these options, the remote system may provide an editor for, say, electronic mail, but because of communication delays, using it will be slow and cumbersome.

Block Checked File Transfers

You might want a program capable of block checked file transfers because you have critical files to transmit or for dealing with binary data. Let's look at both cases.

Parity checking is generally sufficient when you are interacting with a remote computer on-line. Incoming and outgoing characters are checked, and if a parity error is discovered, an asterisk or other special code is displayed. Two bit errors go undetected, but since you are watching the display, you will probably notice them. However, if you will be uploading or downloading critical files, and not watching as the process occurs, look for a program with a block checked file transfer option.

As you recall (Figure 8-14), there are no universal standards for computing block checksums or for handshaking protocols between successive blocks. Therefore, the software at both ends of the file transfer must be compatible.

But minimal compatibility is not enough. A good package will display some indication of the progress of the transmission (perhaps a dot per completed block), keep error statistics, and give you a degree of manual control over the transmission process, for example in determining the number of automatic retries before an error is reported, setting the block size, or turning character display on or off. There will often be operators at both ends of the line, so it is convenient to be able to send messages (e.g., "please insert the budget disk") when in block transfer mode. The ability to transfer groups of files with just one command is also a nice convenience.

Since error checking is provided by the block checksum, it is not necessary to reserve the parity bit in each character being transmitted. For this reason, block checked transmission is also handy for binary data. If you will be transmitting object programs or non-ASCII files created by a word processor, spreadsheet program, or file manager that use all eight bits, look for a program with a block transfer option.

Unattended Operation

In addition to being able to dial up and use remote services, a PC can serve as a remote resource for others dialing it, for example, to receive electronic mail or accept or transmit files. To support remote access, your PC is used in conjunction with an auto-answer modem. There are a number of communication programs that, after answering an incoming call, allow the person calling in to take over the PC that has answered the phone. Commands are executed just as if they were being typed directly into the remote computer. For instance, if you were on a trip, you could dial the PC back at your office and display messages in files that colleagues had left for you, or you could enter sales data by running a data management program that had been set up to expect your call. You could even use a word processing program that was executing in the computer back at the office, although that would be quite slow.

More sophisticated programs for unattended operation are able to act as self-contained bulletin boards or mail systems after they answer the phone. In these cases, you do not have control of the entire PC; you are interacting with the bulletin board or mail program.

In either case, software for unattended operation is not simple. To support unattended operation a program must be able to control an auto-answer modem, execute a series of commands, including conditional statements, for instance hanging up if a broken connection is detected or an unauthorized, mischievous, or poorly trained person calls. It should also watch the time in order to disconnect inactive users and keep the remote user from gaining access to protected files and operating system commands.

In addition to answering the phone while unattended, a PC with the proper modem and software can make calls when no one is around, for example in order to take advantage of reduced phone rates late at night. Your PC might "wake up" in the middle of the night and call your branch offices to obtain payroll data or the day's orders without an operator at either end. Unattended dialing requires that the program be able to dial a number, test for a connection (redialing periodically if none is established), send commands to the remote system, pause while files are being opened, transfer data in both directions, then hang up.

Unattended operation is complex, and it requires technical expertise to set up the system. You should count on getting technical help in software selection and setup if your plans include unattended operation. However, once set up, this, like all other communication procedures, requires minimal operator training and skill.

Terminal Emulation

Everything we have discussed up to this point has assumed that the remote system saw your PC as a dumb terminal, and that will usually be the case. However, at times software on the remote computer will have been written with a specific brand of intelligent terminal in mind. In that case, it will make use of nonprinting control characters for things like controlling the cursor position and the appearance of the display. If you will be using such a system, you will need a special communication program for your PC that emulates the specific terminal, and you can refer back to Chapter 9, in which we discussed the emulation of synchronous terminals, because the problems are similar. Emulation software is available for popular terminals, but you should work closely with whoever supplies the remote service to be sure you maintain compatibility.

HARDWARE

Modem

Modems were introduced in Chapter 8, where we saw that they were used to interface the PC to the telephone line. Since for many years all modems were manufactured by Ma Bell, there are good standards. You don't have to worry about compatibility with the phone network, except in a few rare cases. Your modem should be compatible with the Bell 103 modem for 300 BPS operation and the Bell 212A for 1,200 BPS. Avoid modems compatible with the Bell 202; they are for half-duplex operation.

Asynchronous modem speeds range from 300 to 9,600 BPS, but because of cost, 300 and 1,200 are pervasive at this time. Few remote services are equipped to run at higher rates. Since a 1,200 BPS modem is four times as fast, you will find it noticeably more convenient, and it will save time. However, a 1,200 BPS modem will cost you something extra, and many communication services will charge more for 1,200 BPS operation than for 300 BPS. Still, the higher rate will pay for itself if you plan to spend many hours communicating.

A few remote services, particularly local bulletin boards, may not support 1,200 BPS operation, but the trend is definitely to faster transmission rates. Modem costs are also declining rapidly, since single chip modems are now available. We will see a time when a modem, and even a telephone, are standard equipment in all PCs targeted for the business market.

As we saw, there are two basic ways to connect a modem to your PC—through an RS-232 port or by plugging a modem board into one of the expansion slots. The latter approach saves desk space because the modem is completely inside the PC, but it will take up one of your slots, and you do not have as wide a variety of modems to choose among.

The first approach will probably be somewhat more expensive, unless you already have an extra RS-232 port. The PC-XT comes with one RS-232 port as standard equipment, which can be used by a modem if you have not already decided to use it for a printer or other device with a serial interface. If you will have more than one serial device, many multifunction boards have two or even more ports. In a pinch, you can share one port among two devices by getting a T switch, which alternately connects one and then the other (see Figure 14-2). However, you won't be able to use both simultaneously, and there may be some software and cable compatibility problems.

You must also choose between direct or acoustical coupling with the telephone network. The only advantage to an acoustic coupler is that it can work with any phone with a traditional earpiece and mouthpiece (not, for example, a Princess phone), even if there is not a standard wall jack. It will work in a hotel or even in a phone booth.

Direct connect modems generally include more features ("intelligence") than acoustically coupled modems, for instance auto-dial capability, pulse or tone dialing, programmable pauses during dialing sequences, status feedback to the computer, or the ability to store and redial numbers. Unfortunately, there are no standards as to how these intelligent modem features are implemented; for example, there is no standard modem command for "redial the last number." For this reason, communication programs that are written to take advantage of some of the features provided by a modem often work only with the particular brand. That

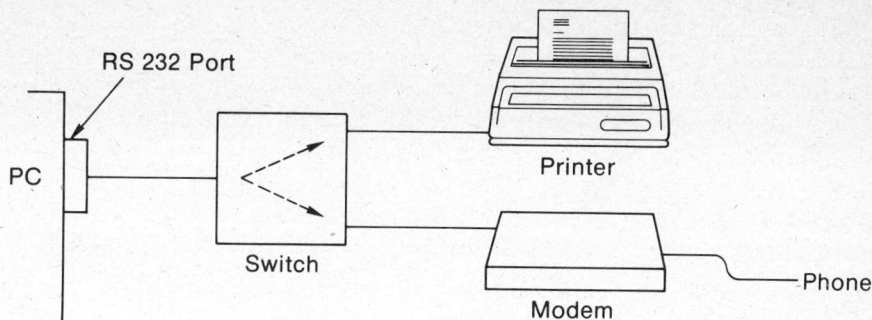

Figure 14-2. If you have only one serial port, you can get an external switch that would let you alternate between two devices, say a printer and a modem. Of course, only one device would be connected to the port at a time. A switch such as this could be used to alternate between other serial devices, for instance between a dot-matrix and formed-character printer.

doesn't mean you can't use the program with other brands of modem, just that the features discussed under the heading "Ease of Making the Connection" may not be available.

Don't forget that if you are planning unattended operation, you will need an auto-answer modem. It would also be nice if it were intelligent enough to detect the speed of the calling modem (300 or 1,200 BPS) automatically and adjust accordingly. Be sure you choose your communication software before buying a modem for unattended operation, because whatever program you pick will almost assuredly be tied to one brand of modem.

Last, but not least in terms of potential aggravation, don't overlook the cable connecting the PC to the modem (assuming that it is an RS-232 modem). As we saw when discussing printer cables in Chapter 3, the cable can cause problems and making them up is a bother, so get your dealer to assume that responsibility.

The Standard Components

Communication places relatively low demands on the rest of your PC hardware. The keyboard is sufficient, it has all of the special keys (control, break, escape) that you need, as long as the software transmits the correct codes. As far as the display goes, even the 40 column TV set display will work with many communication services. (Remember that some of their customers are using very small home computers.)

A 128KB memory should be enough to run any of the stand-alone communication programs. You will need disk space for the largest files that you will be transmitting or receiving, and remember that you will probably want a copy of your word processing program available while you are communicating, so plan your disk requirements accordingly. Two floppy disks will probably be enough for most applications, but if you are thinking of doing a lot of unattended communication, consider a hard disk.

CPU speed is not an important constraint unless your communication software is written in an interpretive language. In that case, 1,200 BPS operation while displaying data on the screen and logging it in a disk file or a printer may be too demanding on the CPU, so run a test before you buy the program.

SERVICES

A growing array of vendors offer communication services. These are generally provided by large time-shared computers that are accessed either by means of direct telephone connection, a voice network such as Sprint or MCI, or a value-added data network such as Tymenet or Telenet. In some cases, communication costs may be inclined as part of the service; in others, they will be billed separately.

Electronic Mail

The most important application for the administrative or managerial user is electronic mail, which can be used for brief messages or large data files and reports. You have three basic choices in setting up an electronic mail system: an in-house time-sharing system, a utility service, and using a PC as a mail server. If your organization has a mainframe computer that is already providing communication service, an electronic mail system can be set up on it. The decision to do so and the selection of the software will be made by the data processing department, and it may turn out that they have already implemented electronic mail.

If you are part of a smaller organization, or if you would like to try electronic mail before making a commitment to it, you should subscribe to one of the many services offered on a utility basis. The billing method varies from system to system, but depending upon your usage, the amount of mail you leave stored in the system, the time of day you use the system, and other factors, you can test electronic mail for as little as, say, $100 per month. In considering electronic mail services, look at more than just the cost. Most mail services are accessible over a value-added network (in fact, the network companies themselves offer mail service), so be sure that all of the locations of your organization are in areas served by the network. If you travel a lot, check into access in areas you visit frequently.

The system should also be easy to use. It should give you a summary of your mail when you log on, and allow you to read, file, discard, or reply to the messages. Check to see if it is possible to transmit many messages in a single batch, so you can do something else while they come in and are logged on disk or printed. Pay attention to the flexibility and ease of use of the message filing system—when messages are filed away, can they be retrieved by subject, keyword, author, date, and so forth? If your communication program does not include an editor, short messages will have to be composed using the editor that is part of the service, so pay particular attention to it. Try it out as you would a word processor, seeing how hard it is to correct errors and review what you have typed. The system should be flexible enough to allow you to set up separate accounts for everyone who will be using it. You will want the ability to forward a message to a colleague, reply immediately after reading a message, or broadcast a message to a group of accounts. You will prepare relatively long messages with your word processing program rather than the mail system's editor, so pay particular attention to compatibility between your word processing files and the mail system. (This is discussed under the heading "File Transmission," above.)

Teleconferencing services, in which a group of people interested in a common topic conduct an asynchronous "meeting," are similar to electronic mail systems. Comments may be input into a growing conference transcript, or directed to individual conferees. Teleconferencing systems may be used for ongoing discussion or for more goal-directed activity, for example the joint authoring of a report or proposal. They overlap somewhat in application with mail systems, but are designed more to facilitate a collaborative effort among a specific group.

If you are part of a relatively small organization located in one geographic area, you might want to use a PC as an electronic mail server. In this case, the issues discussed under the heading Unattended Operation become relevant, and you will need a suitable software package. In comparing PC-based electronic mail programs, look for the same conveniences and features you would if the system were running on a large computer accessed over a network, and don't forget that you will need a hard disk, an intelligent modem, and some technical help in setting the system up.

The mail applications discussed so far have been oriented toward communication among people who are part of the system; however, it is possible to send mail in the broader sense using your PC. You can compose and send messages which are forwarded to Western Union or the U.S. Postal Service. In doing so, you can either deal directly with Western Union or the Post Office, or operate through a utility service with a *gateway* to them. Whether you send your message direct or through an intermediary, it will be delivered as a regular Telex/TWX, Mailgram, E-COM, or Cablegram message. If your volumes are high, it would pay to go directly to the phone company or Western Union; otherwise work through a utility with a gateway.

Databases

A good deal of general information is available on a utility basis from many competing firms. In many cases, the same information is available in other forms, so be a little skeptical. For example, airline schedules, restaurant guides, stock prices, wire service news releases, and abridged encyclopedias are available on many systems. The convenience and cost of using these databases must be compared to calling a travel agent or reading a local newspaper or a magazine.

This sort of current information may be less useful than historical information. While the morning paper may be adequate for today's news, it won't suffice if you are working on a report or proposal and need to research a topic in more depth. Dow Jones, the New York Times, AP, and other wire service articles may be kept for months or even years in some systems.

If your research is in a specific area, for instance a particular industry, profession, or branch of science, database research might be even more profitable. Databases indexing periodicals and research reports are common. Although they may keep the full text of articles and papers on line, it is more common to find abstracts, or just the title and keywords describing the full document. On the basis of this information, you would decide which documents were relevant, and in some cases you could order copies of them directly from the database company, perhaps during the communication session.

There are many specialized databases containing record-oriented information as well as those dealing with documents. There are over 1,000 specialized databases covering topics like company financial data, legal cases, patents, and airplane crashes. A number of companies act as database brokers, and indices are published to help you find data relevant to your interests.

Up to this point, we have spoken only of character-oriented databases, but graphics are also available to a more limited extent. The major activity along these lines has taken place in Europe and Canada, in the development of Prestel and other so-called *videotex* systems. A standard format (called *NAPLPS*, the North American Presentation Level Protocol Syntax) suited to transmitting character and graphic data from central services has been endorsed by IBM and AT&T, so you might see rapid expansion of videotex databases. IBM and many other large companies are using videotex internally, and there are a number of pilot experiments with videotex in private homes. The jury is still out on the future of videotex, but I would look for installations in business organizations sooner than widespread home use. On the other hand, TV sets were in 75% of U.S. households eleven years after they became available. If personal computers were to come into our homes that rapidly, home videotex would get a boost. (By way of contrast, it took 70 years for half of all U.S. households to get telephones.)

Of course, using your PC as a videotex terminal will require software and hardware that can accept NAPLPS data and display it properly, but that is available. Furthermore, there is no reason why a PC cannot be programmed to transmit NAPLPS screens as well as to receive them.

Communication Alternatives

If you spend a lot of time on computer communication, you should also look into your options regarding communication services. As we have mentioned, voice services such as Sprint and MCI can handle data communications as well, although there may be some difficulties with certain modems. The telephone company also offers a number of discount plans for high volume users, such as WATS service. If your communication volumes were sufficiently high, the cheapest rates would be obtained by dealing directly with the value-added networks.

APPENDIX A
Other Applications

This book concentrates on the "big four" applications: word processing, spreadsheet processing, data management, and communication, but you can use your IBM PC for many other things. This appendix briefly outlines several of the other applications that would be of interest to business and professional users, and suggests a few software vendors who should be considered "serious contenders" in each area. We have some experience with the companies and products listed as contenders, but that is not to say they are the best for any application. There are many programs on the market that we have not seen, and we may have only slight experience with some of those listed. Like the vendors mentioned in Appendix E, these are not the only people whose products you should look at, but they will give you a place to start.

GAMES

Although this is a "serious" book, you might be interested in games for learning and (when the boss is not looking) recreation. Computer games can be broken into four general groups: dexterity games, adventure games, simulation and educational games, and strategy games.

I am sure you have seen games involving dexterity in arcades. Atari's Pong was the first, but today there are hundreds of games in which you avoid being eaten by monsters, shoot down rocketships, and so forth. The majority of dexterity games for the IBM PC require the Color/Graphics Display. I have tried a few, but in general I defer to my children's judgment in these matters, because, like all children, they are amazingly adroit players.

The second group comprises adventure games, which put you in imaginary situations. You might be asked to solve a murder mystery, navigate a spaceship, or find your way around in a subterranean cavern filled with bats, dragons, and pots of gold. In that these games typically interact using words rather than images, many of them will work with the

Monochrome Display. Furthermore, as we mentioned in Chapter 1, they are a good starting place for getting a feel for the sorts of things computers can do, if you are a beginner.

Simulations and other educational games have something to teach. A simulation puts you in control of a modeled situation, perhaps a business, government, or nuclear reactor, and the computer is programmed to show the hypothetical results of your decisions. Other educational games might involve question and answer sessions, drill and practice, and so forth.

Finally come strategy games. Common examples are checkers and chess, in which the computer is your opponent. Here you might have a chance of keeping up with your kids.

Game programs should be easy to use, requiring little or no time to learn. Look for those in which you can vary the skill level as you improve, and avoid complex games that force you to learn many arbitrary rules and operating conventions. (I have seen games simulating the Star Trek TV series that would be more difficult to learn than a spreadsheet or word processing program.) Many games require or at least use a joystick. If dexterity games are important, you will probably want a system with a Color/Graphics Display and a joystick.

For a combination of dexterity and simulation, Microsoft's Decathalon game, marketed by IBM, certainly has to be considered a serious contender. For out-and-out dexterity, my children recommend Nightmission Pinball from Sublogic Communications Corp. Those with a monochrome display have very few choices for dexterity games, but my favorites are Slynx and Viper from Ivy Research. For adventure games, look at any of the offerings of Infocom. Their Zork series pioneered the use of quasi-natural language input to games. Executive Suite from Armonk Corporation or Millionaire from Blue Chip Software are two business-oriented simulations you might be interested in looking at. Finally, Sargon from Hayden Software might provide a worthy chess partner.

If you want a joystick, you need both a controller card and the joystick itself. IBM will sell you a controller card, but it is quite expensive and takes up an expansion slot for just one function. You are better off looking for a multifunction board, perhaps a memory board, that incorporates a joystick controller. TG Products, Kraft Systems, and Wico are reputable joystick vendors with good products. The Koala Pad from Koala Technologies is also useful as a game controller.

MAILING LIST MANAGEMENT

These programs are designed specifically for managing mailing lists. They allow you to add names to a list, delete them, make changes, sort the list, print mailing labels, select sublists (such as all people in the computer industry in Southern California), print list rosters, and so forth.

Does that sound familiar? Yes, it would be possible to do the same thing with a more generalized file or database management system such as those discussed in Chapter 7. The advantage of a specialized mailing list program is that it is already set up to do mailing lists, whereas, with a file manager, it would be necessary to define the records as having relevant fields (name, address line 1, address line 2, city, state, zip, etc.), to define reports, to define sort keys, and so forth.

The other side of the coin is that if you create a mailing list application using a file management program, you can tailor it to your own particular needs. For instance, you may need a field that is not included in a certain mailing list package, or the program may not be able to accommodate foreign addresses and phone numbers.

Efficiency can go either way. All things being equal, one would expect that the more specialized programs would be faster and use less storage. However, that will not always be the case because there are differences in program quality. If you will be working with large lists, test the program for such things as file size on the disk, sort times, and time to retrieve a record for viewing or updating. If you will be using the program to merge names and addresses into form letters, make sure it is compatible with your word processing program. Make a test run to confirm that it is.

A serious contender is Mail List Manager, which is available from IBM or Peachtree Software.

GRAPHICS

The most common form of graphics software is for producing business graphics: pie charts, bar graphs, and line plots for illustrating simple numerical relationships graphically. Figure A-1 illustrates a business graph. Note that in addition to the bars representing the growing component complexity in personal computers, there are axes with labels and a title. The ability to annotate a graph is as important as the ability to construct it.

Business graphics software comes in stand-alone packages and is often included as a component of a multi-application program (spreadsheet processors are often offered in combination with graphics software). In evaluating graphic software pay attention to speed, convenience, and capability.

You should be able to preview graphs on the screen before printing or plotting them, since producing hard copy is slow. Even though drawing the graph on the screen will be much faster than printing it, check the time it takes to display it. Display time is important because you will find that you seldom get the graph right on the first try, and you have to go back and change it. When it is finally right, you can print it and save it on disk.

If you will be producing a lot of graphs, for instance setting up a regular reporting system to graph certain data each week or month, look for a package that can input the data automatically from a spreadsheet or database. You don't want to have to key it in each time the graph is produced. When designing graphs, you will appreciate a system with many

thousands of transistors
in a typical system

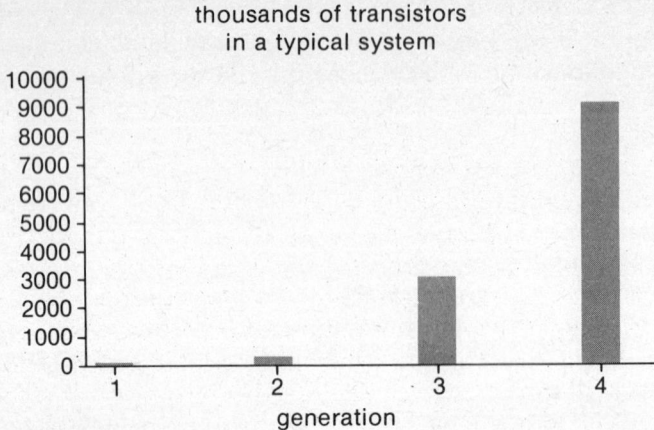

generation

Figure A-1. This bar chart, illustrating the growth in power and complexity of personal computers since 1975, was produced using a business graphics program. Note that in addition to bars showing the number of transistors, the axes are labeled and there is a title on the graph. Flexibility and simplicity in laying out axes and adding titles, labels, and other text may be as important in selecting a graphics program as the options available in drawing the graph itself. Only a few minutes were needed to input the data and headings and preview the result on the display screen.

default parameters, for instance the colors or styles of bars or pie areas, axis label conventions, axis scaling rules, type style for headings, and so forth. A well designed system should enable you to produce a rough graph, accepting those default values, in less than a minute. Starting from that point you can override some of the default values, enter headings and free text comments, and so forth to produce a finished drawing.

The packages also vary considerably in terms of functional choices. A simple program might allow only bar and pie charts, whereas another might allow for three-dimensional graphs showing several variables with different bar colors or textures, scatter diagrams, curve fitting, and statistical computation; such a program might also allow you to change the scale of graphs, rotate them, put several small graphs on one page, change the font and size of the characters used in titles, and so on. Consider your own applications in determining which features are necessary and which would be unused.

In addition to business graphics, you may wish to use graphics for constructing drawings or other material for presentation. You might use your PC to draw an organization chart, to make a series of slides for a presentation, or even to do some very rough animation.

Architects and engineers often use computers as design sketchpads, working interactively until their design is complete. Used in this way, the computer is more than a dynamic drawing medium; it can also perform analysis, giving the designer feedback on the characteristics of the evolving design, for example the strength of an architectural structure or the electrical characteristics of a circuit. The speed, display capability, and software sophistication of the IBM PC make it somewhat marginally useful for this sort of work at this time.

If you plan to do some graphic work with your PC, be sure to try it out. You may be dissatisfied with the size, crispness, and amount of detail possible. The popular image of computer graphics is that of movies like Star Wars or slick television commercials, but those images require hours of mainframe computer time and are made on displays with many times the resolution of the PC. You may find the resolution of the IBM Color/ Graphics display too low for your application, in which case a higher resolution display from another vendor may be in order. In that case, be very careful on the question of compatibility of your graphic software.

For hard copy output, you can use either the IBM Graphics or Color Printer, or printers and plotters from other vendors. Camera-based systems are also available enabling you to make slides with your PC, on either Polaroid or standard 35 millimeter film. Again, be sure your hard copy hardware is compatible with your graphic software.

Two serious contenders for business graphics are Fast Graphs from Innovative Software and Graphmagic from International Software Marketing. For drawing and construction, take a look at Energraphics from Enertronics Research, Inc., 3-Design from 3-Design, Inc., and PC Crayon from PCsoftware.

ACCOUNTING

Accounting software is also available for your PC. There are integrated packages with payroll, payables, receivables, inventory, and general ledger bundled together, or stand-alone programs for a single accounting application.

You should be cautious in approaching the PC as an accounting computer. Don't expect too much, because it is an awkward size for accounting. If you have a fairly large business, you need a multi-user system with a line printer and a large disk, in other words a minicomputer or mainframe. If you have a very small business, it is likely that a pencil and paper accounting system will be a cheaper, simpler solution than any computerized system. If you are just the right size, you should consider using a PC for accounting, perhaps starting off with one application.

Don't forget that the PC will be only one component in your accounting system. When you use your PC to write a memo or create a spreadsheet, you are working independently, but an accounting computer is just one part in a system involving many people, forms, steps, and constraints. If something goes wrong, the orders do not get filled that day. The system must be self-checking, auditable, and accurate, it must save time, and once in place, it should be automatic and invisible. Backup procedures will still have to be available in case you have trouble (hardware failure or operator error) with the system. In short, plan accounting systems carefully, and involve the people who do your accounting and those who will be using it in the planning.

For accounting applications you will amost certainly want a hard disk on your system, and look for a printer that can produce wide reports and run for hours at a time without overheating. There are many accounting programs available for the PC, and serious contenders are offered by Peachtree, Information Unlimited Software, Software Laboratories, Inc., and IBM.

INCOME TAXES

There are many tax preparation programs on the market. The ads begin to appear around the first of the year, and disappear after April. Some programs are written with individuals in mind, others with corporations, and others as tools for professional tax consultants. A few of the individual programs are to be used as "planning" aids, helping you to decide such things as whether to do income averaging and how to depreciate an asset, but most are actually designed to fill in your forms. In all cases, the programs are designed for people who understand taxes already; they are just aids to filing.

The simplest packages are not programs, but spreadsheet templates, set up to resemble tax forms, with the appropriate arithmetic formulas. Others are programs that direct you, typically through a series of menus, in filling out a tax form. In the former case, you need the appropriate spreadsheet program, but the latter programs are generally more complete.

Be skeptical in looking at these packages. We have tried several and found them too slow and cumbersome to bother with for a single return. (This is in the case of an individual with eight schedules.) However, if you will be doing taxes for many people, your PC might save considerable time.

In evaluating tax software make sure it can handle all of the state and federal schedules you will be using. Be sure it was written for the year in which you will be using it, since the forms, regulations, and tables change. (Several vendors offer an annual update service.) Beware of programs written in interpreted BASIC; they can be very slow. When you change an entry on one schedule, be sure that program automatically updates all other schedules that are affected. Make sure the program prints its output in a form suitable for filing. (The 1040 must be on an official printed form.)

Howard Software Services is a serious contender in this area, but it must be noted that this vendor's program was among those I decided were not worth bothering with for a single return.

TRAINING

Since the 1950s enthusiasts have held that computers were tireless, value-free teaching tools that would eventually revolutionize education. Detractors have held that computers were limited, boring teachers and, once the novelty wore off, would prove ineffective. There have been many studies run, and a good deal of computer assisted instruction has taken place, and the results, although still far from conclusive, are between these extremes.

There is a good deal of software on the market designed to teach you about your PC and its applications. There are programs to familiarize you with the keyboard, DOS, and most of the popular application packages such as Wordstar, dBASEII, or VisiCalc. Serious vendors of this sort of PC training material include ATI and Cdex. For an introduction to generic concepts in word processing, file management, and so forth (rather than specific programs) you might also take a look at the offerings of Knoware Inc. Increasing numbers of vendors, for instance Lotus Development, include a tutorial program right along with their packages.

This sort of software might help cut training costs. Those planning to install many PCs in their organizations might maintain a library of such programs for new users. You can also obtain training materials on audio- and videotape, and there are organizations offering training classes and seminars in virtually all large cities. A custom seminar or consultant is probably still the best bet if you are interested in learning how to apply a program or technique in your organization rather than how to use a specific program.

It is also possible to develop specific training software for some task in your organization. For example, a bank might want to put together a computer assisted package for training new tellers in the operation of their terminals and the bank's procedures and policies. To do that, you will need a lot of time, a team with expertise in programming and the task to be taught, and an instructional programming language. Two serious con- tenders for the latter are IBM's Personal Computer Instructional System and The Educator from Spectrum Training Corporation.

CALENDAR MANAGEMENT

Calendar programs can be quite flexible, allowing you to enter either specific appointments or periodic dates like birthdays or regular meetings. The more easily used programs place a simulated calendar on the screen and allow you to enter items on it. The editing functions used to enter and modify calendar entries should be simple to use. It should be possible to print your calendar in a useful format as well as to display it.

The problem with calendar programs is that they must be loaded and running in order to be used. Although a calendar program might be more powerful than pencil and paper, I do not use one because of the inconvenience of having to load the program when I need to use it. That problem would be diminished by a multitasking operating system, in which the calendar program could be called up with a single keystroke or mouse movement. The problem is also partially alleviated by programs combining other functions such as a simple accounting or file-card data management with the calendar program.

A serious contender is IBM's Time Manager.

STATISTICAL ANALYSIS (AND OTHER COMPUTATION-INTENSIVE) PACKAGES

Marketing executives and researchers, business forecasters, social scientists, survey researchers, public health researchers, and others with statistical applications were among the earliest users of large computers. In applications in which display speed is a limiting factor, for instance word processing, a PC will be faster than a mainframe computer that is shared by many users and accessed from a terminal. By contrast, in statistical analysis the time to actually do the computations is the limiting factor; the job is compute bound.

Although your IBM PC cannot be expected to keep up with a mainframe computer in a computationally intensive task like statistical analysis, it can still be a much more cost- and time-effective tool. Perhaps your PC takes five minutes to do a regression analysis that would have taken only a few seconds on a mainframe, but what about the cost? Inputting and editing your data on a PC should be much more convenient, and you won't get a bill at the end of the month if you use a PC for your analysis.

You can expect to see increasing numbers of computationally intensive applications, in engineering and scientific computation as well as in statistical analysis, moving from mainframe computers to personal computers in the future.

There are a number of factors to consider in selecting a statistical analysis package. Unless you have very small problems, you may find hundredfold speed differences among programs. Speed will be affected by factors such as the language in which the program is written (be particularly wary of compute-bound programs written in interpreted BASIC), whether it takes advantage of the 8087 Math Coprocessor, and whether it is able to use all of your PC's memory.

Speed will be related to problem size. If you have very small data sets, any program will be quick. Be sure to run speed benchmarks on problems of typical size, and check to see that the program can handle as many observations and variables as you require. Don't forget that a program that uses disk storage to handle large databases may slow you down considerably.

The packages vary in terms of the statistics they can compute and the tests they can run, so check the list of options. Most statistical programs are written in a modular manner, enabling a programmer to add new statistics with time. Though promises can be broken, a vendor will probably be able to tell you when and if it plans to implement a future option. Accuracy of computation is also a factor with statistical and other analysis programs. To check the accuracy of a PC statistical analysis program, you can compare its results to that of a mainframe package or else run a (tricky) benchmark with a known correct answer. The November 1983 issue of Byte Magazine has a good article on evaluating the accuracy of statistical programs.

Pay attention to the convenience of entering data, editing it, adding new variables or observations, and so forth. It should be easy to create new variables by transforming others as well. You may choose to use a spreadsheet program or file manager to enter and edit your data, transferring it to the statistical program for analysis. In that case, be sure the two programs are compatible, for instance that they can both read and write DIF files.

Finally, pay attention to the output options and their speed and convenience. It should be possible to display and print your results in character or graphic form. Many PC statistical packages have been converted from large computers, and the programmers may not have modified them to exploit the graphics capability of a personal computer.

Serious contenders include SPSS/PC from SPSS, Inc. (this is a version of their well-known mainframe package), Statpro from Wadsworth Electronic Publishing, and Abstat from Anderson Bell.

EQUATION SOLVING

Although I understand that others are forthcoming, TK! Solver is the only program in this category at this time. TK! Solver was developed by Software Arts, the same people who wrote VisiCalc. It is a tool for automating the sorts of computations found in engineering or financial handbooks. A model is specified as a series of equations, and, given values for input variables, a solution, if one exists, is found.

This sort of program can save time for technical people in setting up handbooklike calculations. Although it would save implementation time compared to writing a BASIC program (the probable other option), based upon experience with TK! Solver, the execution would be slower.

Vendors also sell packages of predefined equations, analogous to the application templates sold for spreadsheet programs. For instance, Software Arts offers a disk with financial models and another with mechanical engineering formulas. However, since it is not possible to build a custom interface with operator prompts and help using TK! Solver, the written documentation accompanying these prewritten models is very important. Even if you plan to use prepackaged models, you will have to be quite familiar with the problems you are working on with an equation solver.

PROJECT PLANNING AND CONTROL

There are a number of project management and control programs available for the PC. They are based on the Critical Path Method (CPM) and Program

Evaluation and Review Technique (PERT), which have been available for years on large computers. With these systems, you break a project down into the individual steps needed for its completion, and estimate the resources and time necessary for each step. The computer analyzes the project, showing which steps will delay completion of the entire project if they take longer than anticipated (they are on the "critical path") and which can slip without delaying the project.

Those who have used PERT or CPM programs on larger computers may find the maximum project size (number of activities) allowable with a PC program smaller than what they are used to. On the other hand, the quick interaction will be appreciated. The PC program should be designed for rapid recalculation when the project model is altered. In that way, you can quickly see the effects of possible changes, such as moving workers or machines from a noncritical task to a critical task in order to speed its completion, and perhaps that of the overall project.

Also pay attention to the reports that the program puts out. There will usually be a graphic display and printout showing the activities and their sequencing, as well as columnar reports for more detailed project reporting. Some systems will track a good deal of accounting information, showing how tasks are going with regard to time and cost, and showing the degree of use of available resources like people and equipment.

Two serious contenders for project management and control software are the Milestone program from Digital Marketing and PMS-II from John Wiley and Sons.

WRITING PROGRAMS

Although programming is beyond the scope of this book, you might be interested in learning some programming in the future, or people in your organization may be planning to use the PC for software development. Appendix D suggests steps and resources for beginners who wish to learn something of programming.

If some programmers within your organization will be developing software for the PC, they will find that professional quality software development tools and language processors exist for most programming languages. The following should be considered as sources of professional quality software development tools:

Pascal: Digital Research, Microsoft, IBM
BASIC: Digital Research, Microsoft, IBM, SofTool Systems (development tools only)
FORTRAN: Digital Research, Microsoft
COBOL: Digital Research, Microsoft, IBM
Lisp: Integral Quality
C: Digital Research, Microsoft (Lattice), Mark Williams, Computer Innovations, c-systems, CWare

FORTH: Laboratory Microsystems
Logo: Digital Research, IBM
APL: IBM
Prolog: Springer-Verlag
Modula-2: Springer-Verlag
PL/I: Digital Research

APPENDIX B
Events and Ideas Leading Up to the IBM PC

Personal computers are small but powerful; they are used interactively and are not designed for computer specialists. The idea of interactive computing and interactive applications goes back many years, as does the idea that computers can be useful tools for the man (or child) on the street. The desire to use computers interactively led first to the development of console oriented computers (commercially as well as in laboratories, then to time-sharing. Interpreted languages were developed to facilitate rapid software development on these systems.

Each of the PC components—the CPU, memory, disk, display, printer, and keyboard—has evolved out of early inventions and progress in electronics, as has the capacity to communicate. The following are the approximate dates of some of the important ideas and events that paved the way for your IBM PC.

INTERACTIVE PROBLEM SOLVING

1945: Vannevar Bush writes *As We May Think*.
1962: Douglas Englebart begins work on the "augmentation of human intellect."
1960: J.C.R. Licklider speculates on the development of systems for "man-machine symbiosis."

EARLY INTERACTIVE APPLICATIONS

1951: Whirlwind begins real-time control of radar systems.
1958: William Higinbotham constructs a video game simulating a tennis match.

1958: The SAGE air-defense system becomes operational.
1962: Spacewars, a complex game, is running on the TX-0.
1963: Ivan Sutherland implements Sketchpad, the first interactive graphics system, on the TX-2.
1963: American Airlines' SABRE reservation system goes on-line.

COMPUTERS FOR THE PEOPLE

1961: Bob Albrecht begins teaching programming to children.
1962: John Kemeny and Thomas Kurz initiate a simplified programming experiment at Dartmouth.
1965: Stephan Grey forms the Amateur Computer Society, and starts a newsletter.
1970: Seymour Papert begins work on an environment in which children can internalize the concept of a program, leading to "turtle geometry" and Logo.
1972: Alan Kay begins development of the Dynabook, with children as target users.
1974: The Community Memory project installs public access terminals to a computer bulletin board in San Francisco storefronts.

EARLY CONSOLE ORIENTED COMPUTERS

1956: TX-0 is running at MIT.
1957: TX-2 is running at MIT.
1962: LINC is running at MIT.

TIME-SHARING

1959: Christopher Strachey publishes *Timesharing in Large, Fast Computers.*
1962: PDP-1 time-sharing system is demonstrated at Bolt, Beranek and Newman.
1963: A time-sharing system is running on a modified 7090 at MIT.
1963: A time-sharing system is running on the Q-32 at SDC.
1963: A time-sharing system is running on GE 235 at Dartmouth.
1965: A time-sharing system is running on modified SDS 940 at University of California at Berkeley.

INTERPRETIVE LANGUAGE PROCESSORS

1960: GOTRAN is implemented by Jack Palmer and his colleagues at IBM.

1961: Charles Davidson implements a load and go Fortran at the University of Wisconsin.

1962: DOPE, the Dartmouth Oversimplified Programming Experiment, is implemented by Sidney Marshall under the direction of John Kemeny at Dartmouth College.

1963: JOSS is implemented by Cliff Shaw at Rand.

1963: QUICKTRAN is implemented by John Morrisey *et al.* at IBM.

1963: BASIC is implemented at Dartmouth.

1964: TINT and LISP interpreters are running at SDC.

COMPONENTS

1837: Samuel Morse and Alfred Vail apply for a telegraph patent.

1846: Royal E. House patents a printing telegraph.

1860: Jean Baudot improves teleprinters and transmission and defines a five-level code, which is later revised by Donald Murray.

1867: The first stock tickers appear.

1868: Christopher Sholes, Carlos Glidden, and Samuel Soule patent a typewriter, later marketed by Remington.

1924: The first Teletype machine appears, using Baudot's printing scheme and Murray's "Baudot" code.

1947: William Shockley, John Bardeen, and Walter Brattain demonstrate the transistor effect.

1950: The Whirlwind uses a CRT as an operator's console.

1953: Harwick Johnson applies for a patent on an integrated circuit.

1959: Jack Kilby heads development of first commercial IC at Texas Instruments.

1966: The ASCII code is standardized.

1972: Ted Hoff and colleagues design the Intel 4004 microprocessor.

1973: Al Shugart develops the floppy disk at IBM as a console input device for large computers.

COMMUNICATION

1940: Thornton Fry, George Stibitz, and Samuel Williams demonstrate the Complex Computer, located in New York, at a conference in New Hampshire.

1950: SEAC and Whirlwind process remote data.

1960: J.C.R. Licklider calls for computer networking experiments.

1962: Paul Baran works on a star network at Rand.

1966: TX-2 to Q-32 (in Massachusetts and California) communication experiment is run and protocols are defined.

1969: ARPA-net begins.

1970: Ethernet connects Alto computers at Xerox PARC.

SOME RECENT COMMERCIAL PRODUCTS

1964: IBM's Magnetic Tape Selectric Typewriter is a significant improvement over paper-tape based typewriters, and IBM coins the phrase "word processing."

1965: Wang introduces a programmable electronic calculator, designed by An Wang.

1967: Hewlett-Packard introduces the 9100 desk calculator, designed by Tom Osborne.

1973: IBM announces the 5100, a personal computer that runs BASIC and APL.

1973: Nolan Bushnell forms Atari to market his video game, Pong.

1975: MITS begins marketing the Altair computer, designed by Ed Roberts. It is designed with technical people in mind and is originally sold as a kit.

1975: Bill Gates and Paul Allen write a BASIC interpreter for the Altair and go on to form Microsoft.

1975: Many companies are formed to manufacture boards for the Altair bus.

1976: Processor Technology, Polymorphic Systems, and Compal introduce personal computers designed for the nontechnical manager or professional.

1976: Gary Kildall writes CP/M, an operating system designed for floppy disk. John Torrode of Digital Systems (now Digital Microsystems) markets the first CP/M-based personal computer.

1977: Michael Shrayer, a filmmaker, markets Electric Pencil, the first display-oriented word processing program for a personal computer. It is the first major product developed by a user.

1977: Commodore and Apple introduce personal computers designed for the home and nonprofessional markets.

1979: Dan Bricklin and Bob Frankston develop VisiCalc, a non-word processing program that embodies the metaphor of a personal computer as a window onto a virtual document and exploits the high memory-display bandwidth of the personal computer.

1981: The Sony Typecorder and Osborne I are announced, the first portable products.

1981: IBM announces the PC.

APPENDIX C
A Glimpse at Binary Numbers

An understanding of the way computers store numbers is not needed to follow this book, or even to write many programs. However, if you are a bit curious, the following introduction to binary numbers will give you an idea (though incomplete) of how it is done.

Binary numbers are similar to the decimal numbers we normally use. With the decimal number system, we have ten symbols for digits: 0, 1, 2, 3, 4, 5, 6, 7, 8, and 9. With the binary number system, we have two: 0 and 1. Thus, 10110 or 1101101 are examples of binary numbers, whereas a number like 20726 could not be because it uses "illegal" symbols.

Like decimal numbers, binary numbers use a positional notation. Do you remember learning about positional notation? A decimal number has a digit in the "ones" position, the "tens" position, the "hundreds" position, and so forth. So the decimal number 20726 can be thought of as the addition of:

$$
\begin{aligned}
6 \times 1 &= 6 \\
2 \times 10 &= 20 \\
7 \times 100 &= 700 \\
0 \times 1000 &= 0 \\
2 \times 10000 &= \underline{20000} \\
&\ 20726
\end{aligned}
$$

Note that, in the decimal system, the positions go up as powers of ten. In the binary system, the positions do not go up as powers of ten, they go up as powers of two. So, instead of the "ones," "tens," "hundreds," and so forth, we have the "ones" position, the "twos" position, the "fours" position, the "eights" position, and so forth.

Now for an example. How about the binary number 101101? Adding the places together in the same way as we did with the decimal number above, we get:

$$
\begin{aligned}
1 \times 1 &= 1 \\
0 \times 2 &= 0 \\
1 \times 4 &= 4 \\
1 \times 8 &= 8 \\
0 \times 16 &= 0 \\
1 \times 32 &= \underline{32} \\
&\ 45
\end{aligned}
$$

In other words, the binary number 101101 is the same as the decimal number 45.

At this point you might be wondering what all the fuss is about. You already know how to write 45, so why invent a second way? Besides, isn't 101101 more cumbersome than good old 45? Yes, it is. In fact, because they use only two symbols, binary numbers (above one) are always longer than their decimal equivalents. However, binary numbers have two advantages to offset this inefficiency.

The first is that it is relatively cheap to build circuits to store binary numbers. The 0 and 1 can be represented by two different voltage levels or by a microscopic "switch" being on or off. People have designed computers that used trinary (three symbol) or even decimal numbers, but it turns out that it is simpler to make binary devices.

The second advantage works whether you are a computer or a person. It is easier to learn to do arithmetic on binary numbers than on decimal numbers. How much is 7×9? It's 63, right? You know that because as a child you memorized the multiplication tables. I don't know about you, but I spent the better part of the third grade memorizing the 10 by 10 cell multiplication table. Then, in the fourth grade, I learned how to do long multiplication, using the multiplication facts I had memorized.

But what about binary numbers? If we restrict ourselves to the binary (two symbol) system, the multiplication table is merely:

$$
\begin{aligned}
0 \times 0 &= 0 \\
0 \times 1 &= 0 \\
1 \times 0 &= 0 \\
1 \times 1 &= 1
\end{aligned}
$$

Had I been born in a country where they used binary numbers, I could have learned the multiplication tables in about 30 minutes and devoted the rest of my time in the third grade to playing kickball. It turns out that the long multiplication procedure you learned (multiply, shift, add) works with binary numbers as well as it did with decimal numbers. For instance, we can multiply 10001 by 101 as follows:

```
  10001
    101
  10001
  00000
 10001
 1010101
```

Check that out in decimal if you don't believe it ($17 \times 5 = 85$). It turns out that addition, subtraction, long division, carrying, borrowing, and so forth, all of the things you learned about in the fourth grade, work for binary numbers as well as they do for decimal numbers. That makes binary arithmetic easy for people and computers.

This introduction to the topic should satisfy your curiosity about binary numbers. They facilitate arithmetic calculations and the storage of numbers, simplifying computer design and cutting cost. It turns out that your IBM PC can also store numbers in different ways that are variations on this theme, but I won't go into further detail.

APPENDIX D
The Flavor
of Programming

To learn to program professionally takes most people several years of formal education and several years of apprenticeship. To learn to write small, relatively simple programs, a few months' self-instruction from a book or perhaps a class should suffice. This book is about things you can do with your IBM PC without knowing how to program, but in case you are curious, let me give you a quick glimpse at what a program is.

A program is a list of instructions for a computer to follow. Like any other list of instructions, it must be written in some language or another. Take, for instance, the following program fragment, written in the language BASIC:

```
10 PRINT "Hello"
20 PRINT "I am a computer"
30 PRINT "with a simple program."
40 STOP
```

When it executed this four-instruction program, the computer would display:

```
Hello
I am a computer
with a simple program.
```

on its video screen. Since the instructions would have been executed in order, the lines would have appeared one at a time.

Let's consider a slightly more complicated example, in which the computer accepts some input from the operator while the program is executing:

```
10 PRINT "What is your name?"
20 INPUT NAME$
30 PRINT "Nice to meet you, " + NAME$
40 STOP
```

When statement 10 was executed, the computer would ask the operator what his or her name was. When it got to statement 20, the INPUT statement, it would stop, waiting for the operator to type a name on the keyboard. Whatever the operator typed would then be stored in memory in a location called NAME$. For instance, if I were running the program and typed my name, Larry, when asked, the word "Larry" would be stored in memory location NAME$. Once it had the operator's input, the computer would proceed to instruction 30, where it is told to print the phrase "Nice to meet you," followed by whatever is in memory location NAME$. Since that location contains the word "Larry," it would display "Nice to meet you, Larry."

The entire "conversation" would look like this on the screen:

```
What is your name?
? Larry
Nice to meet you, Larry.
```

Next, let's take an example from another language called Logo. Logo is useful for graphics (drawing pictures) as well as working with words and numbers. With Logo, you give the computer instructions for moving a "pen" around on the screen, thereby producing drawings. The creators of Logo worked with children, so they suggested you imagine that the pen is attached to the tail of an imaginary turtle that is crawling around on the screen. Therefore the Logo program:

```
FORWARD 50
RIGHT 90
FORWARD 100
```

would draw this shape on the screen:

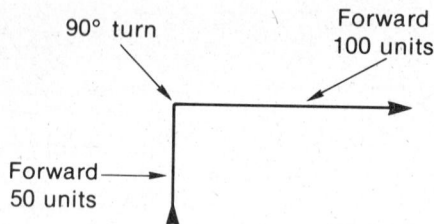

The first instruction moves the turtle forward 50 units, the second tells it to turn 90 degrees to the right, and the third to go forward 100 units. Note that the second instruction does not cause anything to be drawn, it just changes the direction in which the turtle is heading.

Can you figure out what would happen if the following program were executed?

```
RIGHT 90
FORWARD 100
```

```
RIGHT 90
FORWARD 100
RIGHT 90
FORWARD 100
RIGHT 90
FORWARD 100
```

If you trace the execution one step at a time, you will discover that this is a program for drawing a box.

How about this one?

```
RIGHT 30
FORWARD 100
RIGHT 120
FORWARD 100
RIGHT 120
FORWARD 100
RIGHT 90
```

Again, tracing the execution one step at a time, you will discover that this one is a program for drawing a triangle.

The idea is very simple, but you might be thinking to yourself that there is quite a difference between these simple program fragments and a word processing program or a complex spreadsheet processor. Those programs are similar in that they are made up of simple instructions that are executed one at a time, in order, but they are very long. Programs of tens of thousands of instructions that take several person-years to write are common.

Writing long, complex programs necessitates breaking them up into manageable subprograms. We can illustrate this idea with one more Logo program that uses the two we have aleady written. Let's give each of them a name, calling the first one BOX and the second TRIANGLE. In the Logo language, that would be done as follows:

```
TO BOX
     RIGHT 90
     FORWARD 100
     RIGHT 90
     FORWARD 100
     RIGHT 90
     FORWARD 100
     RIGHT 90
     FORWARD 100
END
```

and

```
TO TRIANGLE
     RIGHT 30
     FORWARD 100
     RIGHT 120
     FORWARD 100
     RIGHT 120
     FORWARD 100
     RIGHT 90
END
```

Once the subprograms TRIANGLE and BOX were defined, we would be able to use them as building blocks for larger, perhaps more useful or interesting programs. For example, this program:

```
TO HOUSE
        BOX
        TRIANGLE
END
```

would draw a triangle on top of a box, forming a "house." Trace the execution for yourself, and you will see that you get the following:

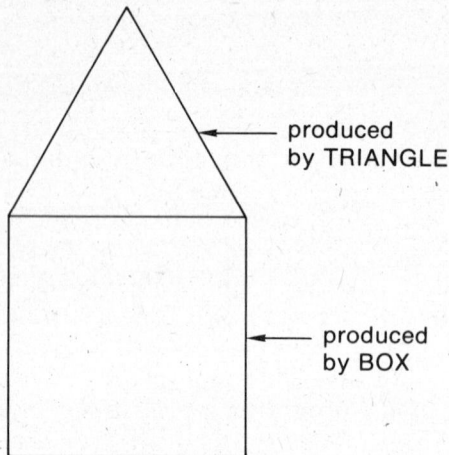

produced by TRIANGLE

produced by BOX

If you would like to learn more about programming, you might start with a book or a course. Four languages, BASIC, Pascal, Modula-2, and Logo, were developed expressly for teaching beginners to program. If you want to learn to write small utility programs, for instance to print a quick report from a data file, BASIC would be a good starting place. If you think you might get ambitious one day and want to write fairly large programs for more complex work with words and numbers, start with Pascal or Modula-2. If your goal is only to learn programming concepts (simple and advanced), I would begin with Logo.

If you decide to begin with BASIC, you have all the software you need to start, because the IBM PC comes with a minimal BASIC interpreter in ROM; if you order the DOS operating system with your PC, IBM includes an extended BASIC interpreter. If you get a bit more involved and start developing software in BASIC, look into the BASIC Development System from Softool Systems. It will save time in writing and debugging programs.

If you begin with Logo, you will need to purchase an interpreter. Serious contenders are a freeware program offered by David Smith of Danbury, Connecticut, IBM's Logo interpreter, and Digital Research's Logo interpreter. You can also get an excellent introduction to Logo with IBM's Turtlepower program.

Pascal compilers generally cost a good deal more than Logo interpreters. IBM and Digital Research both have Pascal compilers, but they are geared and priced for the professional programmer. The p-System, with its Pascal compiler and editor, provides a good learning environment; however, it is necessary to purchase the entire operating system in order to use the compiler. For an excellent, low cost Pascal compiler, contact Borland International.

Modula-2 was defined by Niklaus Wirth, the same man who developed Pascal. It may very well become the next standard teaching language at the university level, since it is simple, like Pascal, yet illustrates important concepts from advanced languages such as Ada. You can learn with a low cost compiler from the Modula Research Institute.

APPENDIX E
Serious Contenders

We have discussed many types of software and hardware. To give you a place to start shopping, this appendix lists products that can be considered serious contenders. For a product to get on the contenders list, we have to have had some experience with it, although in a few cases that experience has been limited. A lot of products we have looked at are not included, so you can have some confidence that these are reputable products from reputable vendors. None are perfect; indeed, some are noticeably flawed, but you should consider them.

Use this list as a starting point. Contact the vendors to get information on the latest versions of their products. Ask them to send brochures, the name of a local dealer, and reprints of any magazine reviews of their product.

There are thousands of vendors offering hardware, software, and services for the PC. We have looked at only a small fraction of these, and if you do not see one on this list, it is probably because we have not had a chance to review it.

WORD PROCESSING

MicroPro International, Wordstar. Since this is the most widely sold package, there is an abundance of supporting material such as tutorial texts and compatible auxiliary programs.

Microsoft, Word. This is a very versatile program, designed to take advantage of a mouse if you have one. Also designed with an eye toward the graphic printers and displays of the future.

Sorcim, Superwriter. Superwriter includes a spelling checker and mail merge facility and is compatible with the rest of Sorcim's products.

IBM or Peachtree Software, Peachtext. Descended from one of the earliest and best word processors, Peachtext does not do on-screen formatting, but is good for writers and those with mailing list applications.

Designer Software, Palantir. A second generation word processor, written by the original author of Peachwriter.

Lifetree Software, Volkswriter. The original version was relatively simple but fast and extremely easy to learn. A more extensive version is now under development.

Mark of the Unicorn, Final Word. A very flexible program, well suited to writers and those who are willing to put time into mastering it.

Quicksoft, PC-Write. A $10.00 word processor.

Word Processing Package, Computer System Resources, Inc. A $24.95 word processor.

Auxiliary Programs

IBM, Wordproof. An excellent spelling checker but, as of this writing, restricted in compatibility with many word processors.

MicroPro International, Correctstar. An excellent spelling corrector for use with the MicroPro's Wordstar word processor.

Oasis Systems, The Word and Punctuation & Style. A spelling checker and proofreading program.

Aspen Software, Grammatik. A proofreading program.

Digital Marketing, Writer's Pack. A group of six auxiliary programs, bundled together at a discount price.

Living Video Text, Think Tank. An excellent outline construction and writing aid.

SPREADSHEET PROCESSING

VisiCorp or IBM, VisiCalc. The original interactive spreadsheet processor. The most advanced version at this time is available only as part of the VisiOn system.

Microsoft or IBM, Multiplan. A powerful, menu oriented program, with a user interface similar to Microsoft's word processor.

Sorcim, Supercalc. A powerful spreadsheet processor, compatible with the rest of the Sorcim line.

Executive Software, Plan-80. A noninteractive program with significant capacity for consolidation of spreadsheets.

DATA MANAGEMENT

Jim Button, PC File. A freeware program.

Micro Data Base Systems, Knowledgeman. A versatile database management system capable of complex applications.

Ashton-Tate, dBASE II. The most widely sold database management system, dBASE II has the most supporting material from other vendors.

Condor Computer Corporation, Condor. A database management system that is relatively easy to use.

Software Publishing Corporation or IBM, pfs File and Report. These two programs, sold separately, are an easy-to-use cardfile system and columnar report generator.

Innovative Software Inc., T.I.M. An easy-to-use file management system.

Eagle Enterprises, Citation. An easy-to-use card file system.

COMMUNICATION

Software

Dynamic Microprocessor Associates, Ascom. This is a flexible package with extensive capability for unattended file transfer, but it requires technical expertise in initial setup.

Headlands Press, PC-Talk. An easy-to-use freeware program designed for interactive sessions.

Persoft Inc., Terminal Emulation Package. A well reputed terminal emulation program.

Microstuff, Crosstalk. A widely sold program that is packaged with several modems. In addition to communication, it has some capability for terminal emulation.

IBM, Personal Communications Manager. An excellent communication program that also includes PC-to-PC electronic mail capability.

Capital PC Software Exchange, RBBS-PC. A public domain program for unattended access by remote users for electronic mail and bulletin boards.

Microcorp, Intelliterm. Oriented toward unattended access by remote users for file transfer.

Software Link, Inc., MultiLink. Oriented toward unattended access by remote users with multitasking so that the PC can be used for something else while it serves as a host. Simultaneous remote users are also allowed.

Online Databases

Cuadra Associates. Their *Directory of Online Databases* is a comprehensive book listing and describing nearly 1,900 databases from nearly 1,000 producers. The directory is revised quarterly.

Dialog Information Retrieval Service. Dialog is a "broker" providing access to over 200 databases. It offers an after-hours service, called

Knowledge Index, whereby you can access several of their most important bibliographic databases at reduced cost.

The Source. The Source offers a variety of online services including databases and electronic mail.

Dow Jones. Dow Jones maintains an extensive database of financial information, including current and historical information on corporations as well as extensive news retrieval.

Compuserve. Compuserve offers a variety of online services including databases and electronic mail.

MULTIPLE APPLICATION PACKAGES

Lotus Development Corporation, 1-2-3. This is a very fast, menu oriented spreadsheet program with modules for business graphics and file management. Word processing and communication modules have been announced.

Context Management Systems, MBA. This, the first integrated package, includes modules for file management, communication, graphics, and word processing in the context of a spreadsheet processor. MBA was originally developed for the p-System, but a DOS version is expected out soon, and that would probably be a better bet.

OPERATING SYSTEM EXTENSIONS

Electronic disk emulation: Jetdrive, Tall Tree Systems

Print spooling: Jspool, Tall Tree Systems

Keyboard redefinition utilities: Keyswapper, Vertex Systems, and Prokey, RoseSoft

Limited multijob extension to DOS: Memory/Shift, North American Business Systems

Windowing extensions for DOS: Windows, Microsoft, and Desq, Quarterdeck Software

Window oriented operating system: VisiOn, VisiCorp
   Although it works in conjunction with DOS, VisiOn is essentially a new operating system. It integrates the spreadsheet, word processing, business graphics, file management programs distributed by Visicorp, but it remains to be seen how many other vendors will offer software written to run under VisiOn.

UTILITY PROGRAMS

For making backup copies of protected software: Copy II PC, Central Point Software and System Backup, Norell Data System

For examining disk files character by character, recreating damaged files, and restoring files that have been inadvertently erased: The Norton Utilities, Peter Norton

For copying files from disks of other computers: Xeno-Copy, Vertex System

For variable font printing: Fancy Font, SoftCraft

HARDWARE

Multifunction boards with input/output ports and memory: AST Research, Microsoft, and Advanced Data Technology

Multifunction boards with memory and a 300/1200 baud modem: US Robotics (includes proprietary communication software)

300/1200 baud internal modems: Hayes Microcomputer Products (bundled with Hayes's proprietary communication software), and intelligent technologies (bundled with software for communication, telephone dialing, electronic mail, and 3270 emulation where dial-in access is supported using a remote computer).

Hayes and US Robotics also manufacture external modems that may be connected to a PC via an RS-232 interface. Hayes was among the first to manufacture a "smart" modem, and hence their modem protocol is used by many other modem manufacturers and is compatible with many communication programs.

Hard disk subsystems: Tecmar and Great Lakes Computer Peripherals. Tecmar manufactures a full line of PC hardware add-ons, including a hard disk that can be shared among several PCs and one with extra expansion slots for those who need more than the PC offers. Great Lakes offers a low cost hard disk as an alternative to the PC-XT.

Graphic Displays: Hercules Computer Technology. The Hercules display board provides relatively high resolution graphics on a monochrome monitor. It includes a parallel printer port.

Mice: Mouse Systems and Microsoft. Mouse Systems's is a three-button optical mouse, and Microsoft's a two-button mechanical mouse. Mouse Systems can be used with Microsoft software.

Maintenance: In addition to IBM, you can get a maintenance agreement from Sorbus Service or, if you are adventurous, order IBM's Hardware Maintenance and Service software and manual or look at "How to Repair and Maintain Your Own IBM PC," from Personal Systems Publications.

OTHER SOURCES

These "serious contenders" are a fraction of all the products on the market. Magazines are a valuable source of pointers to many others. For those who are looking for software and accessory hardware, the most informative, interesting part of these magazines is probably the ads. They also publish review articles (though these are rarely negative). You can also consult any one of several directories to PC hardware and software. These are organized into categories, and contain brief, vendor-supplied descriptions of the programs.

Magazines

PC Magazine, Ziff-Davis Publishing: As of now, this is the largest magazine and so has the most ads.

PC World, PC World Communications: Like PC, a large, mass circulation magazine with many ads. Its annual software review issue is comparable to the published directories.

Softalk for the IBM PC, Softalk Publishing: This magazine is distributed free for one year to PC owners, but it contains excellent articles and reviews as well as the ads, which pay for its publication.

Directories

PC Buyer's Guide, Ziff-Davis Publishing

Guide to IBM Personal Computer Software, Datapro/McGraw-Hill

Annual Software Review, PC World Communications

APPENDIX F

Company Addresses and Phone Numbers

The following are the addresses and phone numbers of companies mentioned in this book and the other appendices.

3-Design
4710 University Way, N.E.
Suite 1512
Seattle, WA 98105
(206) 525-7820

Advanced Data Technology
13600 Ventura Boulevard
Sherman Oaks, CA 91423
(213) 986-6835

Advanced Software Interface
2655 Campus Drive
Suite 260
San Mateo, CA 94403
(415) 572-1347

Anderson-Bell
5336 Crocker Street
Littleton, CO 80120
(303) 794-7509

Armonk Corporation
610 Newport Center Drive, Suite 955
Newport Beach, CA 92660
(714) 760-3955

Ashton-Tate
1050 West Jefferson Boulevard
Culver City, CA 90230
(213) 204-5570

AST Research
2372 Morse Avenue
Irvine, CA 92714
(714) 540-1333

ATI
3770 Highland Avenue, #201
Manhattan Beach, CA 90266
(213) 546-4725

Borland International
4807 Scotts Valley Drive
Scotts Valley, CA 95056
(408) 438-8400

Jim Button
Box 5604
Bellevue, WA 98006

Capital PC Software Exchange
Box 6128
Silver Spring, MD 20906

Cdex Corporation
5050 El Camino Real #200
Los Altos, CA 94022
(415) 964-7600

Central Point Software
Box 19730-203
Portland, OR 97219
(503) 244-5782

Compuserve
Box 20212
Columbus, OH 43220
(800) 848-8990

Condor Computer Corporation
Box 8318
Ann Arbor, MI 48107
(313) 769-3988

Context Management Systems
23868 Hawthorne Boulevard
Torrance, CA 90505
(213) 378-8277

c-Systems
Box 3253
Fullerton, CA 92634
(714) 637-5362

Computer Innovations
10 Mechanic Street, #3
Red Bank, NJ 07701
(201) 530-0995

Computer System Resources
34184-B Coast Highway
Suite 119
Dana Point, CA 92629
(714) 661-9126

Cuadra Associates
2001 Wilshire Boulevard
Suite 305
Santa Monica, CA 90403
(213) 829-9972

CWare
Box 710097
San Jose, CA 95171-0097
(408) 736-6905

Datapro/McGraw-Hill
1805 Underwood Boulevard
Delran, NJ 08075
(609) 764-0100

Designer Software
3400 Montrose, Suite 718
Houston, TX 77006
(713) 520-8221

Dialog Information Retrieval Service
3460 Hillview Avenue
Palo Alto, CA 94304
(800) 227-1927
(800) 982-5838 (in California)

Digital Marketing
2363 Boulevard Circle
Walnut Creek, CA 94595
(800) 826-2222

Digital Research
Box 579
Pacific Grove, CA 93950
(408) 649-3896

Dow Jones News/Retrieval
Box 300
Princeton, NJ 08540
(609) 452-2000

Dynamic Microprocessor Associates
545 Fifth Avenue, #602
New York, NY 10017
(212) 687-7115

Eagle Enterprises
2375 Bush Street
San Francisco, CA 94115
(415) 346-1249

Ecosoft Inc.
Box 68602
Indianapolis, IN 46268-0602
(317) 255-6476

Enertronics Research, Inc.
150 North Meramec, Suite 207
St. Louis, MO 63105
(314) 725-5566

Executive Software, Inc.
255 Delaware Avenue
Buffalo, NY 14202
(705) 722-3373

Great Lakes Computer Peripherals
220 Stonington
Building 220
Hoffman Estates, IL 60195
(312) 884-7272

Hayes Microcomputer Products, Inc.
5923 Peachtree Industrial Boulevard
Norcross, GA 30092
(404) 449-8791

Headlands Press
Box 862
Tiburon, CA 94920

Howard Software Services
8008 Girard Avenue, #310
La Jolla, CA 92037
(619) 454-0121

IBM Corporation
Box 1320
Boca Raton, FL 33432
(800) 447-4700
(800) 447-0890 (in Alaska or Hawaii)

Infocom
55 Wheeler Street
Cambridge, MA 02138
(617) 492-1031

Innovative Software
9300 West 110th Street, Suite 380
Overland Park, KS 66212
(913) 383-1089

Integral Quality
6265 20th Avenue
Seattle, WA 98115
(206) 527-2918

Intelligent Technologies
151 University Avenue
Palo Alto, CA 94301
(415) 328-2411

International Software Marketing
120 East Washington Street
University Building 421
Syracuse, NY 13202
(315) 474-3400

Information Unlimited Software
2401 Marinship Way
Sausalito, CA 94965
(415) 331-6700

Ivy Research
88 Yale Section
New Haven, CT 06520
(203) 789-0676

Knoware
301 Vassar Street
Cambridge, MA 02139
(617) 576-3821

Koala Technologies Corporation
3100 Patrick Henry Drive
Santa Clara, CA 95050
(408) 986-8866

Kraft Systems
450 West California Avenue
Vista, CA 92083

Lifetree Software
411 Pacific Street, Suite 315
Monterey, CA 93940
(408) 373-4718

Living Videotext, Inc.
1000 Elwell Court, #232
Palo Alto, CA 94303
(415) 964-6300

Lotus Development Corporation
180 Franklin Street
Cambridge, MA 02139
(617) 492-7171

Mark of the Unicorn
222 Third Street
Cambridge, MA 02142
(617) 576-2760

Microcorp
913 Walnut Street
Philadelphia, PA 19107
(215) 627-7997

Micro Data Base Systems, Inc.
Box 248
Lafayette, IN 47902
(317) 463-2581

Micrographx
1701 North Greenville, Suite 703
Richardson, TX 75081
(214) 343-4338

MicroPro International
33 San Pablo Avenue
San Rafael, CA 94903
(415) 499-1200

Microsoft
10700 Northrup Way
Bellevue, WA 98004
(206) 828-8080

Microstuff, Inc.
1845 The Exchange
Suite 140
Atlanta, GA 30339
(404) 952-0267

Modula Research Institute
950 North University Avenue
Provo, UT 84604
(801) 375-7402

Mouse Systems
2336H Walsh Avenue
Santa Clara, CA 95051
(408) 988-0211

New York Amateur Computer Club, Inc.
Box 106
New York, NY 10008

Norell Data Systems
3400 Wilshire Boulevard
Box 70127
Los Angeles, CA 90010
(213) 257-2026

North American Business Systems
642 Office Parkway
St. Louis, MO 63141
(314) 432-6106

Oasis Systems
2765 Reynard Way
San Diego, CA 92103
(619) 222-1153

PCsoftware
9120 Grammercy Drive, #416
San Diego, CA 92123
(619) 571-0981

PC World Communications
555 De Haro Street
San Francisco, CA 94107
(415) 861-3861

Peachtree Software
3 Corporate Square, Suite 700
Atlanta, GA 30329
(404) 325-8533

Persoft Inc.
2740 Ski Lane
Madison, WI 53713
(608) 233-1000

Personal Systems Publications
Box 90754
Los Angeles, CA 90009

Peter Norton, Inc.
2210 Wilshire Boulevard
Santa Monica, CA 90403
(213) 399-3948

RoseSoft
4710 University Way, N.E. #601
Seattle, WA 98105
(206) 524-2350

SIG/M
Box 97
Iselin, NJ 08830

David Smith
44 Ole Musket Lane
Danbury, CT 06810

Softalk Publishing, Inc.
11160 McCormick Street
North Hollywood, CA 91603
(213) 980-5074

SoftCraft
8726 South Sepulveda Boulevard
Suite 1641
Los Angeles, CA 90045
(213) 641-3822

SofTool Systems
8972 East Hampden Avenue
Suite 179
Denver, CO 80231
(303) 793-0145

Software Laboratories
6924 Riverside Drive
Dublin, OH 43017
(614) 889-5083

Software Link, Inc.
6700 Roswell Road, #23-B
Atlanta, GA 30328
(404) 255-1254

Software Publishing Corporation
1902 Landings Drive
Mountain View, CA 94043
(415) 962-8910

Sorbus Service
50 East Swedesford Road
Frazer, PA 19355
(215) 296-6241

Sorcim
2310 Lundy Avenue
San Jose, CA 95131
(408) 942-1727

Spectrum Training Corporation
18 Brown Street
Salem, MA 01970
(617) 741-1150

SPSS Inc.
444 North Michigan Avenue
Suite 3000
Chicago, IL 60611
(312) 329-2400

Tall Tree Systems
1032 Elwell, Court 124
Palo Alto, CA 94303
(415) 964-1980

Tecmar
6225 Cochran Road
Cleveland, OH 44139
(216) 349-0600

TG Products
1104 Summit Avenue, Suite 106
Plano, TX 75074
(214) 424-8568

Vertex Systems
7950 West Fourth Street
Los Angeles, CA 90048
(213) 938-0857

VisiCorp
2895 Zanker Road
San Jose, CA 95134
(408) 946-9000

Wadsworth Electronic Publishing Co.
Statler Office Building
20 Park Plaza
Boston, MA 02116
(617) 423-0420

John Wiley and Sons
605 Third Avenue
New York, NY 10158
(212) 850-6000

Ziff-Davis Publishing
One Park Avenue
New York, NY 10016
(212) 725-3500

Index